ISSUE ONE

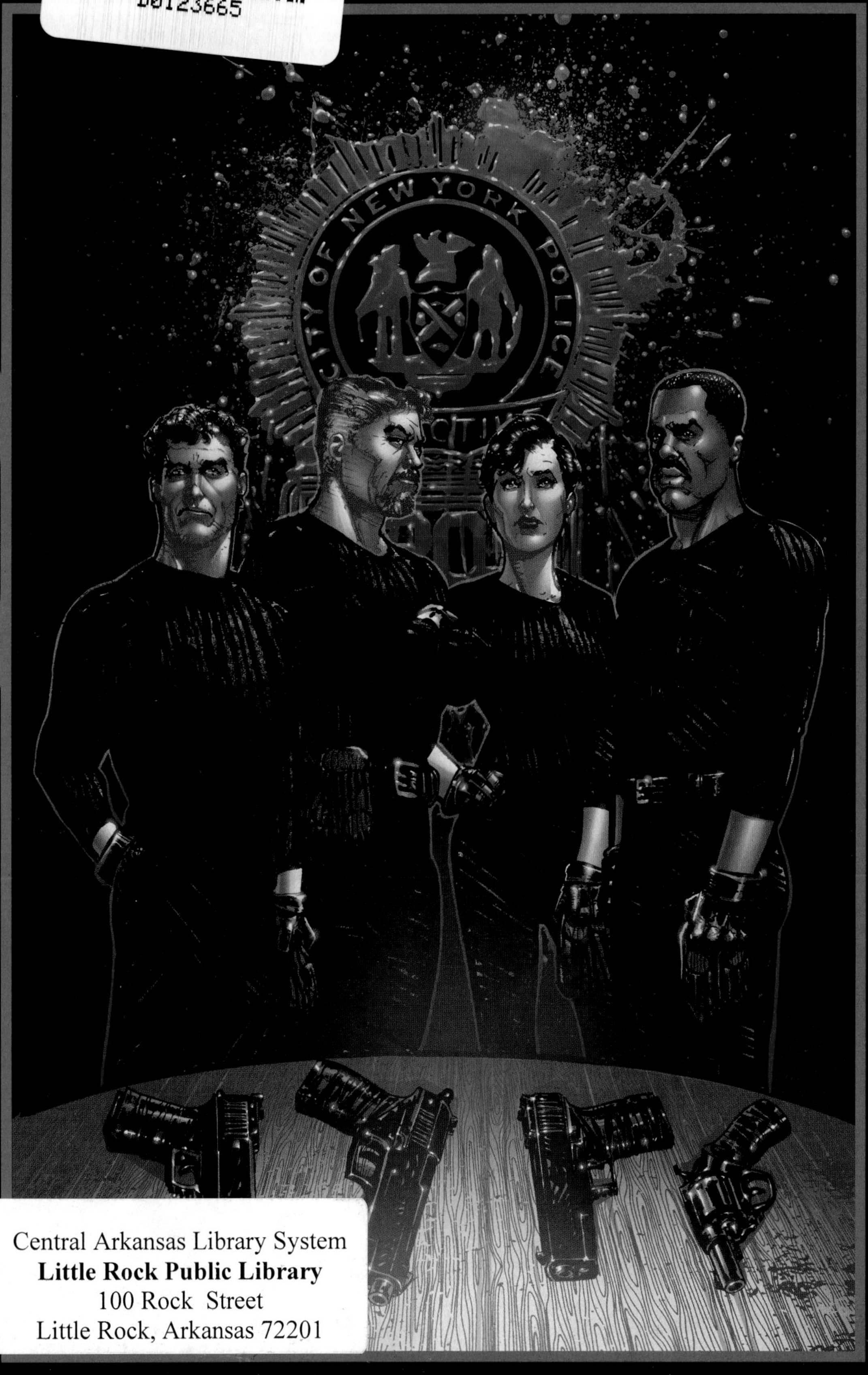

CITY OF NEW YORK POLICE

Issue #1 cover art by **HOWARD CHAYKIN** colors by **JESUS ABURTO**

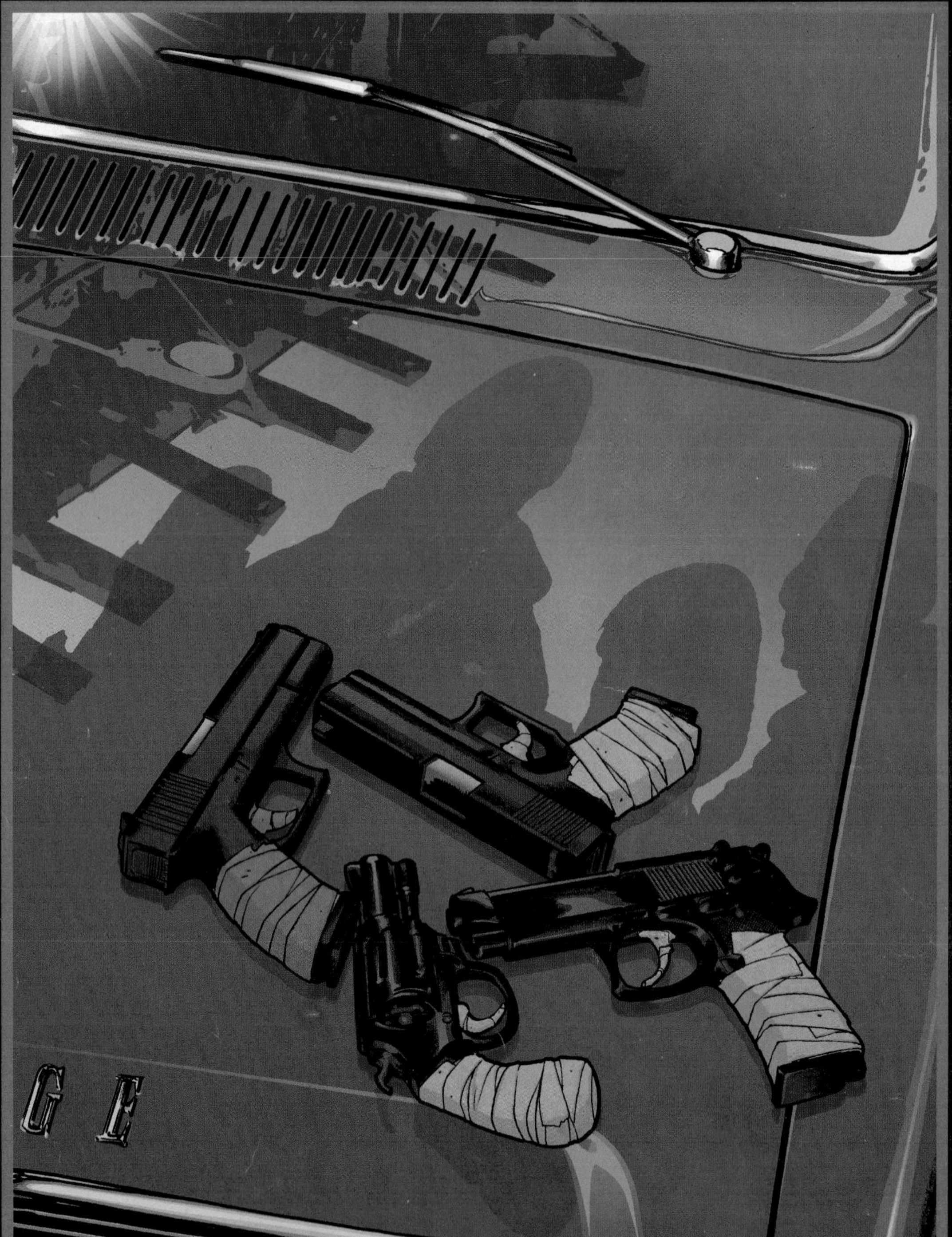
G E
SOOK
Issue #1 alternate cover by **RYAN SOOK**

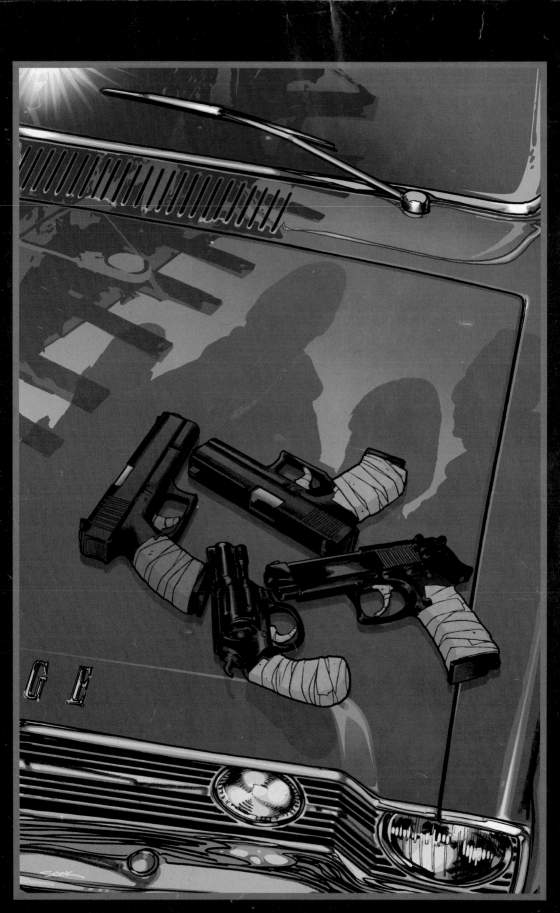

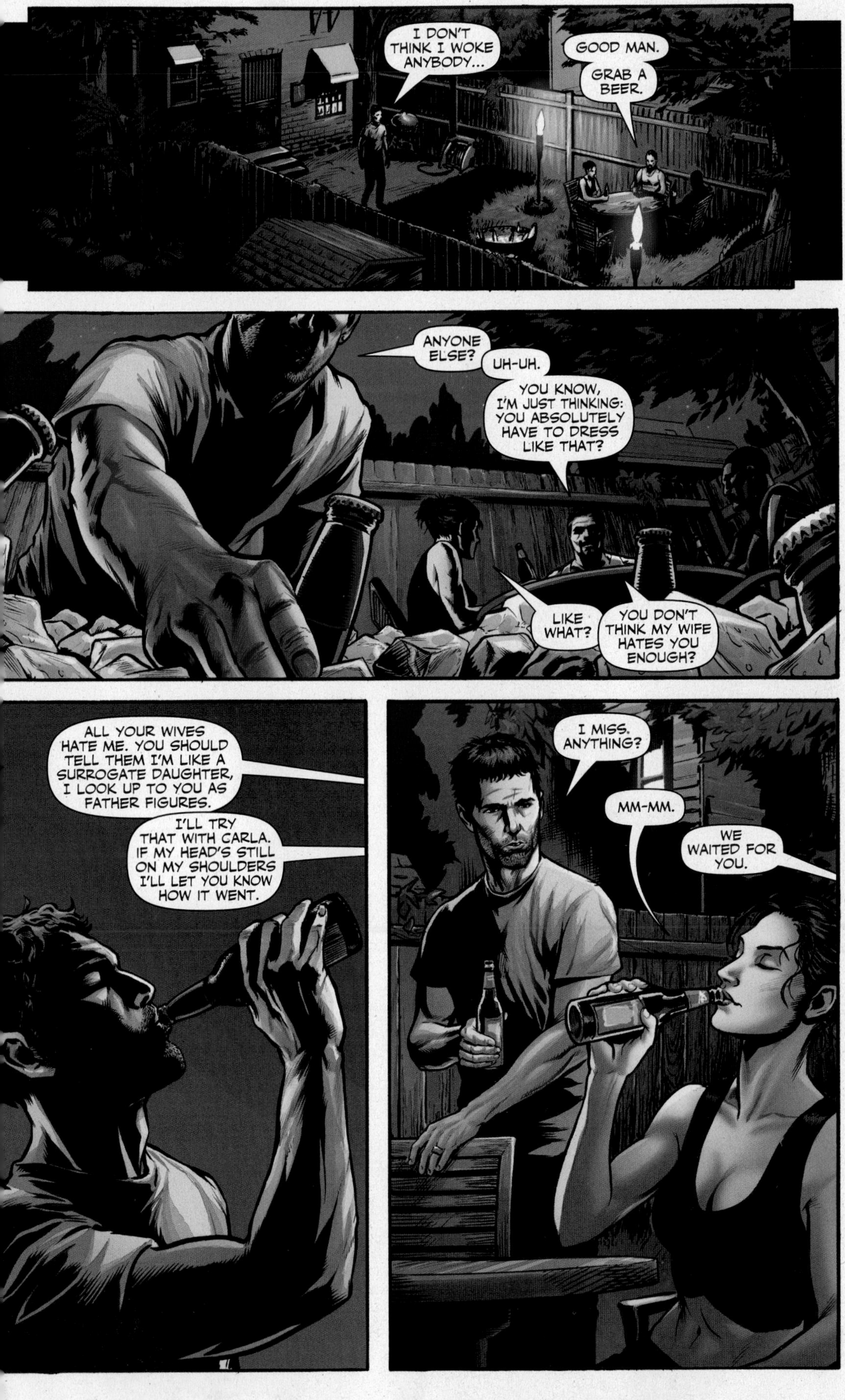
I DON'T THINK I WOKE ANYBODY...
GOOD MAN.
GRAB A BEER.
ANYONE ELSE?
UH-UH.
YOU KNOW, I'M JUST THINKING: YOU ABSOLUTELY HAVE TO DRESS LIKE THAT?
LIKE WHAT?
YOU DON'T THINK MY WIFE HATES YOU ENOUGH?
ALL YOUR WIVES HATE ME. YOU SHOULD TELL THEM I'M LIKE A SURROGATE DAUGHTER, I LOOK UP TO YOU AS FATHER FIGURES.
I'LL TRY THAT WITH CARLA. IF MY HEAD'S STILL ON MY SHOULDERS I'LL LET YOU KNOW HOW IT WENT.
I MISS. ANYTHING?
MM-MM.
WE WAITED FOR YOU.

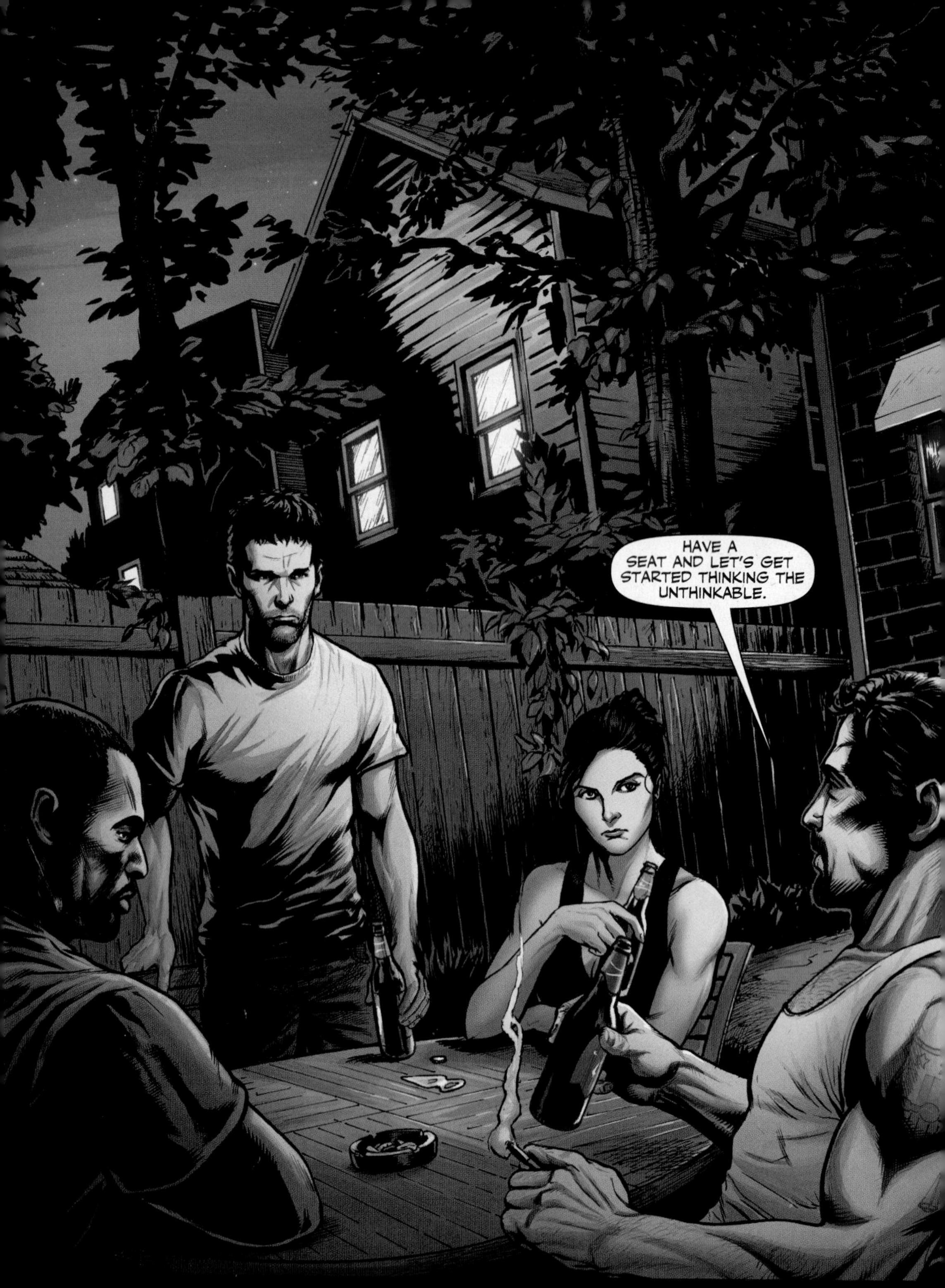
HAVE A SEAT AND LET'S GET STARTED THINKING THE UNTHINKABLE.

1: THE FIRST-TIMERS

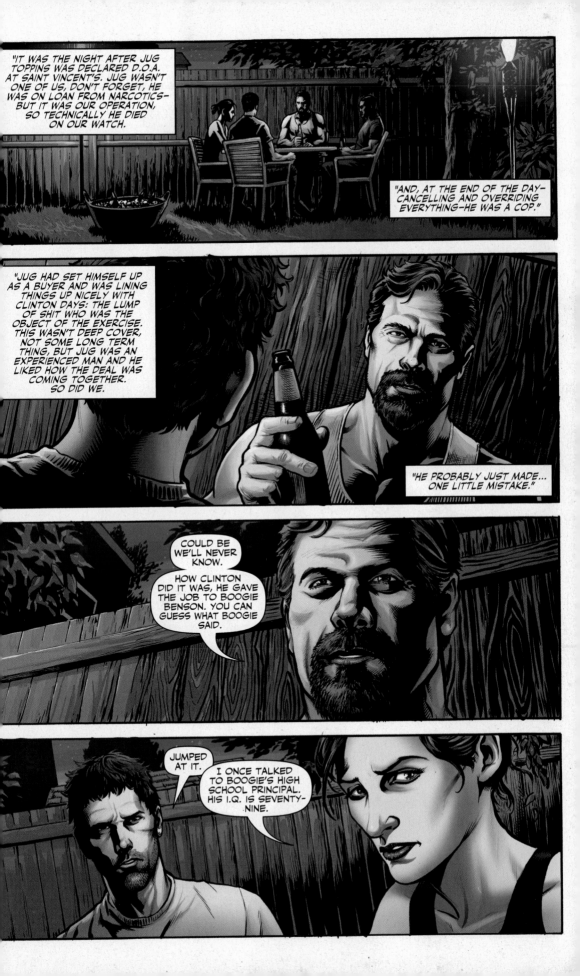

"IT WAS THE NIGHT AFTER JUG TOPPINS WAS DECLARED D.O.A. AT SAINT VINCENT'S. JUG WASN'T ONE OF US, DON'T FORGET, HE WAS ON LOAN FROM NARCOTICS— BUT IT WAS OUR OPERATION, SO TECHNICALLY HE DIED ON OUR WATCH."

"AND, AT THE END OF THE DAY— CANCELLING AND OVERRIDING EVERYTHING—HE WAS A COP."

"JUG HAD SET HIMSELF UP AS A BUYER AND WAS LINING THINGS UP NICELY WITH CLINTON DAYS: THE LUMP OF SHIT WHO WAS THE OBJECT OF THE EXERCISE. THIS WASN'T DEEP COVER, NOT SOME LONG TERM THING, BUT JUG WAS AN EXPERIENCED MAN AND HE LIKED HOW THE DEAL WAS COMING TOGETHER. SO DID WE."

"HE PROBABLY JUST MADE... ONE LITTLE MISTAKE."

COULD BE WE'LL NEVER KNOW.

HOW CLINTON DID IT WAS, HE GAVE THE JOB TO BOOGIE BENSON. YOU CAN GUESS WHAT BOOGIE SAID.

JUMPED AT IT.

I ONCE TALKED TO BOOGIE'S HIGH SCHOOL PRINCIPAL. HIS I.Q. IS SEVENTY-NINE.

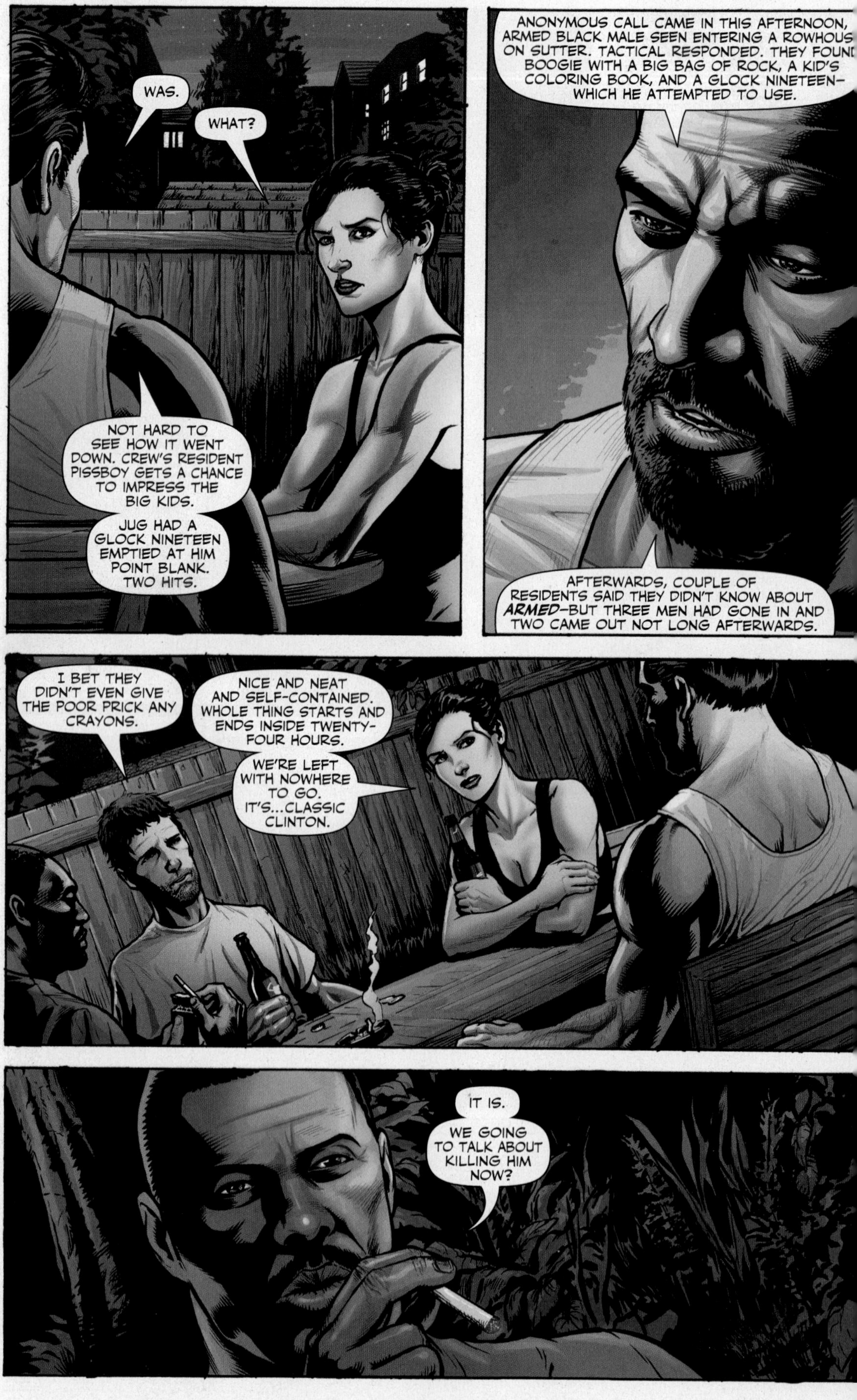
WAS.
WHAT?
NOT HARD TO SEE HOW IT WENT DOWN. CREW'S RESIDENT PISSBOY GETS A CHANCE TO IMPRESS THE BIG KIDS.
JUG HAD A GLOCK NINETEEN EMPTIED AT HIM POINT BLANK. TWO HITS.
ANONYMOUS CALL CAME IN THIS AFTERNOON, ARMED BLACK MALE SEEN ENTERING A ROWHOUS ON SUTTER. TACTICAL RESPONDED. THEY FOUNI BOOGIE WITH A BIG BAG OF ROCK, A KID'S COLORING BOOK, AND A GLOCK NINETEEN— WHICH HE ATTEMPTED TO USE.
AFTERWARDS, COUPLE OF RESIDENTS SAID THEY DIDN'T KNOW ABOUT *ARMED*—BUT THREE MEN HAD GONE IN AND TWO CAME OUT NOT LONG AFTERWARDS.
I BET THEY DIDN'T EVEN GIVE THE POOR PRICK ANY CRAYONS.
NICE AND NEAT AND SELF-CONTAINED. WHOLE THING STARTS AND ENDS INSIDE TWENTY-FOUR HOURS.
WE'RE LEFT WITH NOWHERE TO GO. IT'S...CLASSIC CLINTON.
IT IS.
WE GOING TO TALK ABOUT KILLING HIM NOW?

"THERE IT WAS, RIGHT ON THE TABLE IN FRONT OF US. NOT THAT ANYONE WASN'T EXPECTING IT, OR ELSE WHY WOULD WE COME TO DUKE'S IN THE FIRST PLACE?

"BUT THIS MADE IT REAL. THIS TOOK THE ANGER OVER WHAT HAPPENED TO JUG AND COOLED IT WAY, WAY DOWN, FROM WE HAVE GOT TO DO SOMETHING TO—YEAH? WHAT?"

IS THIS WHERE WE GO ROUND IN A CIRCLE AND SAY IN OR OUT?

IN.

ME TOO.

THAT WAS QUICK...

EDDIE.

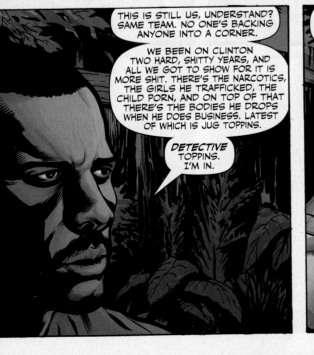

THIS IS STILL US, UNDERSTAND? SAME TEAM. NO ONE'S BACKING ANYONE INTO A CORNER.

WE BEEN ON CLINTON TWO HARD, SHITTY YEARS, AND ALL WE GOT TO SHOW FOR IT IS MORE SHIT. THERE'S THE NARCOTICS, THE GIRLS HE TRAFFICKED, THE CHILD PORN, AND ON TOP OF THAT THERE'S THE BODIES HE DROPS WHEN HE DOES BUSINESS. LATEST OF WHICH IS JUG TOPPINS.

DETECTIVE TOPPINS. I'M IN.

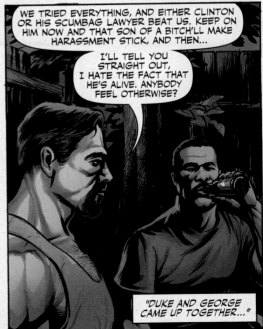

WE TRIED EVERYTHING, AND EITHER CLINTON OR HIS SCUMBAG LAWYER BEAT US. KEEP ON HIM NOW AND THAT SON OF A BITCH'LL MAKE HARASSMENT STICK, AND THEN...

I'LL TELL YOU STRAIGHT OUT, I HATE THE FACT THAT HE'S ALIVE. ANYBODY FEEL OTHERWISE?

"DUKE AND GEORGE CAME UP TOGETHER..."

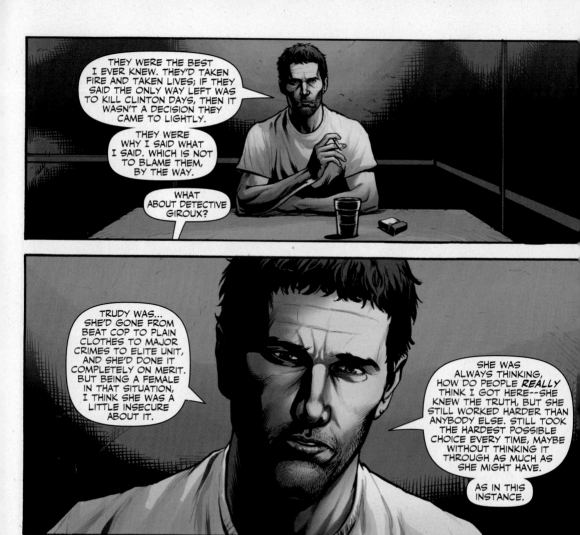

THEY WERE THE BEST I EVER KNEW. THEY'D TAKEN FIRE AND TAKEN LIVES; IF THEY SAID THE ONLY WAY LEFT WAS TO KILL CLINTON DAYS, THEN IT WASN'T A DECISION THEY CAME TO LIGHTLY.

THEY WERE WHY I SAID WHAT I SAID. WHICH IS NOT TO BLAME THEM, BY THE WAY.

WHAT ABOUT DETECTIVE GIROUX?

TRUDY WAS... SHE'D GONE FROM BEAT COP TO PLAIN CLOTHES TO MAJOR CRIMES TO ELITE UNIT, AND SHE'D DONE IT COMPLETELY ON MERIT. BUT BEING A FEMALE IN THAT SITUATION, I THINK SHE WAS A LITTLE INSECURE ABOUT IT.

SHE WAS ALWAYS THINKING, HOW DO PEOPLE REALLY THINK I GOT HERE--SHE KNEW THE TRUTH, BUT SHE STILL WORKED HARDER THAN ANYBODY ELSE. STILL TOOK THE HARDEST POSSIBLE CHOICE EVERY TIME, MAYBE WITHOUT THINKING IT THROUGH AS MUCH AS SHE MIGHT HAVE.

AS IN THIS INSTANCE.

INTERESTING VIEWPOINT.

JUST MY OPINION.

SO WHAT DID YOU SAY, WHEN YOU SAID WHAT YOU SAID?

YES.

EVENTUALLY.

WHY EVENTUALLY?

BECAUSE IT WAS FUCKING WRONG...!

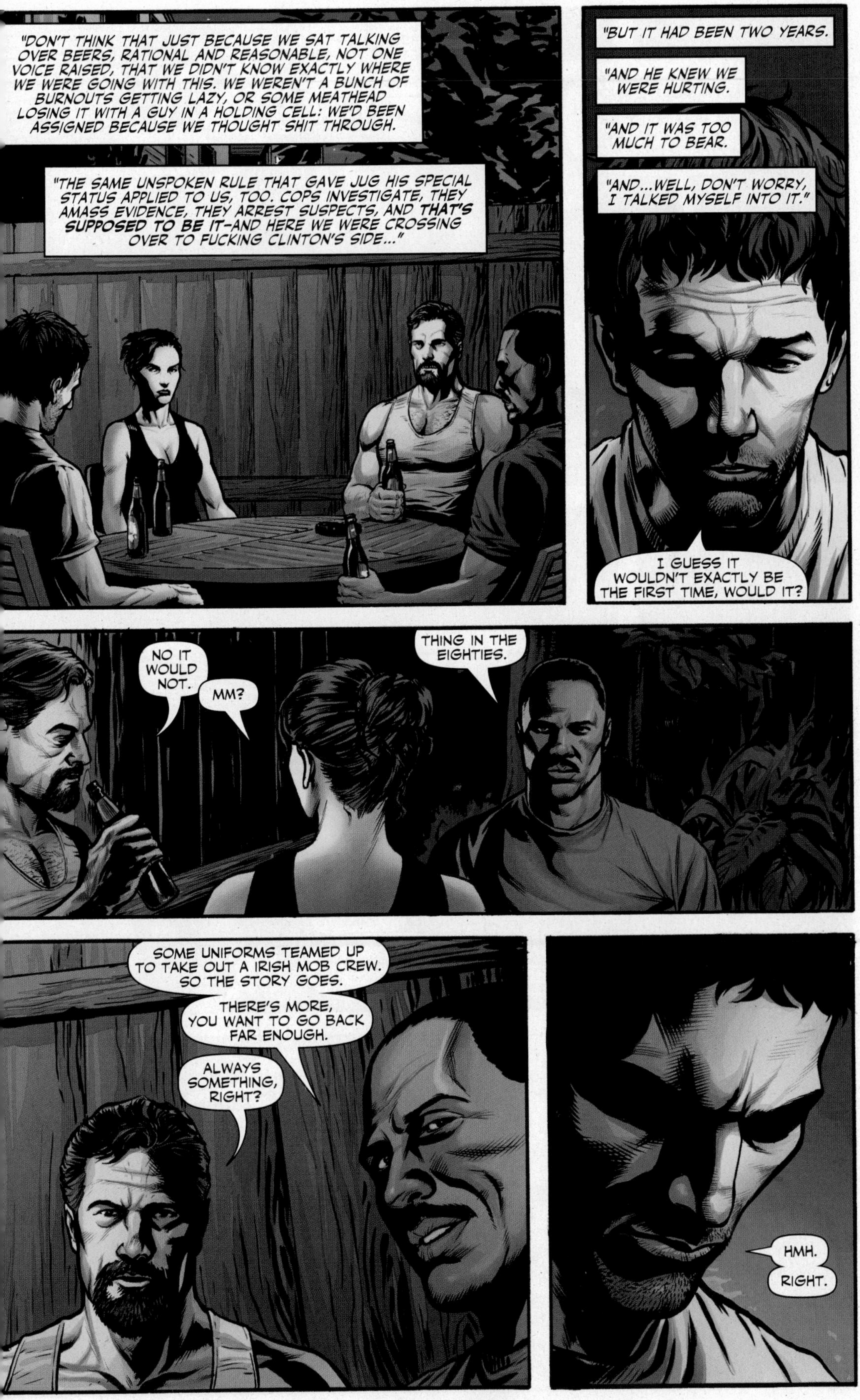
"DON'T THINK THAT JUST BECAUSE WE SAT TALKING OVER BEERS, RATIONAL AND REASONABLE, NOT ONE VOICE RAISED, THAT WE DIDN'T KNOW EXACTLY WHERE WE WERE GOING WITH THIS. WE WEREN'T A BUNCH OF BURNOUTS GETTING LAZY, OR SOME MEATHEAD LOSING IT WITH A GUY IN A HOLDING CELL: WE'D BEEN ASSIGNED BECAUSE WE THOUGHT SHIT THROUGH.
"THE SAME UNSPOKEN RULE THAT GAVE JUG HIS SPECIAL STATUS APPLIED TO US, TOO. COPS INVESTIGATE, THEY AMASS EVIDENCE, THEY ARREST SUSPECTS, AND **THAT'S SUPPOSED TO BE IT**–AND HERE WE WERE CROSSING OVER TO FUCKING CLINTON'S SIDE..."
"BUT IT HAD BEEN TWO YEARS.
"AND HE KNEW WE WERE HURTING.
"AND IT WAS TOO MUCH TO BEAR.
"AND...WELL, DON'T WORRY, I TALKED MYSELF INTO IT."
I GUESS IT WOULDN'T EXACTLY BE THE FIRST TIME, WOULD IT?
NO IT WOULD NOT.
MM?
THING IN THE EIGHTIES.
SOME UNIFORMS TEAMED UP TO TAKE OUT A IRISH MOB CREW. SO THE STORY GOES.
THERE'S MORE, YOU WANT TO GO BACK FAR ENOUGH.
ALWAYS SOMETHING, RIGHT?
HMH.
RIGHT.

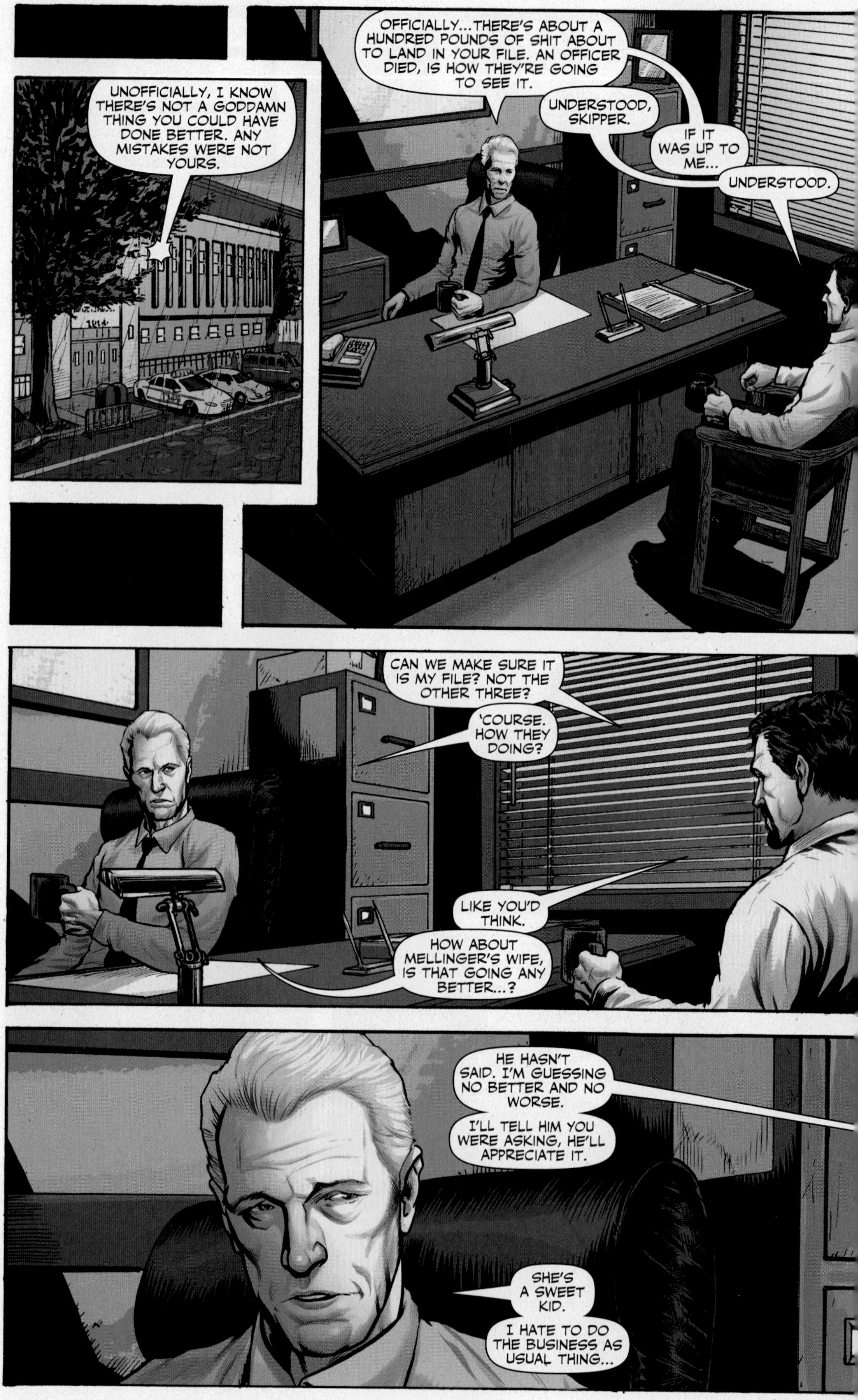
UNOFFICIALLY, I KNOW THERE'S NOT A GODDAMN THING YOU COULD HAVE DONE BETTER. ANY MISTAKES WERE NOT YOURS.
OFFICIALLY...THERE'S ABOUT A HUNDRED POUNDS OF SHIT ABOUT TO LAND IN YOUR FILE. AN OFFICER DIED, IS HOW THEY'RE GOING TO SEE IT.
UNDERSTOOD, SKIPPER.
IF IT WAS UP TO ME...
UNDERSTOOD.
CAN WE MAKE SURE IT IS MY FILE? NOT THE OTHER THREE?
'COURSE. HOW THEY DOING?
LIKE YOU'D THINK.
HOW ABOUT MELLINGER'S WIFE, IS THAT GOING ANY BETTER...?
HE HASN'T SAID. I'M GUESSING NO BETTER AND NO WORSE.
I'LL TELL HIM YOU WERE ASKING, HE'LL APPRECIATE IT.
SHE'S A SWEET KID.
I HATE TO DO THE BUSINESS AS USUAL THING...

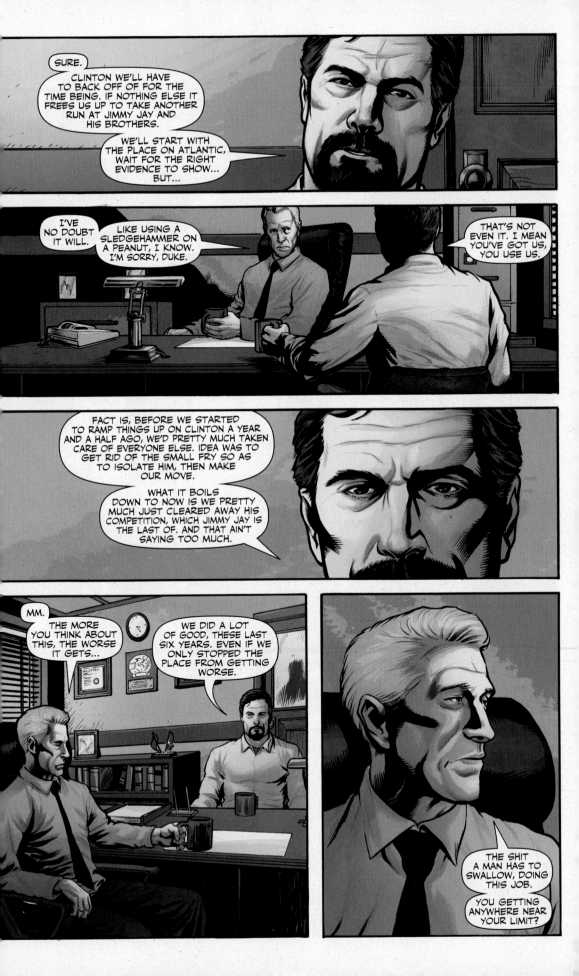

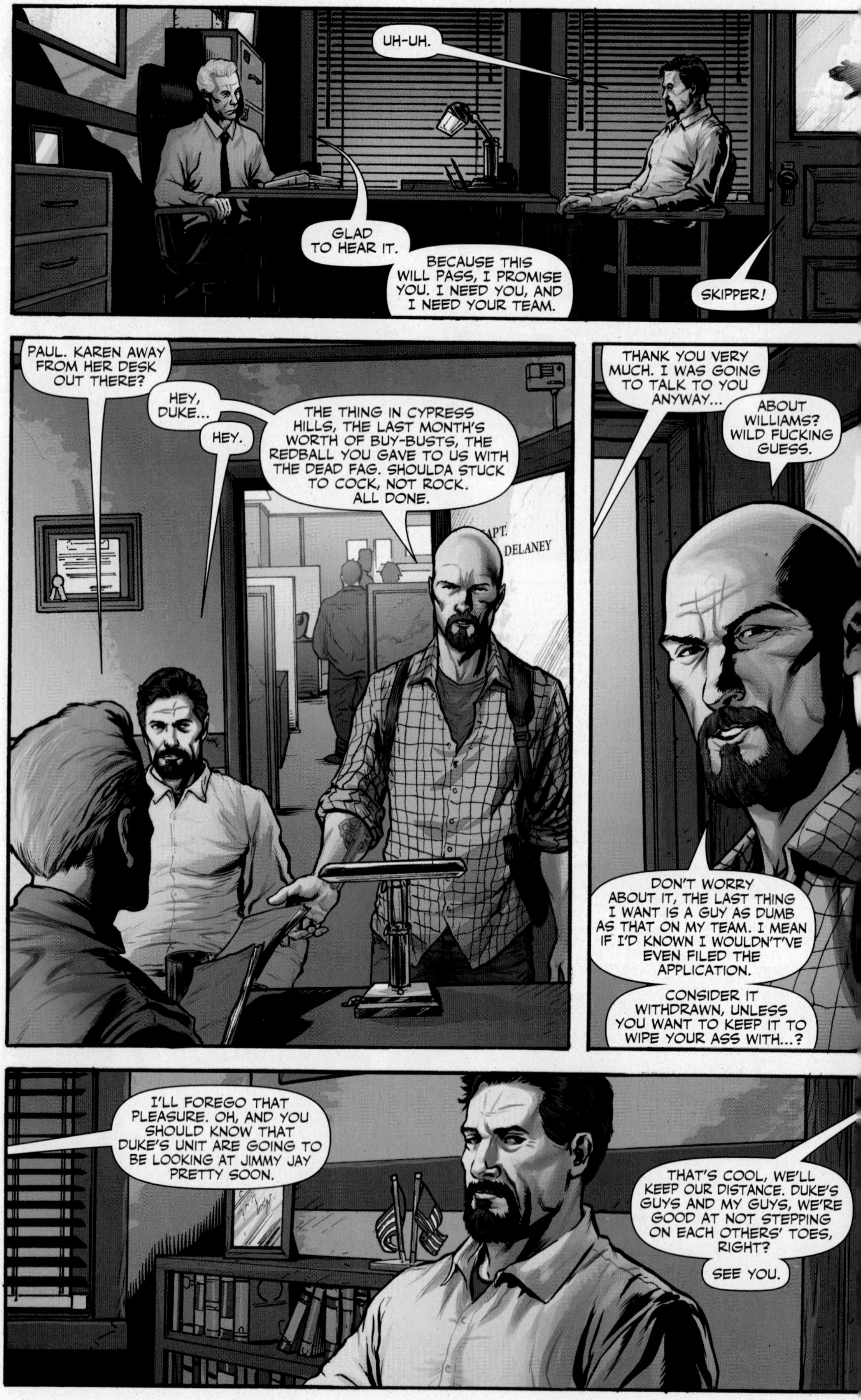
UH-UH.
GLAD TO HEAR IT.
BECAUSE THIS WILL PASS, I PROMISE YOU. I NEED YOU, AND I NEED YOUR TEAM.
SKIPPER!
PAUL. KAREN AWAY FROM HER DESK OUT THERE?
HEY, DUKE...
HEY.
THE THING IN CYPRESS HILLS, THE LAST MONTH'S WORTH OF BUY-BUSTS, THE REDBALL YOU GAVE TO US WITH THE DEAD FAG. SHOULDA STUCK TO COCK, NOT ROCK. ALL DONE.
APT.
DELANEY
THANK YOU VERY MUCH. I WAS GOING TO TALK TO YOU ANYWAY...
ABOUT WILLIAMS? WILD FUCKING GUESS.
DON'T WORRY ABOUT IT, THE LAST THING I WANT IS A GUY AS DUMB AS THAT ON MY TEAM. I MEAN IF I'D KNOWN I WOULDN'T'VE EVEN FILED THE APPLICATION.
CONSIDER IT WITHDRAWN, UNLESS YOU WANT TO KEEP IT TO WIPE YOUR ASS WITH...?
I'LL FOREGO THAT PLEASURE. OH, AND YOU SHOULD KNOW THAT DUKE'S UNIT ARE GOING TO BE LOOKING AT JIMMY JAY PRETTY SOON.
THAT'S COOL, WE'LL KEEP OUR DISTANCE. DUKE'S GUYS AND MY GUYS, WE'RE GOOD AT NOT STEPPING ON EACH OTHERS' TOES, RIGHT?
SEE YOU.

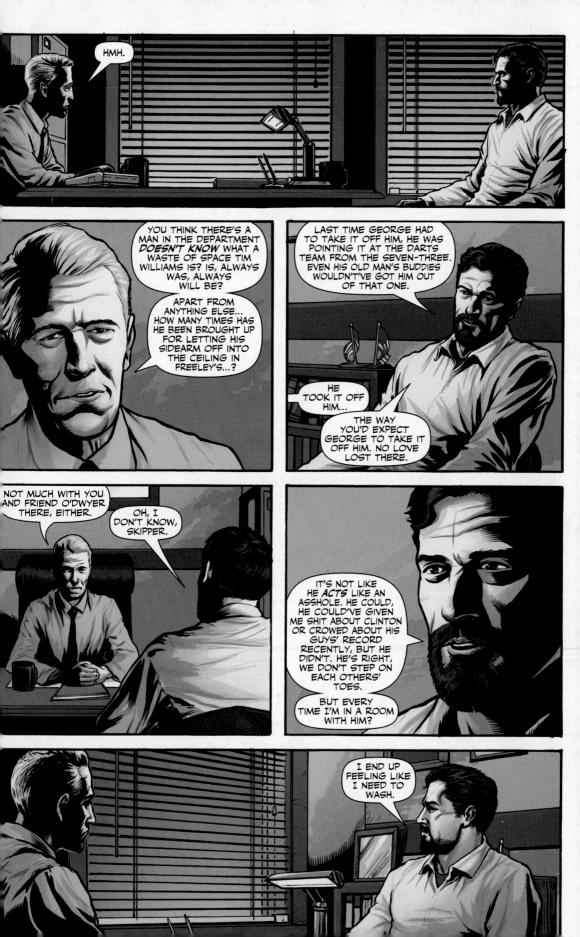

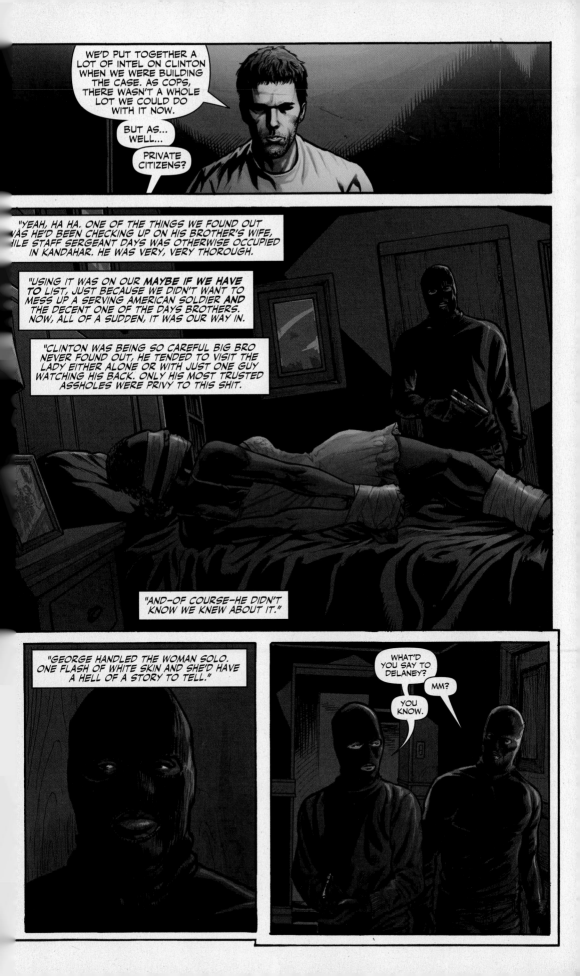

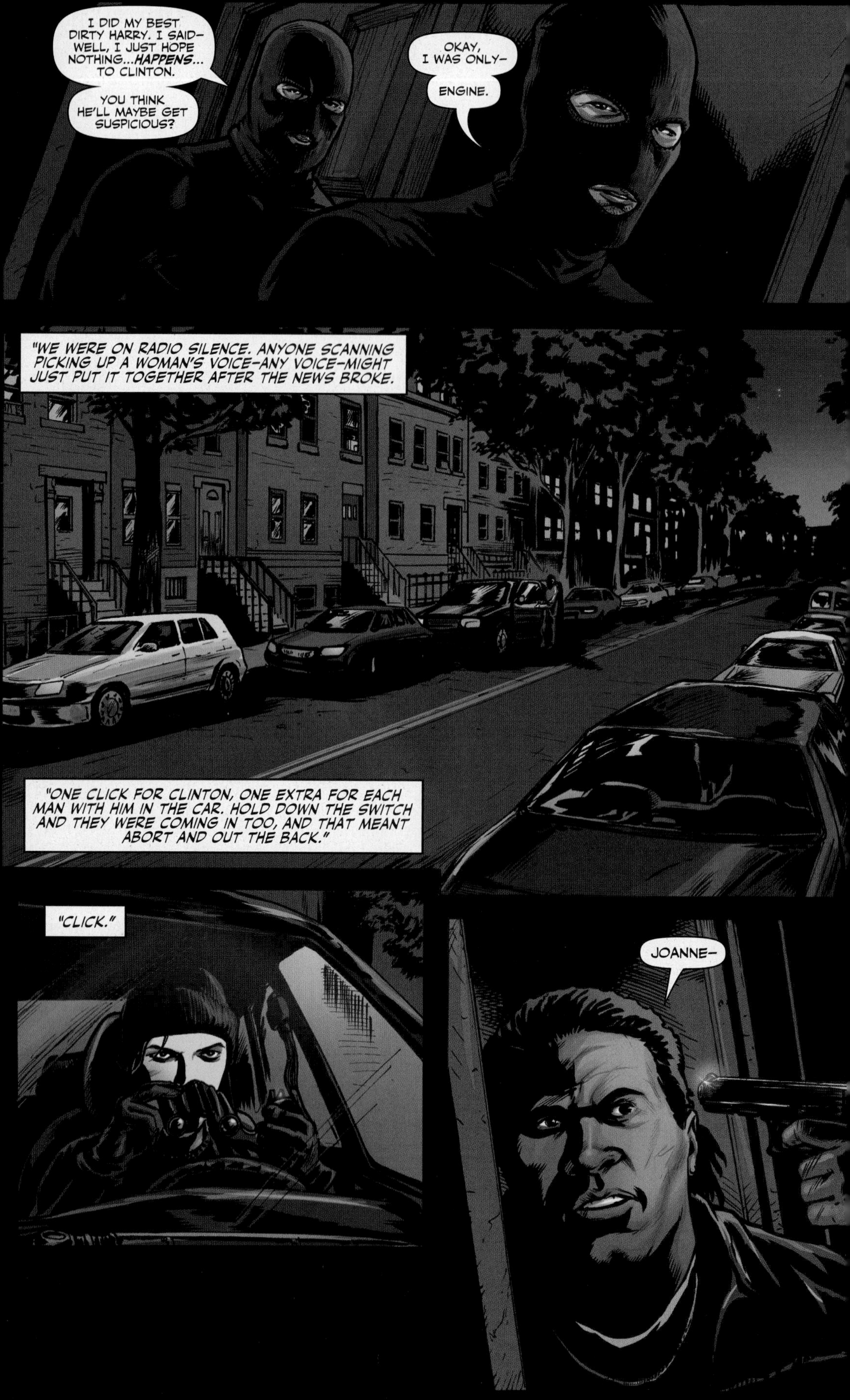
I DID MY BEST DIRTY HARRY. I SAID— WELL, I JUST HOPE NOTHING...*HAPPENS*... TO CLINTON.
YOU THINK HE'LL MAYBE GET SUSPICIOUS?
OKAY, I WAS ONLY—
ENGINE.
"WE WERE ON RADIO SILENCE. ANYONE SCANNING PICKING UP A WOMAN'S VOICE—ANY VOICE—MIGHT JUST PUT IT TOGETHER AFTER THE NEWS BROKE.
"ONE CLICK FOR CLINTON, ONE EXTRA FOR EACH MAN WITH HIM IN THE CAR. HOLD DOWN THE SWITCH AND THEY WERE COMING IN TOO, AND THAT MEANT ABORT AND OUT THE BACK."
"CLICK."
JOANNE—

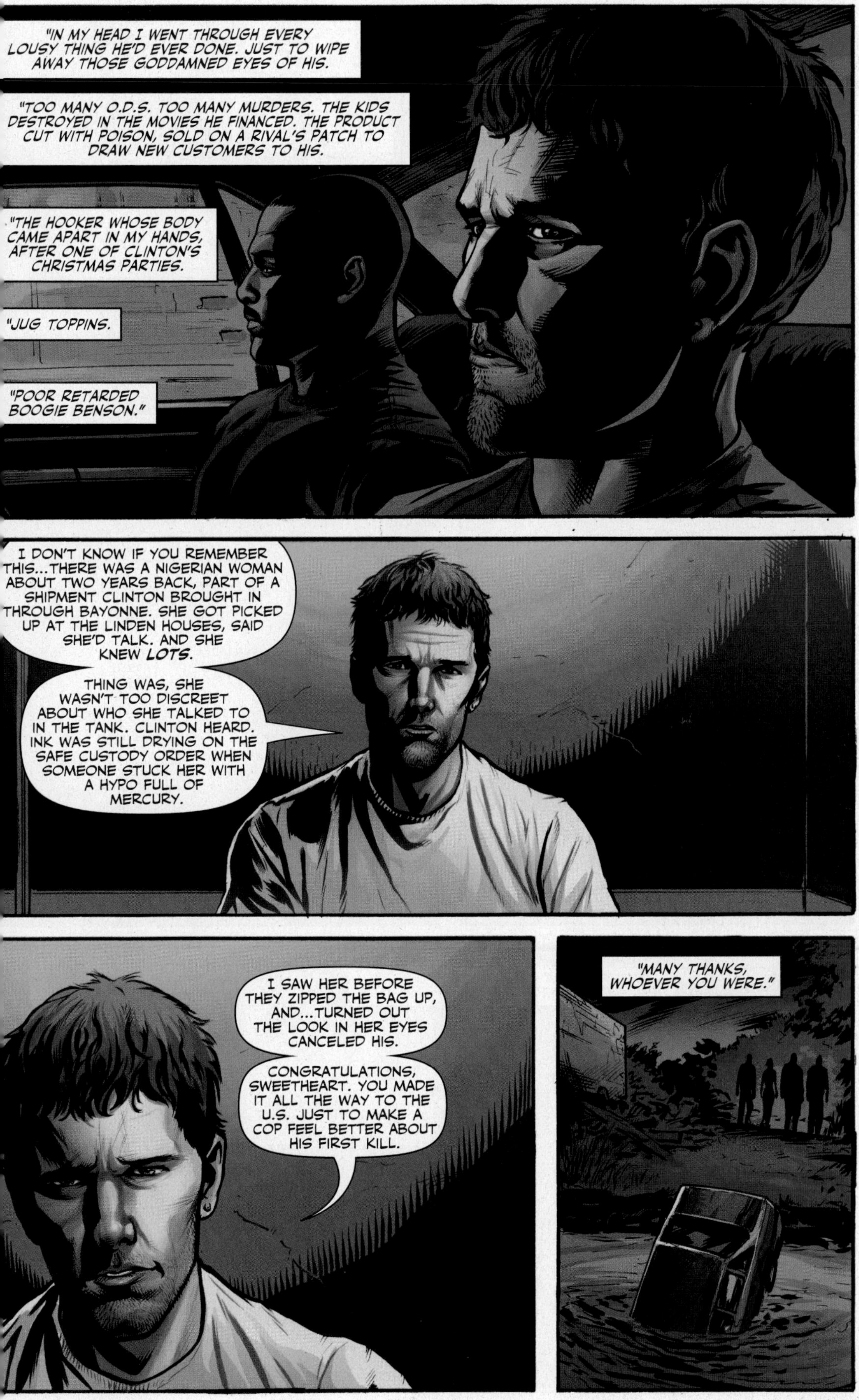
"IN MY HEAD I WENT THROUGH EVERY LOUSY THING HE'D EVER DONE. JUST TO WIPE AWAY THOSE GODDAMNED EYES OF HIS.
"TOO MANY O.D.S. TOO MANY MURDERS. THE KIDS DESTROYED IN THE MOVIES HE FINANCED. THE PRODUCT CUT WITH POISON, SOLD ON A RIVAL'S PATCH TO DRAW NEW CUSTOMERS TO HIS.
"THE HOOKER WHOSE BODY CAME APART IN MY HANDS, AFTER ONE OF CLINTON'S CHRISTMAS PARTIES.
"JUG TOPPINS.
"POOR RETARDED BOOGIE BENSON."
I DON'T KNOW IF YOU REMEMBER THIS...THERE WAS A NIGERIAN WOMAN ABOUT TWO YEARS BACK, PART OF A SHIPMENT CLINTON BROUGHT IN THROUGH BAYONNE. SHE GOT PICKED UP AT THE LINDEN HOUSES, SAID SHE'D TALK. AND SHE KNEW *LOTS*.
THING WAS, SHE WASN'T TOO DISCREET ABOUT WHO SHE TALKED TO IN THE TANK. CLINTON HEARD. INK WAS STILL DRYING ON THE SAFE CUSTODY ORDER WHEN SOMEONE STUCK HER WITH A HYPO FULL OF MERCURY.
I SAW HER BEFORE THEY ZIPPED THE BAG UP, AND...TURNED OUT THE LOOK IN HER EYES CANCELED HIS.
CONGRATULATIONS, SWEETHEART. YOU MADE IT ALL THE WAY TO THE U.S. JUST TO MAKE A COP FEEL BETTER ABOUT HIS FIRST KILL.
"MANY THANKS, WHOEVER YOU WERE."

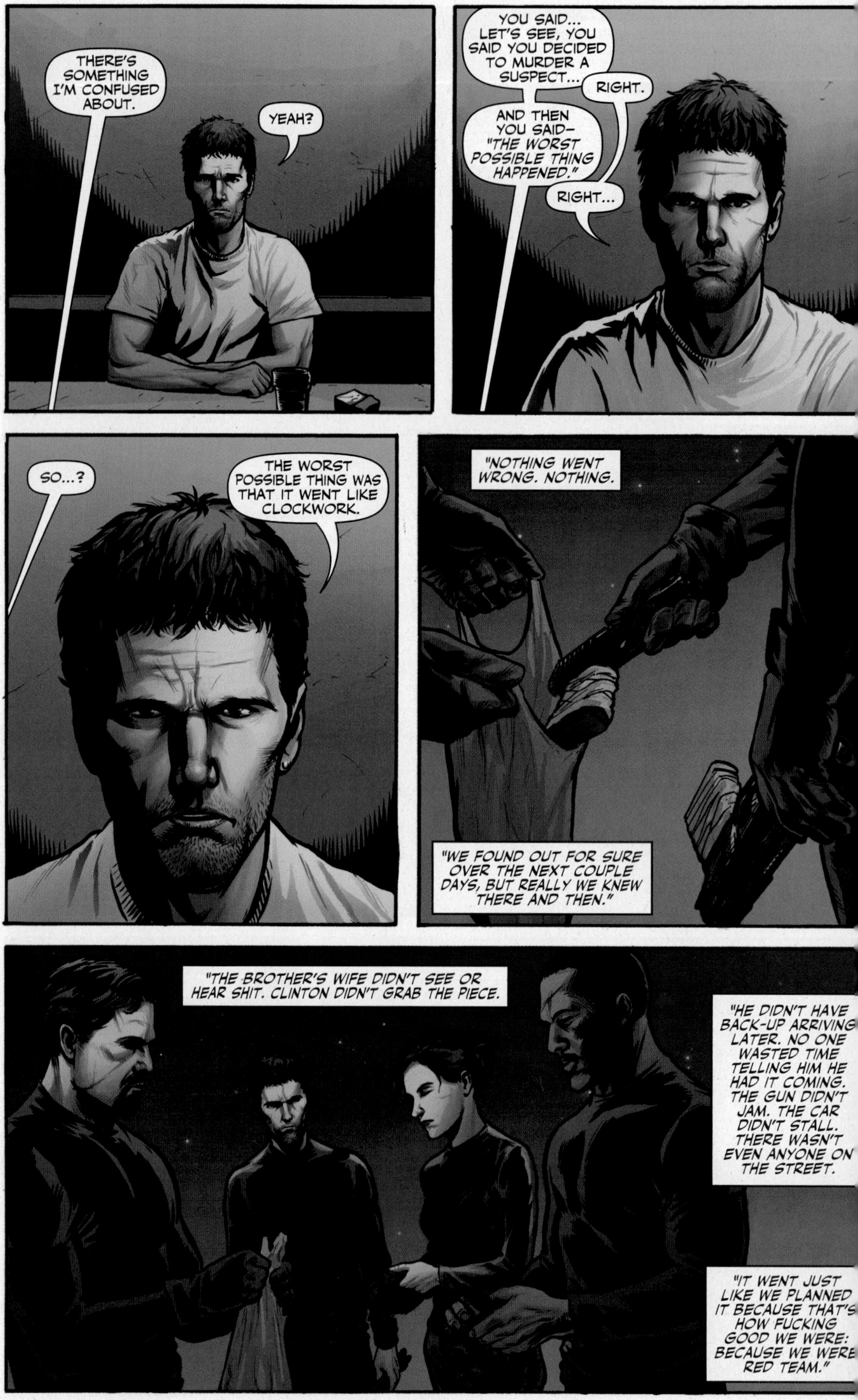
THERE'S SOMETHING I'M CONFUSED ABOUT.
YEAH?
YOU SAID... LET'S SEE, YOU SAID YOU DECIDED TO MURDER A SUSPECT...
RIGHT.
AND THEN YOU SAID– "THE WORST POSSIBLE THING HAPPENED."
RIGHT...
SO...?
THE WORST POSSIBLE THING WAS THAT IT WENT LIKE CLOCKWORK.
"NOTHING WENT WRONG. NOTHING.
"WE FOUND OUT FOR SURE OVER THE NEXT COUPLE DAYS, BUT REALLY WE KNEW THERE AND THEN."
"THE BROTHER'S WIFE DIDN'T SEE OR HEAR SHIT. CLINTON DIDN'T GRAB THE PIECE.
"HE DIDN'T HAVE BACK-UP ARRIVING LATER. NO ONE WASTED TIME TELLING HIM HE HAD IT COMING. THE GUN DIDN'T JAM. THE CAR DIDN'T STALL. THERE WASN'T EVEN ANYONE ON THE STREET.
"IT WENT JUST LIKE WE PLANNED IT BECAUSE THAT'S HOW FUCKING GOOD WE WERE: BECAUSE WE WERE RED TEAM."

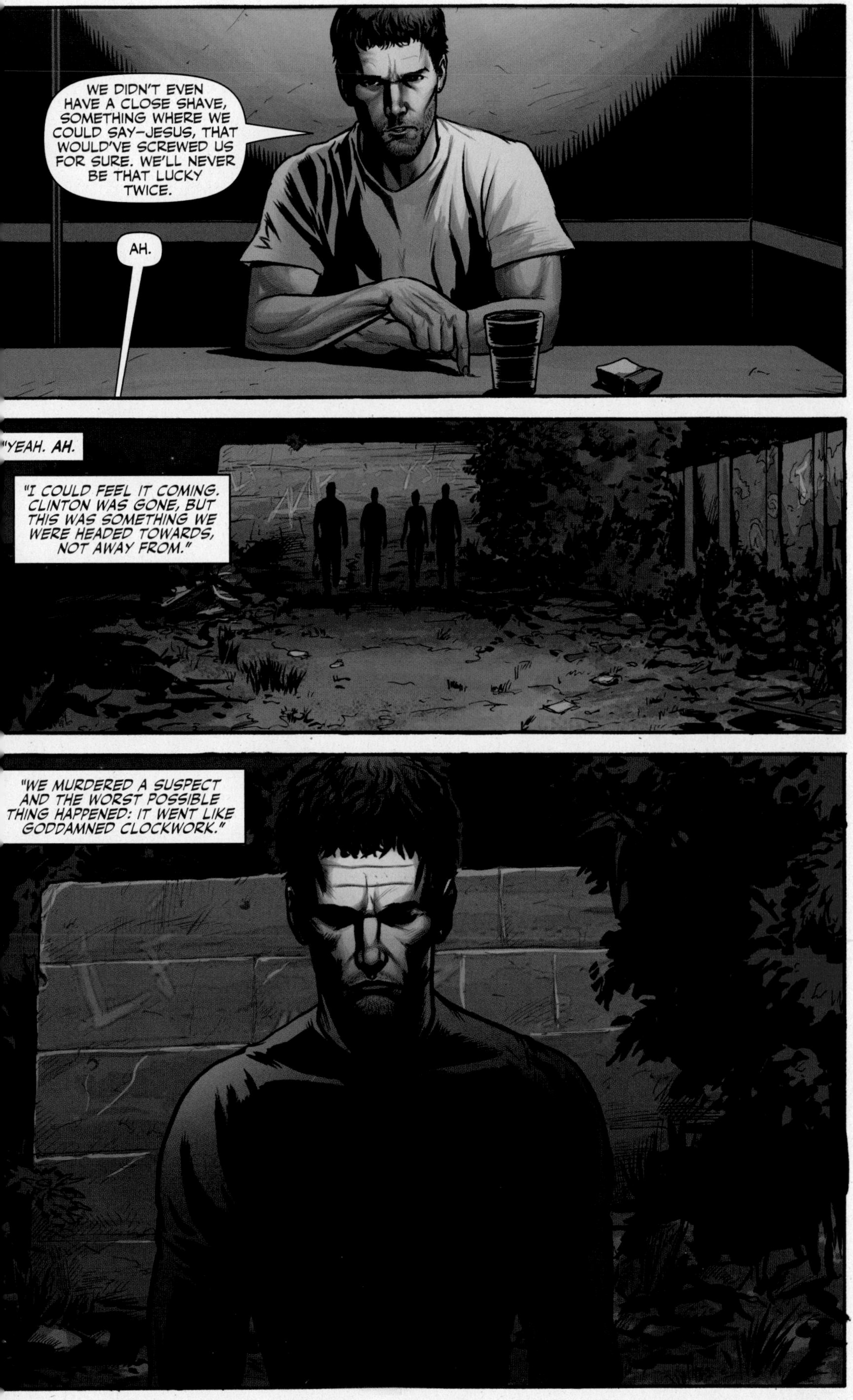
WE DIDN'T EVEN HAVE A CLOSE SHAVE, SOMETHING WHERE WE COULD SAY–JESUS, THAT WOULD'VE SCREWED US FOR SURE. WE'LL NEVER BE THAT LUCKY TWICE.
AH.
"YEAH. AH.
"I COULD FEEL IT COMING. CLINTON WAS GONE, BUT THIS WAS SOMETHING WE WERE HEADED TOWARDS, NOT AWAY FROM."
"WE MURDERED A SUSPECT AND THE WORST POSSIBLE THING HAPPENED: IT WENT LIKE GODDAMNED CLOCKWORK."

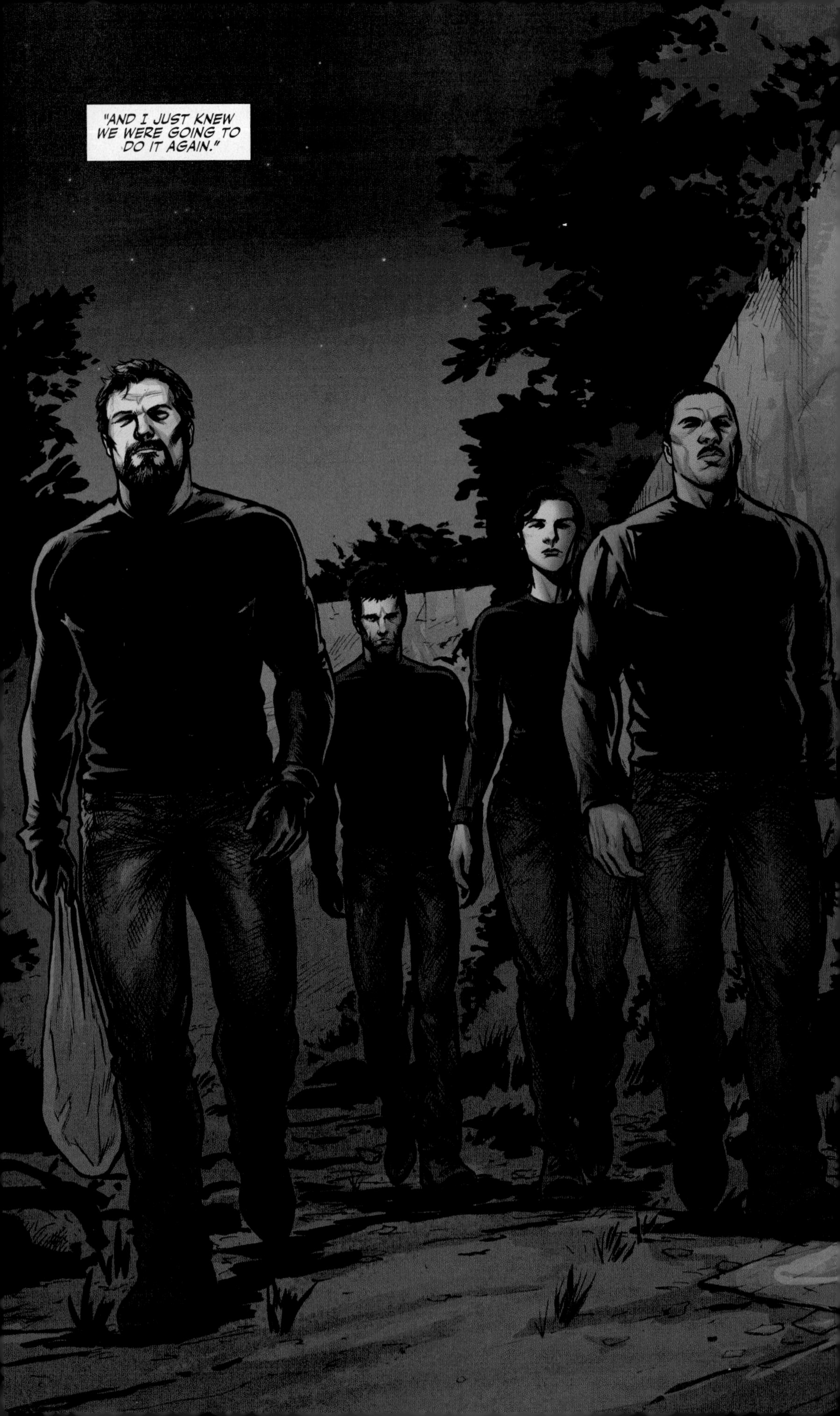
"AND I JUST KNEW WE WERE GOING TO DO IT AGAIN."

ISSUE TWO

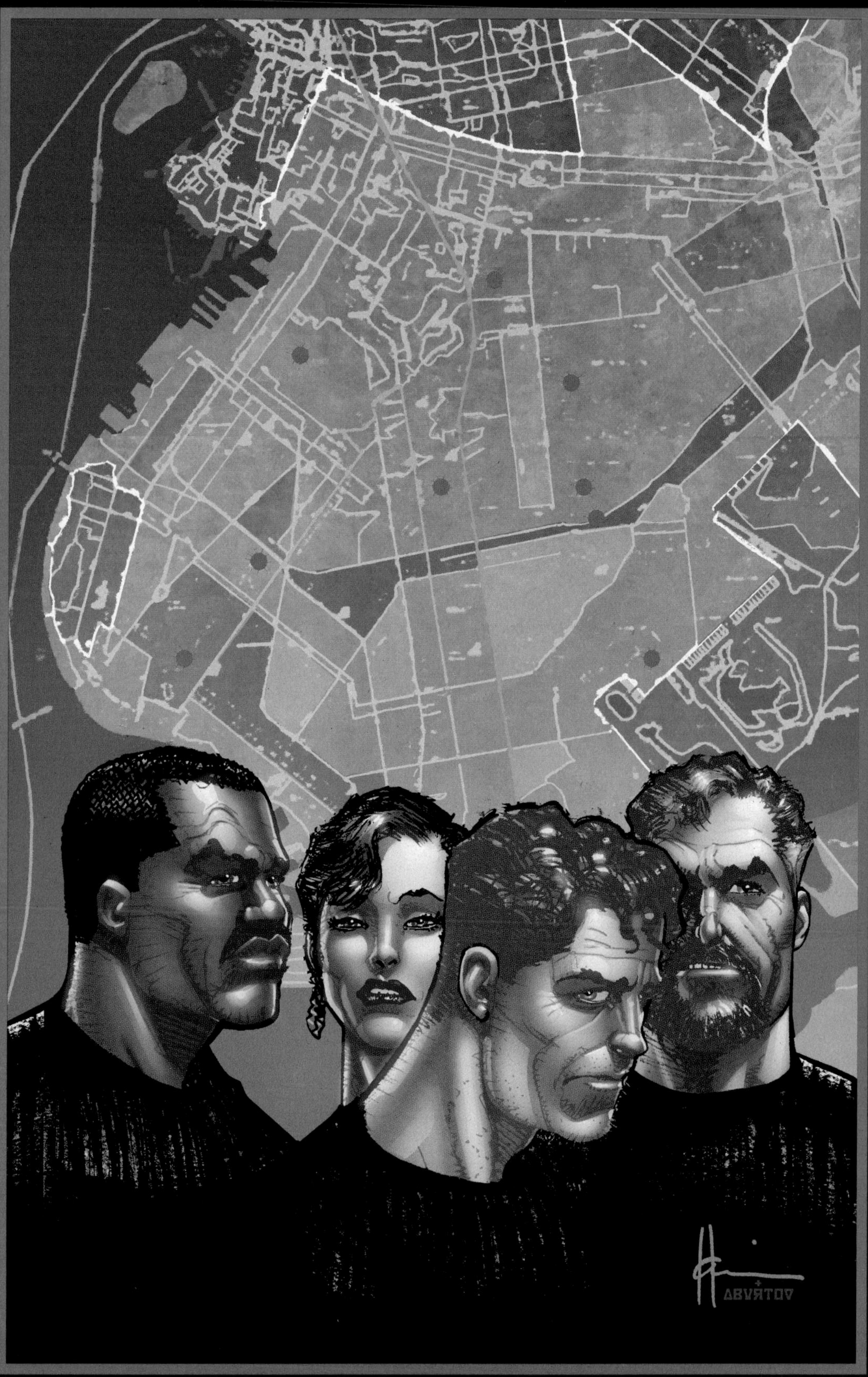
ABURTO

Issue #2 cover art by **HOWARD CHAYKIN** colors by **JESUS ABURTO**

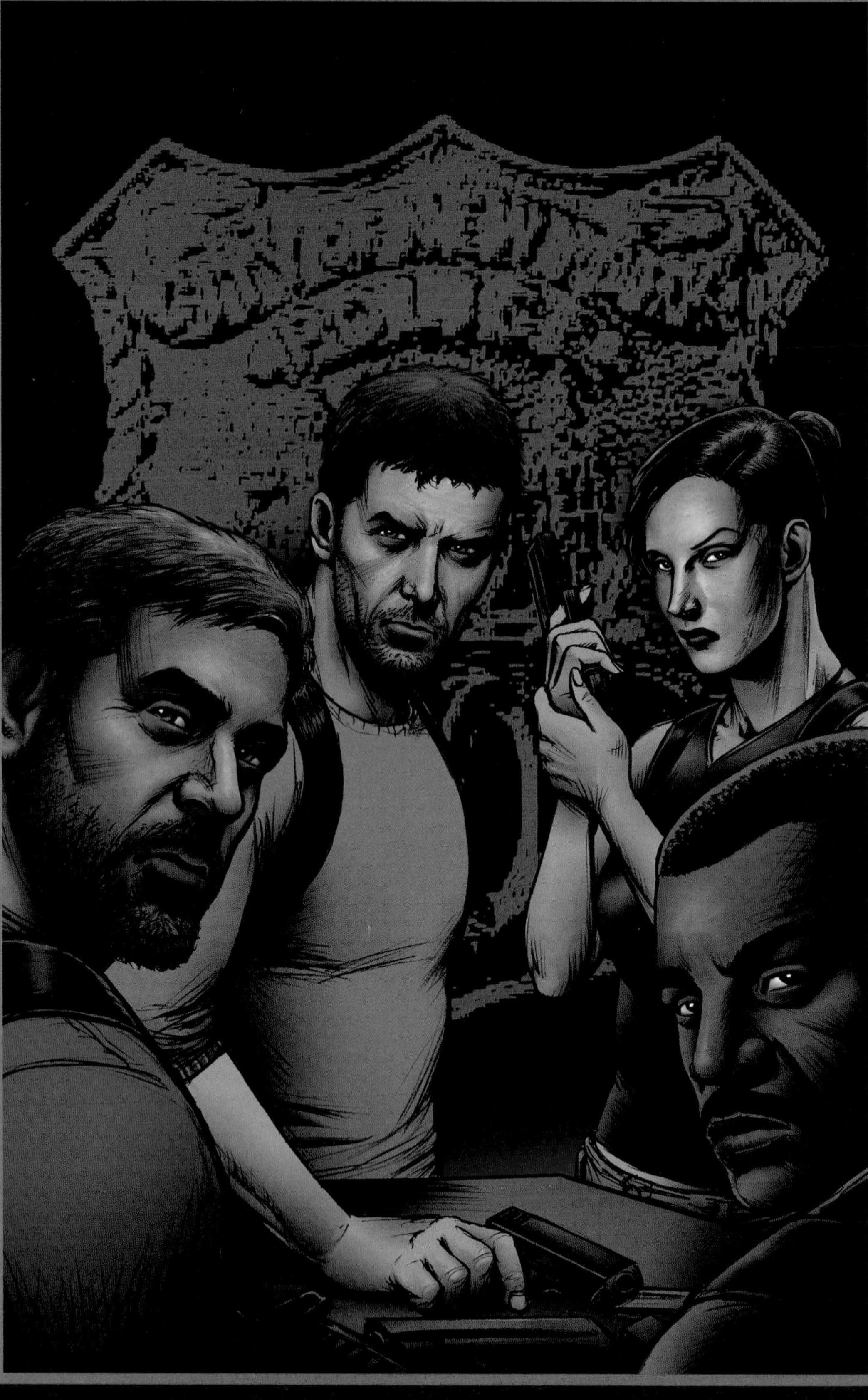

Issue #1 alternate cover by **RUSS BRAUN**

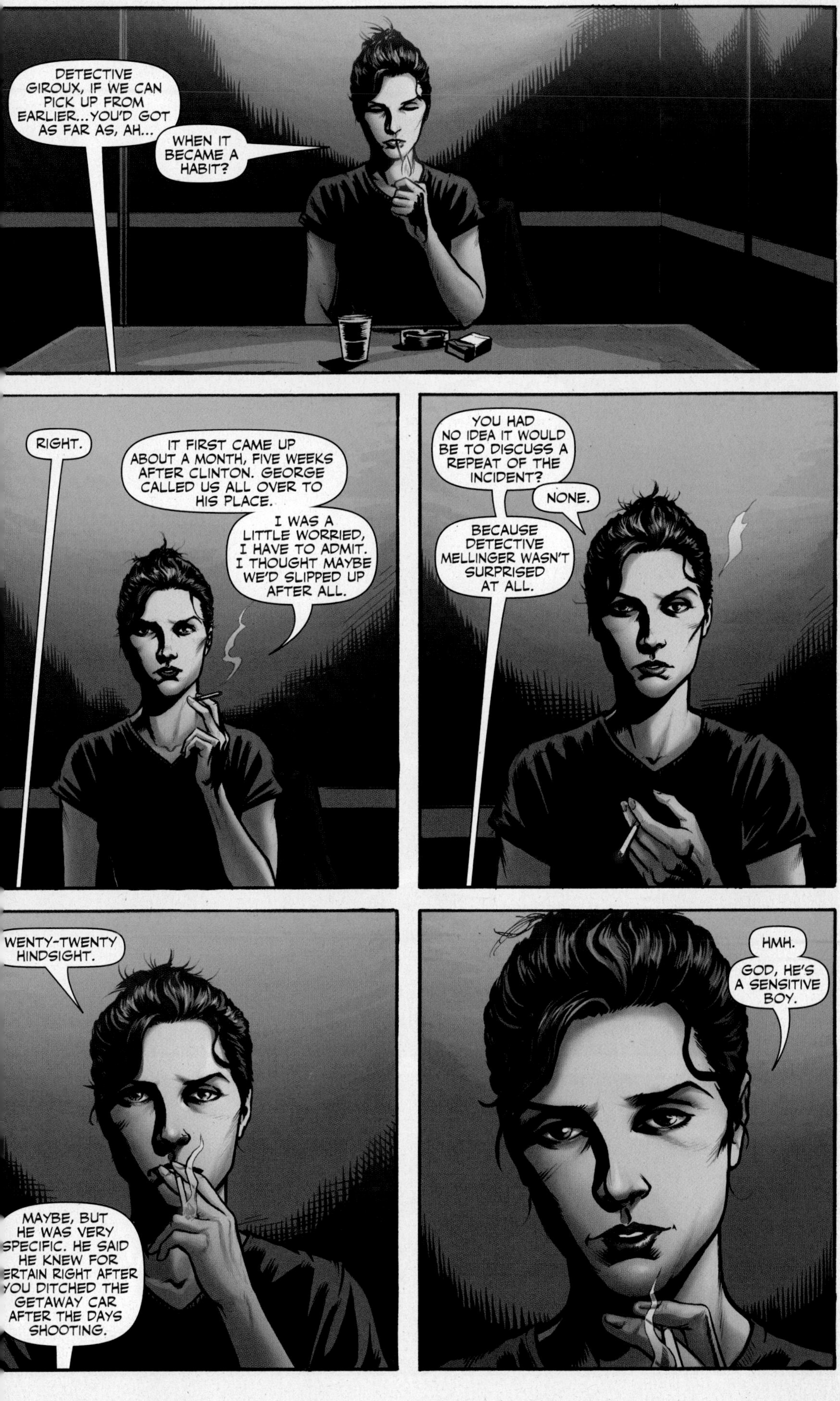
DETECTIVE GIROUX, IF WE CAN PICK UP FROM EARLIER...YOU'D GOT AS FAR AS, AH...
WHEN IT BECAME A HABIT?
RIGHT.
IT FIRST CAME UP ABOUT A MONTH, FIVE WEEKS AFTER CLINTON. GEORGE CALLED US ALL OVER TO HIS PLACE.
I WAS A LITTLE WORRIED, I HAVE TO ADMIT. I THOUGHT MAYBE WE'D SLIPPED UP AFTER ALL.
YOU HAD NO IDEA IT WOULD BE TO DISCUSS A REPEAT OF THE INCIDENT?
NONE.
BECAUSE DETECTIVE MELLINGER WASN'T SURPRISED AT ALL.
WENTY-TWENTY HINDSIGHT.
MAYBE, BUT HE WAS VERY SPECIFIC. HE SAID HE KNEW FOR ERTAIN RIGHT AFTER YOU DITCHED THE GETAWAY CAR AFTER THE DAYS SHOOTING.
HMH.
GOD, HE'S A SENSITIVE BOY.

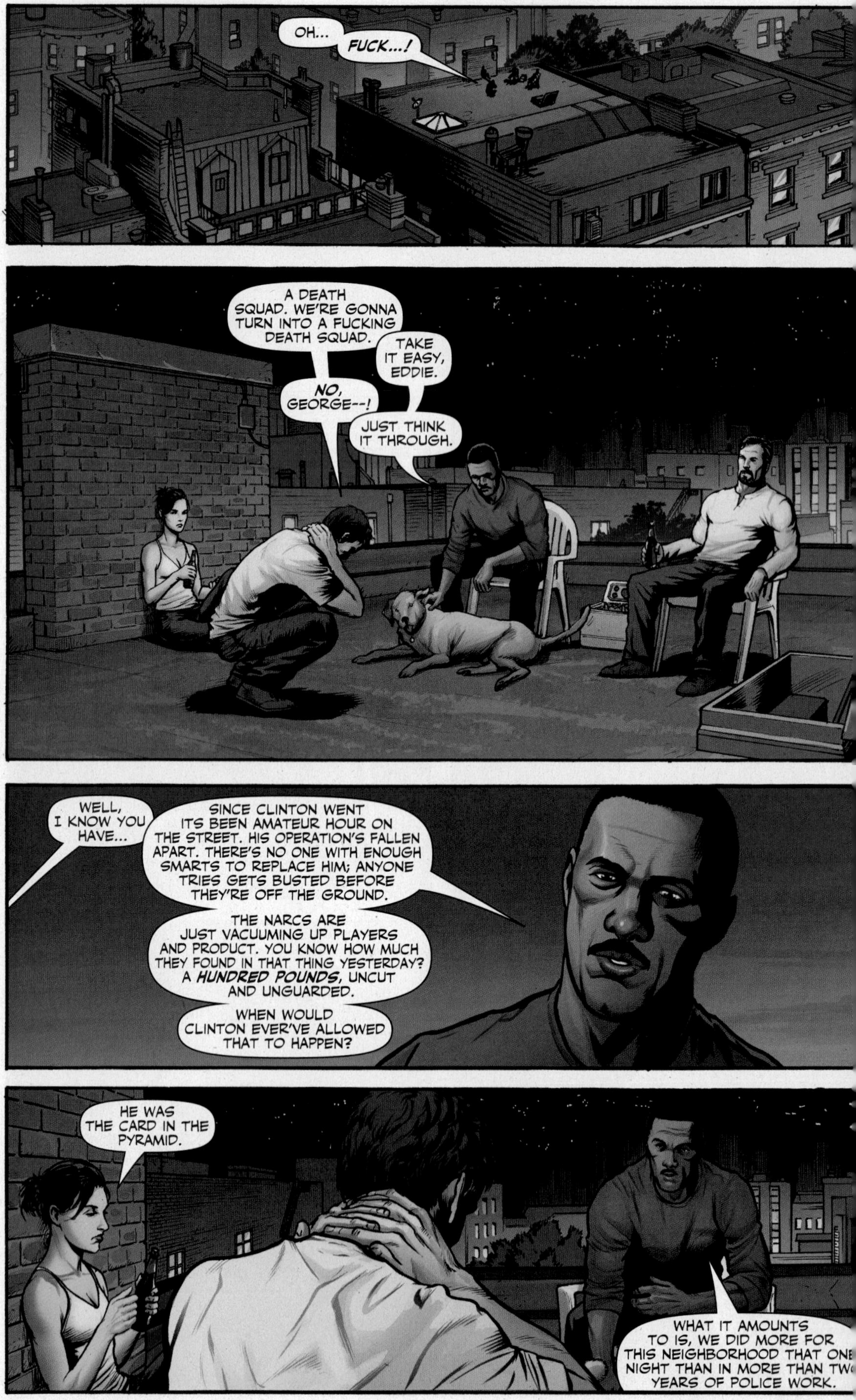
OH...
FUCK...!
A DEATH SQUAD. WE'RE GONNA TURN INTO A FUCKING DEATH SQUAD.
TAKE IT EASY, EDDIE.
NO, GEORGE--!
JUST THINK IT THROUGH.
WELL, I KNOW YOU HAVE...
SINCE CLINTON WENT ITS BEEN AMATEUR HOUR ON THE STREET. HIS OPERATION'S FALLEN APART. THERE'S NO ONE WITH ENOUGH SMARTS TO REPLACE HIM; ANYONE TRIES GETS BUSTED BEFORE THEY'RE OFF THE GROUND.
THE NARCS ARE JUST VACUUMING UP PLAYERS AND PRODUCT. YOU KNOW HOW MUCH THEY FOUND IN THAT THING YESTERDAY? A HUNDRED POUNDS, UNCUT AND UNGUARDED.
WHEN WOULD CLINTON EVER'VE ALLOWED THAT TO HAPPEN?
HE WAS THE CARD IN THE PYRAMID.
WHAT IT AMOUNTS TO IS, WE DID MORE FOR THIS NEIGHBORHOOD THAT ONE NIGHT THAN IN MORE THAN TWO YEARS OF POLICE WORK.

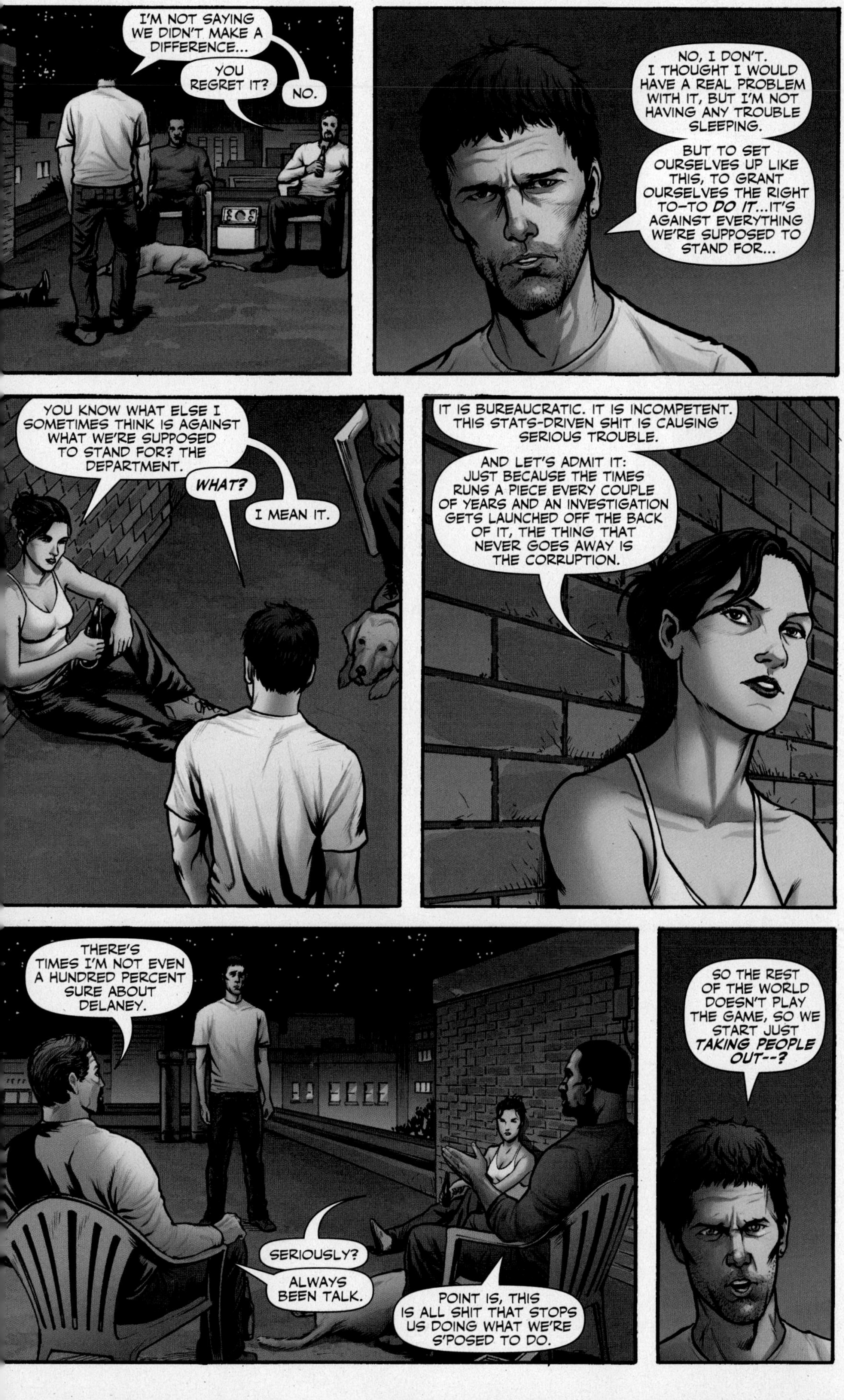

I'M NOT SAYING WE DIDN'T MAKE A DIFFERENCE...
YOU REGRET IT?
NO.
NO, I DON'T. I THOUGHT I WOULD HAVE A REAL PROBLEM WITH IT, BUT I'M NOT HAVING ANY TROUBLE SLEEPING.
BUT TO SET OURSELVES UP LIKE THIS, TO GRANT OURSELVES THE RIGHT TO--TO DO IT...IT'S AGAINST EVERYTHING WE'RE SUPPOSED TO STAND FOR...
YOU KNOW WHAT ELSE I SOMETIMES THINK IS AGAINST WHAT WE'RE SUPPOSED TO STAND FOR? THE DEPARTMENT.
WHAT?
I MEAN IT.
IT IS BUREAUCRATIC. IT IS INCOMPETENT. THIS STATS-DRIVEN SHIT IS CAUSING SERIOUS TROUBLE.
AND LET'S ADMIT IT: JUST BECAUSE THE TIMES RUNS A PIECE EVERY COUPLE OF YEARS AND AN INVESTIGATION GETS LAUNCHED OFF THE BACK OF IT, THE THING THAT NEVER GOES AWAY IS THE CORRUPTION.
THERE'S TIMES I'M NOT EVEN A HUNDRED PERCENT SURE ABOUT DELANEY.
SERIOUSLY?
ALWAYS BEEN TALK.
POINT IS, THIS IS ALL SHIT THAT STOPS US DOING WHAT WE'RE S'POSED TO DO.
SO THE REST OF THE WORLD DOESN'T PLAY THE GAME, SO WE START JUST TAKING PEOPLE OUT--?

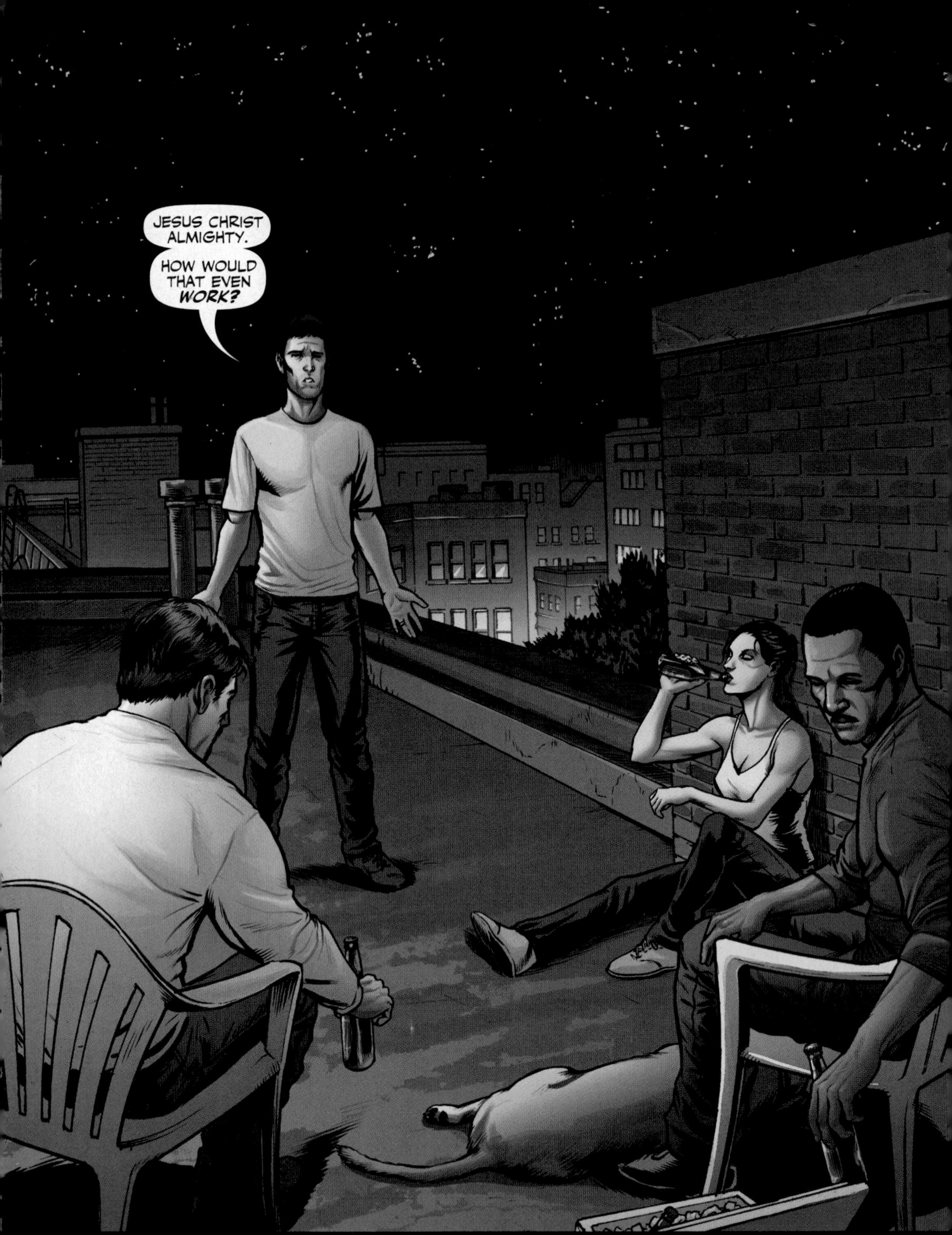
JESUS CHRIST ALMIGHTY.
HOW WOULD THAT EVEN *WORK?*

2: THE RULES

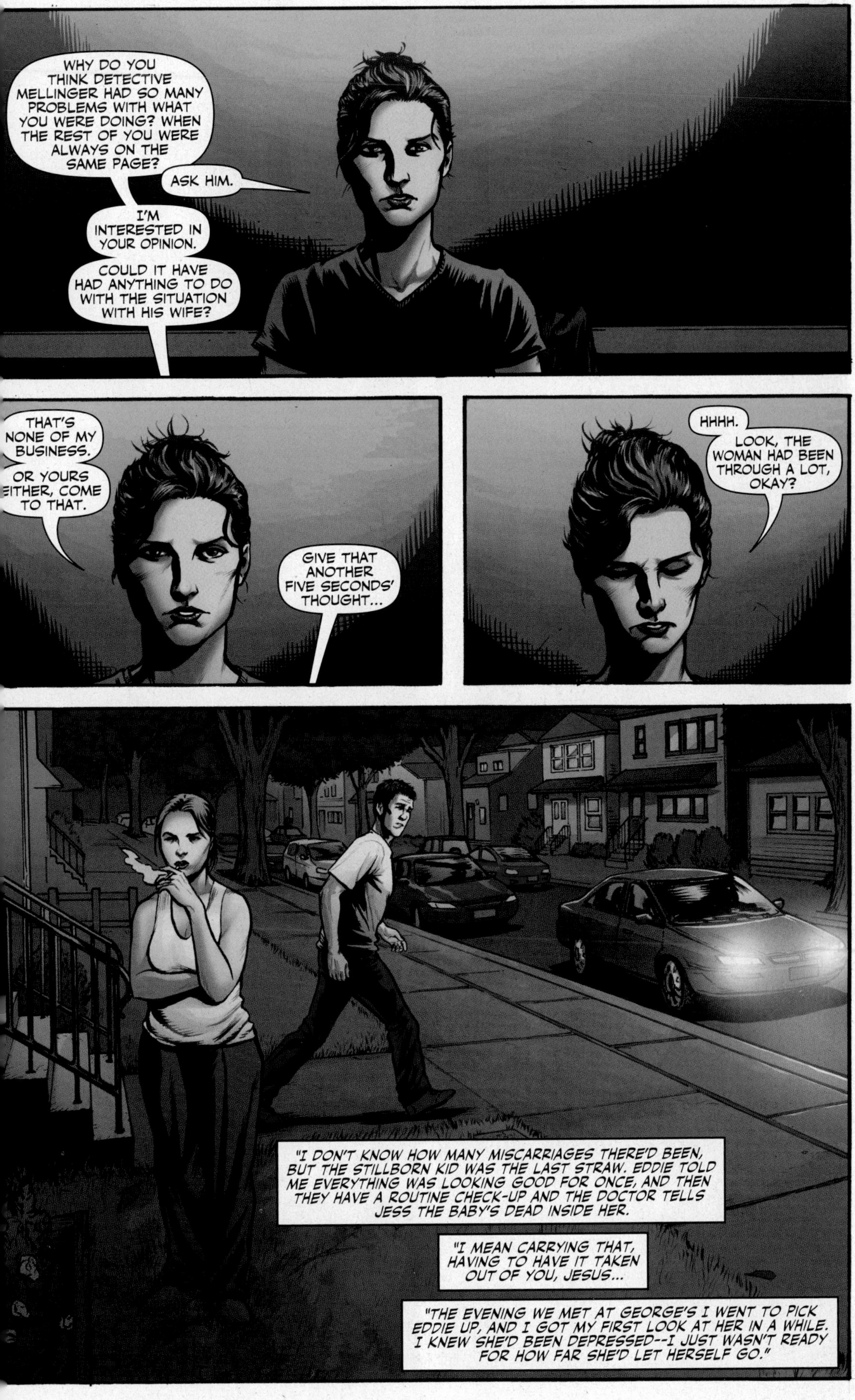
WHY DO YOU THINK DETECTIVE MELLINGER HAD SO MANY PROBLEMS WITH WHAT YOU WERE DOING? WHEN THE REST OF YOU WERE ALWAYS ON THE SAME PAGE?
ASK HIM.
I'M INTERESTED IN YOUR OPINION.
COULD IT HAVE HAD ANYTHING TO DO WITH THE SITUATION WITH HIS WIFE?
THAT'S NONE OF MY BUSINESS.
OR YOURS EITHER, COME TO THAT.
GIVE THAT ANOTHER FIVE SECONDS' THOUGHT...
HHHH.
LOOK, THE WOMAN HAD BEEN THROUGH A LOT, OKAY?
"I DON'T KNOW HOW MANY MISCARRIAGES THERE'D BEEN, BUT THE STILLBORN KID WAS THE LAST STRAW. EDDIE TOLD ME EVERYTHING WAS LOOKING GOOD FOR ONCE, AND THEN THEY HAVE A ROUTINE CHECK-UP AND THE DOCTOR TELLS JESS THE BABY'S DEAD INSIDE HER.
"I MEAN CARRYING THAT, HAVING TO HAVE IT TAKEN OUT OF YOU, JESUS...
"THE EVENING WE MET AT GEORGE'S I WENT TO PICK EDDIE UP, AND I GOT MY FIRST LOOK AT HER IN A WHILE. I KNEW SHE'D BEEN DEPRESSED--I JUST WASN'T READY FOR HOW FAR SHE'D LET HERSELF GO."

"SHE HATED ME MORE THAN THE OTHER WIVES. IT MIGHT'VE BEEN JUST THAT I WAS EDDIE'S PARTNER, IT MIGHT'VE BEEN THAT WE'RE AROUND THE SAME AGE—SO THE WAY SHE SAW IT, EDDIE HAD MORE OF A SHOT THAN DUKE OR GEORGE. WHO KNOWS?

"BEFORE THEN I DIDN'T SEE HER THAT MUCH, BUT WHEN I DID SHE LOOKED LIKE A MILLION BUCKS: MAKE-UP, HAIR, CLEAVAGE ON SHOW. JUST SO THE THREE OF US ALL KNEW WHERE WE STOOD, IF YOU TAKE MY MEANING.

"NOW SHE LOOKED...SHE LOOKED LIKE SHIT, AND IT WAS OBVIOUS IT'D BEEN LIKE THAT FOR A WHILE. AND WHAT MADE IT EVEN MORE SHOCKING WAS SHE KNEW THAT I KNEW—

"AND SHE HONESTLY COULDN'T CARE LESS."

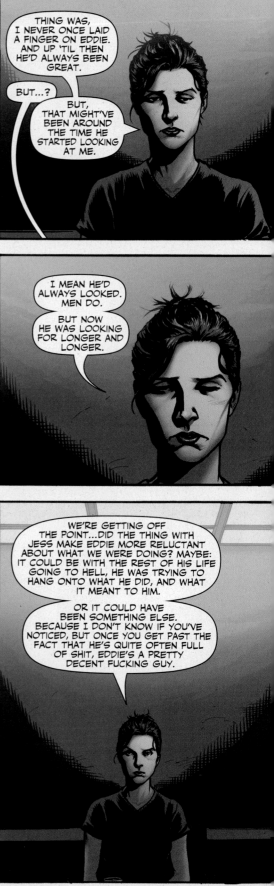

THING WAS, I NEVER ONCE LAID A FINGER ON EDDIE. AND UP 'TIL THEN HE'D ALWAYS BEEN GREAT.

BUT...?

BUT, THAT MIGHT'VE BEEN AROUND THE TIME HE STARTED LOOKING AT ME.

I MEAN HE'D ALWAYS LOOKED. MEN DO.

BUT NOW HE WAS LOOKING FOR LONGER AND LONGER.

WE'RE GETTING OFF THE POINT...DID THE THING WITH JESS MAKE EDDIE MORE RELUCTANT ABOUT WHAT WE WERE DOING? MAYBE: IT COULD BE WITH THE REST OF HIS LIFE GOING TO HELL, HE WAS TRYING TO HANG ONTO WHAT HE DID, AND WHAT IT MEANT TO HIM.

OR IT COULD HAVE BEEN SOMETHING ELSE. BECAUSE I DON'T KNOW IF YOU'VE NOTICED, BUT ONCE YOU GET PAST THE FACT THAT HE'S QUITE OFTEN FULL OF SHIT, EDDIE'S A PRETTY DECENT FUCKING GUY.

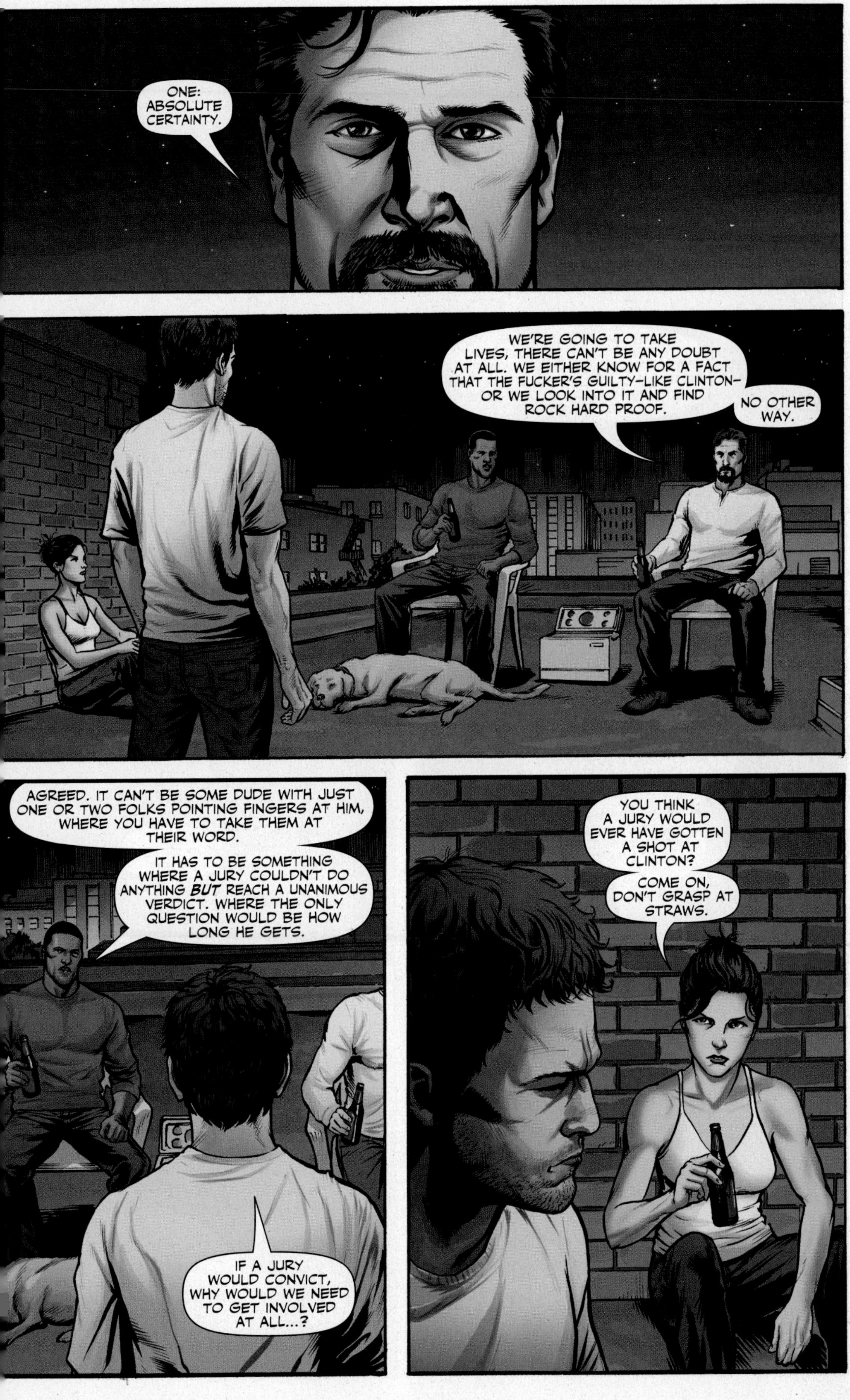

ONE: ABSOLUTE CERTAINTY.
WE'RE GOING TO TAKE LIVES, THERE CAN'T BE ANY DOUBT AT ALL. WE EITHER KNOW FOR A FACT THAT THE FUCKER'S GUILTY–LIKE CLINTON– OR WE LOOK INTO IT AND FIND ROCK HARD PROOF.
NO OTHER WAY.
AGREED. IT CAN'T BE SOME DUDE WITH JUST ONE OR TWO FOLKS POINTING FINGERS AT HIM, WHERE YOU HAVE TO TAKE THEM AT THEIR WORD.
IT HAS TO BE SOMETHING WHERE A JURY COULDN'T DO ANYTHING *BUT* REACH A UNANIMOUS VERDICT. WHERE THE ONLY QUESTION WOULD BE HOW LONG HE GETS.
IF A JURY WOULD CONVICT, WHY WOULD WE NEED TO GET INVOLVED AT ALL...?
YOU THINK A JURY WOULD EVER HAVE GOTTEN A SHOT AT CLINTON?
COME ON, DON'T GRASP AT STRAWS.

TWO: NEVER MAKE IT PERSONAL.

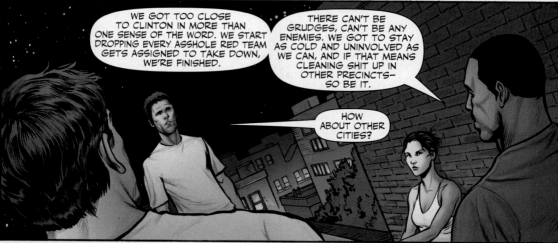

WE GOT TOO CLOSE TO CLINTON IN MORE THAN ONE SENSE OF THE WORD. WE START DROPPING EVERY ASSHOLE RED TEAM GETS ASSIGNED TO TAKE DOWN, WE'RE FINISHED.

THERE CAN'T BE GRUDGES, CAN'T BE ANY ENEMIES. WE GOT TO STAY AS COLD AND UNINVOLVED AS WE CAN, AND IF THAT MEANS CLEANING SHIT UP IN OTHER PRECINCTS— SO BE IT.

HOW ABOUT OTHER CITIES?

I'M NOT GRASPING AT ANYTHING, I JUST WANT TO KNOW HOW FAR WE'RE GOING TO TAKE THIS.

LIKE ARE WE GOING TO BE GOING AFTER AMERICA'S MOST WANTED, OR...?

THAT'S ONE WE CAN REVISIT.

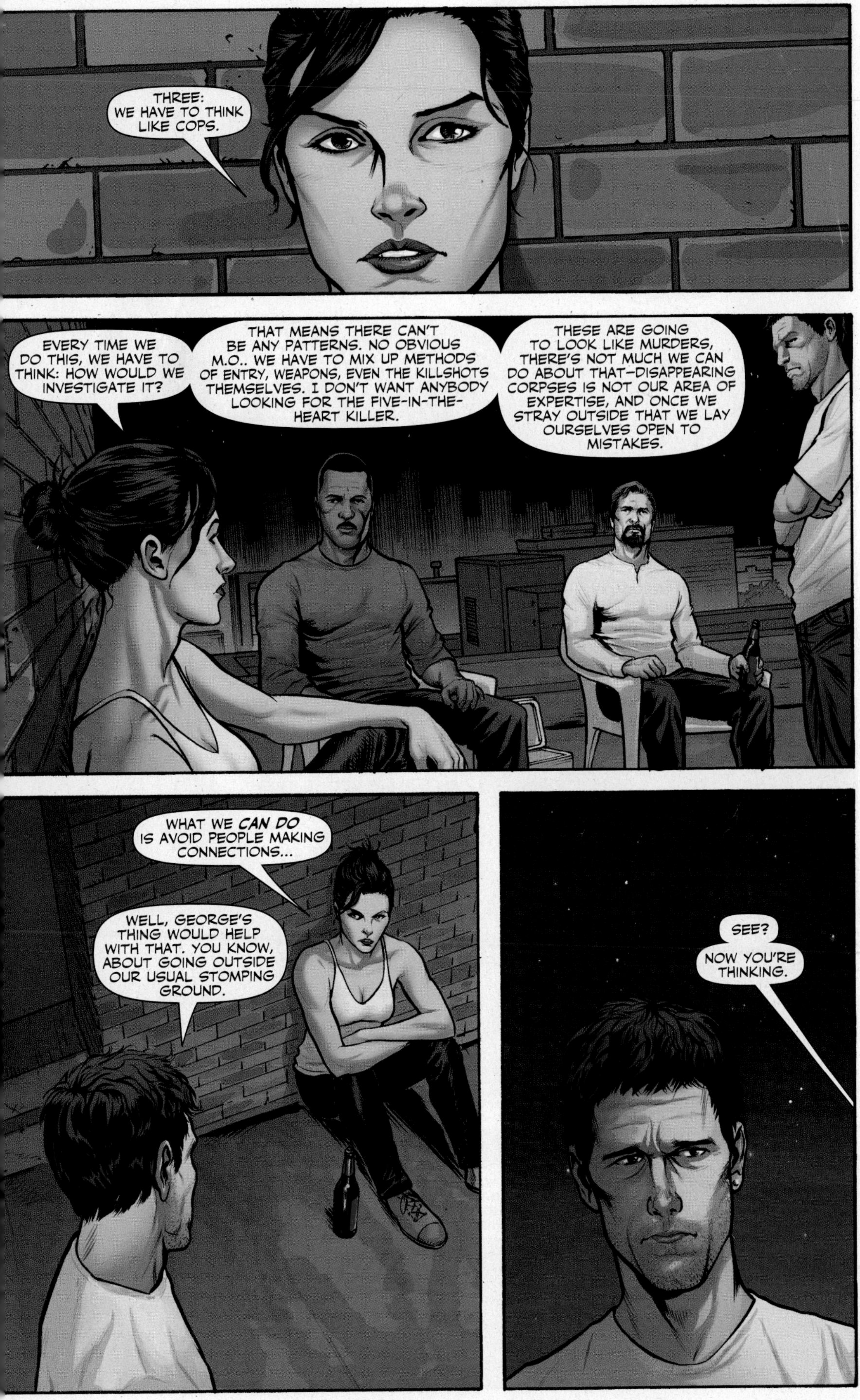
THREE: WE HAVE TO THINK LIKE COPS.
EVERY TIME WE DO THIS, WE HAVE TO THINK: HOW WOULD WE INVESTIGATE IT?
THAT MEANS THERE CAN'T BE ANY PATTERNS. NO OBVIOUS M.O.. WE HAVE TO MIX UP METHODS OF ENTRY, WEAPONS, EVEN THE KILLSHOTS THEMSELVES. I DON'T WANT ANYBODY LOOKING FOR THE FIVE-IN-THE-HEART KILLER.
THESE ARE GOING TO LOOK LIKE MURDERS, THERE'S NOT MUCH WE CAN DO ABOUT THAT—DISAPPEARING CORPSES IS NOT OUR AREA OF EXPERTISE, AND ONCE WE STRAY OUTSIDE THAT WE LAY OURSELVES OPEN TO MISTAKES.
WHAT WE *CAN DO* IS AVOID PEOPLE MAKING CONNECTIONS...
WELL, GEORGE'S THING WOULD HELP WITH THAT. YOU KNOW, ABOUT GOING OUTSIDE OUR USUAL STOMPING GROUND.
SEE?
NOW YOU'RE THINKING.

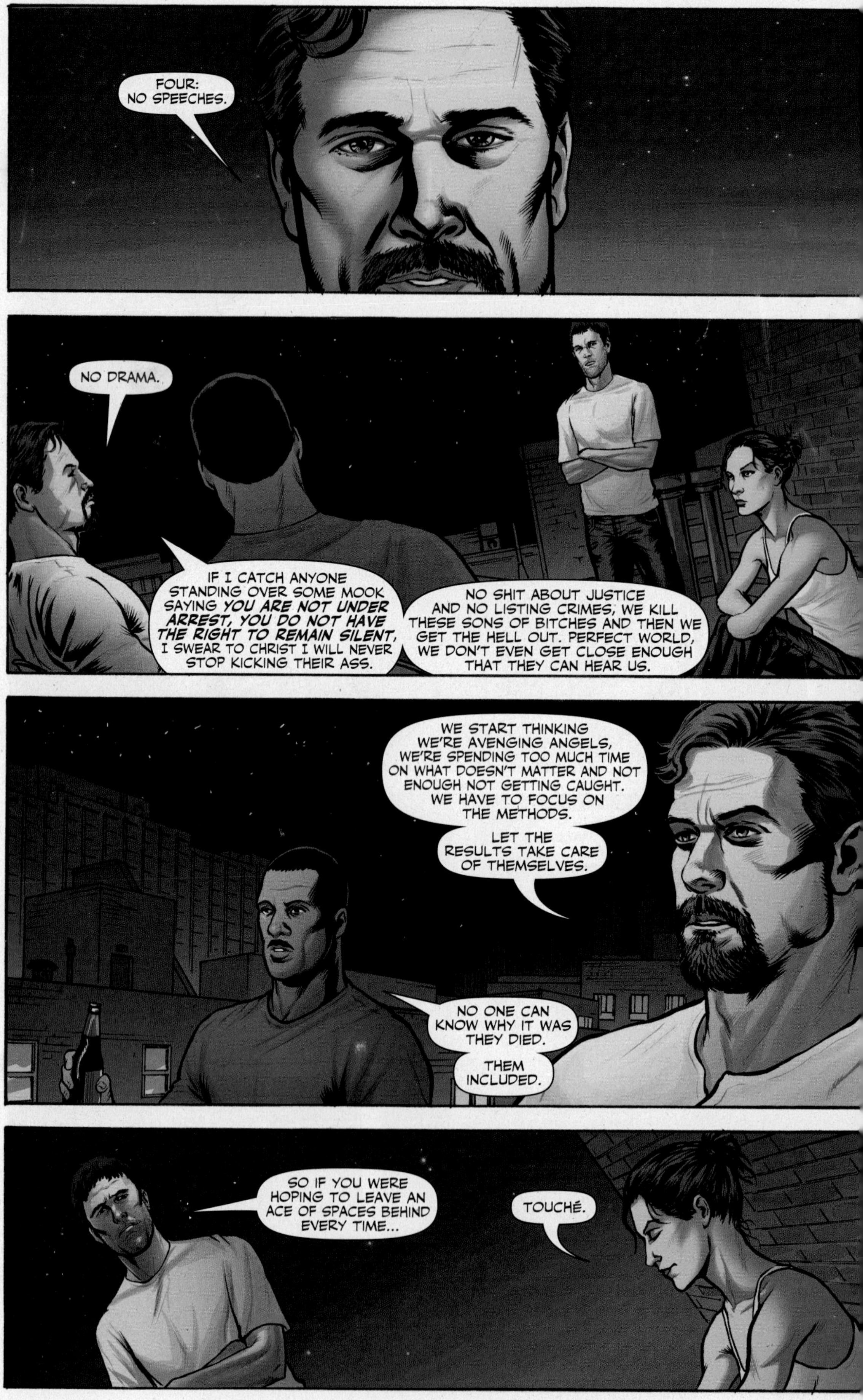

FOUR: NO SPEECHES.
NO DRAMA.
IF I CATCH ANYONE STANDING OVER SOME MOOK SAYING *YOU ARE NOT UNDER ARREST, YOU DO NOT HAVE THE RIGHT TO REMAIN SILENT*, I SWEAR TO CHRIST I WILL NEVER STOP KICKING THEIR ASS.
NO SHIT ABOUT JUSTICE AND NO LISTING CRIMES; WE KILL THESE SONS OF BITCHES AND THEN WE GET THE HELL OUT. PERFECT WORLD, WE DON'T EVEN GET CLOSE ENOUGH THAT THEY CAN HEAR US.
WE START THINKING WE'RE AVENGING ANGELS, WE'RE SPENDING TOO MUCH TIME ON WHAT DOESN'T MATTER AND NOT ENOUGH NOT GETTING CAUGHT. WE HAVE TO FOCUS ON THE METHODS.
LET THE RESULTS TAKE CARE OF THEMSELVES.
NO ONE CAN KNOW WHY IT WAS THEY DIED.
THEM INCLUDED.
SO IF YOU WERE HOPING TO LEAVE AN ACE OF SPACES BEHIND EVERY TIME...
TOUCHÉ.

FIVE: WE CAN'T BE COPS.

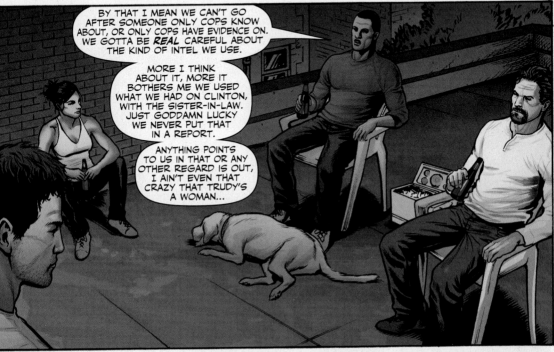

BY THAT I MEAN WE CAN'T GO AFTER SOMEONE ONLY COPS KNOW ABOUT, OR ONLY COPS HAVE EVIDENCE ON. WE GOTTA BE *REAL* CAREFUL ABOUT THE KIND OF INTEL WE USE.

MORE I THINK ABOUT IT, MORE IT BOTHERS ME WE USED WHAT WE HAD ON CLINTON, WITH THE SISTER-IN-LAW. JUST GODDAMN LUCKY WE NEVER PUT THAT IN A REPORT.

ANYTHING POINTS TO US IN THAT OR ANY OTHER REGARD IS OUT, I AIN'T EVEN THAT CRAZY THAT TRUDY'S A WOMAN...

AH, THAT CAME OUT WRONG. I MEAN IN THE SENSE THAT WE'RE KNOWN TO BE THREE MALE OFFICERS AND ONE FEMALE, AND IF A WITNESS—

I KNOW WHAT YOU MEAN.

SO HOW YOU DOING THERE, EDDIE?

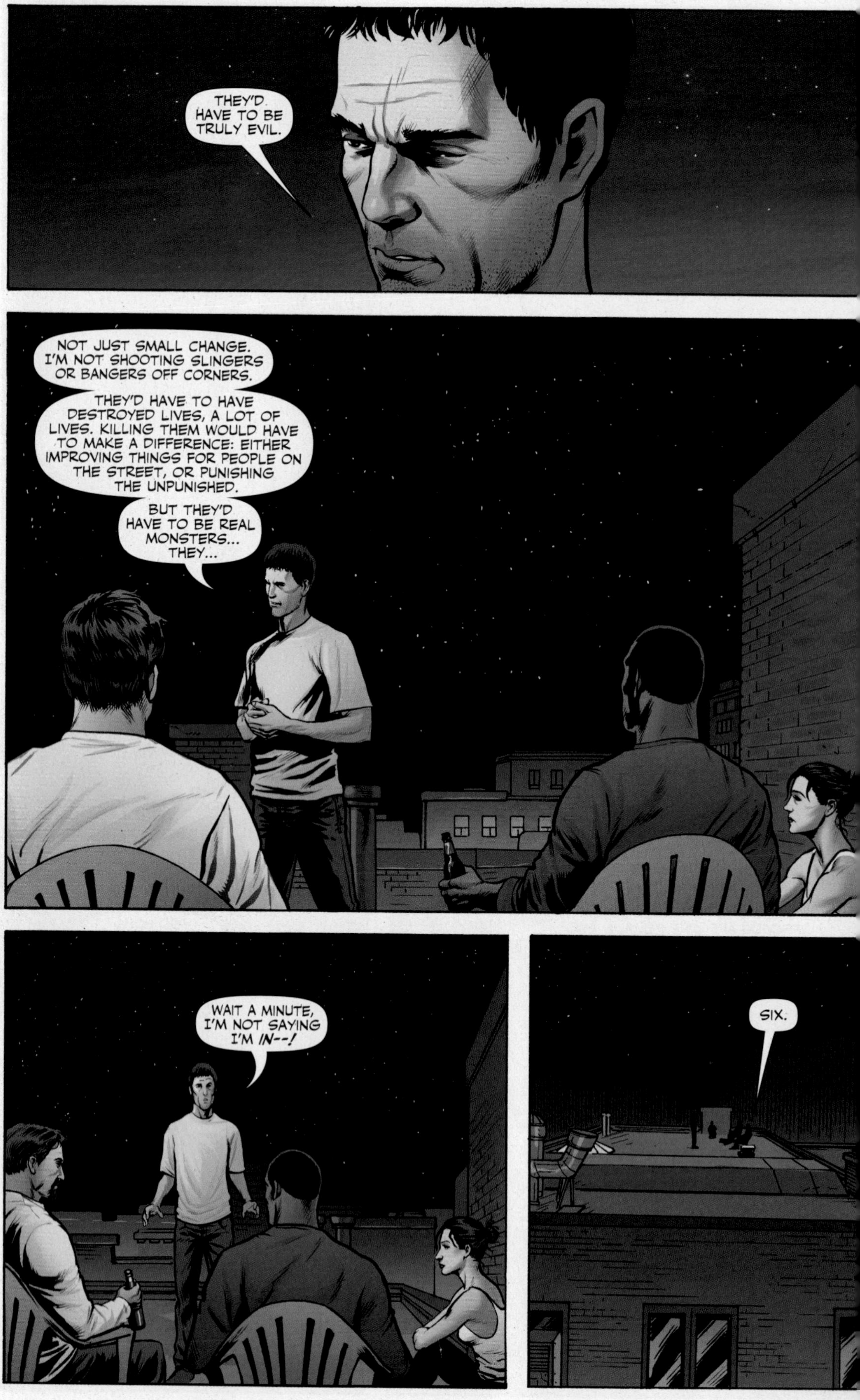
THEY'D HAVE TO BE TRULY EVIL.
NOT JUST SMALL CHANGE. I'M NOT SHOOTING SLINGERS OR BANGERS OFF CORNERS.
THEY'D HAVE TO HAVE DESTROYED LIVES, A LOT OF LIVES. KILLING THEM WOULD HAVE TO MAKE A DIFFERENCE: EITHER IMPROVING THINGS FOR PEOPLE ON THE STREET, OR PUNISHING THE UNPUNISHED.
BUT THEY'D HAVE TO BE REAL MONSTERS... THEY...
WAIT A MINUTE, I'M NOT SAYING I'M *IN--!*
SIX.

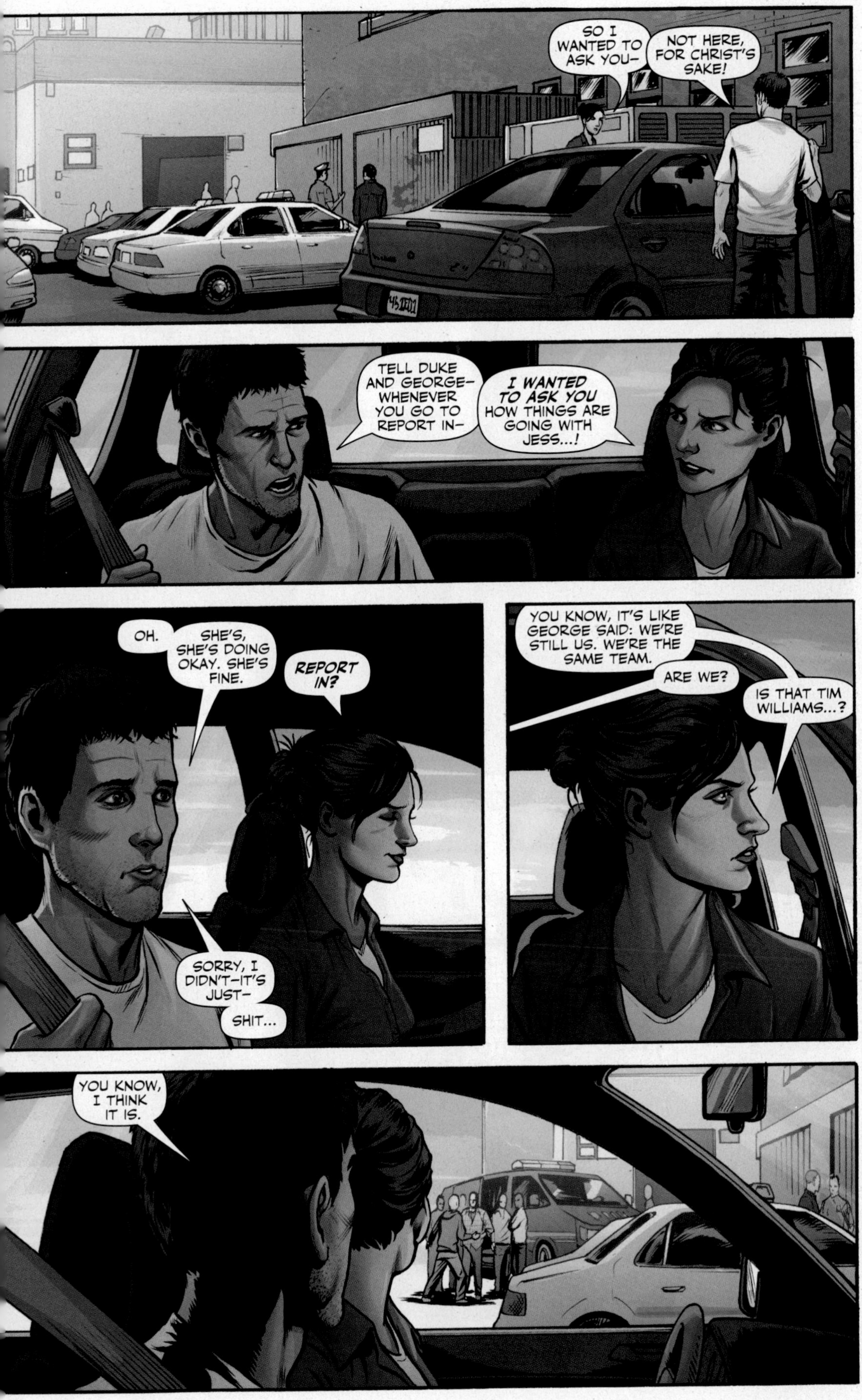
SO I WANTED TO ASK YOU-
NOT HERE, FOR CHRIST'S SAKE!
TELL DUKE AND GEORGE- WHENEVER YOU GO TO REPORT IN-
I WANTED TO ASK YOU HOW THINGS ARE GOING WITH JESS...!
OH.
SHE'S, SHE'S DOING OKAY. SHE'S FINE.
REPORT IN?
SORRY, I DIDN'T-IT'S JUST-
SHIT...
YOU KNOW, IT'S LIKE GEORGE SAID: WE'RE STILL US. WE'RE THE SAME TEAM.
ARE WE?
IS THAT TIM WILLIAMS...?
YOU KNOW, I THINK IT IS.

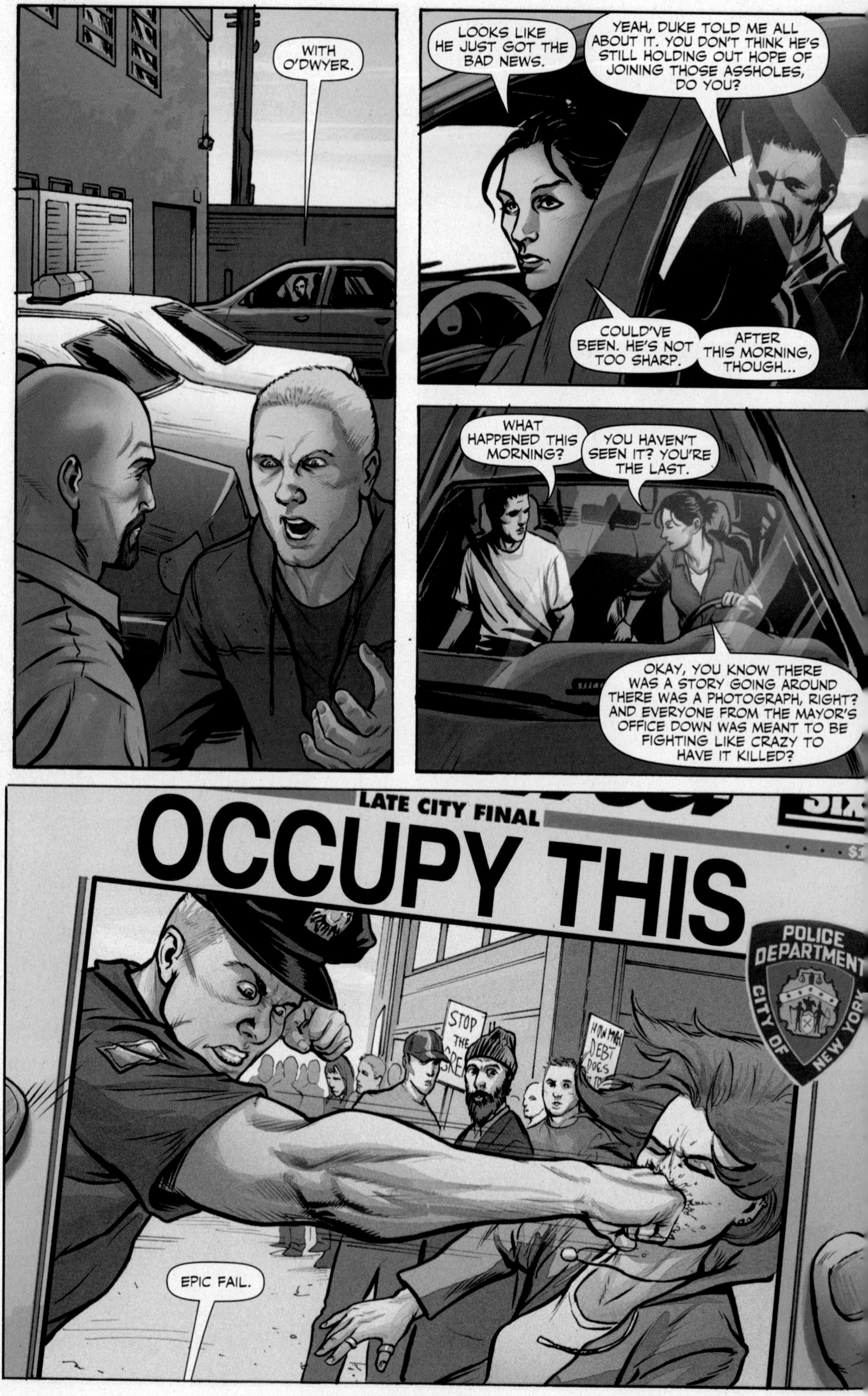
WITH O'DWYER.
LOOKS LIKE HE JUST GOT THE BAD NEWS.
YEAH, DUKE TOLD ME ALL ABOUT IT. YOU DON'T THINK HE'S STILL HOLDING OUT HOPE OF JOINING THOSE ASSHOLES, DO YOU?
COULD'VE BEEN. HE'S NOT TOO SHARP.
AFTER THIS MORNING, THOUGH...
WHAT HAPPENED THIS MORNING?
YOU HAVEN'T SEEN IT? YOU'RE THE LAST.
OKAY, YOU KNOW THERE WAS A STORY GOING AROUND THERE WAS A PHOTOGRAPH, RIGHT? AND EVERYONE FROM THE MAYOR'S OFFICE DOWN WAS MEANT TO BE FIGHTING LIKE CRAZY TO HAVE IT KILLED?
LATE CITY FINAL
OCCUPY THIS
POLICE DEPARTMENT
CITY OF NEW YORK
STOP THE
EPIC FAIL.

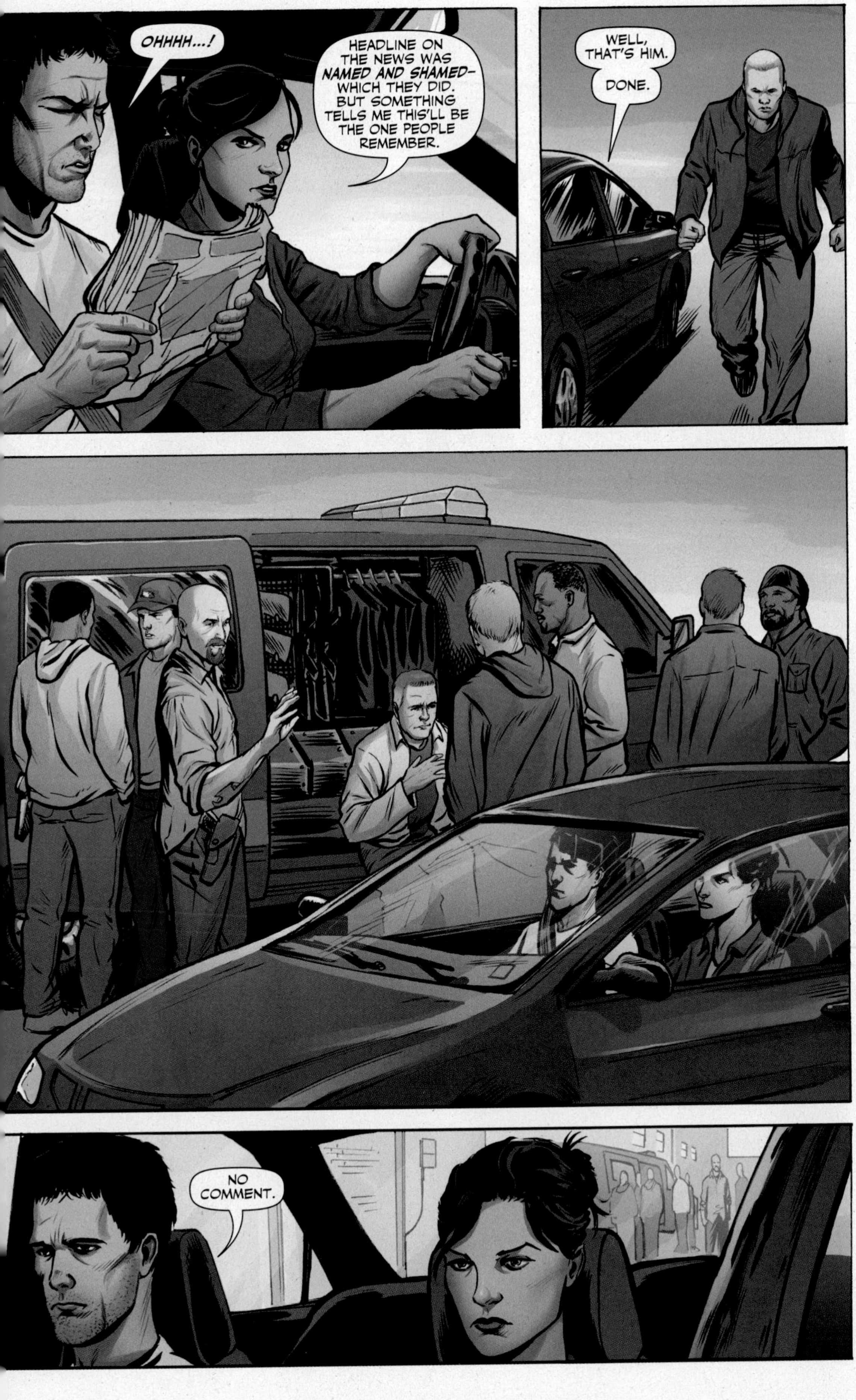
OHHHH...!
HEADLINE ON THE NEWS WAS NAMED AND SHAMED— WHICH THEY DID. BUT SOMETHING TELLS ME THIS'LL BE THE ONE PEOPLE REMEMBER.
WELL, THAT'S HIM.
DONE.
NO COMMENT.

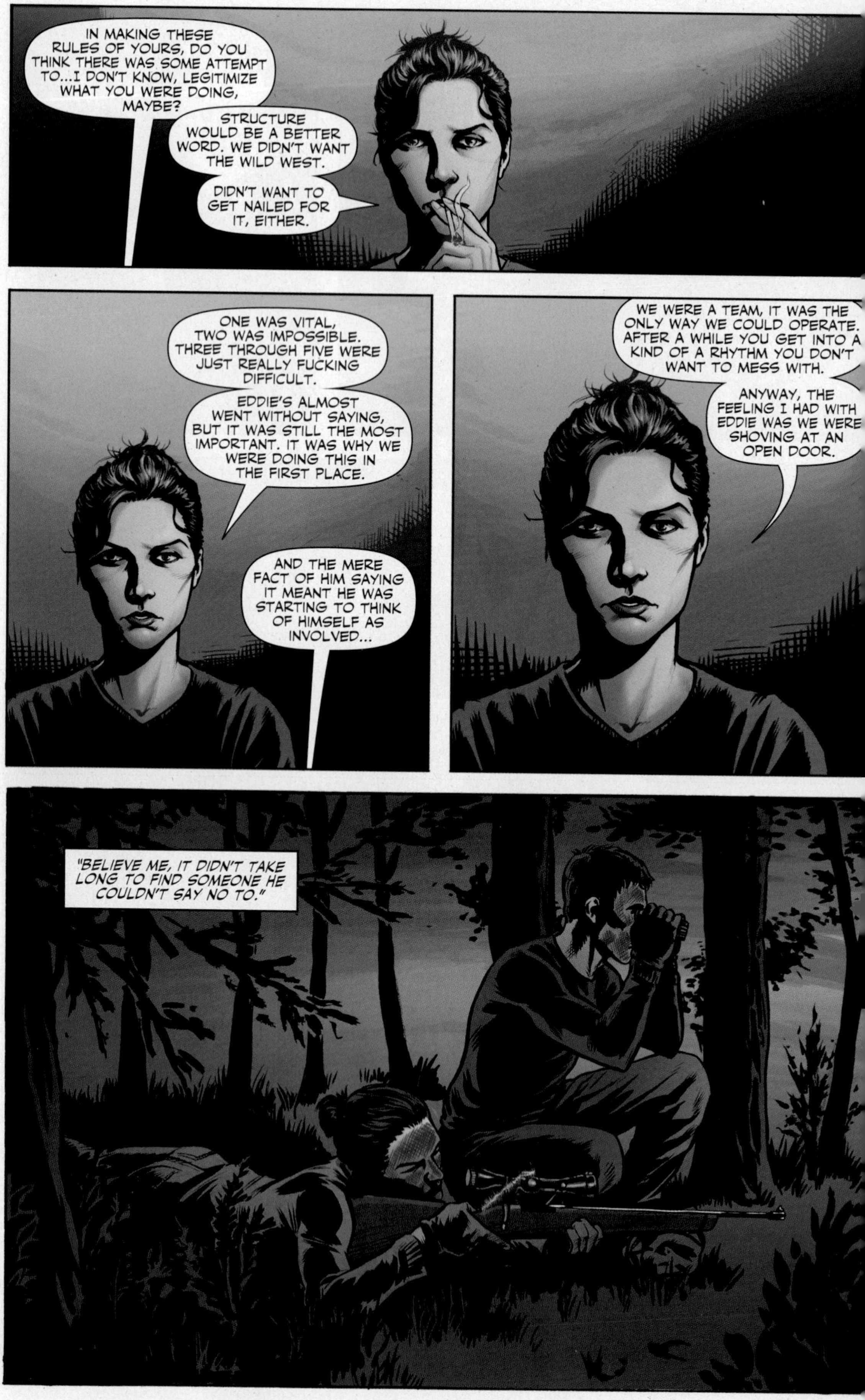
IN MAKING THESE RULES OF YOURS, DO YOU THINK THERE WAS SOME ATTEMPT TO...I DON'T KNOW, LEGITIMIZE WHAT YOU WERE DOING, MAYBE?
STRUCTURE WOULD BE A BETTER WORD. WE DIDN'T WANT THE WILD WEST.
DIDN'T WANT TO GET NAILED FOR IT, EITHER.
ONE WAS VITAL, TWO WAS IMPOSSIBLE. THREE THROUGH FIVE WERE JUST REALLY FUCKING DIFFICULT.
EDDIE'S ALMOST WENT WITHOUT SAYING, BUT IT WAS STILL THE MOST IMPORTANT. IT WAS WHY WE WERE DOING THIS IN THE FIRST PLACE.
AND THE MERE FACT OF HIM SAYING IT MEANT HE WAS STARTING TO THINK OF HIMSELF AS INVOLVED...
WE WERE A TEAM, IT WAS THE ONLY WAY WE COULD OPERATE. AFTER A WHILE YOU GET INTO A KIND OF A RHYTHM YOU DON'T WANT TO MESS WITH.
ANYWAY, THE FEELING I HAD WITH EDDIE WAS WE WERE SHOVING AT AN OPEN DOOR.
"BELIEVE ME, IT DIDN'T TAKE LONG TO FIND SOMEONE HE COULDN'T SAY NO TO."

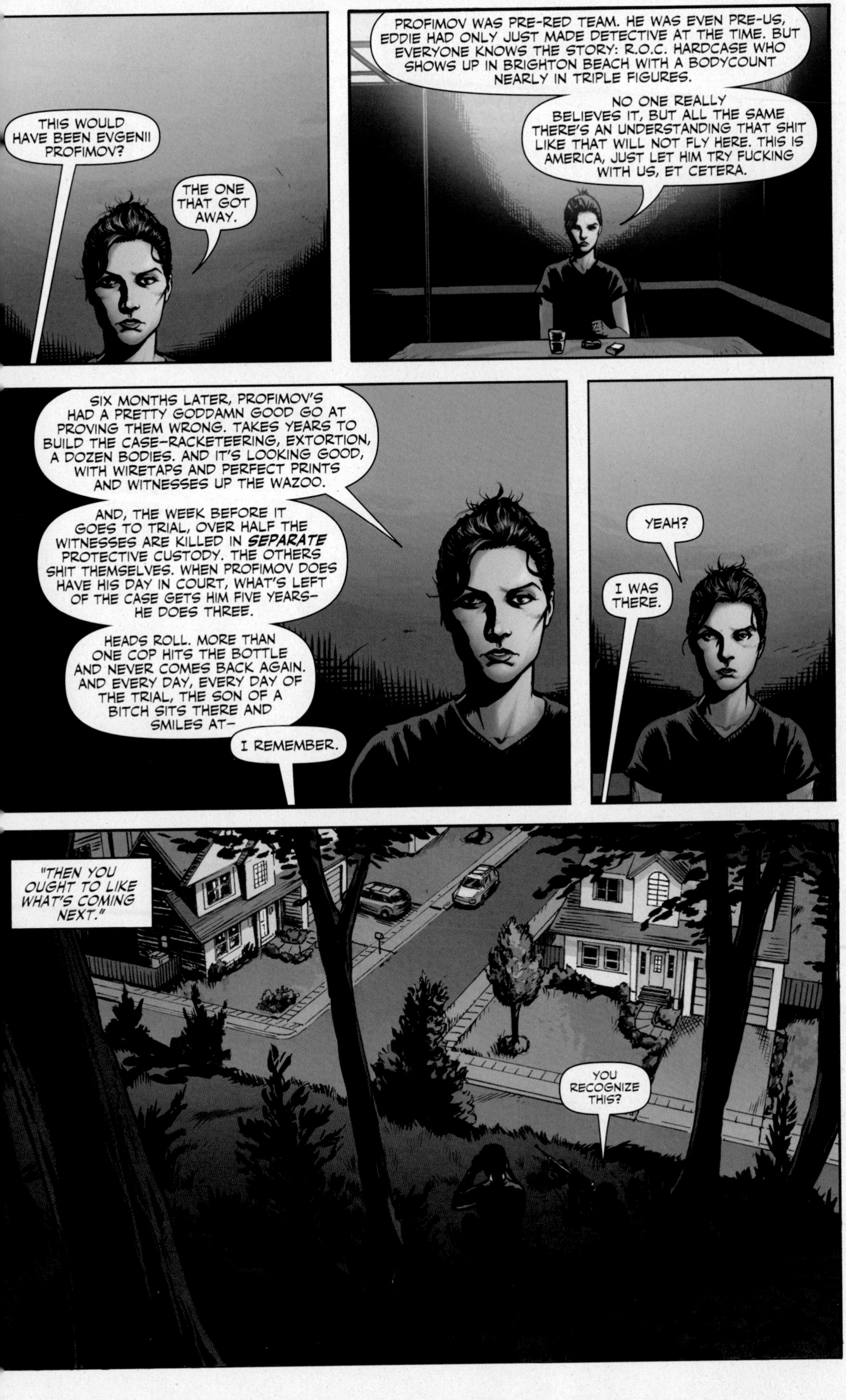
THIS WOULD HAVE BEEN EVGENII PROFIMOV?
THE ONE THAT GOT AWAY.
PROFIMOV WAS PRE-RED TEAM. HE WAS EVEN PRE-US, EDDIE HAD ONLY JUST MADE DETECTIVE AT THE TIME. BUT EVERYONE KNOWS THE STORY: R.O.C. HARDCASE WHO SHOWS UP IN BRIGHTON BEACH WITH A BODYCOUNT NEARLY IN TRIPLE FIGURES.
NO ONE REALLY BELIEVES IT, BUT ALL THE SAME THERE'S AN UNDERSTANDING THAT SHIT LIKE THAT WILL NOT FLY HERE. THIS IS AMERICA, JUST LET HIM TRY FUCKING WITH US, ET CETERA.
SIX MONTHS LATER, PROFIMOV'S HAD A PRETTY GODDAMN GOOD GO AT PROVING THEM WRONG. TAKES YEARS TO BUILD THE CASE–RACKETEERING, EXTORTION, A DOZEN BODIES. AND IT'S LOOKING GOOD, WITH WIRETAPS AND PERFECT PRINTS AND WITNESSES UP THE WAZOO.
AND, THE WEEK BEFORE IT GOES TO TRIAL, OVER HALF THE WITNESSES ARE KILLED IN ***SEPARATE*** PROTECTIVE CUSTODY. THE OTHERS SHIT THEMSELVES. WHEN PROFIMOV DOES HAVE HIS DAY IN COURT, WHAT'S LEFT OF THE CASE GETS HIM FIVE YEARS–HE DOES THREE.
HEADS ROLL. MORE THAN ONE COP HITS THE BOTTLE AND NEVER COMES BACK AGAIN. AND EVERY DAY, EVERY DAY OF THE TRIAL, THE SON OF A BITCH SITS THERE AND SMILES AT–
I REMEMBER.
YEAH?
I WAS THERE.
"THEN YOU OUGHT TO LIKE WHAT'S COMING NEXT."
YOU RECOGNIZE THIS?

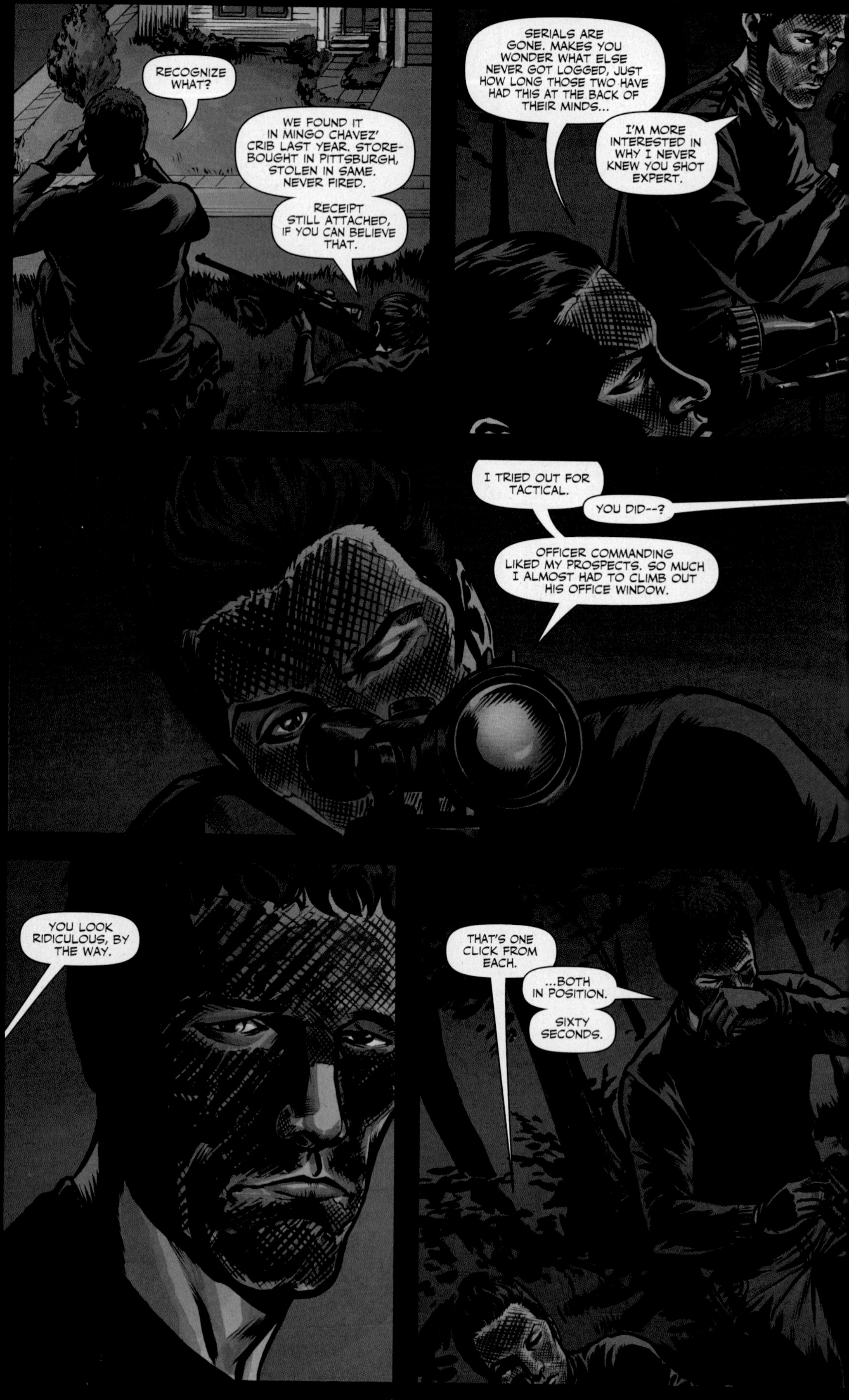
RECOGNIZE WHAT?
WE FOUND IT IN MINGO CHAVEZ' CRIB LAST YEAR. STORE-BOUGHT IN PITTSBURGH, STOLEN IN SAME. NEVER FIRED.
RECEIPT STILL ATTACHED, IF YOU CAN BELIEVE THAT.
SERIALS ARE GONE. MAKES YOU WONDER WHAT ELSE NEVER GOT LOGGED, JUST HOW LONG THOSE TWO HAVE HAD THIS AT THE BACK OF THEIR MINDS...
I'M MORE INTERESTED IN WHY I NEVER KNEW YOU SHOT EXPERT.
I TRIED OUT FOR TACTICAL.
YOU DID--?
OFFICER COMMANDING LIKED MY PROSPECTS. SO MUCH I ALMOST HAD TO CLIMB OUT HIS OFFICE WINDOW.
YOU LOOK RIDICULOUS, BY THE WAY.
THAT'S ONE CLICK FROM EACH.
...BOTH IN POSITION.
SIXTY SECONDS.

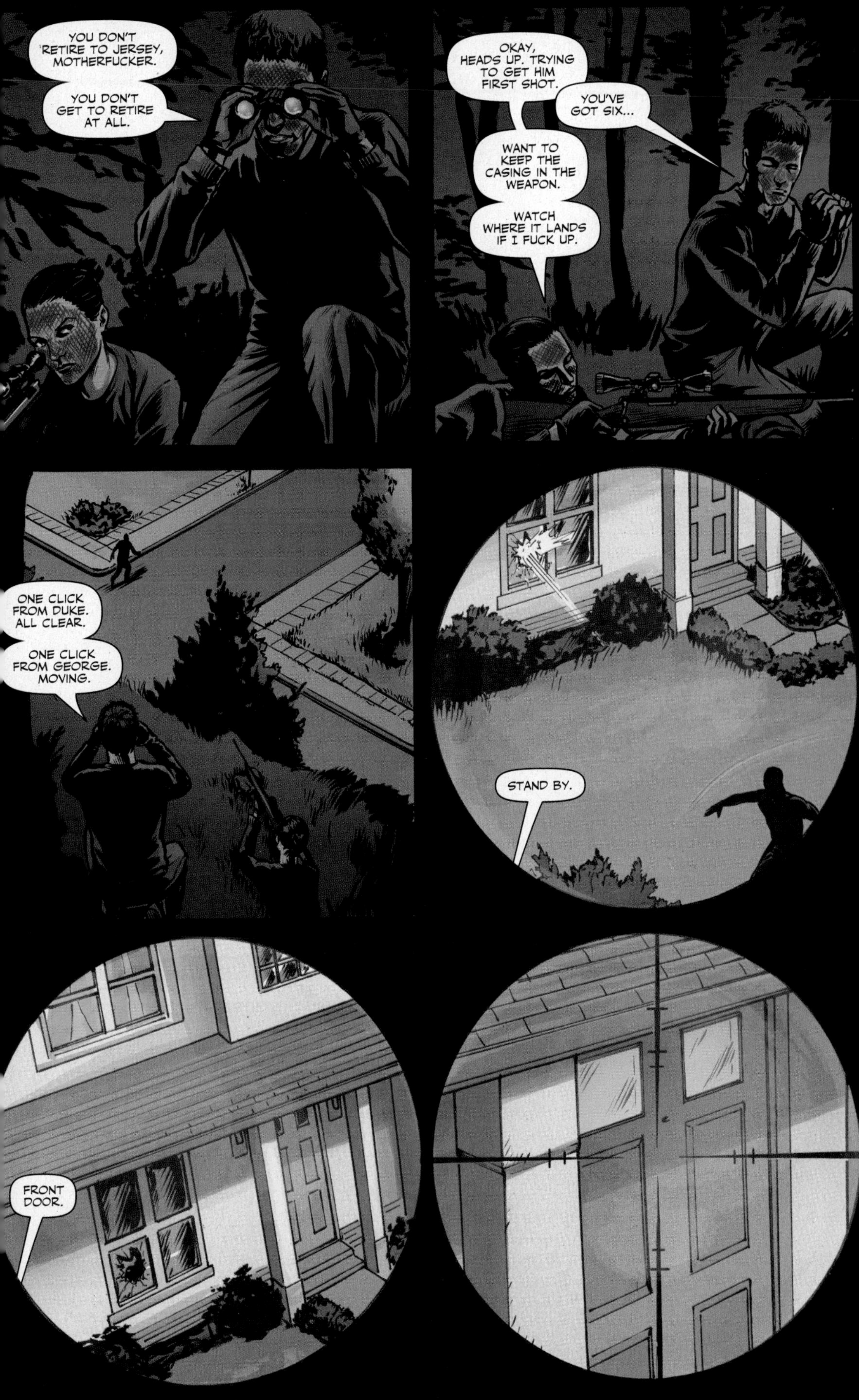
YOU DON'T RETIRE TO JERSEY, MOTHERFUCKER.
YOU DON'T GET TO RETIRE AT ALL.
OKAY, HEADS UP. TRYING TO GET HIM FIRST SHOT.
YOU'VE GOT SIX...
WANT TO KEEP THE CASING IN THE WEAPON.
WATCH WHERE IT LANDS IF I FUCK UP.
ONE CLICK FROM DUKE. ALL CLEAR.
ONE CLICK FROM GEORGE. MOVING.
STAND BY.
FRONT DOOR.

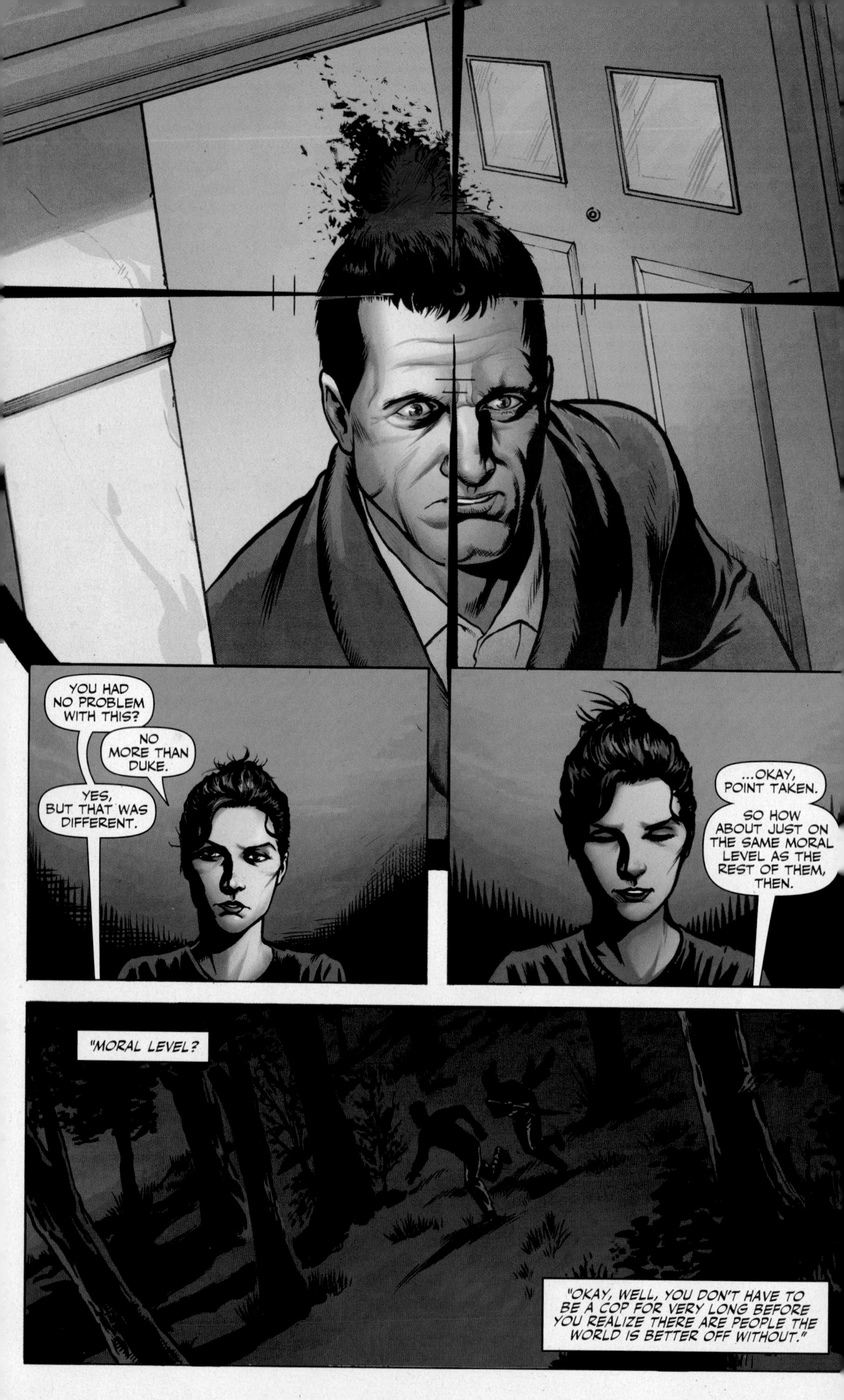
YOU HAD NO PROBLEM WITH THIS?
NO MORE THAN DUKE.
YES, BUT THAT WAS DIFFERENT.
...OKAY, POINT TAKEN.
SO HOW ABOUT JUST ON THE SAME MORAL LEVEL AS THE REST OF THEM, THEN.
"MORAL LEVEL?
"OKAY, WELL, YOU DON'T HAVE TO BE A COP FOR VERY LONG BEFORE YOU REALIZE THERE ARE PEOPLE THE WORLD IS BETTER OFF WITHOUT."

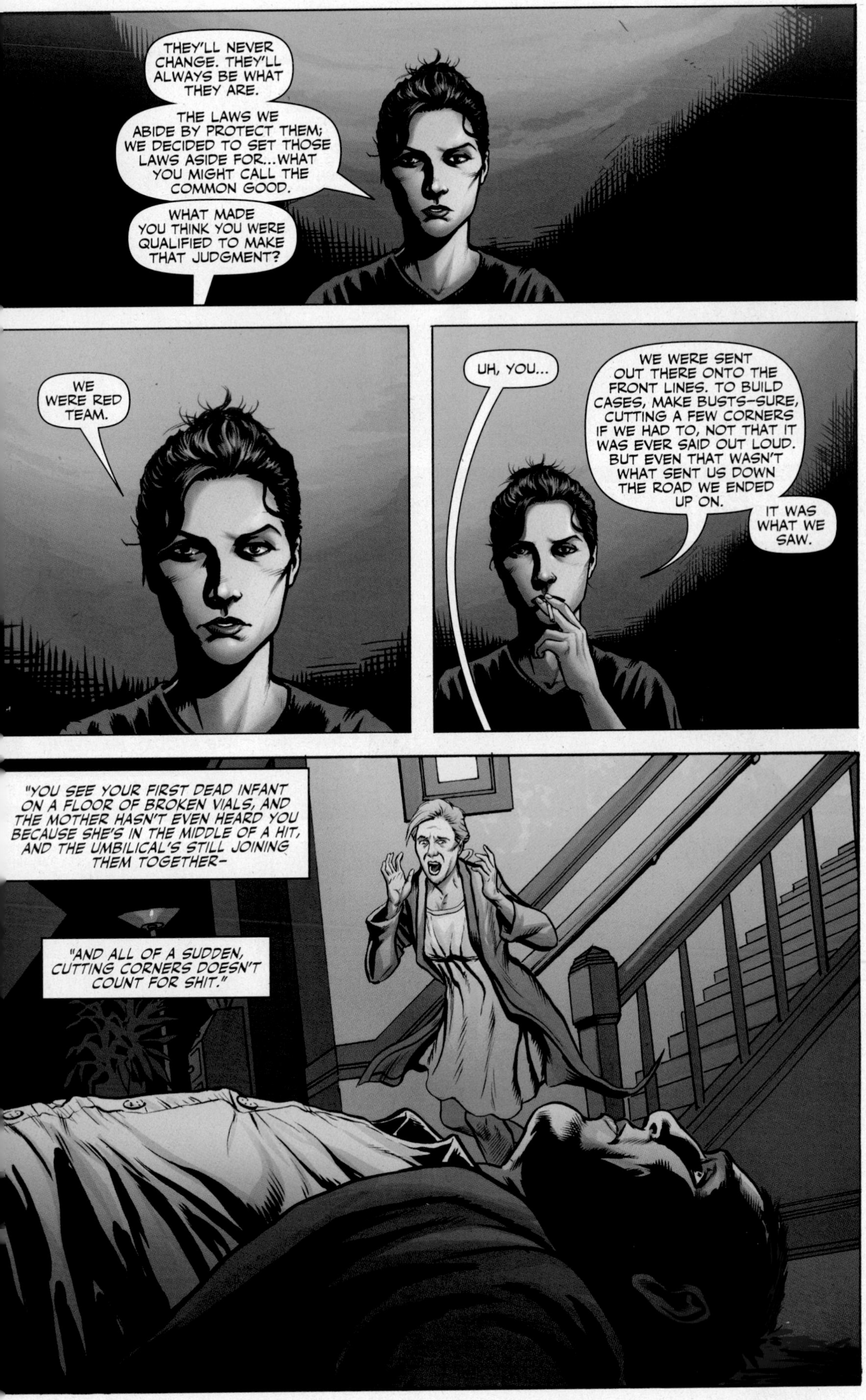
THEY'LL NEVER CHANGE. THEY'LL ALWAYS BE WHAT THEY ARE.
THE LAWS WE ABIDE BY PROTECT THEM; WE DECIDED TO SET THOSE LAWS ASIDE FOR...WHAT YOU MIGHT CALL THE COMMON GOOD.
WHAT MADE YOU THINK YOU WERE QUALIFIED TO MAKE THAT JUDGMENT?
WE WERE RED TEAM.
UH, YOU...
WE WERE SENT OUT THERE ONTO THE FRONT LINES. TO BUILD CASES, MAKE BUSTS--SURE, CUTTING A FEW CORNERS IF WE HAD TO, NOT THAT IT WAS EVER SAID OUT LOUD. BUT EVEN THAT WASN'T WHAT SENT US DOWN THE ROAD WE ENDED UP ON.
IT WAS WHAT WE SAW.
"YOU SEE YOUR FIRST DEAD INFANT ON A FLOOR OF BROKEN VIALS, AND THE MOTHER HASN'T EVEN HEARD YOU BECAUSE SHE'S IN THE MIDDLE OF A HIT, AND THE UMBILICAL'S STILL JOINING THEM TOGETHER--
"AND ALL OF A SUDDEN, CUTTING CORNERS DOESN'T COUNT FOR SHIT."

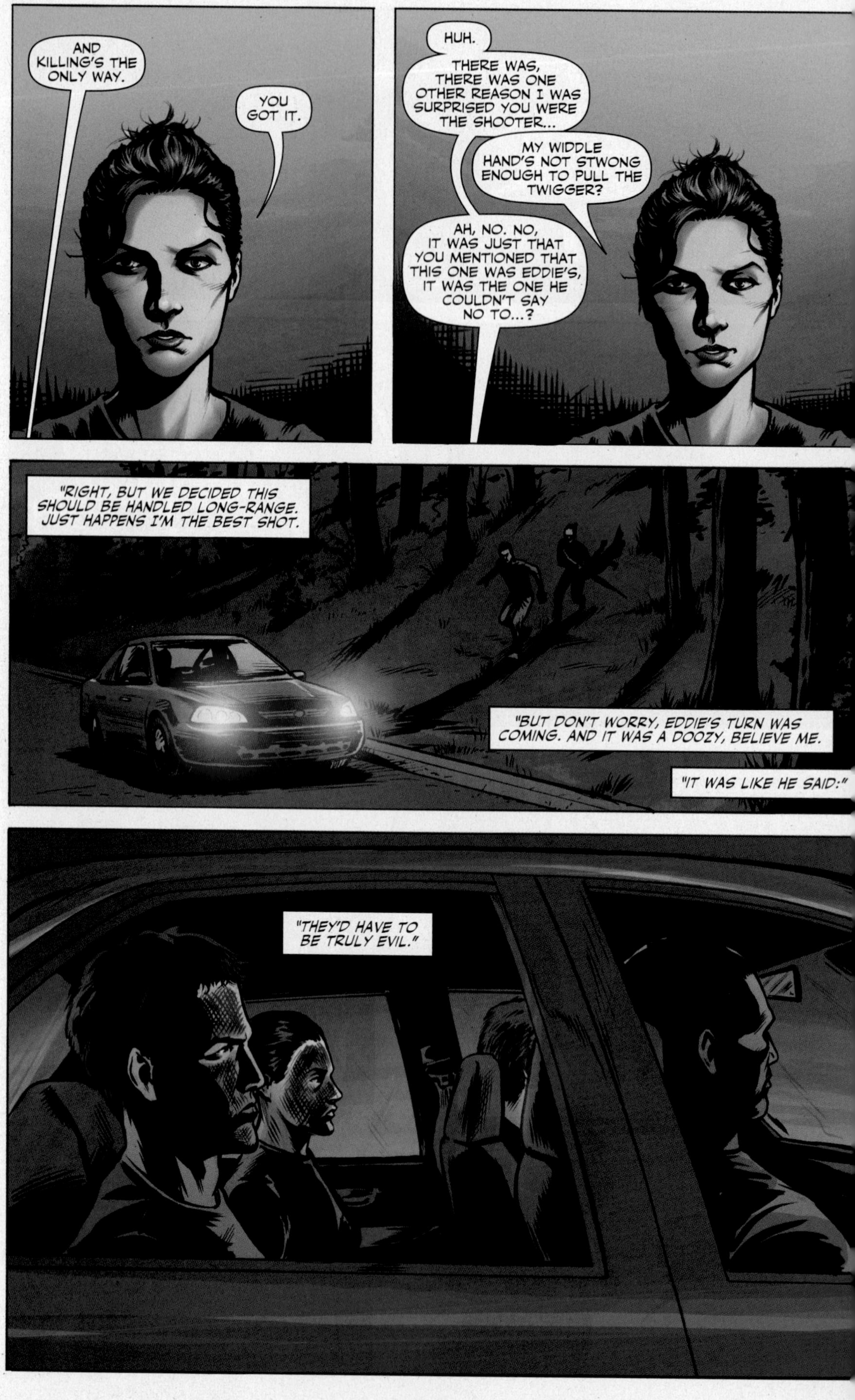
AND KILLING'S THE ONLY WAY.
YOU GOT IT.
HUH.
THERE WAS, THERE WAS ONE OTHER REASON I WAS SURPRISED YOU WERE THE SHOOTER...
MY WIDDLE HAND'S NOT STWONG ENOUGH TO PULL THE TWIGGER?
AH, NO. NO, IT WAS JUST THAT YOU MENTIONED THAT THIS ONE WAS EDDIE'S, IT WAS THE ONE HE COULDN'T SAY NO TO...?
"RIGHT, BUT WE DECIDED THIS SHOULD BE HANDLED LONG-RANGE. JUST HAPPENS I'M THE BEST SHOT.
"BUT DON'T WORRY, EDDIE'S TURN WAS COMING. AND IT WAS A DOOZY, BELIEVE ME.
"IT WAS LIKE HE SAID:"
"THEY'D HAVE TO BE TRULY EVIL."

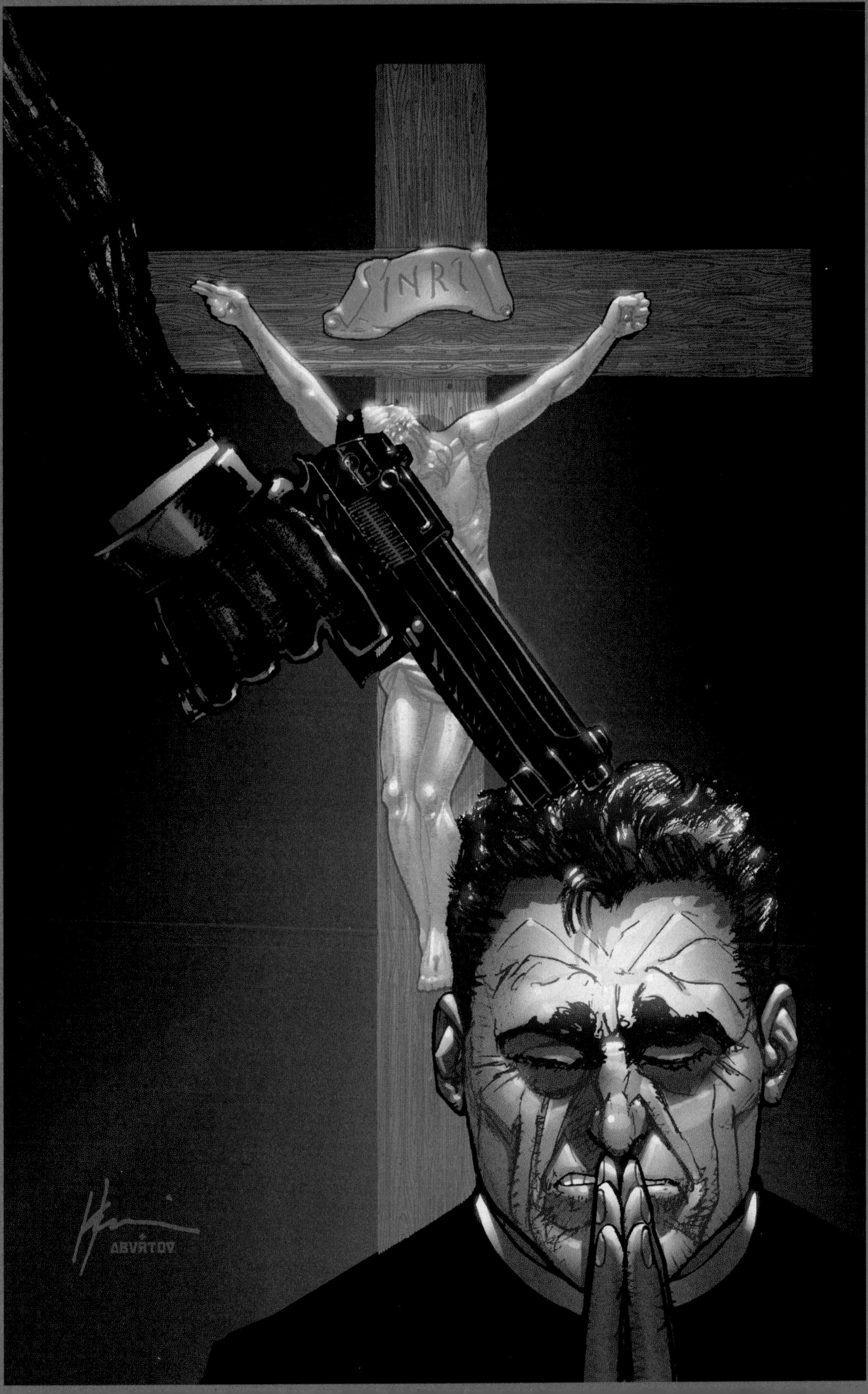
INRI

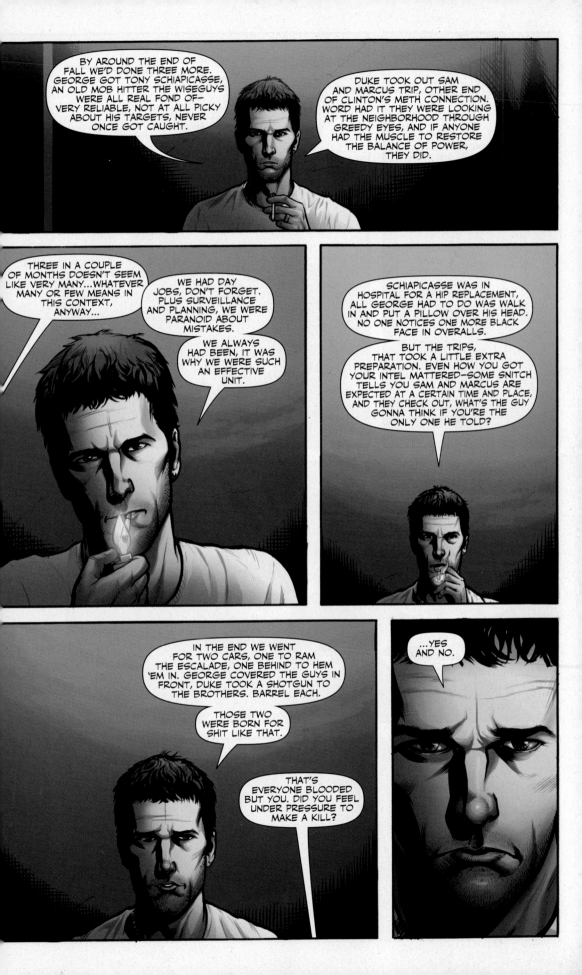

BY AROUND THE END OF FALL WE'D DONE THREE MORE. GEORGE GOT TONY SCHIAPICASSE, AN OLD MOB HITTER THE WISEGUYS WERE ALL REAL FOND OF—VERY RELIABLE, NOT AT ALL PICKY ABOUT HIS TARGETS, NEVER ONCE GOT CAUGHT.

DUKE TOOK OUT SAM AND MARCUS TRIP, OTHER END OF CLINTON'S METH CONNECTION. WORD HAD IT THEY WERE LOOKING AT THE NEIGHBORHOOD THROUGH GREEDY EYES, AND IF ANYONE HAD THE MUSCLE TO RESTORE THE BALANCE OF POWER, THEY DID.

THREE IN A COUPLE OF MONTHS DOESN'T SEEM LIKE VERY MANY...WHATEVER MANY OR FEW MEANS IN THIS CONTEXT, ANYWAY...

WE HAD DAY JOBS, DON'T FORGET. PLUS SURVEILLANCE AND PLANNING, WE WERE PARANOID ABOUT MISTAKES.

WE ALWAYS HAD BEEN, IT WAS WHY WE WERE SUCH AN EFFECTIVE UNIT.

SCHIAPICASSE WAS IN HOSPITAL FOR A HIP REPLACEMENT, ALL GEORGE HAD TO DO WAS WALK IN AND PUT A PILLOW OVER HIS HEAD. NO ONE NOTICES ONE MORE BLACK FACE IN OVERALLS.

BUT THE TRIPS, THAT TOOK A LITTLE EXTRA PREPARATION. EVEN HOW YOU GOT YOUR INTEL MATTERED—SOME SNITCH TELLS YOU SAM AND MARCUS ARE EXPECTED AT A CERTAIN TIME AND PLACE, AND THEY CHECK OUT, WHAT'S THE GUY GONNA THINK IF YOU'RE THE ONLY ONE HE TOLD?

IN THE END WE WENT FOR TWO CARS, ONE TO RAM THE ESCALADE, ONE BEHIND TO HEM 'EM IN. GEORGE COVERED THE GUYS IN FRONT, DUKE TOOK A SHOTGUN TO THE BROTHERS. BARREL EACH.

THOSE TWO WERE BORN FOR SHIT LIKE THAT.

THAT'S EVERYONE BLOODED BUT YOU. DID YOU FEEL UNDER PRESSURE TO MAKE A KILL?

...YES AND NO.

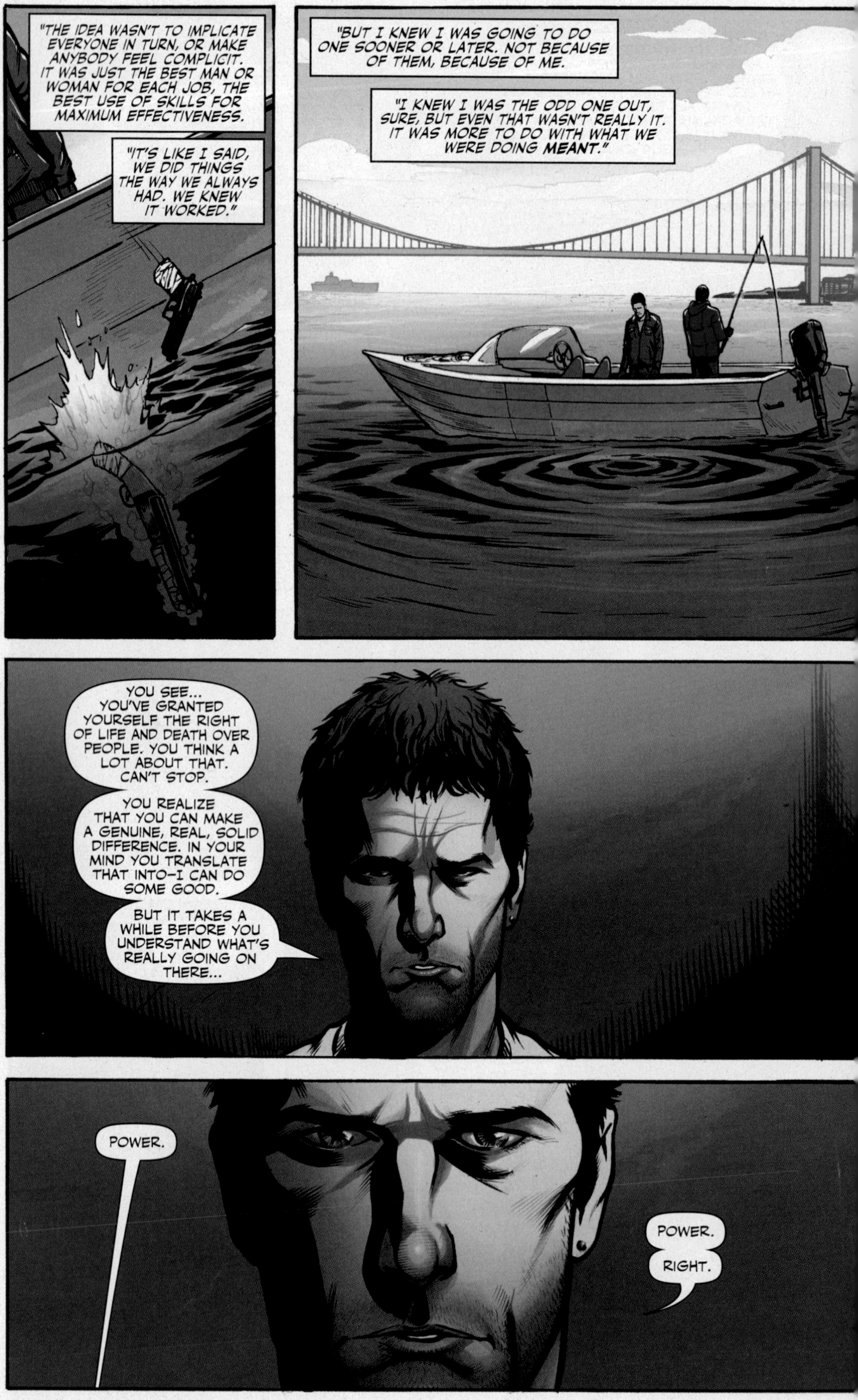
"THE IDEA WASN'T TO IMPLICATE EVERYONE IN TURN, OR MAKE ANYBODY FEEL COMPLICIT. IT WAS JUST THE BEST MAN OR WOMAN FOR EACH JOB, THE BEST USE OF SKILLS FOR MAXIMUM EFFECTIVENESS.
"IT'S LIKE I SAID, WE DID THINGS THE WAY WE ALWAYS HAD. WE KNEW IT WORKED."
"BUT I KNEW I WAS GOING TO DO ONE SOONER OR LATER. NOT BECAUSE OF THEM, BECAUSE OF ME.
"I KNEW I WAS THE ODD ONE OUT, SURE, BUT EVEN THAT WASN'T REALLY IT. IT WAS MORE TO DO WITH WHAT WE WERE DOING MEANT."
YOU SEE... YOU'VE GRANTED YOURSELF THE RIGHT OF LIFE AND DEATH OVER PEOPLE. YOU THINK A LOT ABOUT THAT. CAN'T STOP.
YOU REALIZE THAT YOU CAN MAKE A GENUINE, REAL, SOLID DIFFERENCE. IN YOUR MIND YOU TRANSLATE THAT INTO—I CAN DO SOME GOOD.
BUT IT TAKES A WHILE BEFORE YOU UNDERSTAND WHAT'S REALLY GOING ON THERE...
POWER.
POWER.
RIGHT.

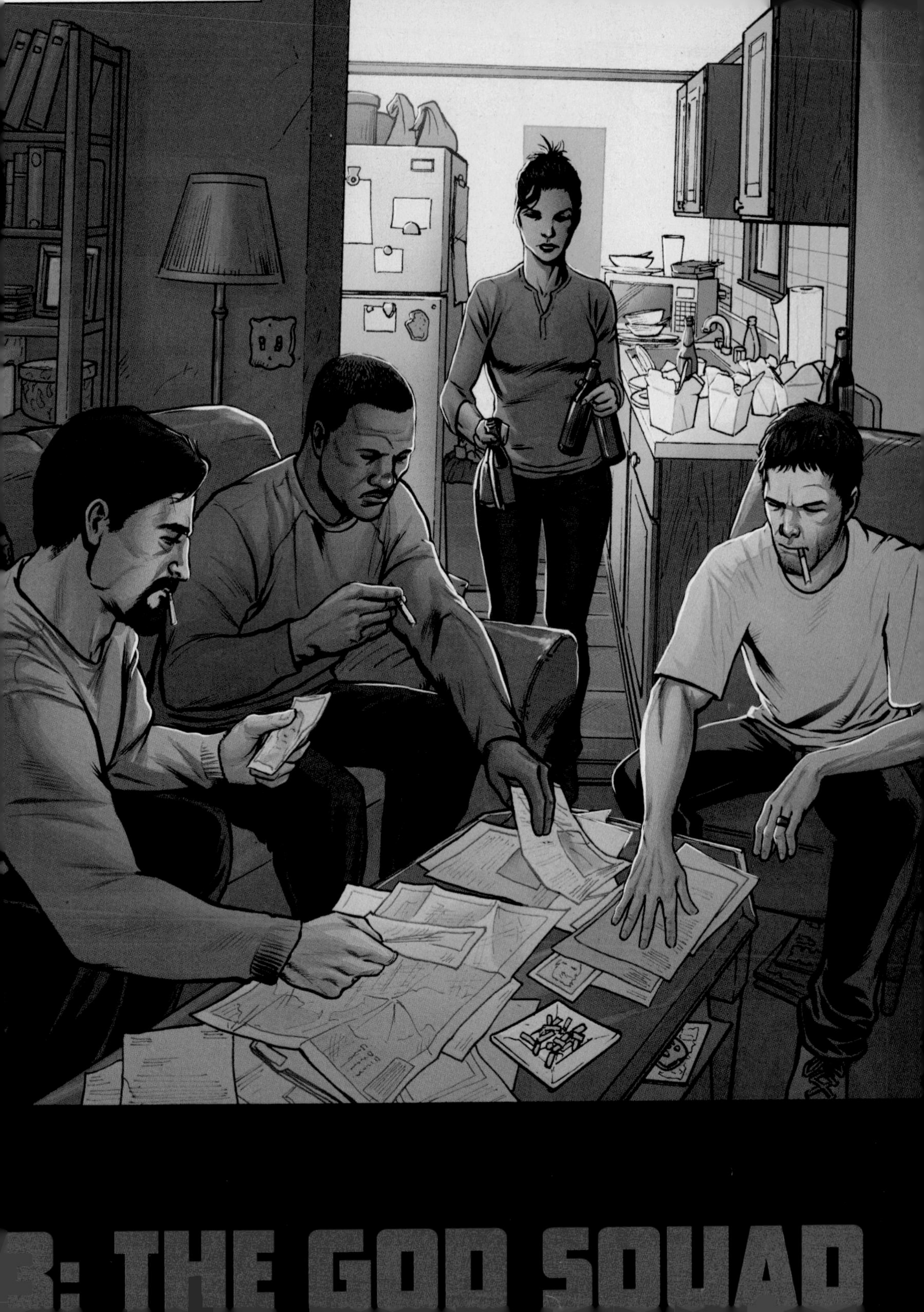

3: THE GOD SQUAD

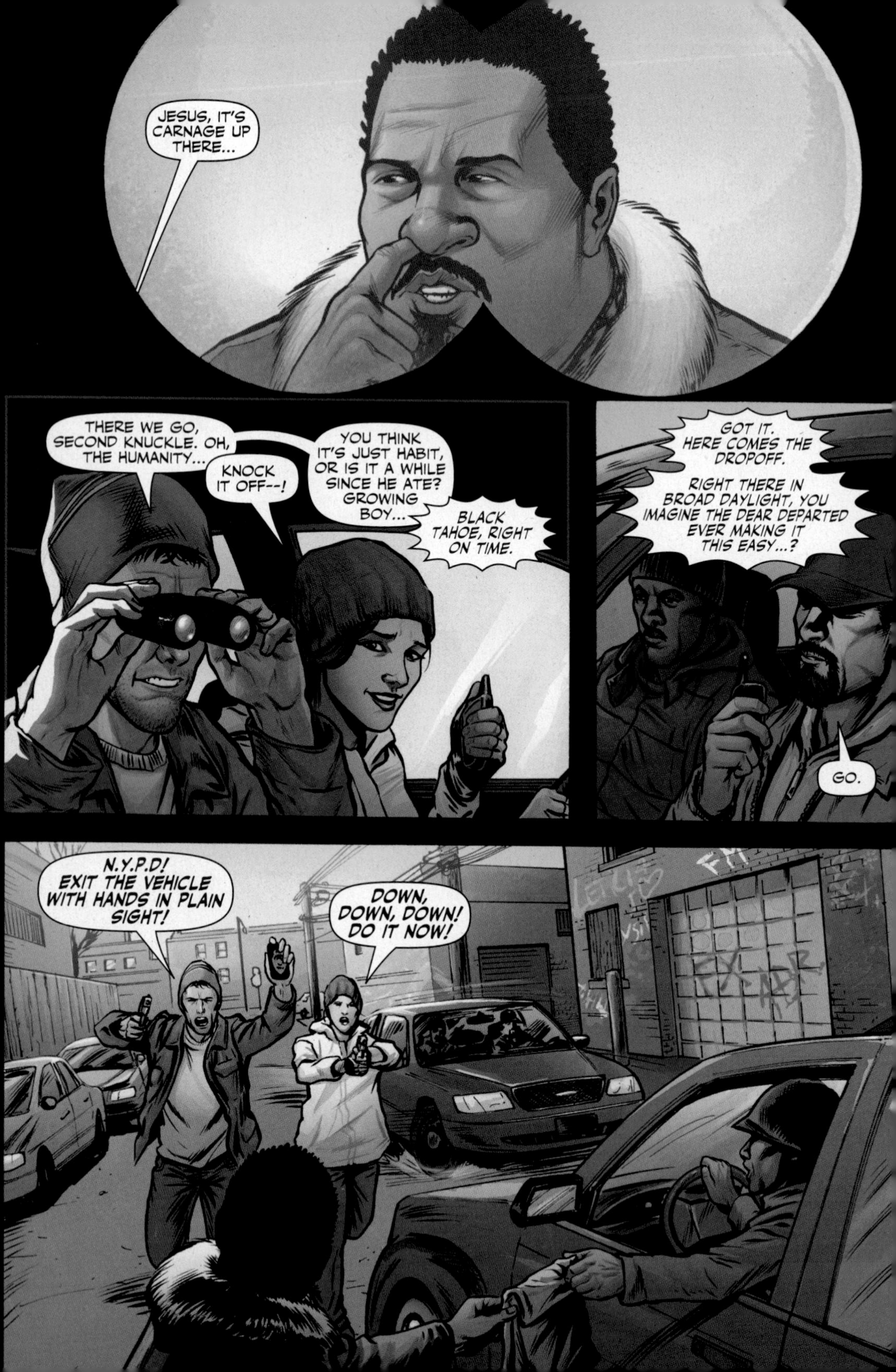
JESUS, IT'S CARNAGE UP THERE...
THERE WE GO, SECOND KNUCKLE. OH, THE HUMANITY...
KNOCK IT OFF--!
YOU THINK IT'S JUST HABIT, OR IS IT A WHILE SINCE HE ATE? GROWING BOY...
BLACK TAHOE, RIGHT ON TIME.
GOT IT. HERE COMES THE DROPOFF.
RIGHT THERE IN BROAD DAYLIGHT, YOU IMAGINE THE DEAR DEPARTED EVER MAKING IT THIS EASY...?
GO.
N.Y.P.D! EXIT THE VEHICLE WITH HANDS IN PLAIN SIGHT!
DOWN, DOWN, DOWN! DO IT NOW!

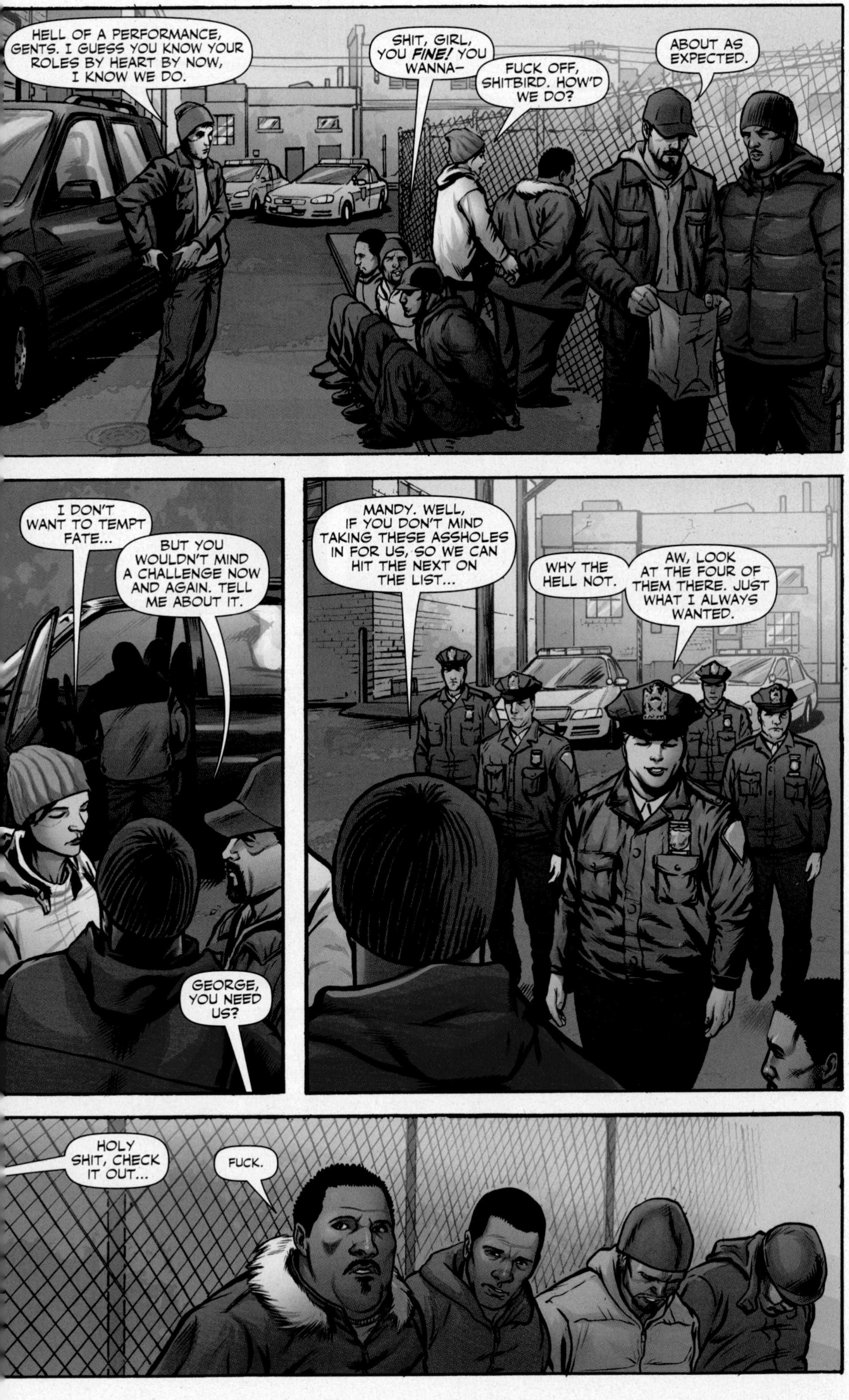

HELL OF A PERFORMANCE, GENTS. I GUESS YOU KNOW YOUR ROLES BY HEART BY NOW, I KNOW WE DO.
SHIT, GIRL, YOU *FINE!* YOU WANNA–
FUCK OFF, SHITBIRD. HOW'D WE DO?
ABOUT AS EXPECTED.
I DON'T WANT TO TEMPT FATE...
BUT YOU WOULDN'T MIND A CHALLENGE NOW AND AGAIN. TELL ME ABOUT IT.
GEORGE, YOU NEED US?
MANDY. WELL, IF YOU DON'T MIND TAKING THESE ASSHOLES IN FOR US, SO WE CAN HIT THE NEXT ON THE LIST...
WHY THE HELL NOT.
AW, LOOK AT THE FOUR OF THEM THERE. JUST WHAT I ALWAYS WANTED.
HOLY SHIT, CHECK IT OUT...
FUCK.

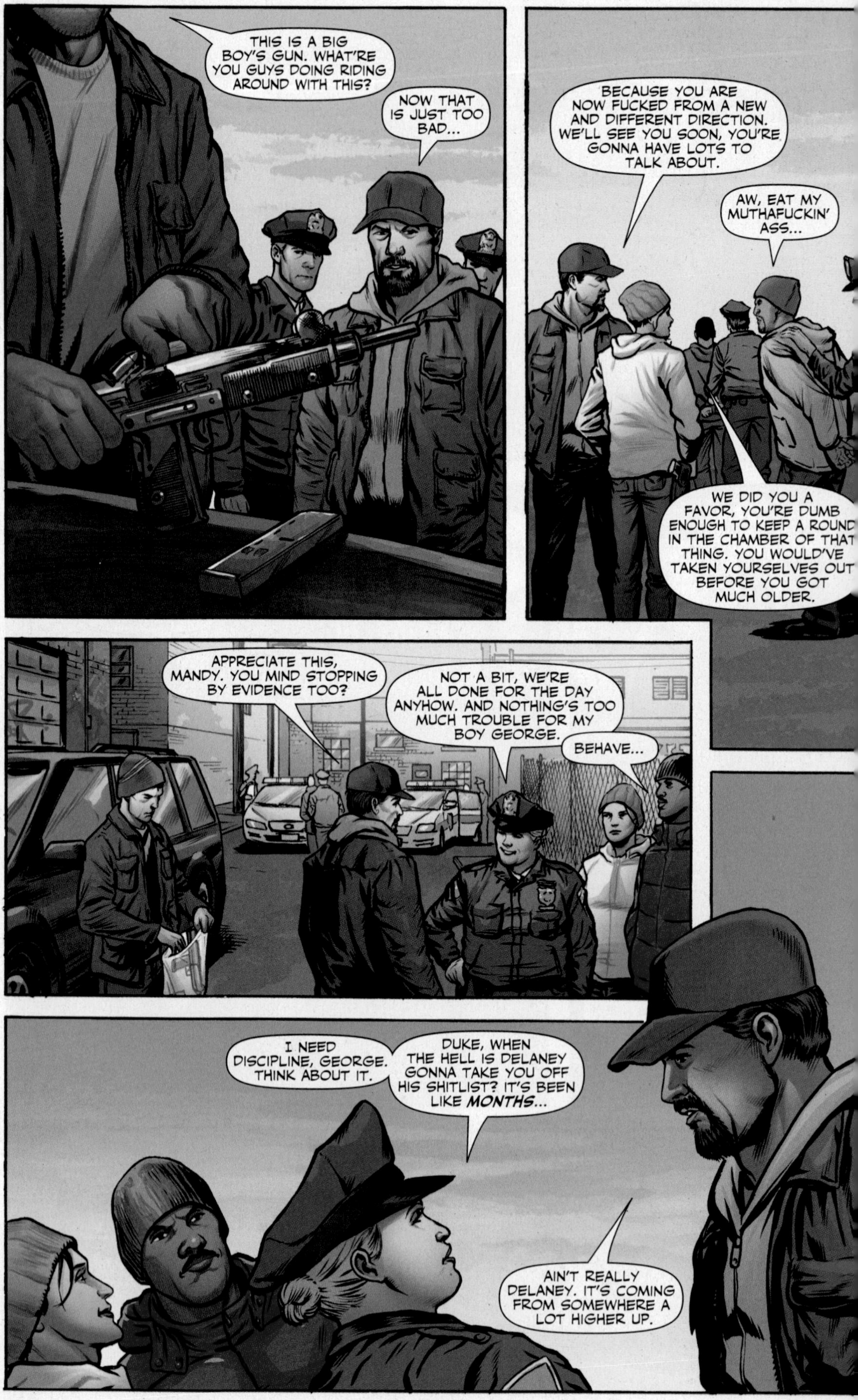
THIS IS A BIG BOY'S GUN. WHAT'RE YOU GUYS DOING RIDING AROUND WITH THIS?
NOW THAT IS JUST TOO BAD...
BECAUSE YOU ARE NOW FUCKED FROM A NEW AND DIFFERENT DIRECTION. WE'LL SEE YOU SOON, YOU'RE GONNA HAVE LOTS TO TALK ABOUT.
AW, EAT MY MUTHAFUCKIN' ASS...
WE DID YOU A FAVOR, YOU'RE DUMB ENOUGH TO KEEP A ROUND IN THE CHAMBER OF THAT THING. YOU WOULD'VE TAKEN YOURSELVES OUT BEFORE YOU GOT MUCH OLDER.
APPRECIATE THIS, MANDY. YOU MIND STOPPING BY EVIDENCE TOO?
NOT A BIT, WE'RE ALL DONE FOR THE DAY ANYHOW. AND NOTHING'S TOO MUCH TROUBLE FOR MY BOY GEORGE.
BEHAVE...
I NEED DISCIPLINE, GEORGE. THINK ABOUT IT.
DUKE, WHEN THE HELL IS DELANEY GONNA TAKE YOU OFF HIS SHITLIST? IT'S BEEN LIKE *MONTHS*...
AIN'T REALLY DELANEY. IT'S COMING FROM SOMEWHERE A LOT HIGHER UP.

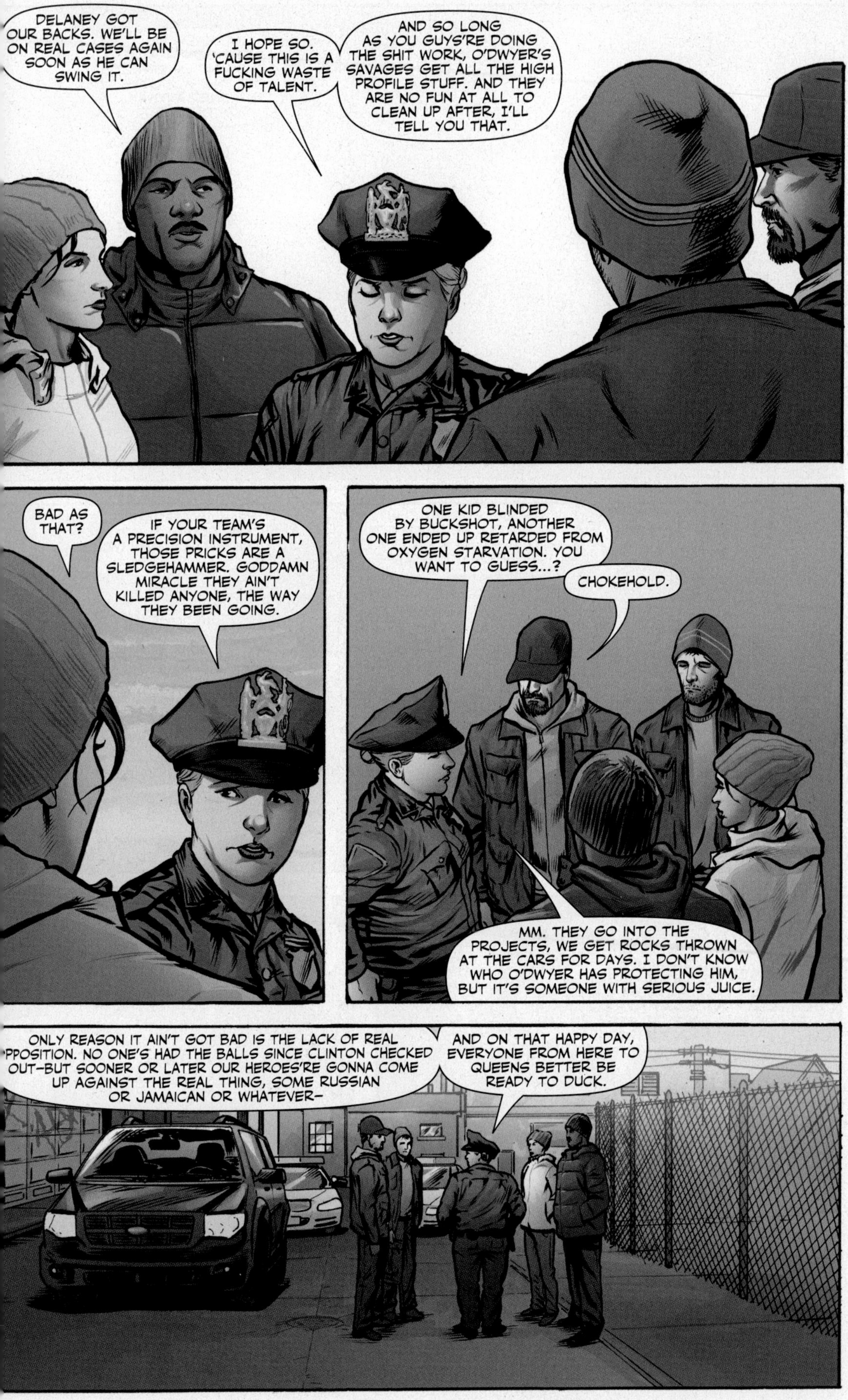
DELANEY GOT OUR BACKS. WE'LL BE ON REAL CASES AGAIN SOON AS HE CAN SWING IT.
I HOPE SO. 'CAUSE THIS IS A FUCKING WASTE OF TALENT.
AND SO LONG AS YOU GUYS'RE DOING THE SHIT WORK, O'DWYER'S SAVAGES GET ALL THE HIGH PROFILE STUFF. AND THEY ARE NO FUN AT ALL TO CLEAN UP AFTER, I'LL TELL YOU THAT.
BAD AS THAT?
IF YOUR TEAM'S A PRECISION INSTRUMENT, THOSE PRICKS ARE A SLEDGEHAMMER. GODDAMN MIRACLE THEY AIN'T KILLED ANYONE, THE WAY THEY BEEN GOING.
ONE KID BLINDED BY BUCKSHOT, ANOTHER ONE ENDED UP RETARDED FROM OXYGEN STARVATION. YOU WANT TO GUESS...?
CHOKEHOLD.
MM. THEY GO INTO THE PROJECTS, WE GET ROCKS THROWN AT THE CARS FOR DAYS. I DON'T KNOW WHO O'DWYER HAS PROTECTING HIM, BUT IT'S SOMEONE WITH SERIOUS JUICE.
ONLY REASON IT AIN'T GOT BAD IS THE LACK OF REAL OPPOSITION. NO ONE'S HAD THE BALLS SINCE CLINTON CHECKED OUT–BUT SOONER OR LATER OUR HEROES'RE GONNA COME UP AGAINST THE REAL THING, SOME RUSSIAN OR JAMAICAN OR WHATEVER–
AND ON THAT HAPPY DAY, EVERYONE FROM HERE TO QUEENS BETTER BE READY TO DUCK.

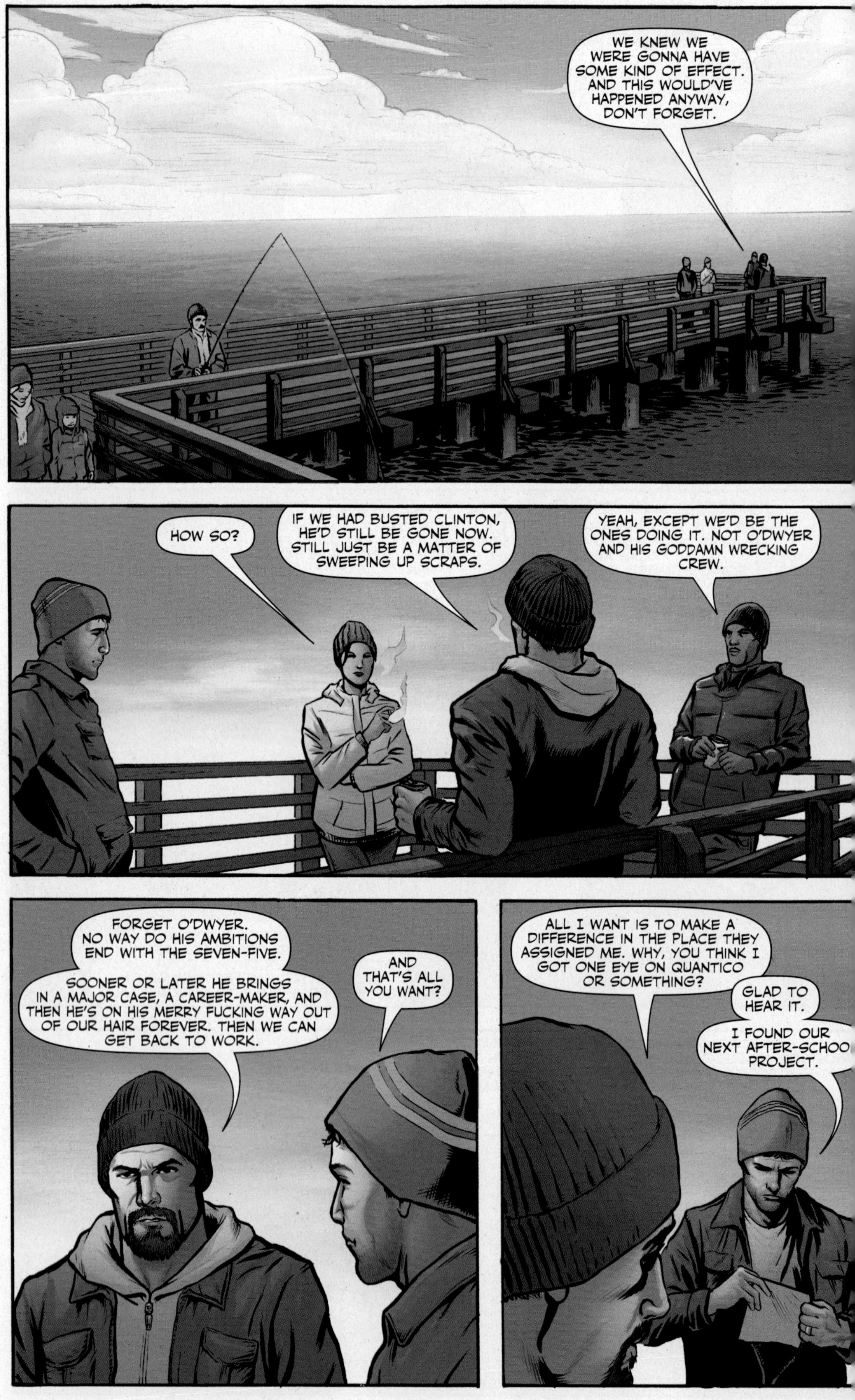
WE KNEW WE WERE GONNA HAVE SOME KIND OF EFFECT. AND THIS WOULD'VE HAPPENED ANYWAY, DON'T FORGET.
HOW SO?
IF WE HAD BUSTED CLINTON, HE'D STILL BE GONE NOW. STILL JUST BE A MATTER OF SWEEPING UP SCRAPS.
YEAH, EXCEPT WE'D BE THE ONES DOING IT. NOT O'DWYER AND HIS GODDAMN WRECKING CREW.
FORGET O'DWYER. NO WAY DO HIS AMBITIONS END WITH THE SEVEN-FIVE.
SOONER OR LATER HE BRINGS IN A MAJOR CASE, A CAREER-MAKER, AND THEN HE'S ON HIS MERRY FUCKING WAY OUT OF OUR HAIR FOREVER. THEN WE CAN GET BACK TO WORK.
AND THAT'S ALL YOU WANT?
ALL I WANT IS TO MAKE A DIFFERENCE IN THE PLACE THEY ASSIGNED ME. WHY, YOU THINK I GOT ONE EYE ON QUANTICO OR SOMETHING?
GLAD TO HEAR IT.
I FOUND OUR NEXT AFTER-SCHOO PROJECT.

I SAID WE CAN'T JUST GO HUNTING IN THE GHETTO WHEN WE FEEL LIKE IT, IT HAS TO BE ABOUT MORE THAN THAT. WELL, THIS IS GERALD McEWAN—

FATHER GERALD McEWAN.

HE'S A PRIEST.

THAT HE IS.

HE WAS AT SAINT MALACHY'S ON VAN SICLEN FROM NINETY TO NINETY-SIX. THEY GOT COMPLAINTS FROM PARENTS— JUST LIKE AT THE PARISH HE WAS AT BEFORE, JUST LIKE THE TWO SINCE. ALL THE CHURCH DID WAS MOVE HIM.

ONE BOY COMMITTED SUICIDE, ANOTHER TRIED.

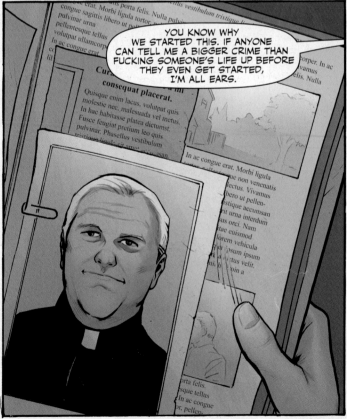

YOU KNOW WHY WE STARTED THIS. IF ANYONE CAN TELL ME A BIGGER CRIME THAN FUCKING SOMEONE'S LIFE UP BEFORE THEY EVEN GET STARTED, I'M ALL EARS.

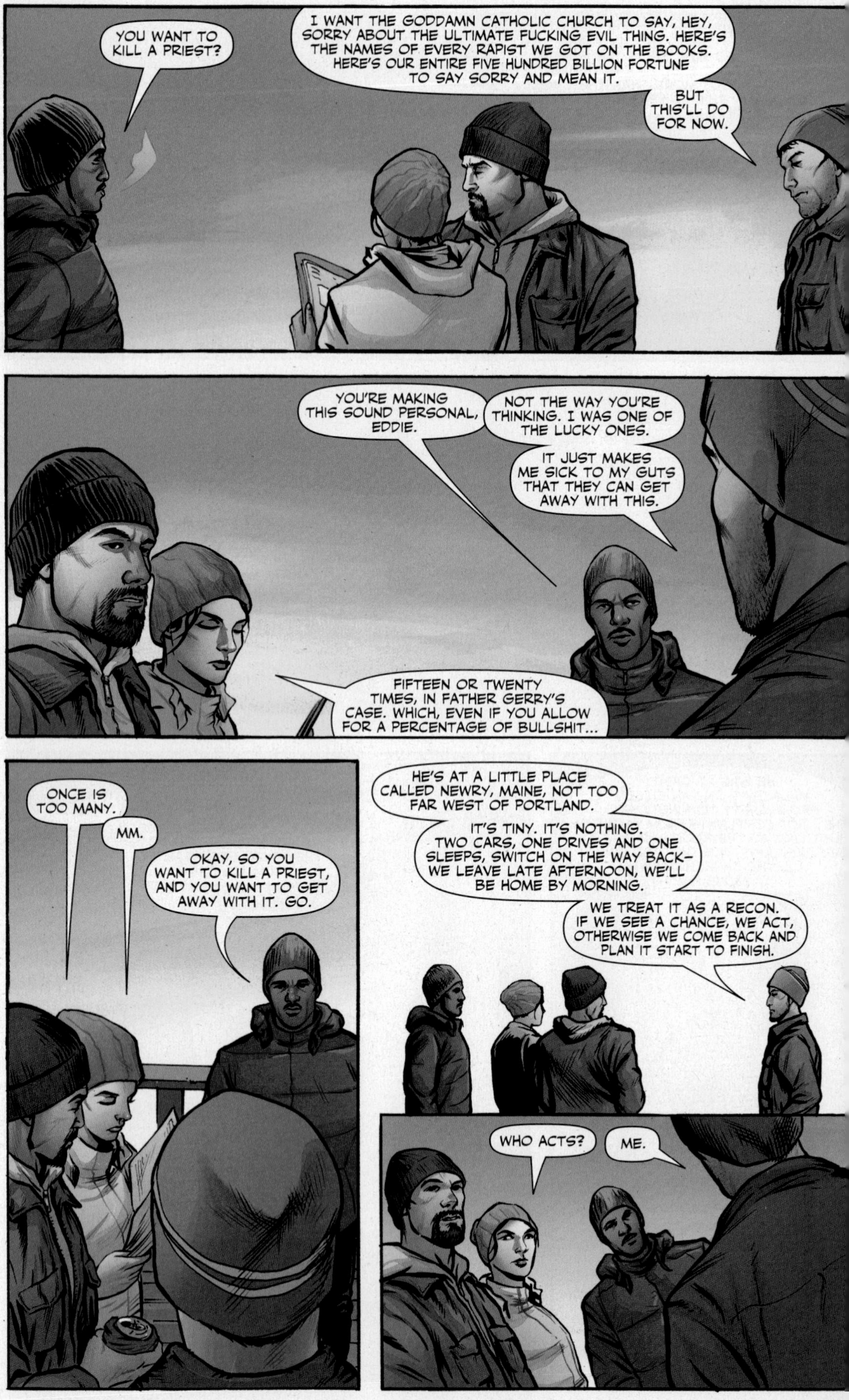
YOU WANT TO KILL A PRIEST?
I WANT THE GODDAMN CATHOLIC CHURCH TO SAY, HEY, SORRY ABOUT THE ULTIMATE FUCKING EVIL THING. HERE'S THE NAMES OF EVERY RAPIST WE GOT ON THE BOOKS. HERE'S OUR ENTIRE FIVE HUNDRED BILLION FORTUNE TO SAY SORRY AND MEAN IT.
BUT THIS'LL DO FOR NOW.
YOU'RE MAKING THIS SOUND PERSONAL, EDDIE.
NOT THE WAY YOU'RE THINKING. I WAS ONE OF THE LUCKY ONES.
IT JUST MAKES ME SICK TO MY GUTS THAT THEY CAN GET AWAY WITH THIS.
FIFTEEN OR TWENTY TIMES, IN FATHER GERRY'S CASE. WHICH, EVEN IF YOU ALLOW FOR A PERCENTAGE OF BULLSHIT...
ONCE IS TOO MANY.
MM.
OKAY, SO YOU WANT TO KILL A PRIEST, AND YOU WANT TO GET AWAY WITH IT. GO.
HE'S AT A LITTLE PLACE CALLED NEWRY, MAINE, NOT TOO FAR WEST OF PORTLAND.
IT'S TINY. IT'S NOTHING. TWO CARS, ONE DRIVES AND ONE SLEEPS, SWITCH ON THE WAY BACK– WE LEAVE LATE AFTERNOON, WE'LL BE HOME BY MORNING.
WE TREAT IT AS A RECON. IF WE SEE A CHANCE, WE ACT, OTHERWISE WE COME BACK AND PLAN IT START TO FINISH.
WHO ACTS?
ME.

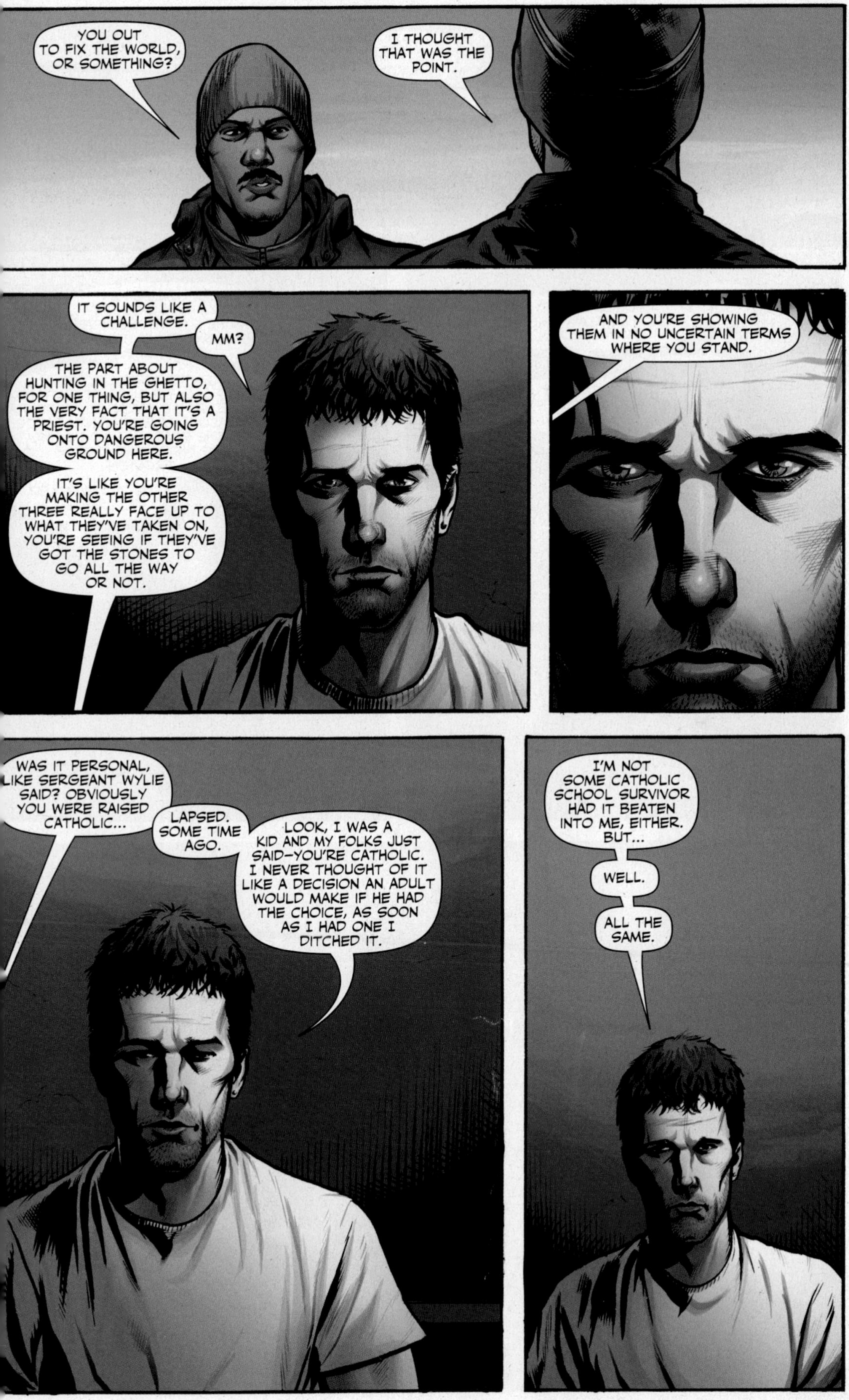
YOU OUT TO FIX THE WORLD, OR SOMETHING?
I THOUGHT THAT WAS THE POINT.
IT SOUNDS LIKE A CHALLENGE.
MM?
THE PART ABOUT HUNTING IN THE GHETTO, FOR ONE THING, BUT ALSO THE VERY FACT THAT IT'S A PRIEST. YOU'RE GOING ONTO DANGEROUS GROUND HERE.
IT'S LIKE YOU'RE MAKING THE OTHER THREE REALLY FACE UP TO WHAT THEY'VE TAKEN ON, YOU'RE SEEING IF THEY'VE GOT THE STONES TO GO ALL THE WAY OR NOT.
AND YOU'RE SHOWING THEM IN NO UNCERTAIN TERMS WHERE YOU STAND.
WAS IT PERSONAL, LIKE SERGEANT WYLIE SAID? OBVIOUSLY YOU WERE RAISED CATHOLIC...
LAPSED. SOME TIME AGO.
LOOK, I WAS A KID AND MY FOLKS JUST SAID–YOU'RE CATHOLIC. I NEVER THOUGHT OF IT LIKE A DECISION AN ADULT WOULD MAKE IF HE HAD THE CHOICE, AS SOON AS I HAD ONE I DITCHED IT.
I'M NOT SOME CATHOLIC SCHOOL SURVIVOR HAD IT BEATEN INTO ME, EITHER. BUT...
WELL.
ALL THE SAME.

THINK HE'S IN THE CHURCH.

YEAH?

SOMEBODY IS. PRETTY CERTAIN THEY'RE ON THEIR OWN.

IT'S TWO A.M....

ACTUALLY SOUNDS LIKE HE'S PRAYING.

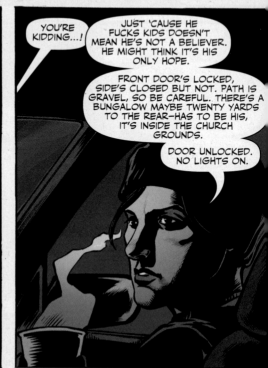

YOU'RE KIDDING...!

JUST 'CAUSE HE FUCKS KIDS DOESN'T MEAN HE'S NOT A BELIEVER. HE MIGHT THINK IT'S HIS ONLY HOPE.

FRONT DOOR'S LOCKED, SIDE'S CLOSED BUT NOT. PATH IS GRAVEL, SO BE CAREFUL. THERE'S A BUNGALOW MAYBE TWENTY YARDS TO THE REAR—HAS TO BE HIS, IT'S INSIDE THE CHURCH GROUNDS.

DOOR UNLOCKED. NO LIGHTS ON.

OKAY, FUCK IT.

GIVE 'EM TWO CLICKS.

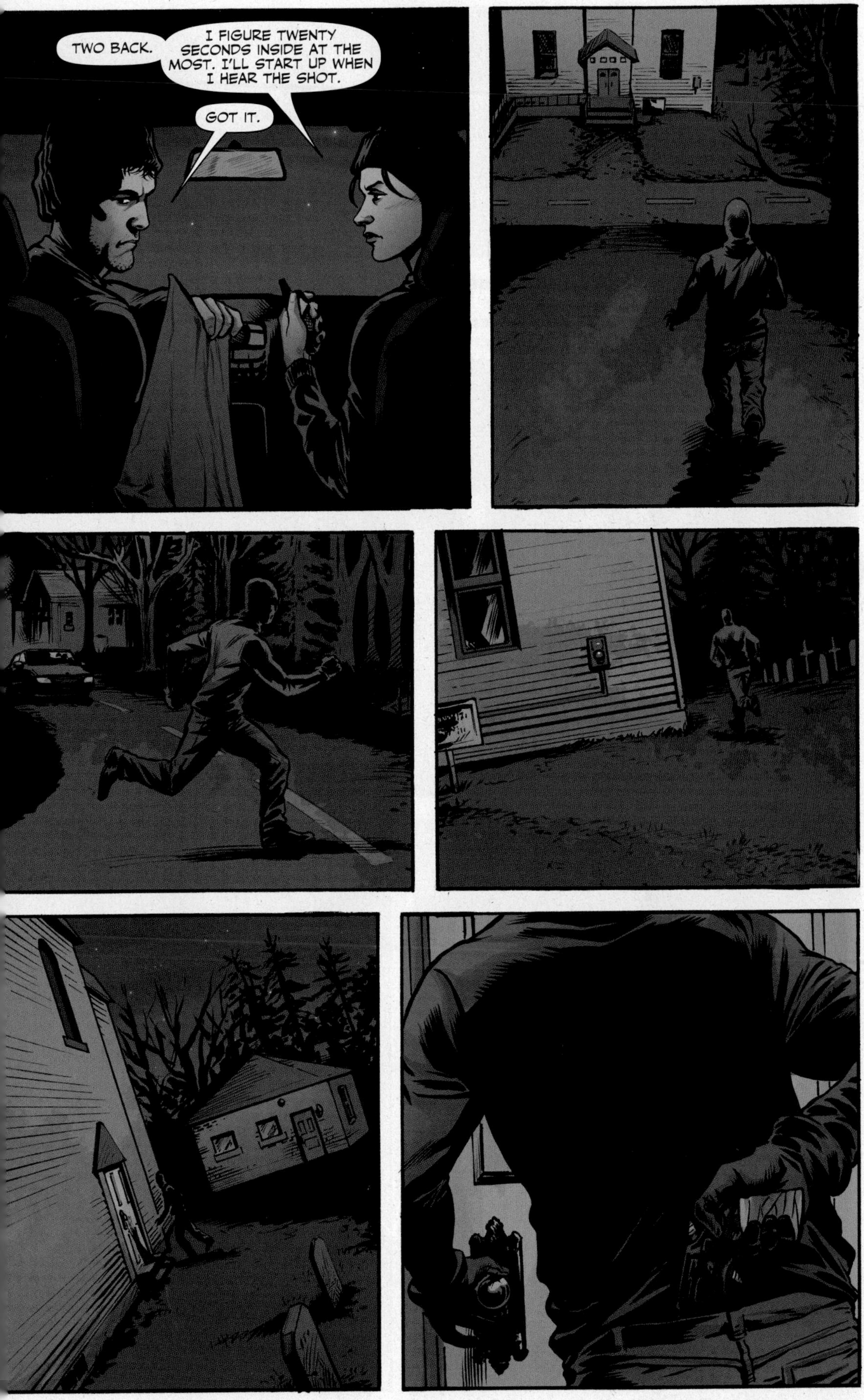
TWO BACK.
I FIGURE TWENTY SECONDS INSIDE AT THE MOST. I'LL START UP WHEN I HEAR THE SHOT.
GOT IT.

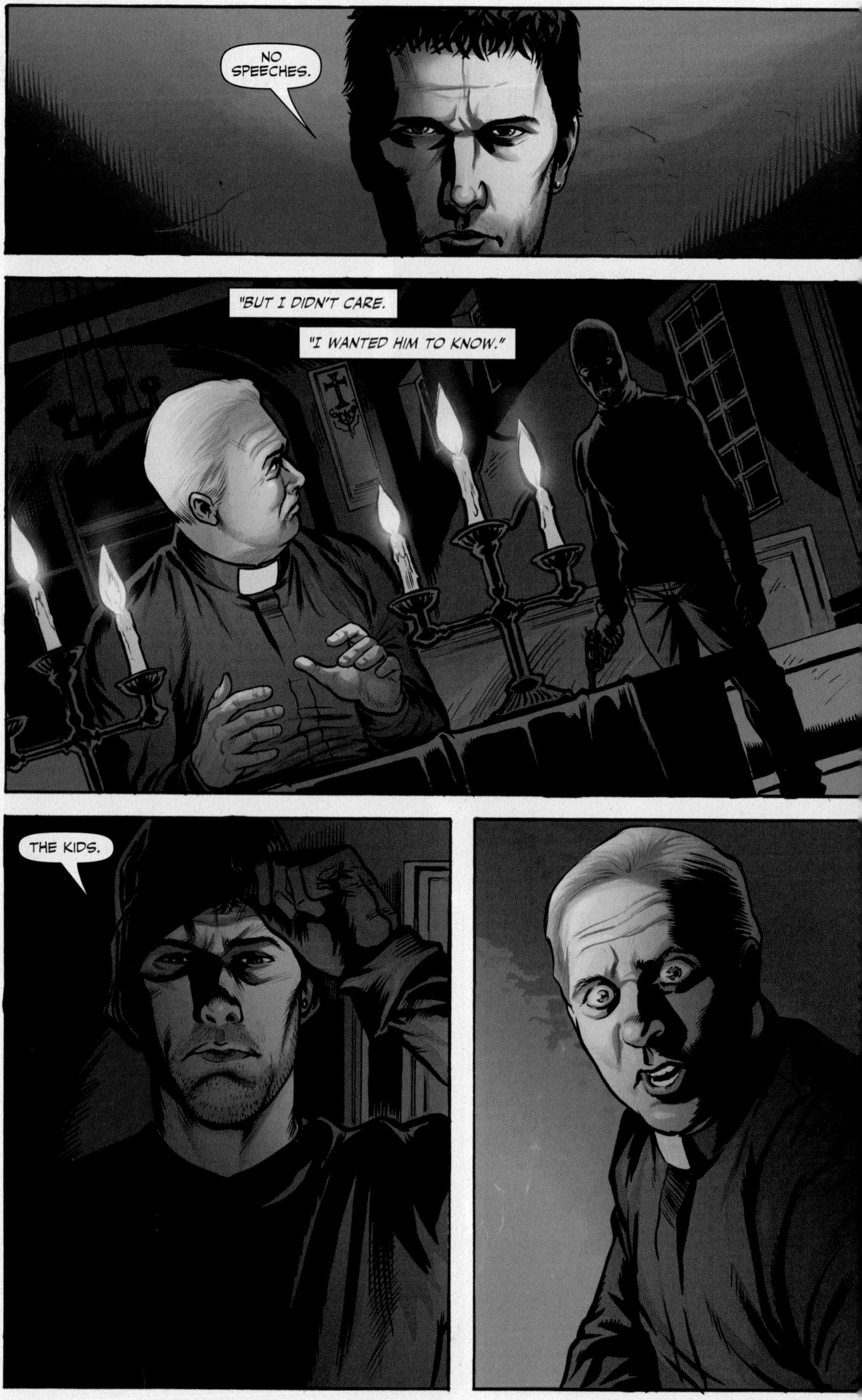
NO SPEECHES.
"BUT I DIDN'T CARE.
"I WANTED HIM TO KNOW."
THE KIDS.

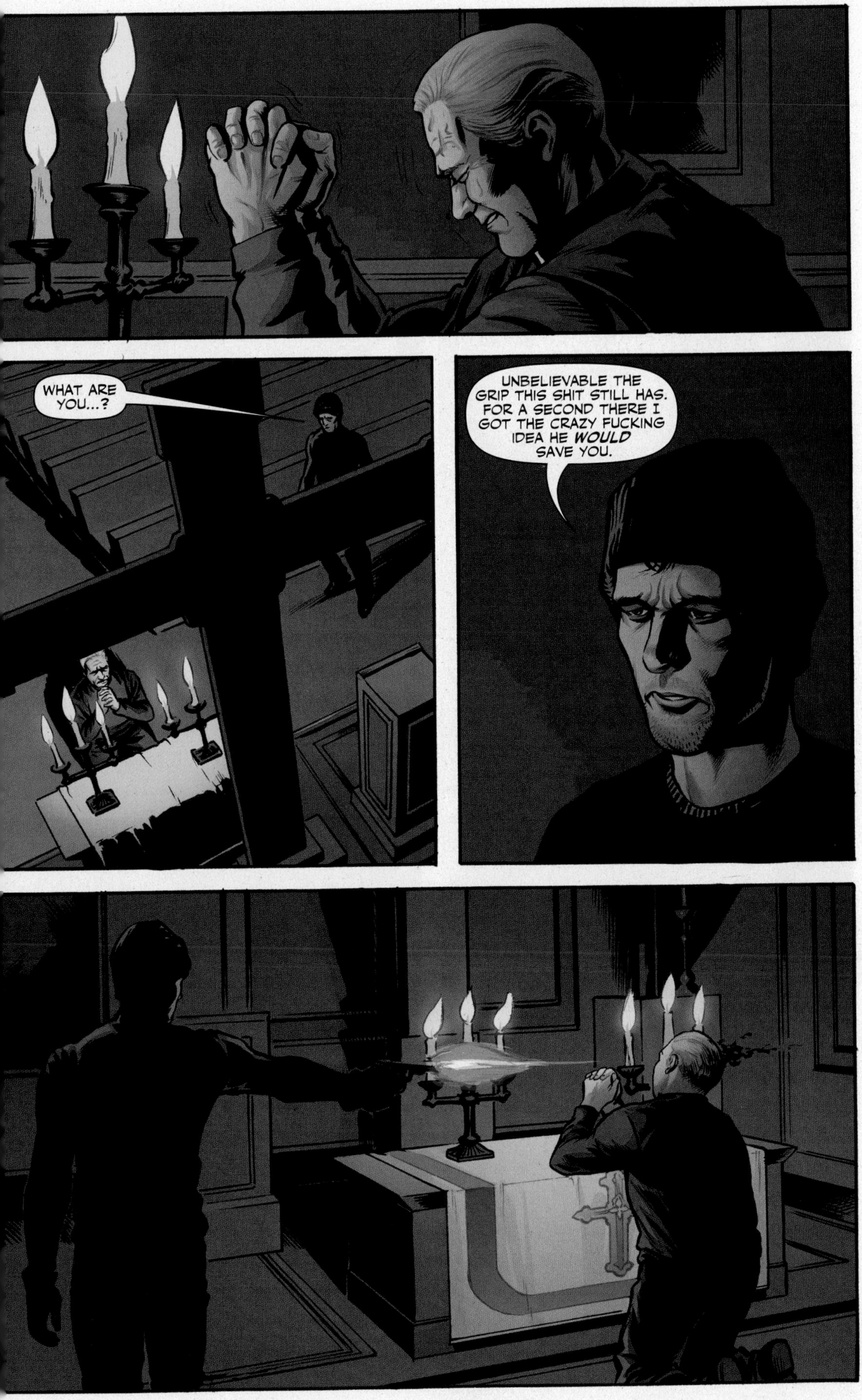
WHAT ARE YOU...?
UNBELIEVABLE THE GRIP THIS SHIT STILL HAS. FOR A SECOND THERE I GOT THE CRAZY FUCKING IDEA HE *WOULD* SAVE YOU.

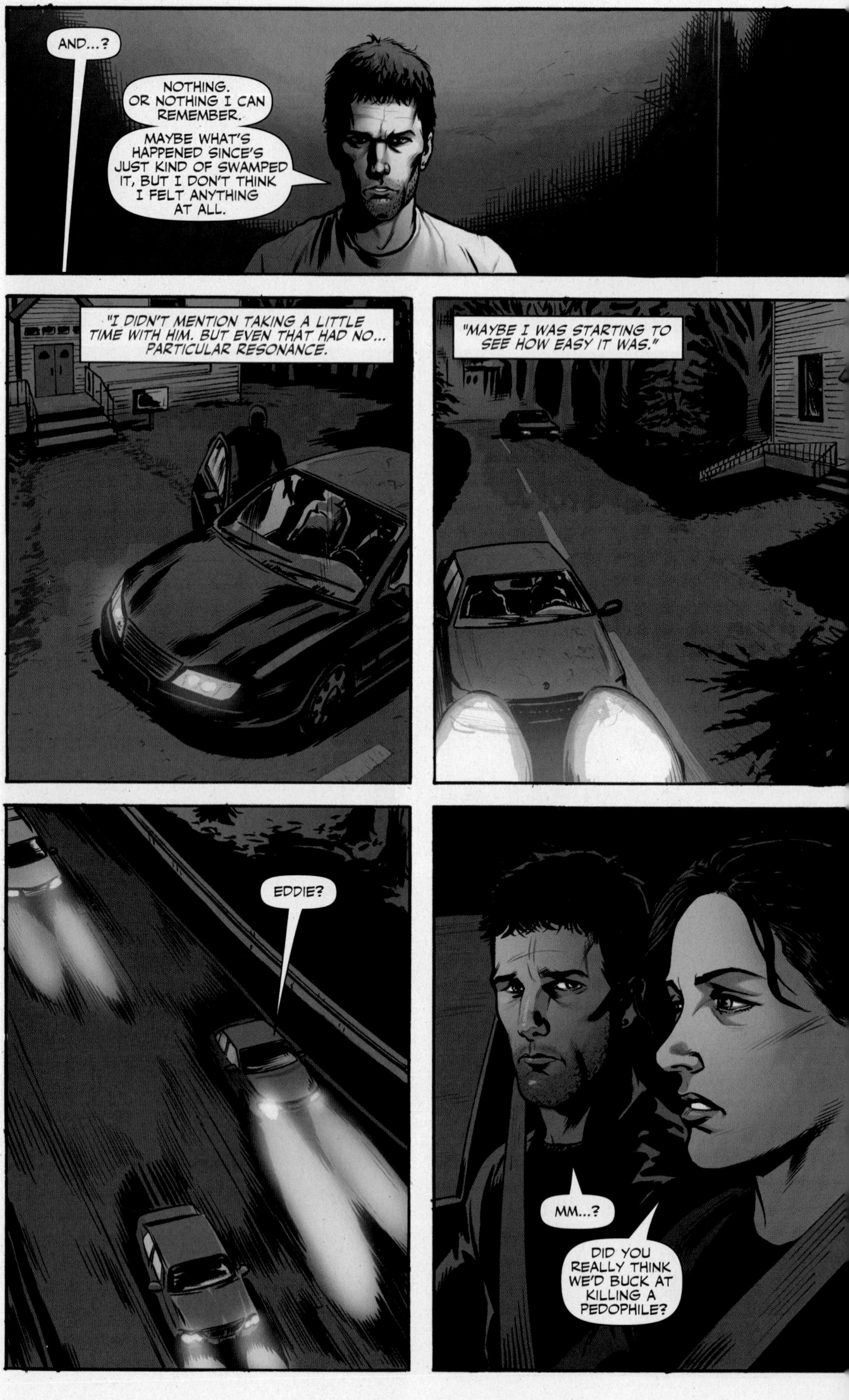
AND...?
NOTHING. OR NOTHING I CAN REMEMBER.
MAYBE WHAT'S HAPPENED SINCE'S JUST KIND OF SWAMPED IT, BUT I DON'T THINK I FELT ANYTHING AT ALL.
"I DIDN'T MENTION TAKING A LITTLE TIME WITH HIM. BUT EVEN THAT HAD NO... PARTICULAR RESONANCE.
"MAYBE I WAS STARTING TO SEE HOW EASY IT WAS."
EDDIE?
MM...?
DID YOU REALLY THINK WE'D BUCK AT KILLING A PEDOPHILE?

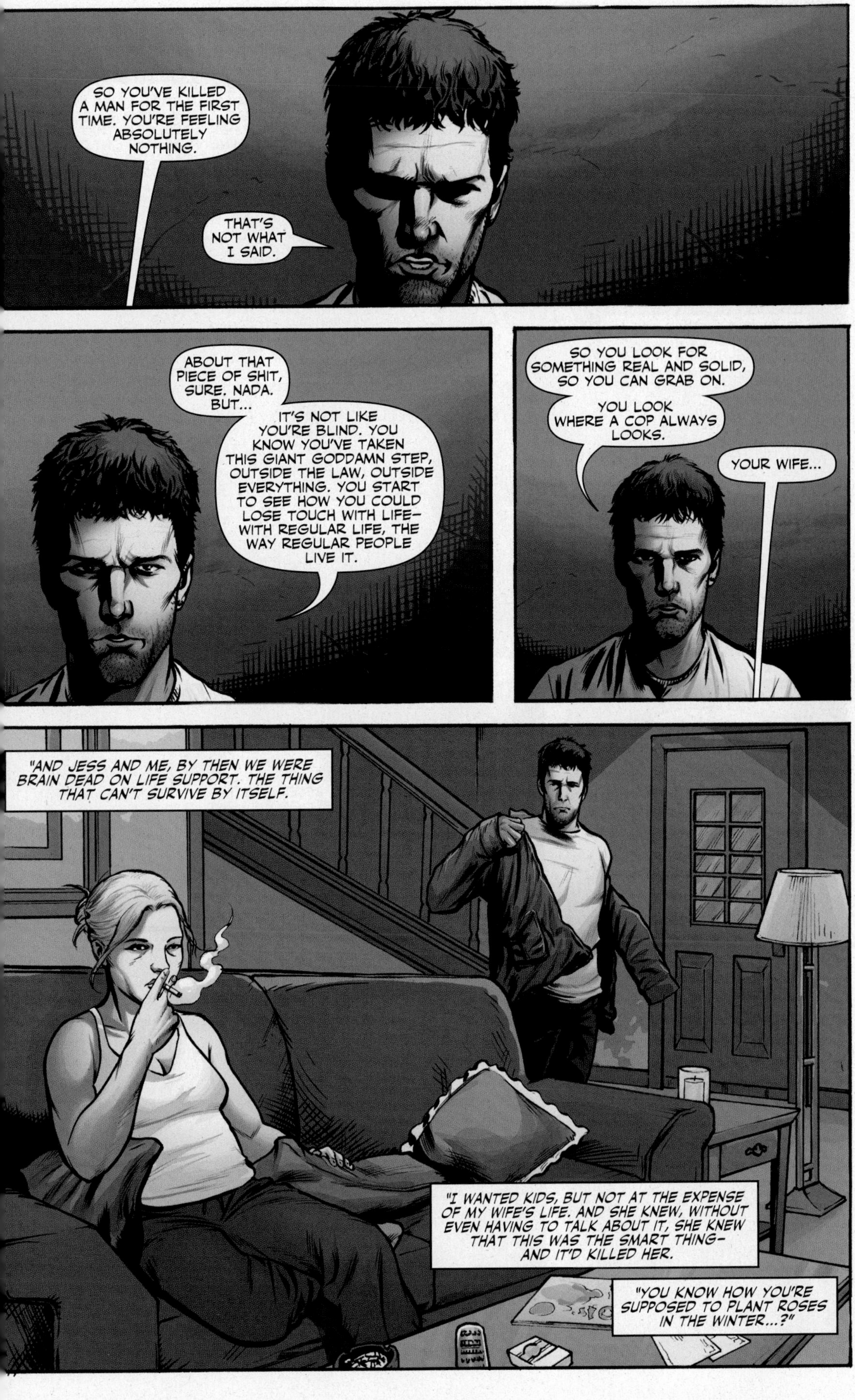
SO YOU'VE KILLED A MAN FOR THE FIRST TIME. YOU'RE FEELING ABSOLUTELY NOTHING.
THAT'S NOT WHAT I SAID.
ABOUT THAT PIECE OF SHIT, SURE. NADA. BUT...
IT'S NOT LIKE YOU'RE BLIND. YOU KNOW YOU'VE TAKEN THIS GIANT GODDAMN STEP, OUTSIDE THE LAW, OUTSIDE EVERYTHING. YOU START TO SEE HOW YOU COULD LOSE TOUCH WITH LIFE-WITH REGULAR LIFE, THE WAY REGULAR PEOPLE LIVE IT.
SO YOU LOOK FOR SOMETHING REAL AND SOLID, SO YOU CAN GRAB ON.
YOU LOOK WHERE A COP ALWAYS LOOKS.
YOUR WIFE...
"AND JESS AND ME, BY THEN WE WERE BRAIN DEAD ON LIFE SUPPORT. THE THING THAT CAN'T SURVIVE BY ITSELF.
"I WANTED KIDS, BUT NOT AT THE EXPENSE OF MY WIFE'S LIFE. AND SHE KNEW, WITHOUT EVEN HAVING TO TALK ABOUT IT, SHE KNEW THAT THIS WAS THE SMART THING-AND IT'D KILLED HER.
"YOU KNOW HOW YOU'RE SUPPOSED TO PLANT ROSES IN THE WINTER...?"

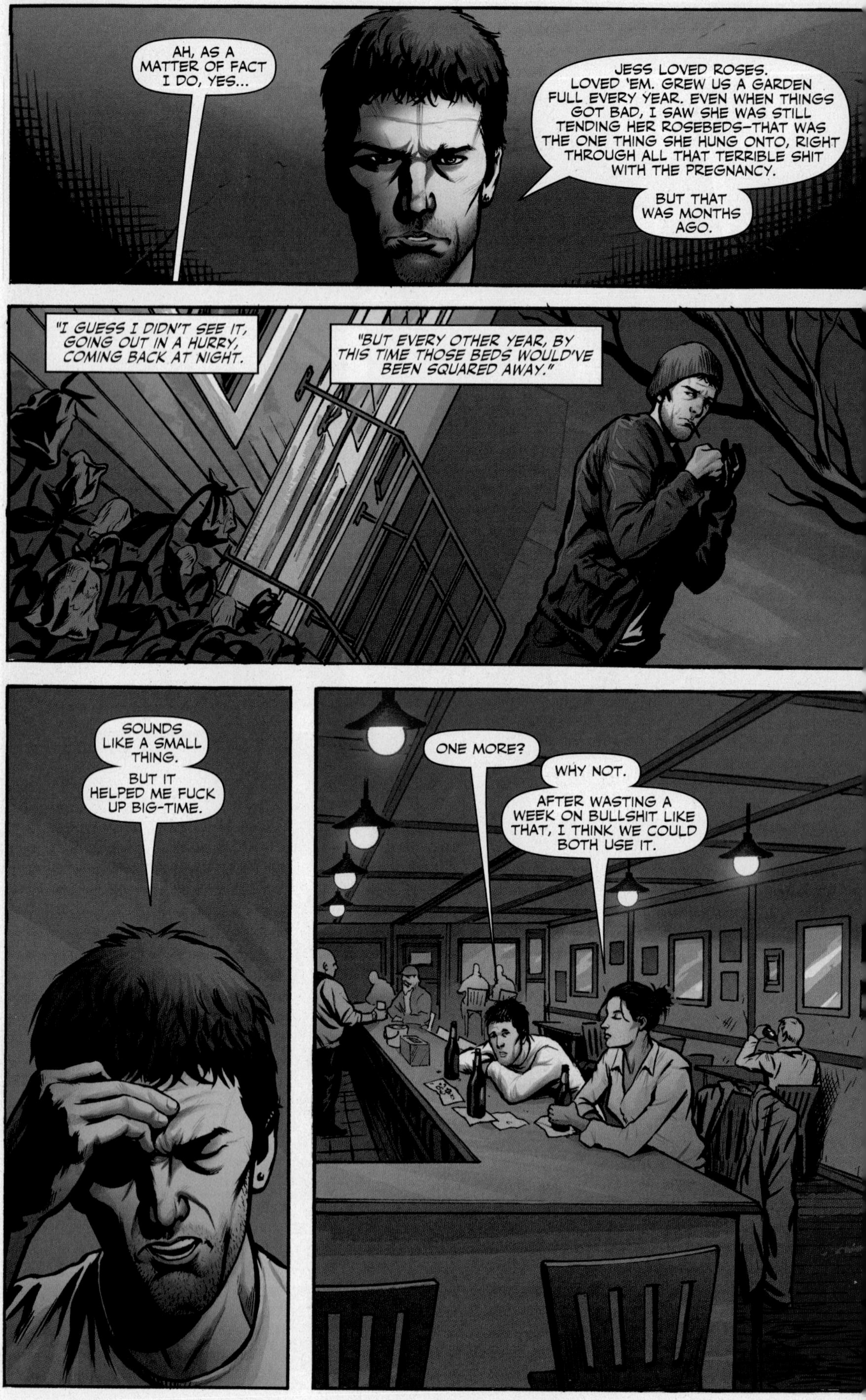
AH, AS A MATTER OF FACT I DO, YES...
JESS LOVED ROSES. LOVED 'EM. GREW US A GARDEN FULL EVERY YEAR. EVEN WHEN THINGS GOT BAD, I SAW SHE WAS STILL TENDING HER ROSEBEDS—THAT WAS THE ONE THING SHE HUNG ONTO, RIGHT THROUGH ALL THAT TERRIBLE SHIT WITH THE PREGNANCY.
BUT THAT WAS MONTHS AGO.
"I GUESS I DIDN'T SEE IT, GOING OUT IN A HURRY, COMING BACK AT NIGHT.
"BUT EVERY OTHER YEAR, BY THIS TIME THOSE BEDS WOULD'VE BEEN SQUARED AWAY."
SOUNDS LIKE A SMALL THING.
BUT IT HELPED ME FUCK UP BIG-TIME.
ONE MORE?
WHY NOT.
AFTER WASTING A WEEK ON BULLSHIT LIKE THAT, I THINK WE COULD BOTH USE IT.

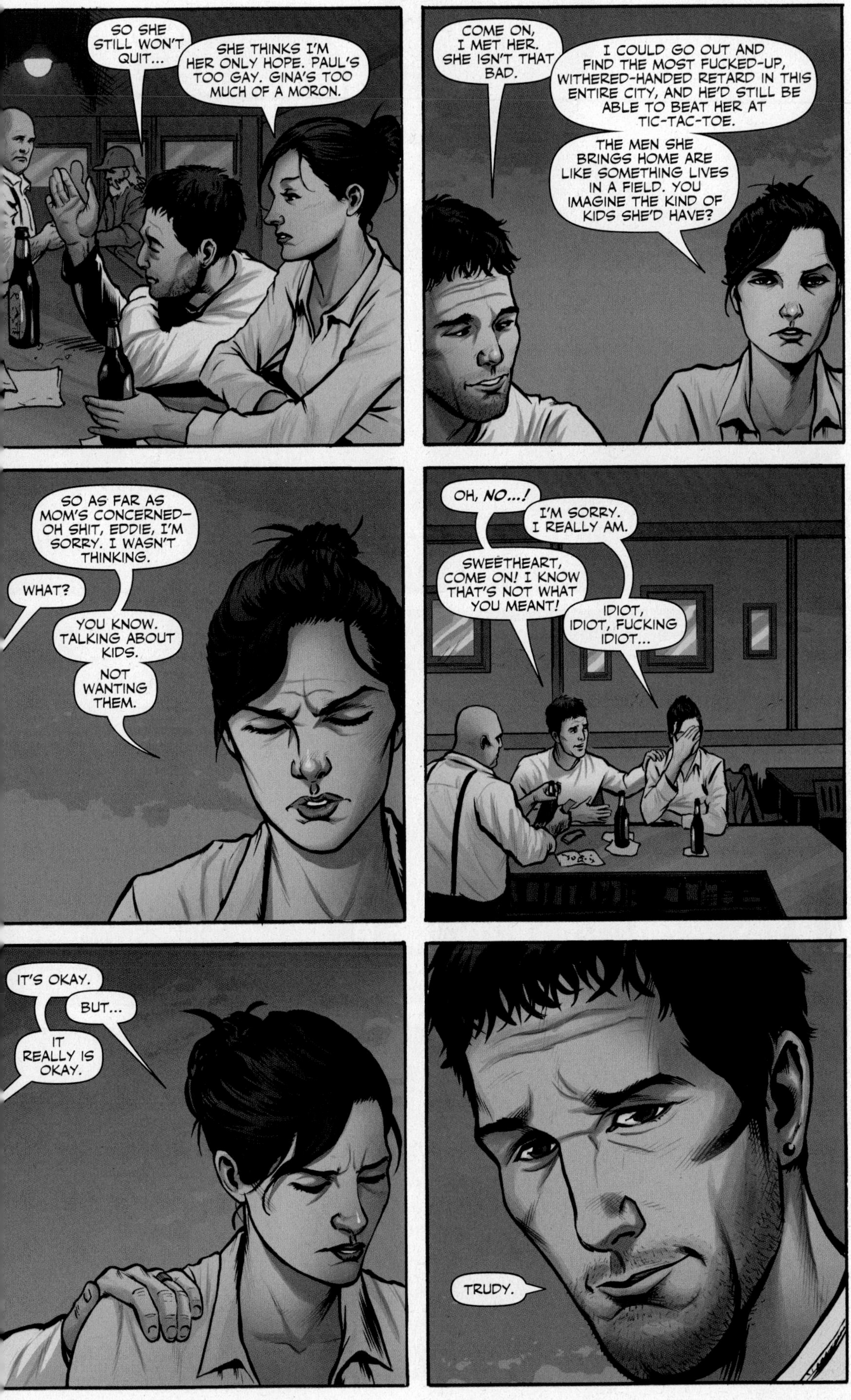
SO SHE STILL WON'T QUIT...
SHE THINKS I'M HER ONLY HOPE. PAUL'S TOO GAY. GINA'S TOO MUCH OF A MORON.
COME ON, I MET HER. SHE ISN'T THAT BAD.
I COULD GO OUT AND FIND THE MOST FUCKED-UP, WITHERED-HANDED RETARD IN THIS ENTIRE CITY, AND HE'D STILL BE ABLE TO BEAT HER AT TIC-TAC-TOE.
THE MEN SHE BRINGS HOME ARE LIKE SOMETHING LIVES IN A FIELD. YOU IMAGINE THE KIND OF KIDS SHE'D HAVE?
SO AS FAR AS MOM'S CONCERNED-- OH SHIT, EDDIE, I'M SORRY. I WASN'T THINKING.
WHAT?
YOU KNOW. TALKING ABOUT KIDS.
NOT WANTING THEM.
OH, NO...!
I'M SORRY. I REALLY AM.
SWEETHEART, COME ON! I KNOW THAT'S NOT WHAT YOU MEANT!
IDIOT, IDIOT, FUCKING IDIOT...
IT'S OKAY.
BUT...
IT REALLY IS OKAY.
TRUDY.

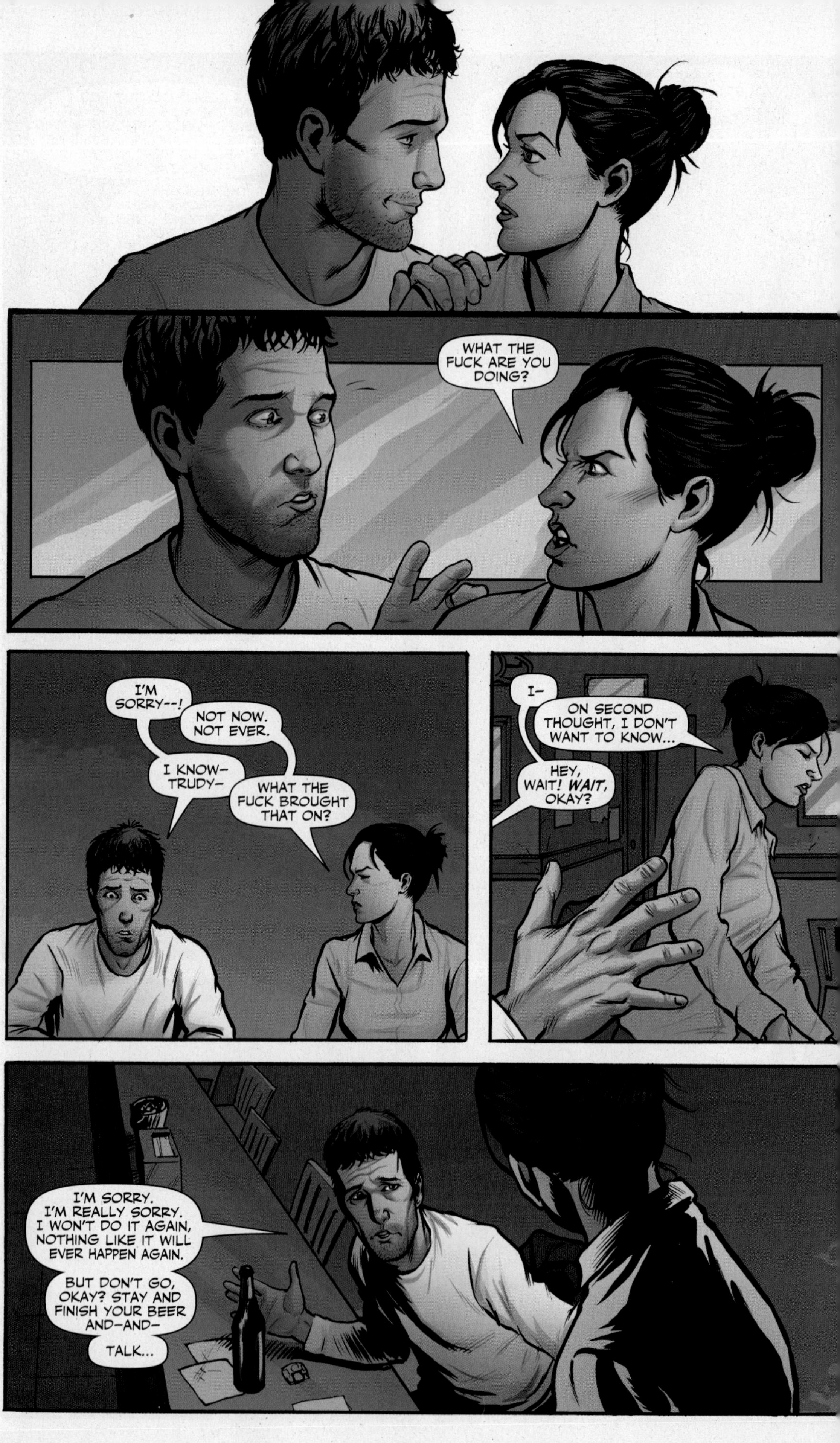
WHAT THE FUCK ARE YOU DOING?
I'M SORRY--!
NOT NOW. NOT EVER.
I KNOW-TRUDY-
WHAT THE FUCK BROUGHT THAT ON?
I-
ON SECOND THOUGHT, I DON'T WANT TO KNOW...
HEY, WAIT! *WAIT*, OKAY?
I'M SORRY. I'M REALLY SORRY. I WON'T DO IT AGAIN, NOTHING LIKE IT WILL EVER HAPPEN AGAIN.
BUT DON'T GO, OKAY? STAY AND FINISH YOUR BEER AND-AND-
TALK...

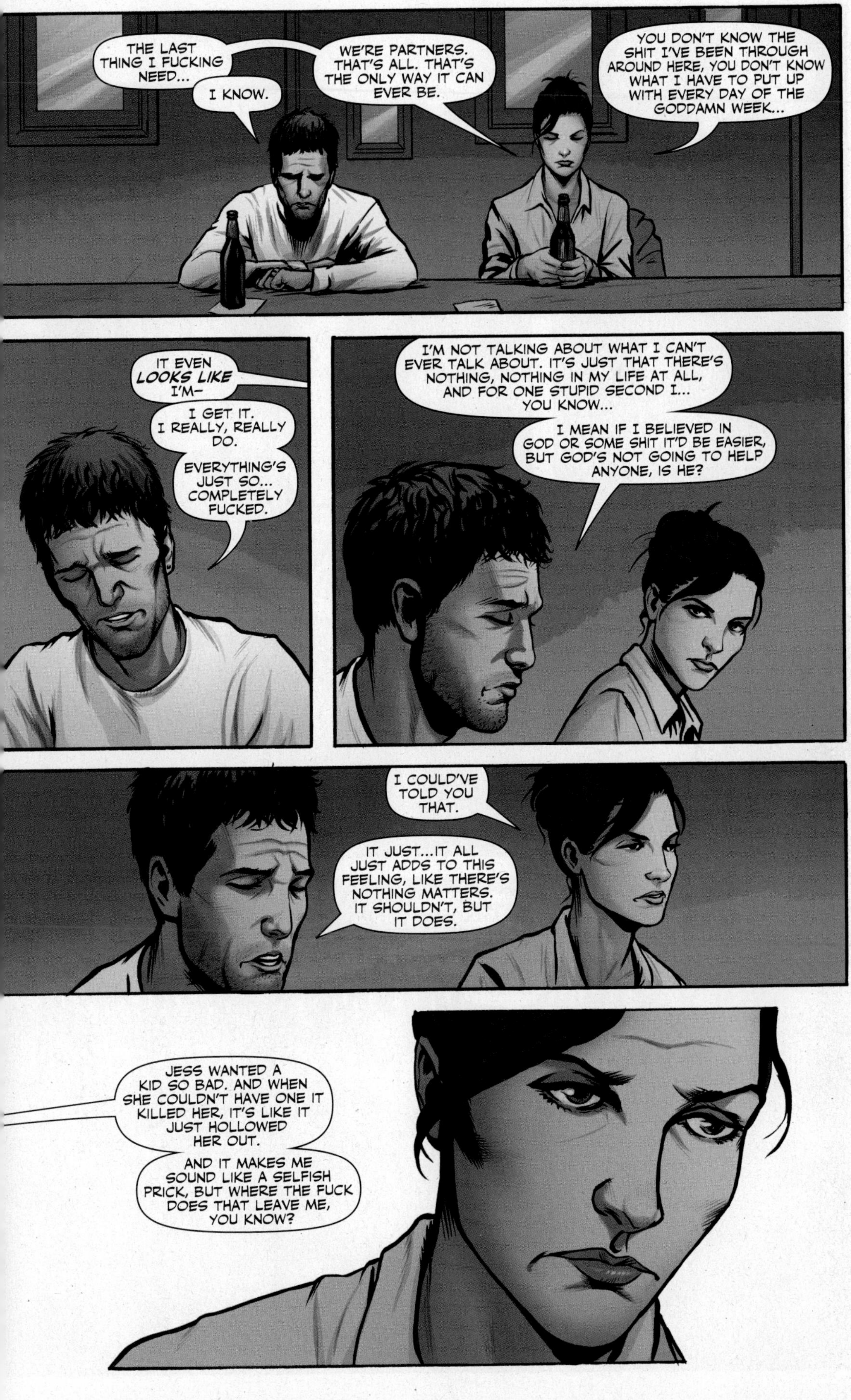
THE LAST THING I FUCKING NEED...
I KNOW.
WE'RE PARTNERS. THAT'S ALL. THAT'S THE ONLY WAY IT CAN EVER BE.
YOU DON'T KNOW THE SHIT I'VE BEEN THROUGH AROUND HERE, YOU DON'T KNOW WHAT I HAVE TO PUT UP WITH EVERY DAY OF THE GODDAMN WEEK...
IT EVEN LOOKS LIKE I'M–
I GET IT. I REALLY, REALLY DO.
EVERYTHING'S JUST SO... COMPLETELY FUCKED.
I'M NOT TALKING ABOUT WHAT I CAN'T EVER TALK ABOUT. IT'S JUST THAT THERE'S NOTHING, NOTHING IN MY LIFE AT ALL, AND FOR ONE STUPID SECOND I... YOU KNOW...
I MEAN IF I BELIEVED IN GOD OR SOME SHIT IT'D BE EASIER, BUT GOD'S NOT GOING TO HELP ANYONE, IS HE?
I COULD'VE TOLD YOU THAT.
IT JUST...IT ALL JUST ADDS TO THIS FEELING, LIKE THERE'S NOTHING MATTERS. IT SHOULDN'T, BUT IT DOES.
JESS WANTED A KID SO BAD. AND WHEN SHE COULDN'T HAVE ONE IT KILLED HER, IT'S LIKE IT JUST HOLLOWED HER OUT.
AND IT MAKES ME SOUND LIKE A SELFISH PRICK, BUT WHERE THE FUCK DOES THAT LEAVE ME, YOU KNOW?

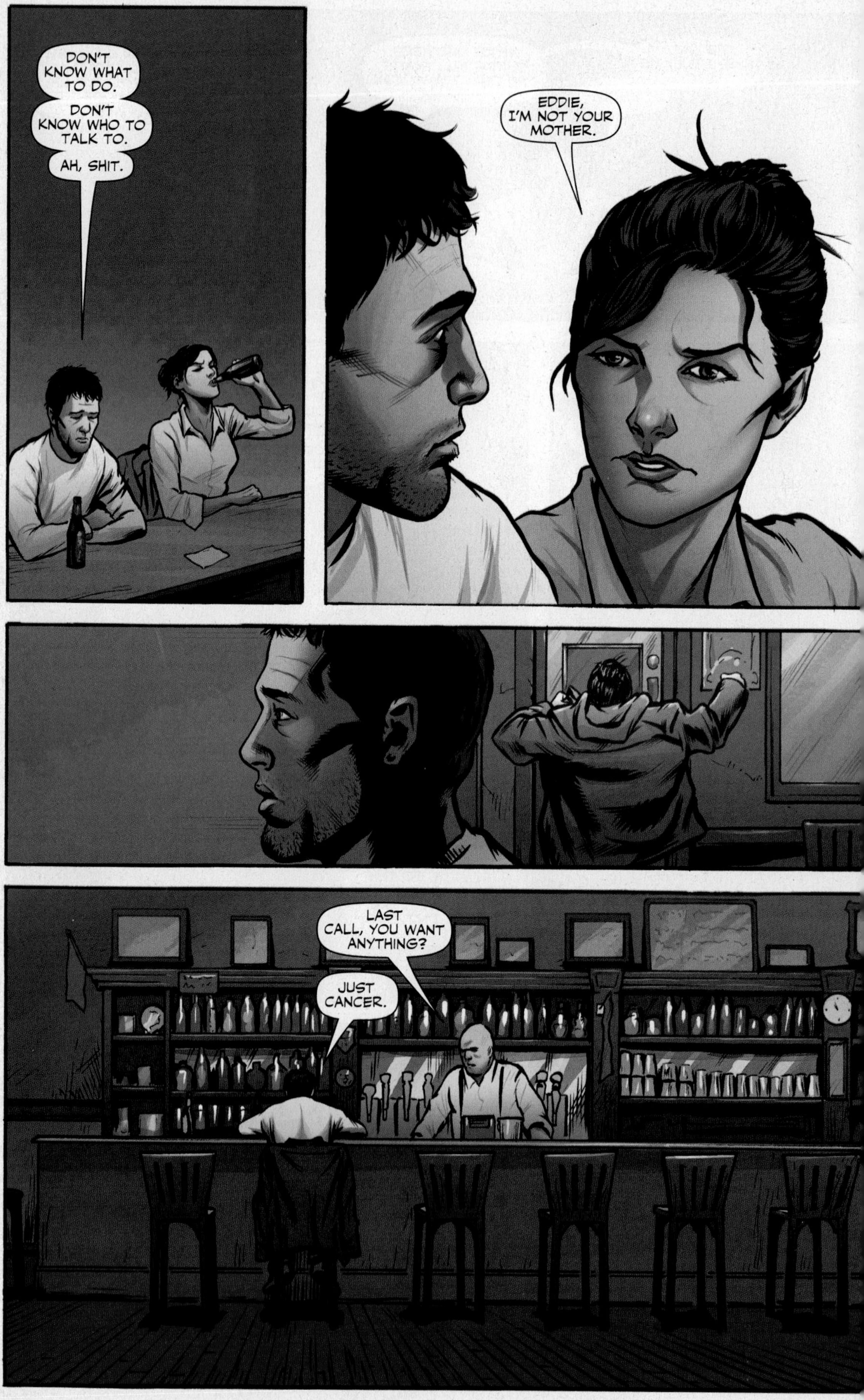
DON'T KNOW WHAT TO DO.
DON'T KNOW WHO TO TALK TO.
AH, SHIT.
EDDIE, I'M NOT YOUR MOTHER.
LAST CALL, YOU WANT ANYTHING?
JUST CANCER.

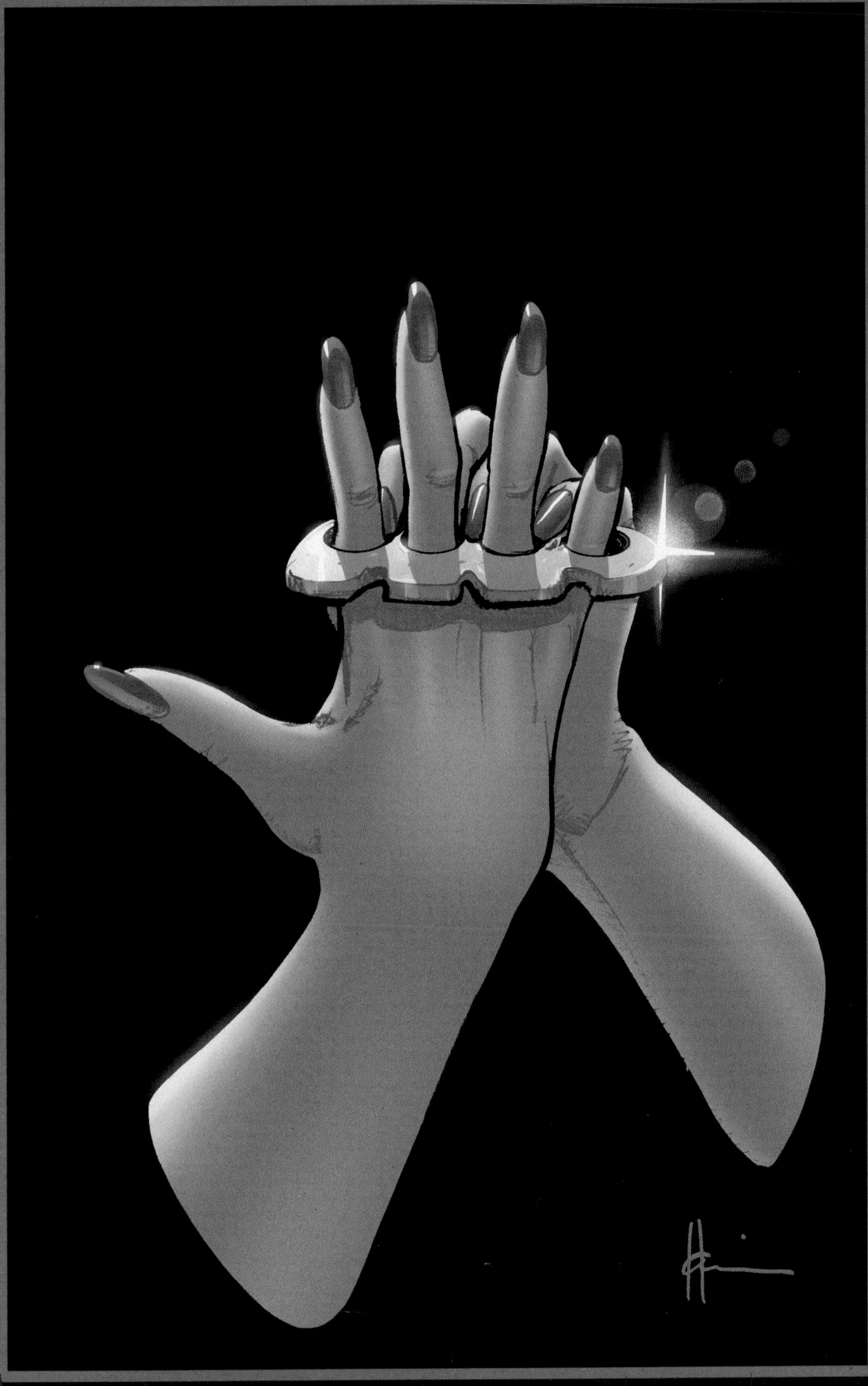

YKIN colors by JESUS ABURTO

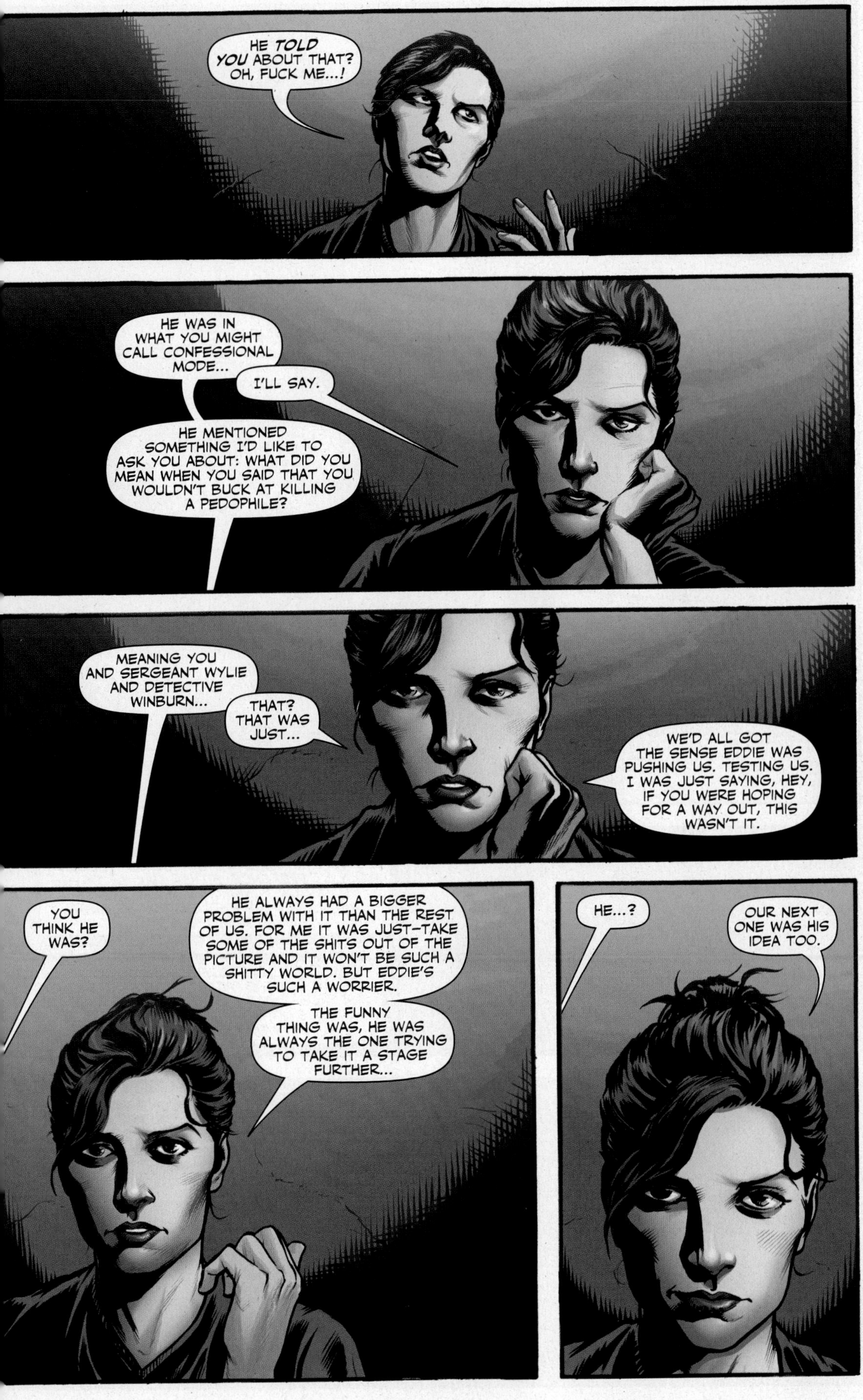
HE TOLD YOU ABOUT THAT? OH, FUCK ME...!
HE WAS IN WHAT YOU MIGHT CALL CONFESSIONAL MODE...
I'LL SAY.
HE MENTIONED SOMETHING I'D LIKE TO ASK YOU ABOUT: WHAT DID YOU MEAN WHEN YOU SAID THAT YOU WOULDN'T BUCK AT KILLING A PEDOPHILE?
MEANING YOU AND SERGEANT WYLIE AND DETECTIVE WINBURN...
THAT? THAT WAS JUST...
WE'D ALL GOT THE SENSE EDDIE WAS PUSHING US. TESTING US. I WAS JUST SAYING, HEY, IF YOU WERE HOPING FOR A WAY OUT, THIS WASN'T IT.
YOU THINK HE WAS?
HE ALWAYS HAD A BIGGER PROBLEM WITH IT THAN THE REST OF US. FOR ME IT WAS JUST—TAKE SOME OF THE SHITS OUT OF THE PICTURE AND IT WON'T BE SUCH A SHITTY WORLD. BUT EDDIE'S SUCH A WORRIER.
THE FUNNY THING WAS, HE WAS ALWAYS THE ONE TRYING TO TAKE IT A STAGE FURTHER...
HE...?
OUR NEXT ONE WAS HIS IDEA TOO.

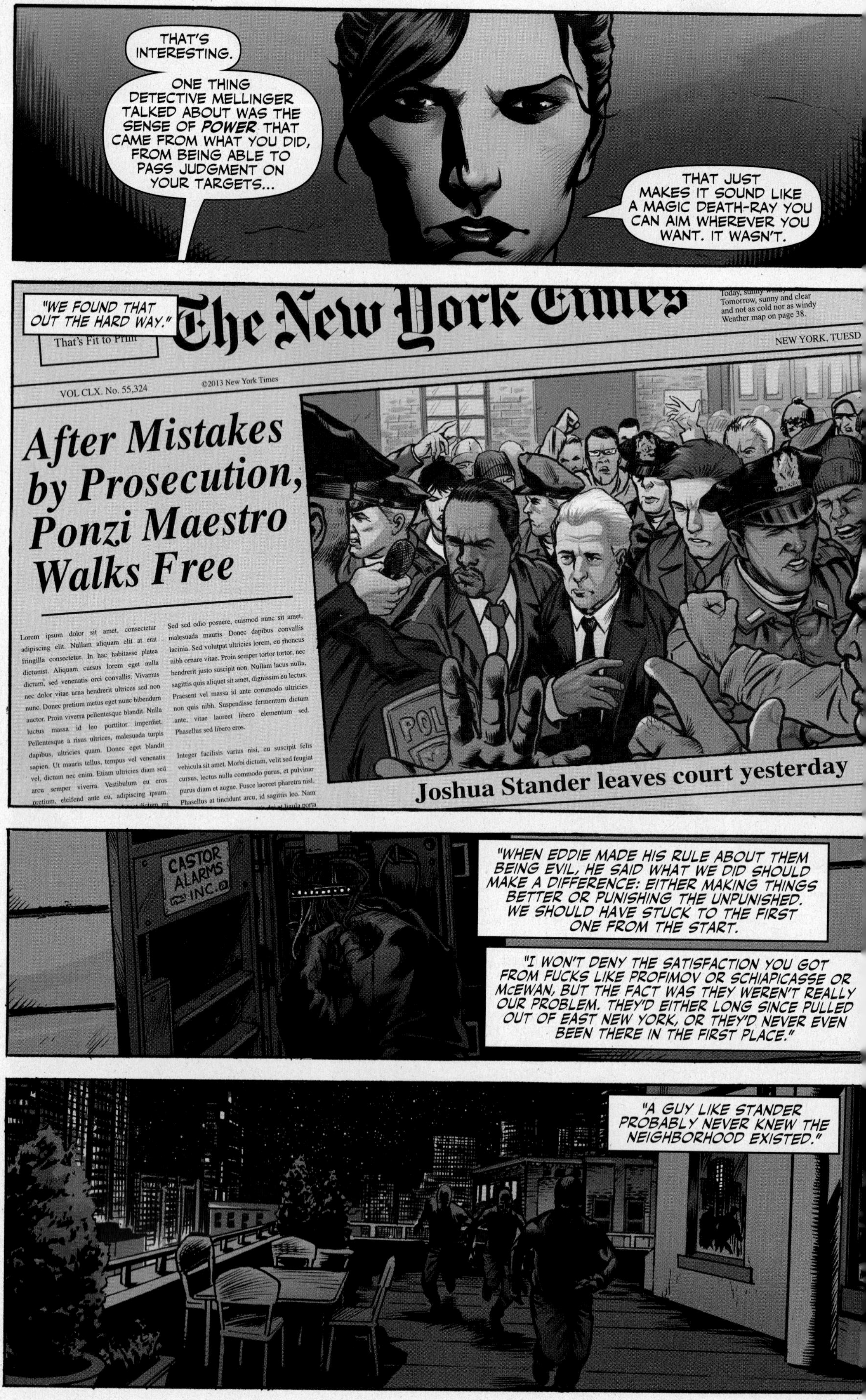

THAT'S INTERESTING.
ONE THING DETECTIVE MELLINGER TALKED ABOUT WAS THE SENSE OF *POWER* THAT CAME FROM WHAT YOU DID, FROM BEING ABLE TO PASS JUDGMENT ON YOUR TARGETS...
THAT JUST MAKES IT SOUND LIKE A MAGIC DEATH-RAY YOU CAN AIM WHEREVER YOU WANT. IT WASN'T.
"WE FOUND THAT OUT THE HARD WAY."
That's Fit to Print
The New York Times
Tomorrow, sunny and clear and not as cold nor as windy
Weather map on page 38.
NEW YORK, TUESD
VOL CLX. No. 55,324
©2013 New York Times
After Mistakes by Prosecution, Ponzi Maestro Walks Free
POL
Joshua Stander leaves court yesterday
CASTOR ALARMS INC.
"WHEN EDDIE MADE HIS RULE ABOUT THEM BEING EVIL, HE SAID WHAT WE DID SHOULD MAKE A DIFFERENCE: EITHER MAKING THINGS BETTER OR PUNISHING THE UNPUNISHED. WE SHOULD HAVE STUCK TO THE FIRST ONE FROM THE START.
"I WON'T DENY THE SATISFACTION YOU GOT FROM FUCKS LIKE PROFIMOV OR SCHIAPICASSE OR McEWAN, BUT THE FACT WAS THEY WEREN'T REALLY OUR PROBLEM. THEY'D EITHER LONG SINCE PULLED OUT OF EAST NEW YORK, OR THEY'D NEVER EVEN BEEN THERE IN THE FIRST PLACE."
"A GUY LIKE STANDER PROBABLY NEVER KNEW THE NEIGHBORHOOD EXISTED."

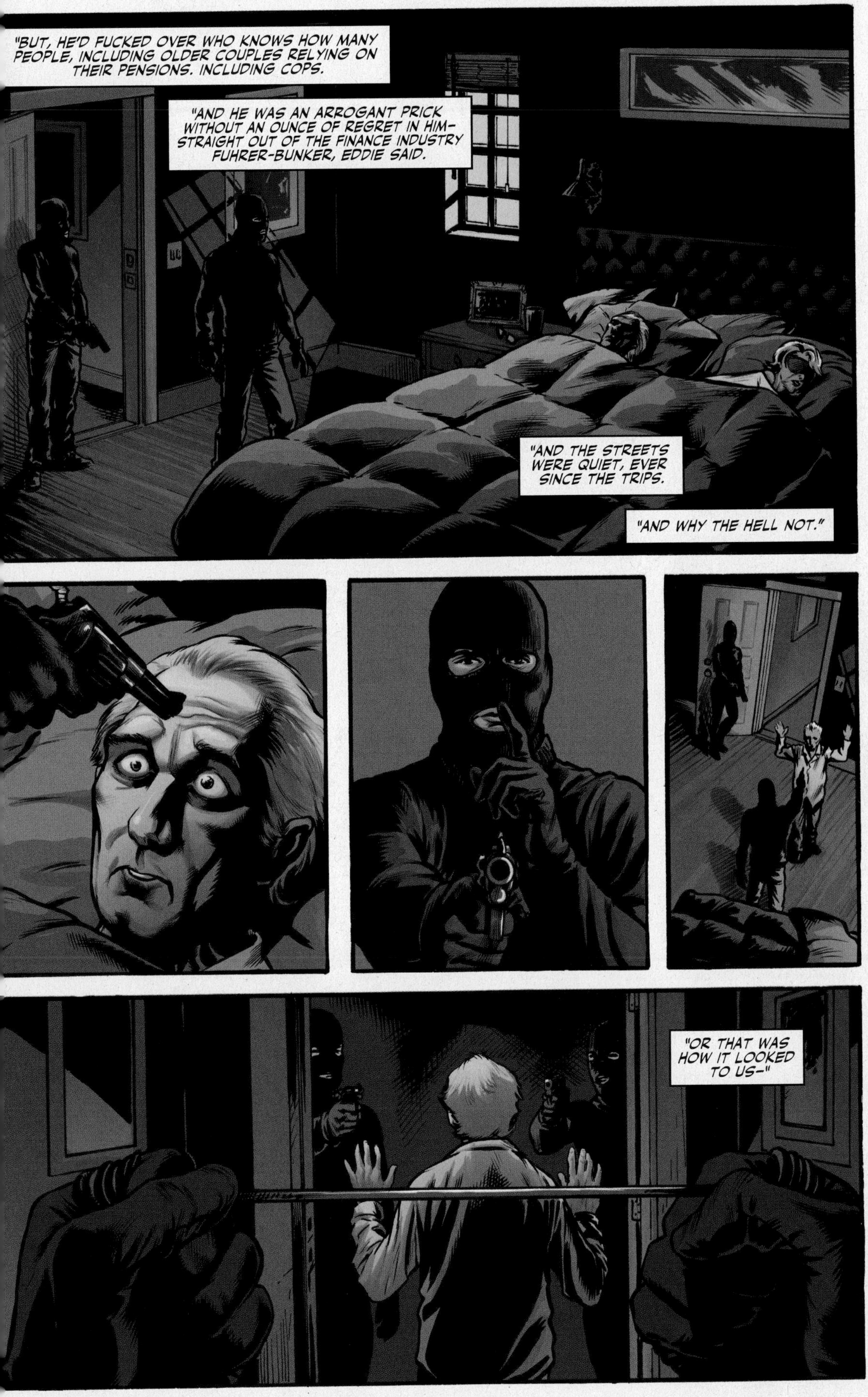
"BUT, HE'D FUCKED OVER WHO KNOWS HOW MANY PEOPLE, INCLUDING OLDER COUPLES RELYING ON THEIR PENSIONS. INCLUDING COPS.
"AND HE WAS AN ARROGANT PRICK WITHOUT AN OUNCE OF REGRET IN HIM-STRAIGHT OUT OF THE FINANCE INDUSTRY FUHRER-BUNKER, EDDIE SAID.
"AND THE STREETS WERE QUIET, EVER SINCE THE TRIPS.
"AND WHY THE HELL NOT."
"OR THAT WAS HOW IT LOOKED TO US–"

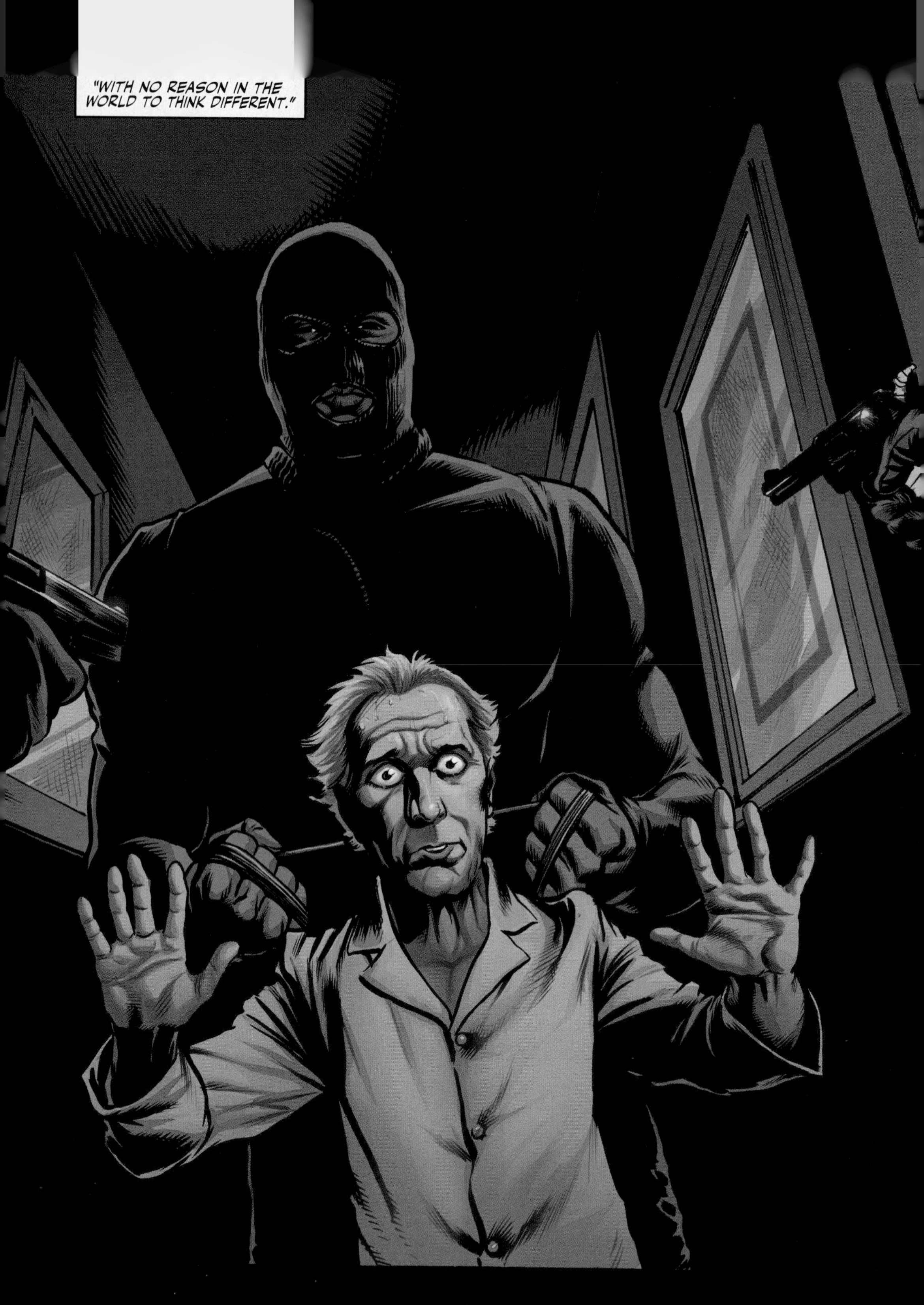
"WITH NO REASON IN THE WORLD TO THINK DIFFERENT."

4: THE BULLET-DODGERS

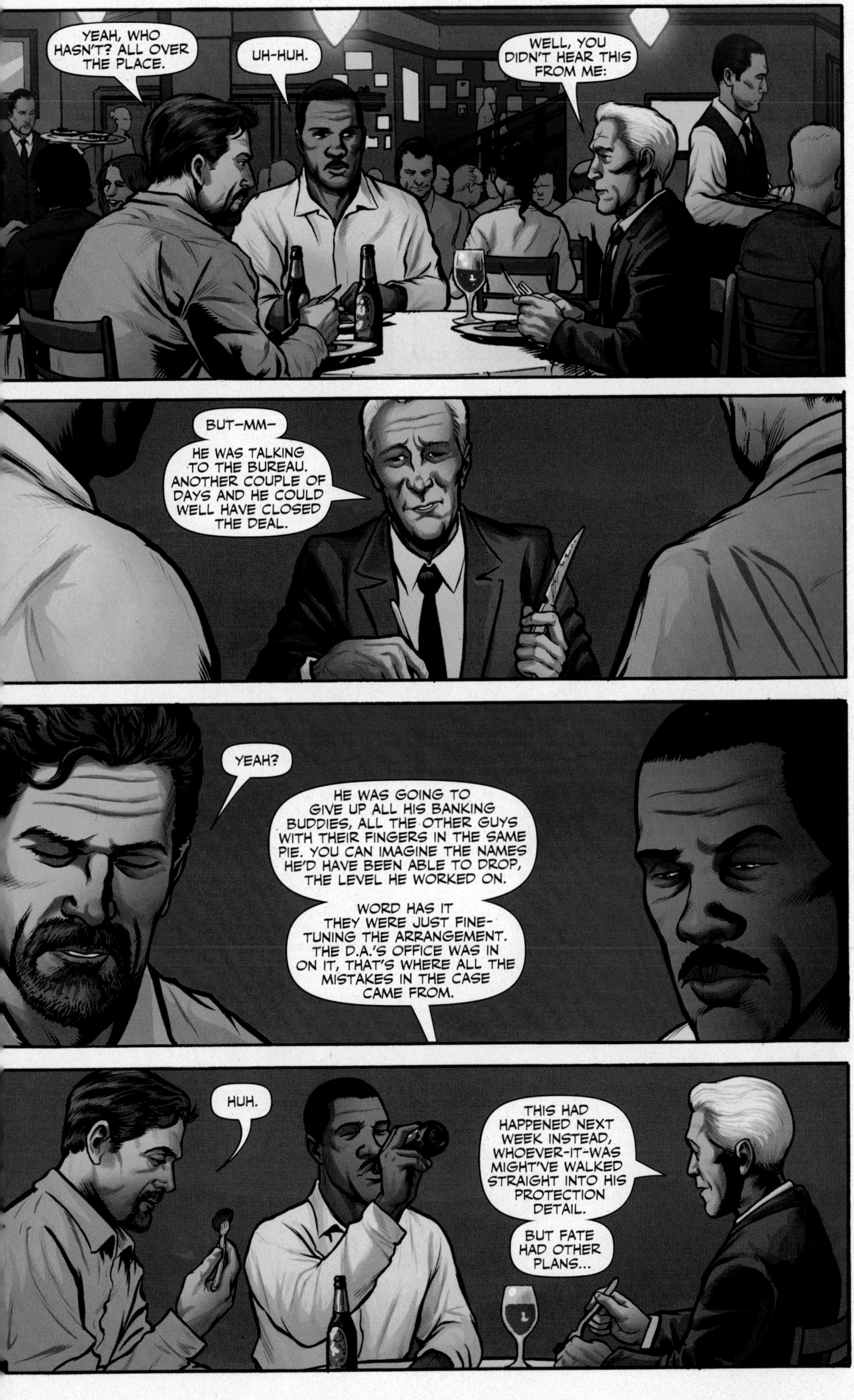
YEAH, WHO HASN'T? ALL OVER THE PLACE.
UH-HUH.
WELL, YOU DIDN'T HEAR THIS FROM ME:
BUT–MM–
HE WAS TALKING TO THE BUREAU. ANOTHER COUPLE OF DAYS AND HE COULD WELL HAVE CLOSED THE DEAL.
YEAH?
HE WAS GOING TO GIVE UP ALL HIS BANKING BUDDIES, ALL THE OTHER GUYS WITH THEIR FINGERS IN THE SAME PIE. YOU CAN IMAGINE THE NAMES HE'D HAVE BEEN ABLE TO DROP, THE LEVEL HE WORKED ON.
WORD HAS IT THEY WERE JUST FINE-TUNING THE ARRANGEMENT. THE D.A.'S OFFICE WAS IN ON IT, THAT'S WHERE ALL THE MISTAKES IN THE CASE CAME FROM.
HUH.
THIS HAD HAPPENED NEXT WEEK INSTEAD, WHOEVER-IT-WAS MIGHT'VE WALKED STRAIGHT INTO HIS PROTECTION DETAIL.
BUT FATE HAD OTHER PLANS...

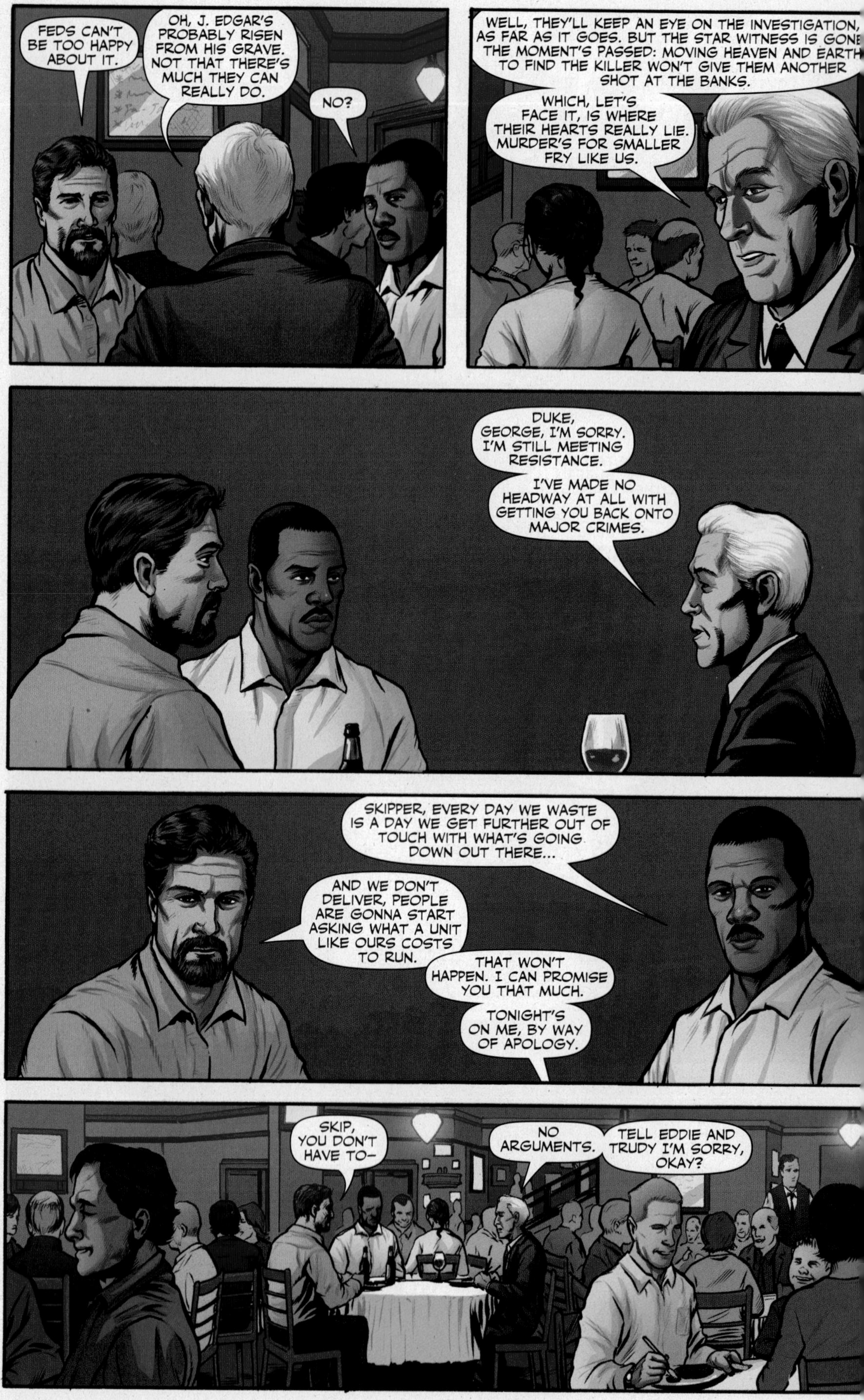

FEDS CAN'T BE TOO HAPPY ABOUT IT.
OH, J. EDGAR'S PROBABLY RISEN FROM HIS GRAVE. NOT THAT THERE'S MUCH THEY CAN REALLY DO.
NO?
WELL, THEY'LL KEEP AN EYE ON THE INVESTIGATION, AS FAR AS IT GOES. BUT THE STAR WITNESS IS GONE THE MOMENT'S PASSED: MOVING HEAVEN AND EARTH TO FIND THE KILLER WON'T GIVE THEM ANOTHER SHOT AT THE BANKS.
WHICH, LET'S FACE IT, IS WHERE THEIR HEARTS REALLY LIE. MURDER'S FOR SMALLER FRY LIKE US.
DUKE, GEORGE, I'M SORRY. I'M STILL MEETING RESISTANCE.
I'VE MADE NO HEADWAY AT ALL WITH GETTING YOU BACK ONTO MAJOR CRIMES.
SKIPPER, EVERY DAY WE WASTE IS A DAY WE GET FURTHER OUT OF TOUCH WITH WHAT'S GOING DOWN OUT THERE...
AND WE DON'T DELIVER, PEOPLE ARE GONNA START ASKING WHAT A UNIT LIKE OURS COSTS TO RUN.
THAT WON'T HAPPEN. I CAN PROMISE YOU THAT MUCH.
TONIGHT'S ON ME, BY WAY OF APOLOGY.
SKIP, YOU DON'T HAVE TO–
NO ARGUMENTS.
TELL EDDIE AND TRUDY I'M SORRY, OKAY?

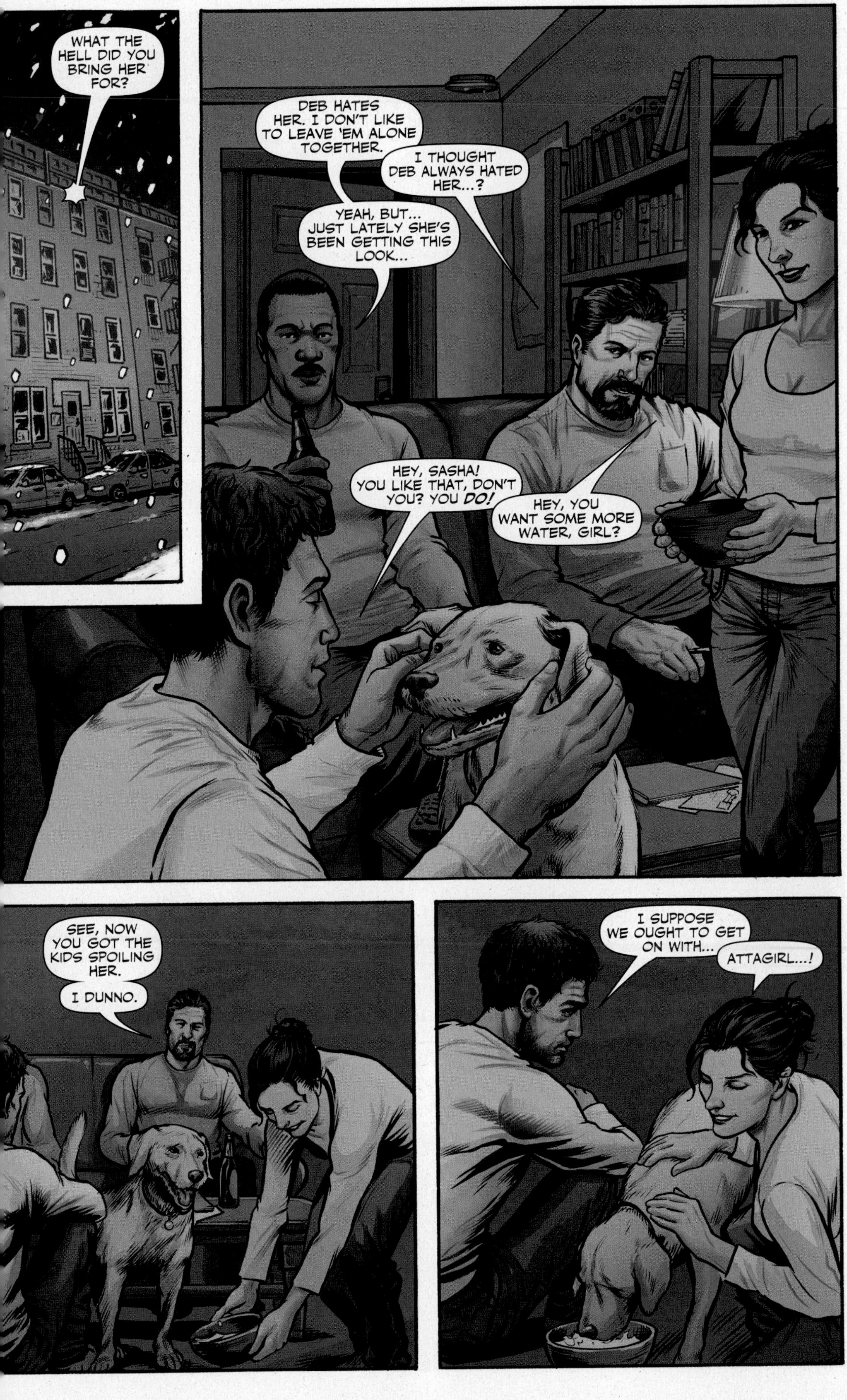

WHAT THE HELL DID YOU BRING HER FOR?
DEB HATES HER. I DON'T LIKE TO LEAVE 'EM ALONE TOGETHER.
I THOUGHT DEB ALWAYS HATED HER...?
YEAH, BUT... JUST LATELY SHE'S BEEN GETTING THIS LOOK...
HEY, SASHA! YOU LIKE THAT, DON'T YOU? YOU *DO!*
HEY, YOU WANT SOME MORE WATER, GIRL?
SEE, NOW YOU GOT THE KIDS SPOILING HER.
I DUNNO.
I SUPPOSE WE OUGHT TO GET ON WITH...
ATTAGIRL...!

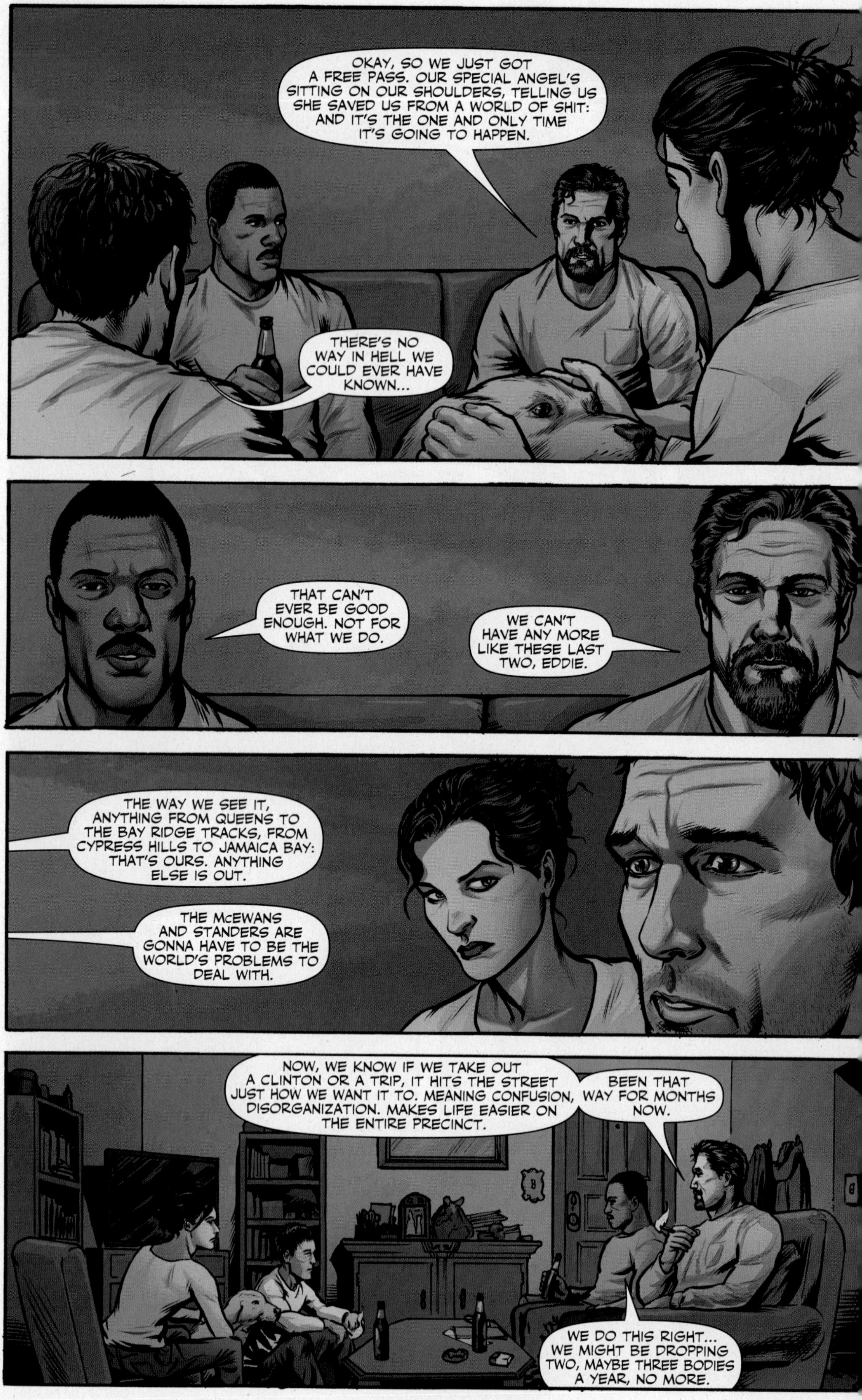
OKAY, SO WE JUST GOT A FREE PASS. OUR SPECIAL ANGEL'S SITTING ON OUR SHOULDERS, TELLING US SHE SAVED US FROM A WORLD OF SHIT: AND IT'S THE ONE AND ONLY TIME IT'S GOING TO HAPPEN.
THERE'S NO WAY IN HELL WE COULD EVER HAVE KNOWN...
THAT CAN'T EVER BE GOOD ENOUGH. NOT FOR WHAT WE DO.
WE CAN'T HAVE ANY MORE LIKE THESE LAST TWO, EDDIE.
THE WAY WE SEE IT, ANYTHING FROM QUEENS TO THE BAY RIDGE TRACKS, FROM CYPRESS HILLS TO JAMAICA BAY: THAT'S OURS. ANYTHING ELSE IS OUT.
THE McEWANS AND STANDERS ARE GONNA HAVE TO BE THE WORLD'S PROBLEMS TO DEAL WITH.
NOW, WE KNOW IF WE TAKE OUT A CLINTON OR A TRIP, IT HITS THE STREET JUST HOW WE WANT IT TO. MEANING CONFUSION, DISORGANIZATION. MAKES LIFE EASIER ON THE ENTIRE PRECINCT.
BEEN THAT WAY FOR MONTHS NOW.
WE DO THIS RIGHT... WE MIGHT BE DROPPING TWO, MAYBE THREE BODIES A YEAR, NO MORE.

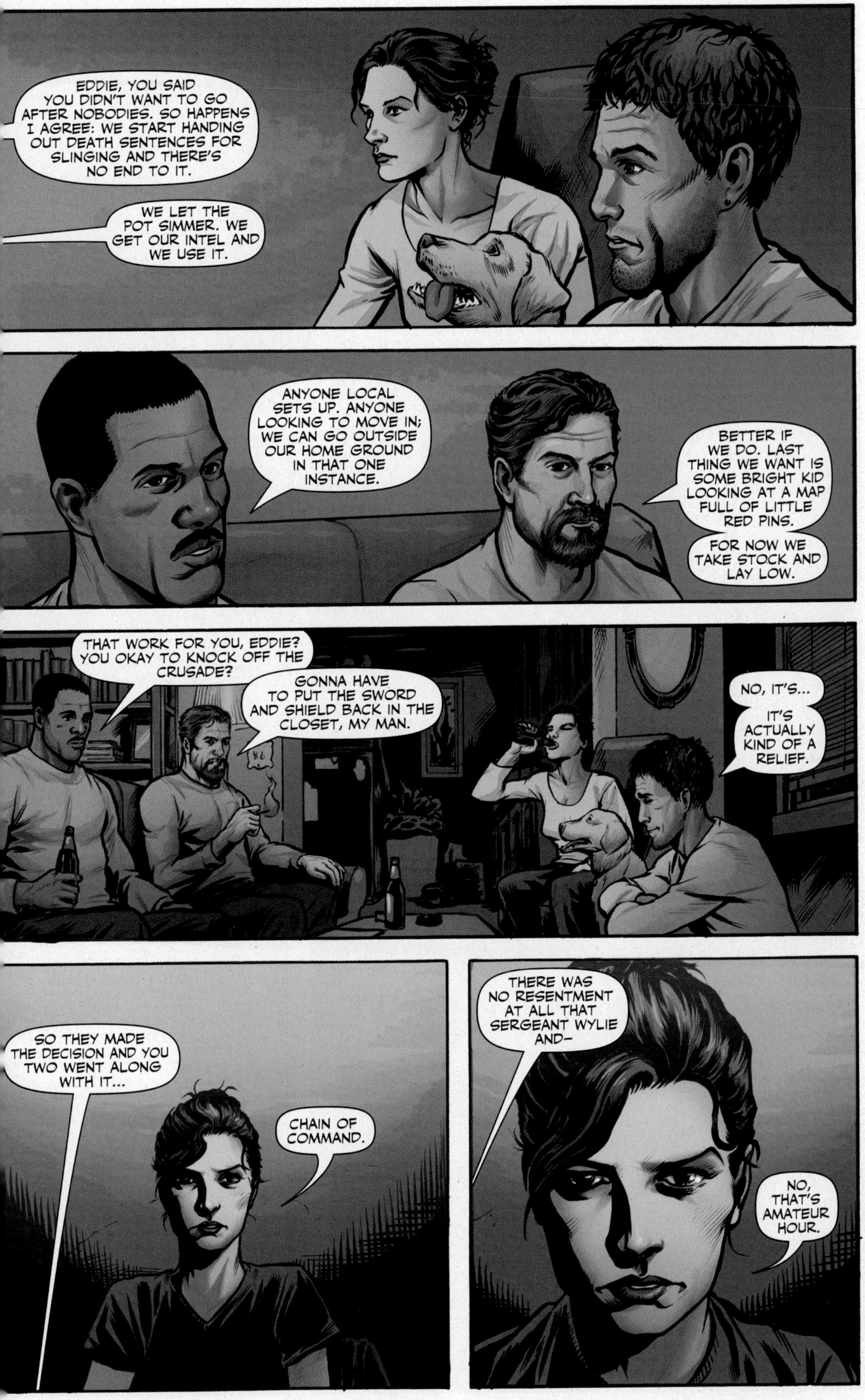
EDDIE, YOU SAID YOU DIDN'T WANT TO GO AFTER NOBODIES. SO HAPPENS I AGREE: WE START HANDING OUT DEATH SENTENCES FOR SLINGING AND THERE'S NO END TO IT.
WE LET THE POT SIMMER. WE GET OUR INTEL AND WE USE IT.
ANYONE LOCAL SETS UP. ANYONE LOOKING TO MOVE IN; WE CAN GO OUTSIDE OUR HOME GROUND IN THAT ONE INSTANCE.
BETTER IF WE DO. LAST THING WE WANT IS SOME BRIGHT KID LOOKING AT A MAP FULL OF LITTLE RED PINS.
FOR NOW WE TAKE STOCK AND LAY LOW.
THAT WORK FOR YOU, EDDIE? YOU OKAY TO KNOCK OFF THE CRUSADE?
GONNA HAVE TO PUT THE SWORD AND SHIELD BACK IN THE CLOSET, MY MAN.
NO, IT'S...
IT'S ACTUALLY KIND OF A RELIEF.
SO THEY MADE THE DECISION AND YOU TWO WENT ALONG WITH IT...
CHAIN OF COMMAND.
THERE WAS NO RESENTMENT AT ALL THAT SERGEANT WYLIE AND–
NO, THAT'S AMATEUR HOUR.

JEALOUS SHIT LIKE THAT SINKS CREWS FULL OF IDIOTS, NOT US.

DUKE RAN THE TEAM, GEORGE BACKED HIM UP. WE LISTENED. SURE, THE FOUR OF US WOULD TALK THROUGH THE BEST WAY TO DO THINGS, BUT IN THE END IT CAME DOWN TO DOING THE JOB YOU WERE GIVEN.

AND WHO *WOULDN'T* LISTEN TO THE TWO OF THEM?

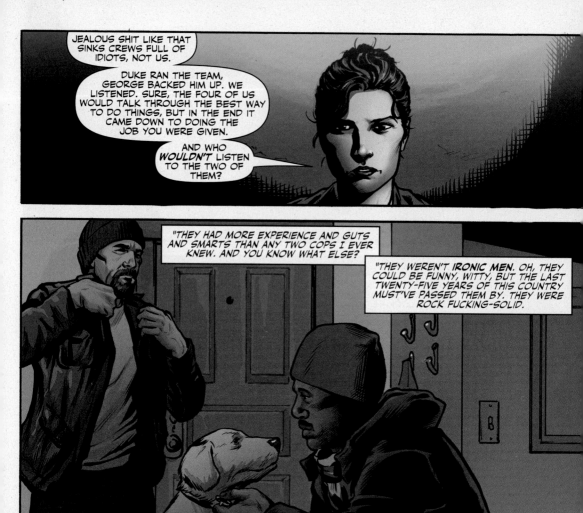

"THEY HAD MORE EXPERIENCE AND GUTS AND SMARTS THAN ANY TWO COPS I EVER KNEW. AND YOU KNOW WHAT ELSE?

"THEY WEREN'T *IRONIC MEN.* OH, THEY COULD BE FUNNY, WITTY, BUT THE LAST TWENTY-FIVE YEARS OF THIS COUNTRY MUST'VE PASSED THEM BY. THEY WERE ROCK FUCKING-SOLID.

"I SOMETIMES THOUGHT THEY BOTH SAW THE SAME JOHN WAYNE MOVIE AT JUST THE RIGHT AGE, AND THOUGHT: YEAH. THAT'S HOW A MAN'S SUPPOSED TO BE."

"EDDIE NOT SO MUCH."

WAS HE STILL...?

OH, FUCK, NO... ALL HE WANTED WAS TO APOLOGIZE.

BUT I CAN'T STAND CONVERSATIONS WHERE YOU KNOW WHAT THEIR LINES'LL BE AS WELL AS YOUR OWN, I JUST FUCKING CRINGE THE WHOLE TIME. LET'S NOT AND SAY WE DID, YOU KNOW?

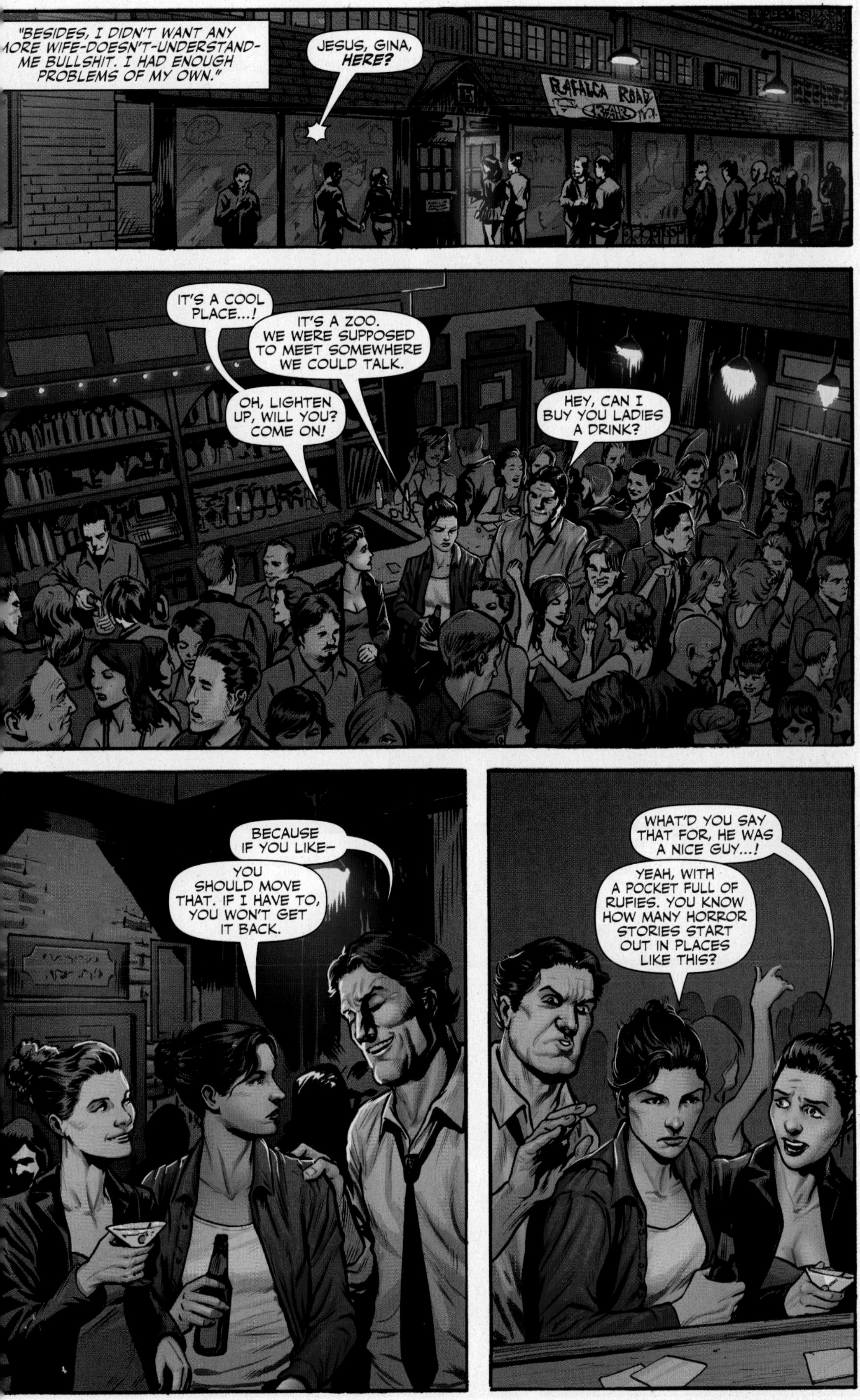
"BESIDES, I DIDN'T WANT ANY MORE WIFE-DOESN'T-UNDERSTAND-ME BULLSHIT. I HAD ENOUGH PROBLEMS OF MY OWN."
JESUS, GINA, HERE?
RAFALCA ROAD
IT'S A COOL PLACE...!
IT'S A ZOO. WE WERE SUPPOSED TO MEET SOMEWHERE WE COULD TALK.
OH, LIGHTEN UP, WILL YOU? COME ON!
HEY, CAN I BUY YOU LADIES A DRINK?
BECAUSE IF YOU LIKE–
YOU SHOULD MOVE THAT. IF I HAVE TO, YOU WON'T GET IT BACK.
WHAT'D YOU SAY THAT FOR, HE WAS A NICE GUY...!
YEAH, WITH A POCKET FULL OF RUFIES. YOU KNOW HOW MANY HORROR STORIES START OUT IN PLACES LIKE THIS?

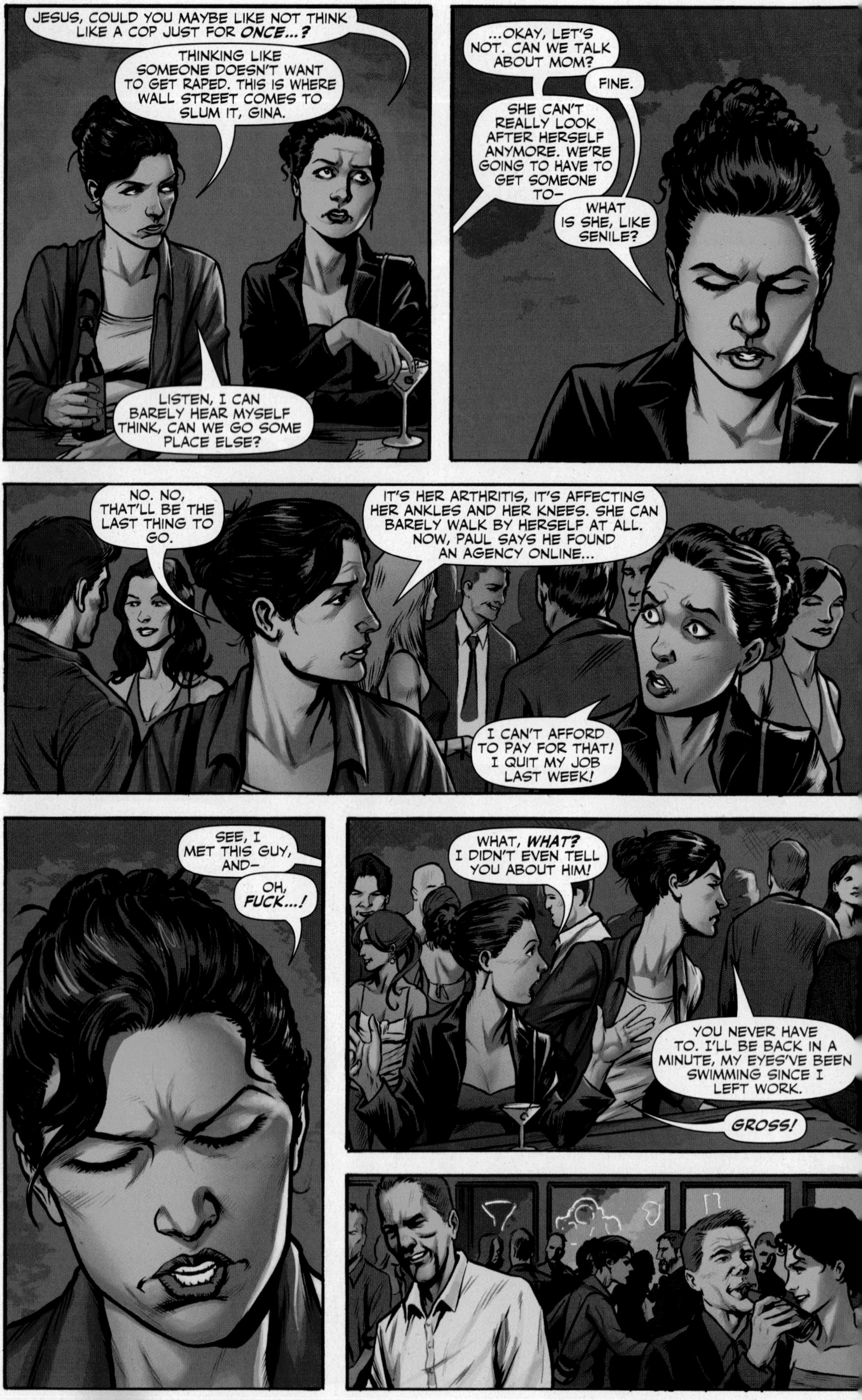
JESUS, COULD YOU MAYBE LIKE NOT THINK LIKE A COP JUST FOR *ONCE...?*
THINKING LIKE SOMEONE DOESN'T WANT TO GET RAPED. THIS IS WHERE WALL STREET COMES TO SLUM IT, GINA.
LISTEN, I CAN BARELY HEAR MYSELF THINK, CAN WE GO SOME PLACE ELSE?
...OKAY, LET'S NOT. CAN WE TALK ABOUT MOM?
FINE.
SHE CAN'T REALLY LOOK AFTER HERSELF ANYMORE. WE'RE GOING TO HAVE TO GET SOMEONE TO–
WHAT IS SHE, LIKE SENILE?
NO. NO, THAT'LL BE THE LAST THING TO GO.
IT'S HER ARTHRITIS, IT'S AFFECTING HER ANKLES AND HER KNEES. SHE CAN BARELY WALK BY HERSELF AT ALL. NOW, PAUL SAYS HE FOUND AN AGENCY ONLINE...
I CAN'T AFFORD TO PAY FOR THAT! I QUIT MY JOB LAST WEEK!
SEE, I MET THIS GUY, AND–
OH, *FUCK...!*
WHAT, *WHAT?* I DIDN'T EVEN TELL YOU ABOUT HIM!
YOU NEVER HAVE TO. I'LL BE BACK IN A MINUTE, MY EYES'VE BEEN SWIMMING SINCE I LEFT WORK.
GROSS!

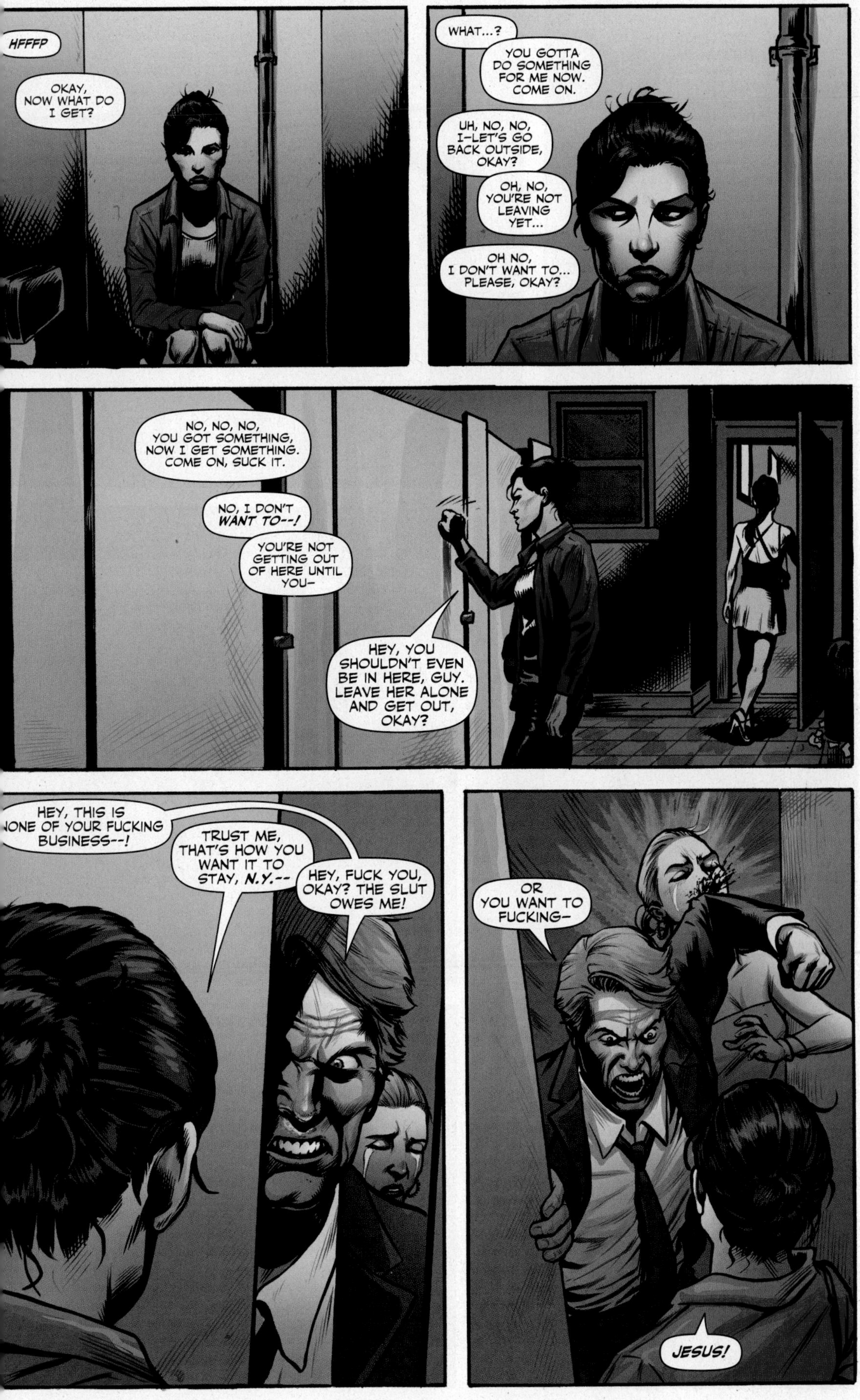
HFFFP
OKAY, NOW WHAT DO I GET?
WHAT...?
YOU GOTTA DO SOMETHING FOR ME NOW. COME ON.
UH, NO, NO, I--LET'S GO BACK OUTSIDE, OKAY?
OH, NO, YOU'RE NOT LEAVING YET...
OH NO, I DON'T WANT TO... PLEASE, OKAY?
NO, NO, NO, YOU GOT SOMETHING, NOW I GET SOMETHING. COME ON, SUCK IT.
NO, I DON'T WANT TO--!
YOU'RE NOT GETTING OUT OF HERE UNTIL YOU-
HEY, YOU SHOULDN'T EVEN BE IN HERE, GUY. LEAVE HER ALONE AND GET OUT, OKAY?
HEY, THIS IS NONE OF YOUR FUCKING BUSINESS--!
TRUST ME, THAT'S HOW YOU WANT IT TO STAY, N.Y.--
HEY, FUCK YOU, OKAY? THE SLUT OWES ME!
OR YOU WANT TO FUCKING-
JESUS!

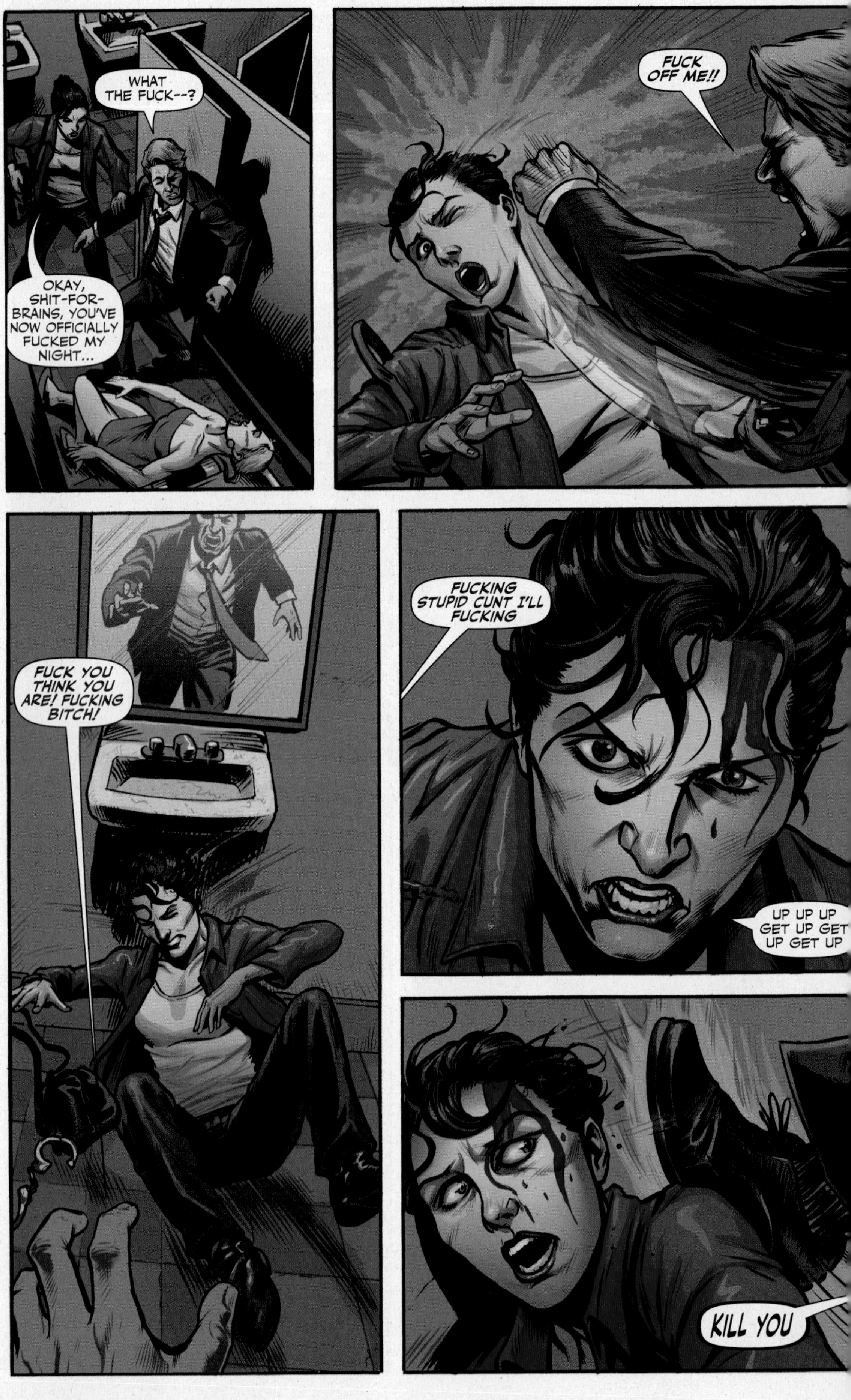
WHAT THE FUCK--?
OKAY, SHIT-FOR-BRAINS, YOU'VE NOW OFFICIALLY FUCKED MY NIGHT...
FUCK OFF ME!!
FUCK YOU THINK YOU ARE! FUCKING BITCH!
FUCKING STUPID CUNT I'LL FUCKING
UP UP UP GET UP GET UP GET UP
KILL YOU

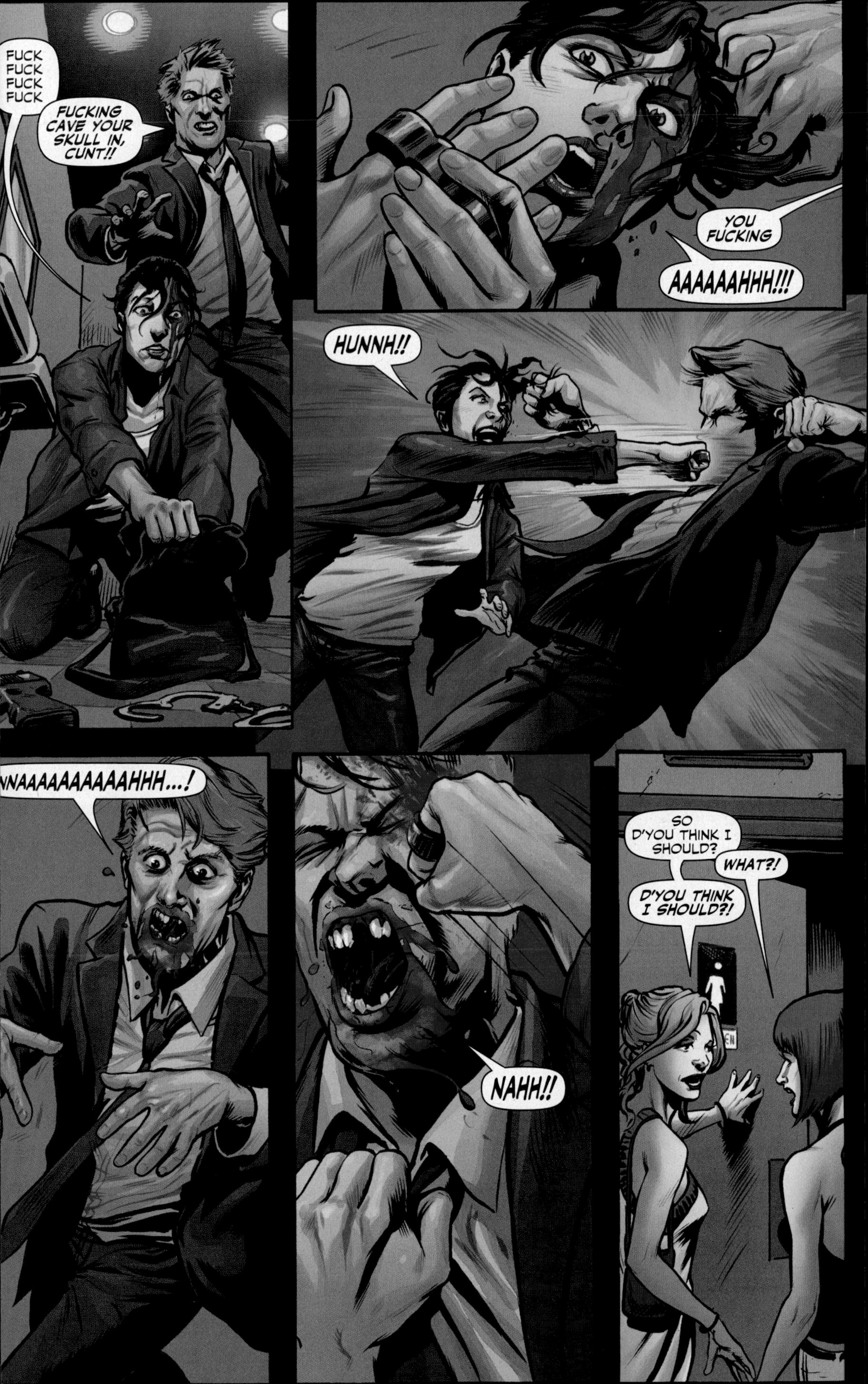
FUCK FUCK FUCK FUCK
FUCKING CAVE YOUR SKULL IN, CUNT!!
YOU FUCKING
AAAAAAHHH!!!
HUNNH!!
NNAAAAAAAAAAHHH...!
NAHH!!
SO D'YOU THINK I SHOULD?
WHAT?!
D'YOU THINK I SHOULD?!

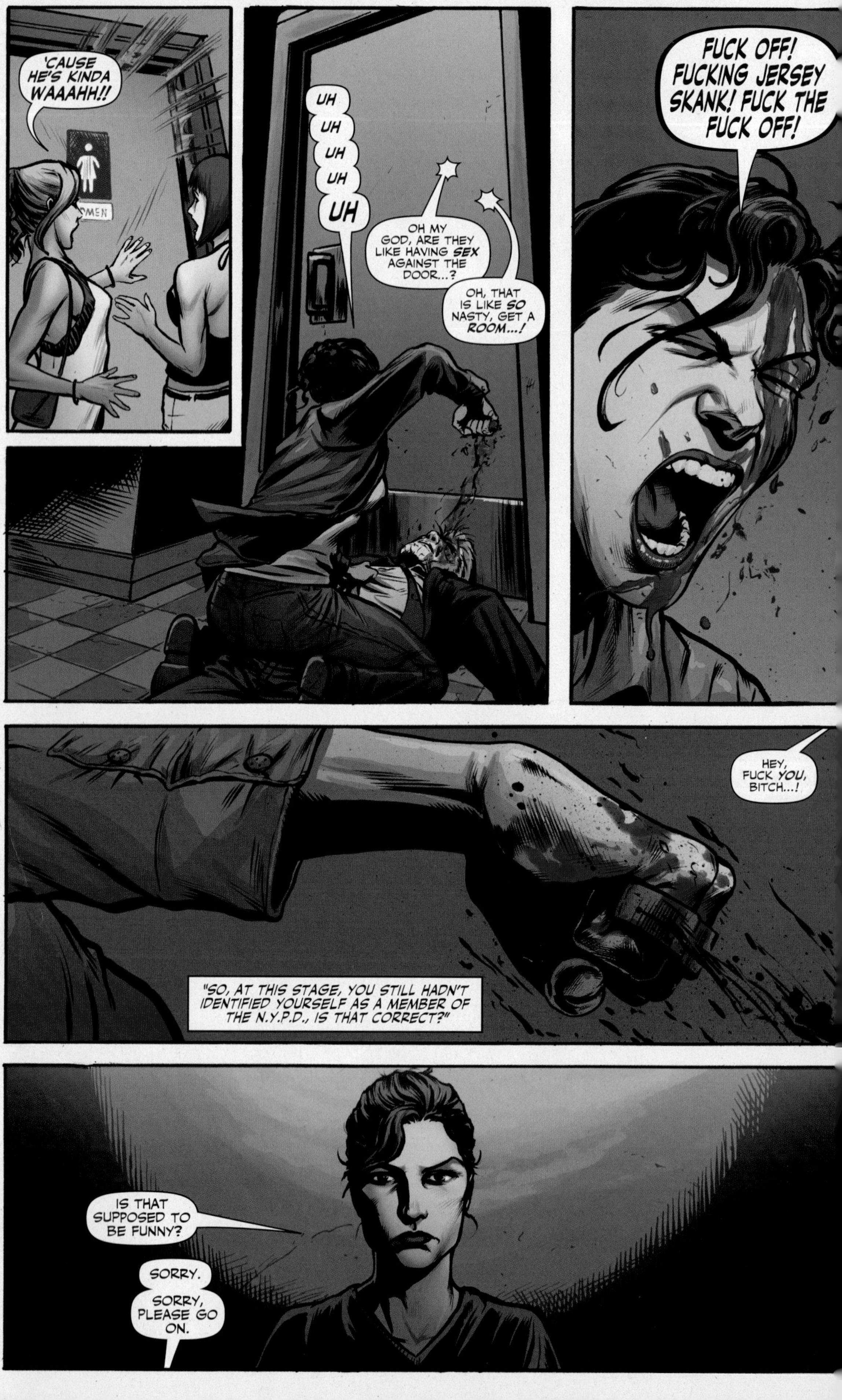
'CAUSE HE'S KINDA WAAAHH!!
UH
UH
UH
UH
UH
OH MY GOD, ARE THEY LIKE HAVING SEX AGAINST THE DOOR...?
OH, THAT IS LIKE SO NASTY, GET A ROOM...!
FUCK OFF! FUCKING JERSEY SKANK! FUCK THE FUCK OFF!
HEY, FUCK YOU, BITCH...!
"SO, AT THIS STAGE, YOU STILL HADN'T IDENTIFIED YOURSELF AS A MEMBER OF THE N.Y.P.D., IS THAT CORRECT?"
IS THAT SUPPOSED TO BE FUNNY?
SORRY.
SORRY, PLEASE GO ON.

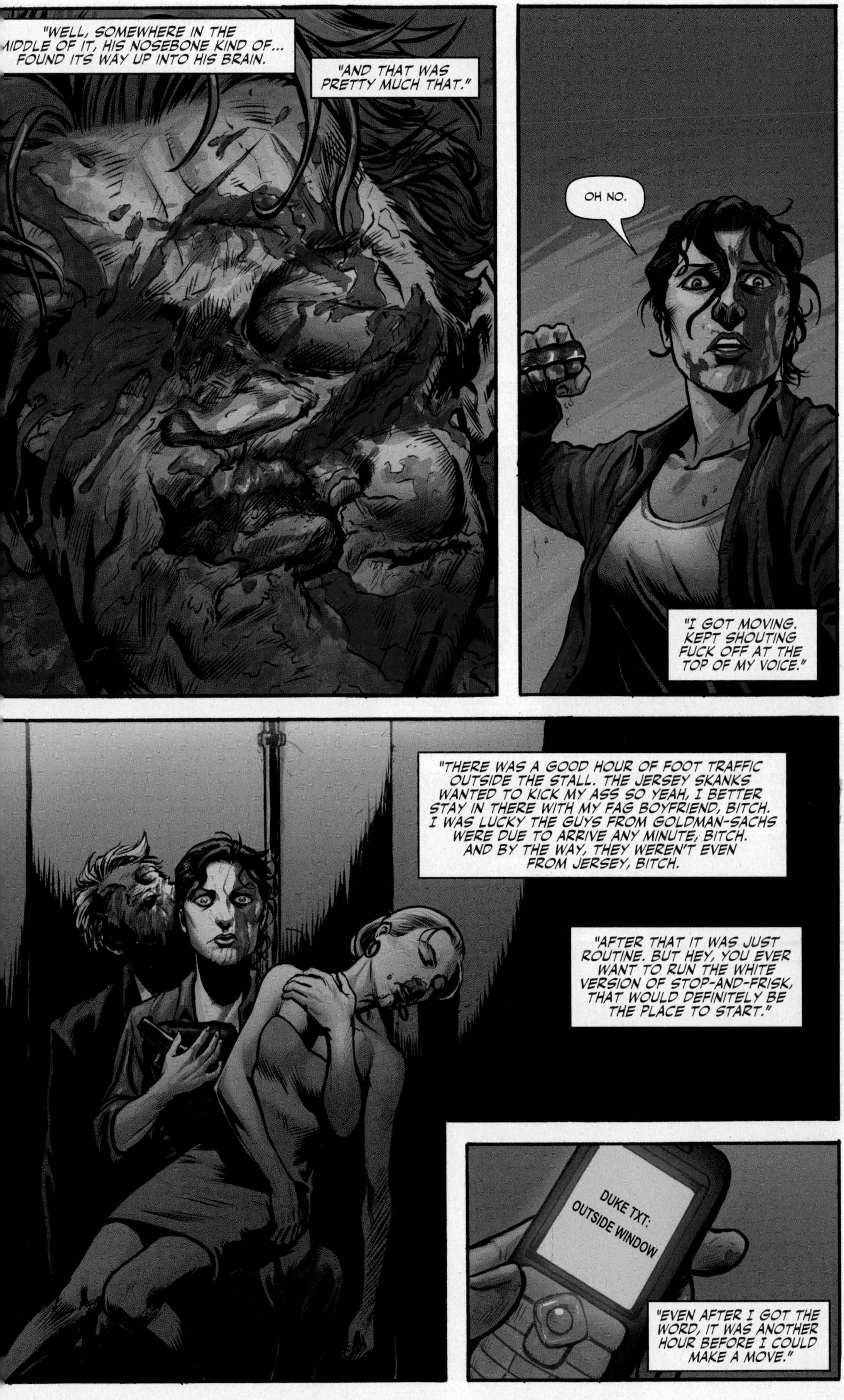
"WELL, SOMEWHERE IN THE MIDDLE OF IT, HIS NOSEBONE KIND OF... FOUND ITS WAY UP INTO HIS BRAIN.
"AND THAT WAS PRETTY MUCH THAT."
OH NO.
"I GOT MOVING. KEPT SHOUTING FUCK OFF AT THE TOP OF MY VOICE."
"THERE WAS A GOOD HOUR OF FOOT TRAFFIC OUTSIDE THE STALL. THE JERSEY SKANKS WANTED TO KICK MY ASS SO YEAH, I BETTER STAY IN THERE WITH MY FAG BOYFRIEND, BITCH. I WAS LUCKY THE GUYS FROM GOLDMAN-SACHS WERE DUE TO ARRIVE ANY MINUTE, BITCH. AND BY THE WAY, THEY WEREN'T EVEN FROM JERSEY, BITCH.
"AFTER THAT IT WAS JUST ROUTINE. BUT HEY, YOU EVER WANT TO RUN THE WHITE VERSION OF STOP-AND-FRISK, THAT WOULD DEFINITELY BE THE PLACE TO START."
DUKE TXT: OUTSIDE WINDOW
"EVEN AFTER I GOT THE WORD, IT WAS ANOTHER HOUR BEFORE I COULD MAKE A MOVE."

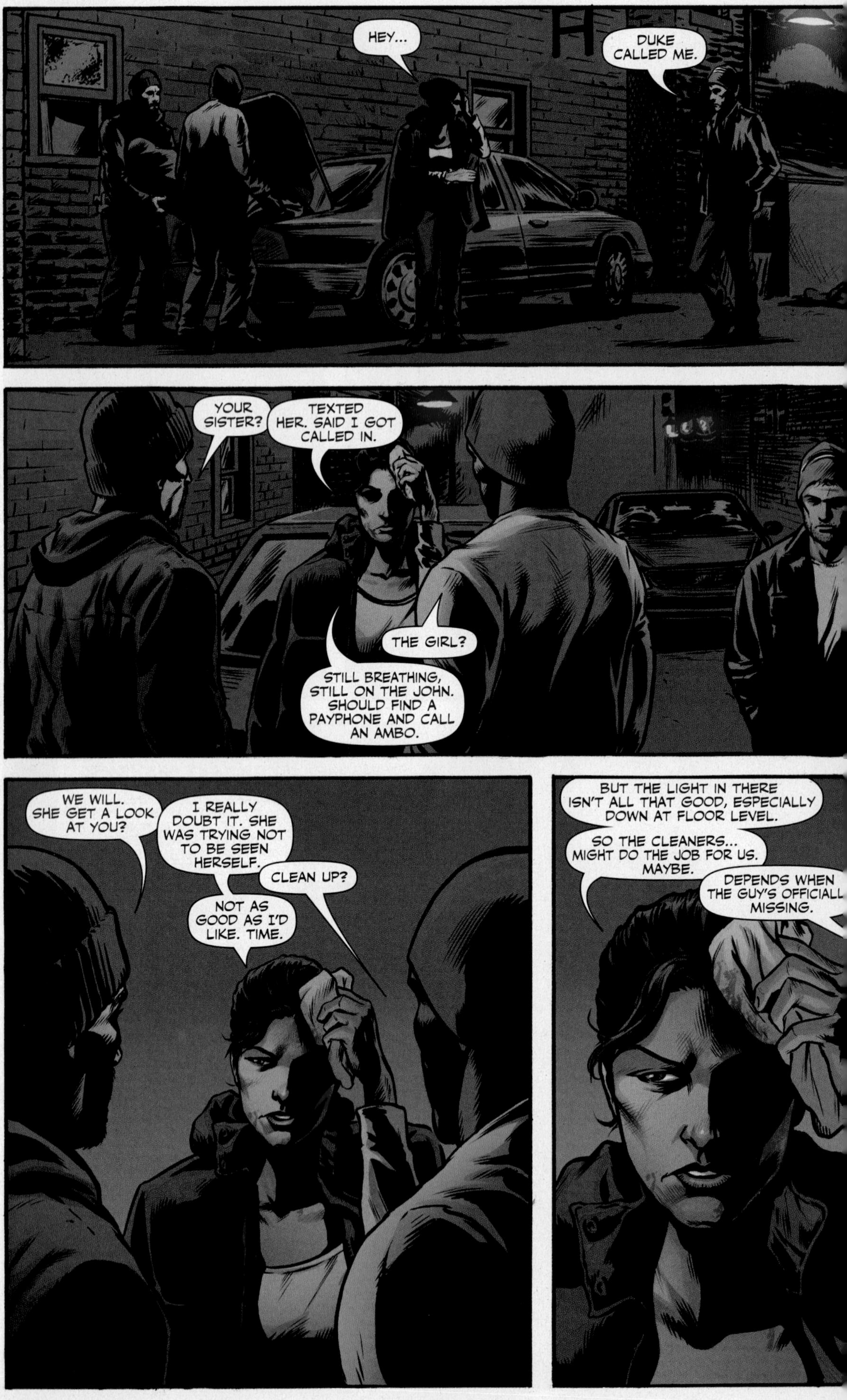
HEY...
DUKE CALLED ME.
YOUR SISTER?
TEXTED HER. SAID I GOT CALLED IN.
THE GIRL?
STILL BREATHING, STILL ON THE JOHN. SHOULD FIND A PAYPHONE AND CALL AN AMBO.
WE WILL. SHE GET A LOOK AT YOU?
I REALLY DOUBT IT. SHE WAS TRYING NOT TO BE SEEN HERSELF.
CLEAN UP?
NOT AS GOOD AS I'D LIKE. TIME.
BUT THE LIGHT IN THERE ISN'T ALL THAT GOOD, ESPECIALLY DOWN AT FLOOR LEVEL.
SO THE CLEANERS... MIGHT DO THE JOB FOR US. MAYBE.
DEPENDS WHEN THE GUY'S OFFICIALL MISSING.

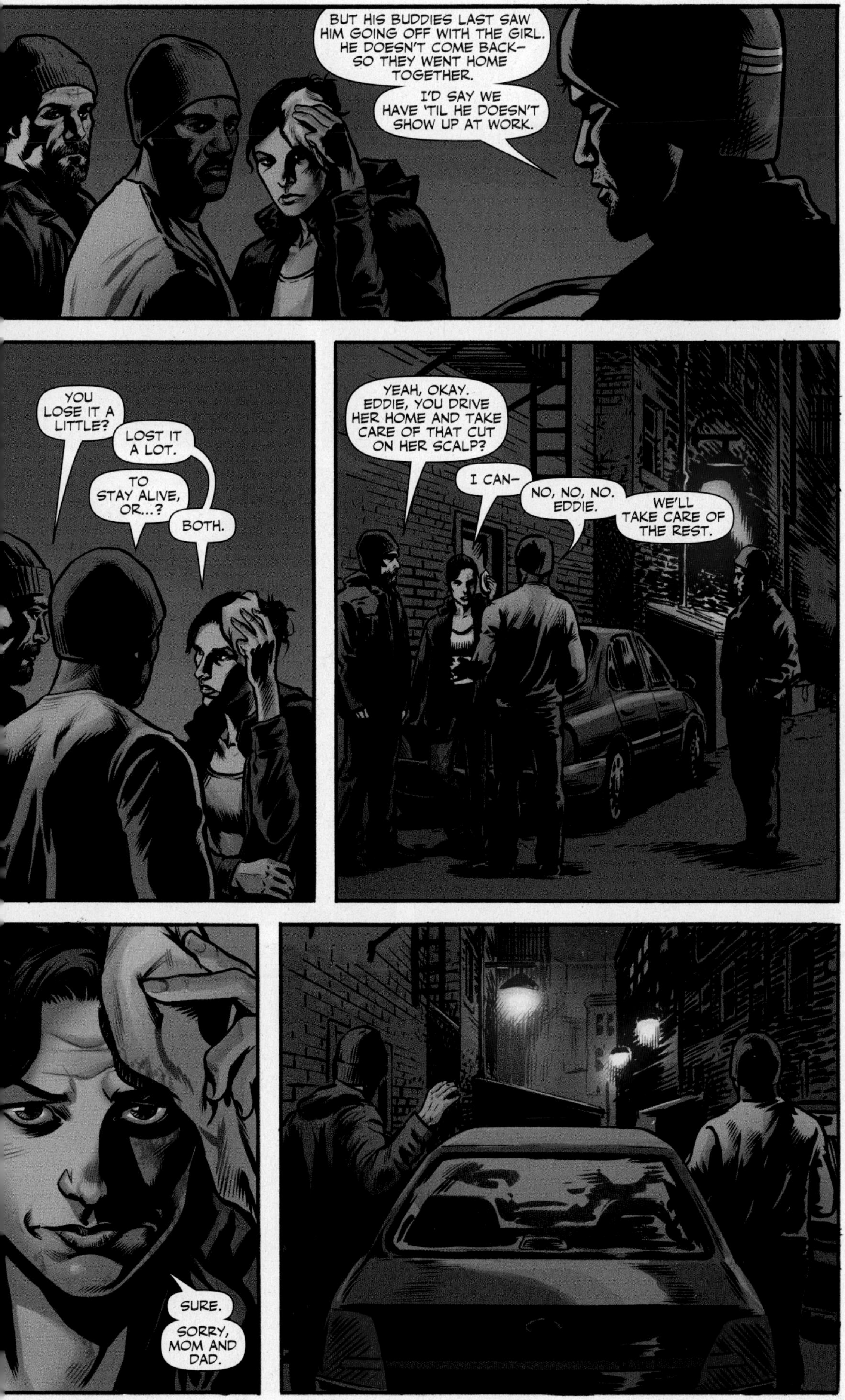
BUT HIS BUDDIES LAST SAW HIM GOING OFF WITH THE GIRL. HE DOESN'T COME BACK– SO THEY WENT HOME TOGETHER.
I'D SAY WE HAVE 'TIL HE DOESN'T SHOW UP AT WORK.
YOU LOSE IT A LITTLE?
LOST IT A LOT.
TO STAY ALIVE, OR...?
BOTH.
YEAH, OKAY. EDDIE, YOU DRIVE HER HOME AND TAKE CARE OF THAT CUT ON HER SCALP?
I CAN–
NO, NO, NO. EDDIE.
WE'LL TAKE CARE OF THE REST.
SURE.
SORRY, MOM AND DAD.

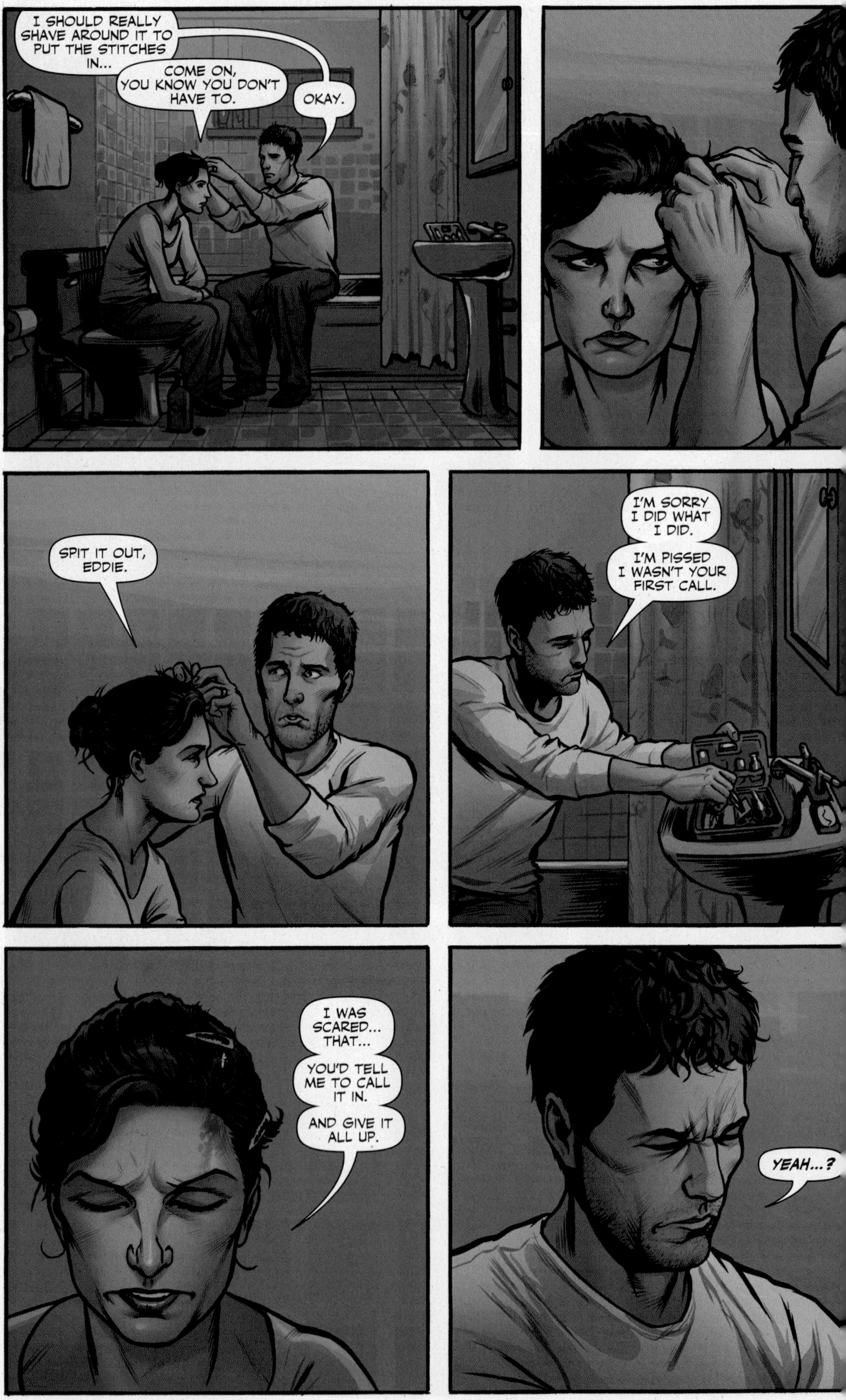
I SHOULD REALLY SHAVE AROUND IT TO PUT THE STITCHES IN...
COME ON, YOU KNOW YOU DON'T HAVE TO.
OKAY.
SPIT IT OUT, EDDIE.
I'M SORRY I DID WHAT I DID.
I'M PISSED I WASN'T YOUR FIRST CALL.
I WAS SCARED... THAT...
YOU'D TELL ME TO CALL IT IN.
AND GIVE IT ALL UP.
YEAH...?

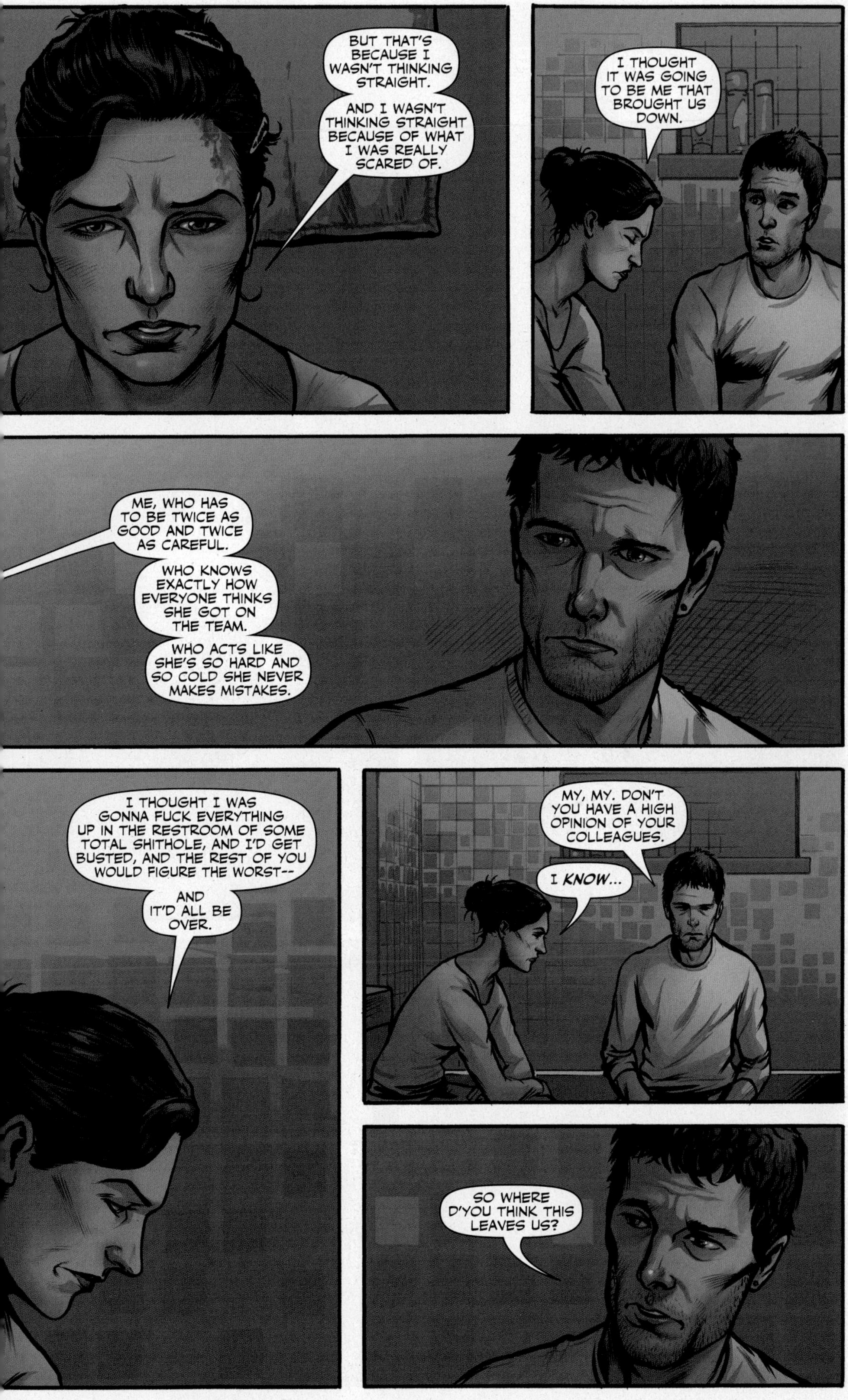
BUT THAT'S BECAUSE I WASN'T THINKING STRAIGHT.
AND I WASN'T THINKING STRAIGHT BECAUSE OF WHAT I WAS REALLY SCARED OF.
I THOUGHT IT WAS GOING TO BE ME THAT BROUGHT US DOWN.
ME, WHO HAS TO BE TWICE AS GOOD AND TWICE AS CAREFUL.
WHO KNOWS EXACTLY HOW EVERYONE THINKS SHE GOT ON THE TEAM.
WHO ACTS LIKE SHE'S SO HARD AND SO COLD SHE NEVER MAKES MISTAKES.
I THOUGHT I WAS GONNA FUCK EVERYTHING UP IN THE RESTROOM OF SOME TOTAL SHITHOLE, AND I'D GET BUSTED, AND THE REST OF YOU WOULD FIGURE THE WORST--
AND IT'D ALL BE OVER.
MY, MY. DON'T YOU HAVE A HIGH OPINION OF YOUR COLLEAGUES.
I *KNOW*...
SO WHERE D'YOU THINK THIS LEAVES US?

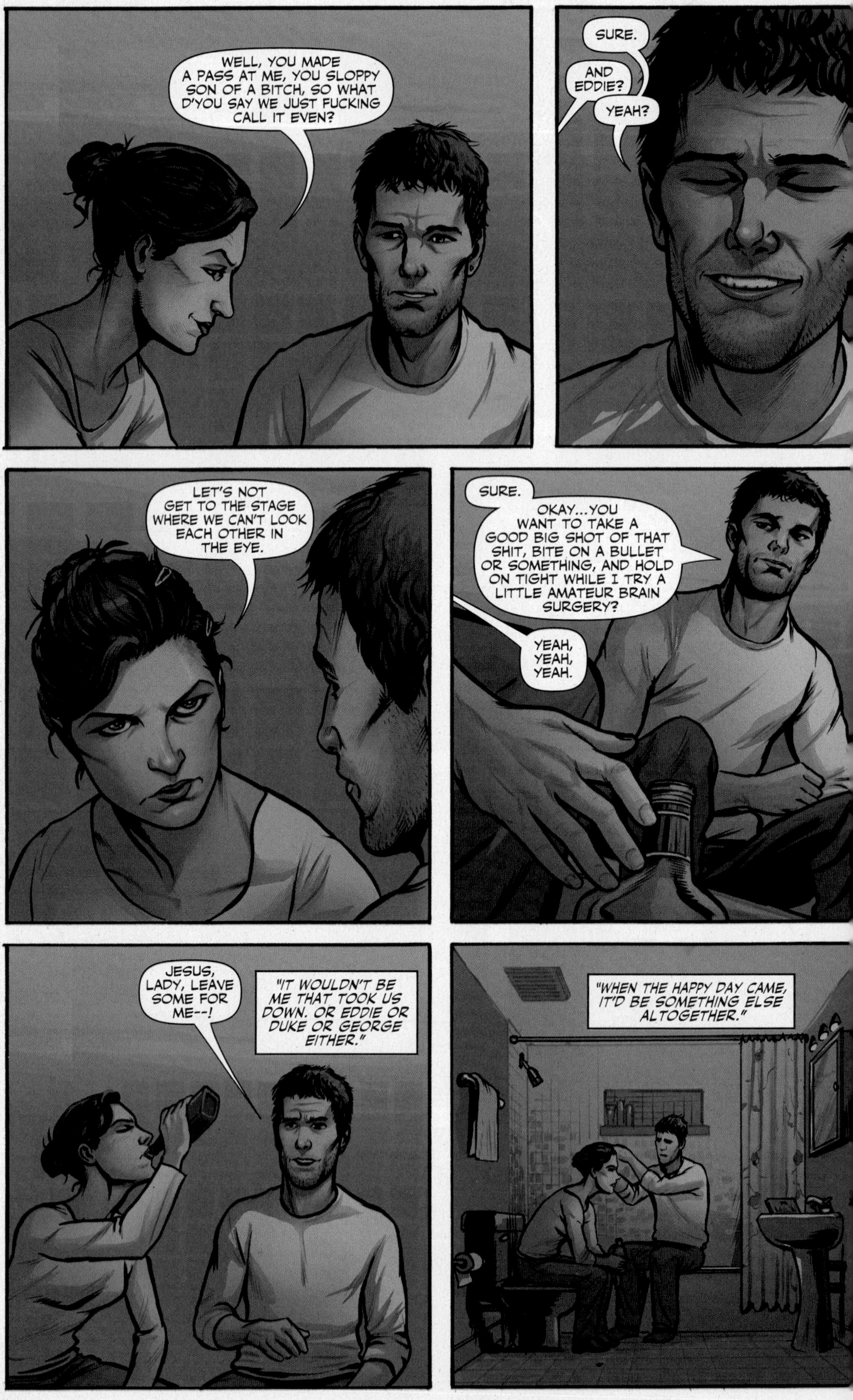
WELL, YOU MADE A PASS AT ME, YOU SLOPPY SON OF A BITCH, SO WHAT D'YOU SAY WE JUST FUCKING CALL IT EVEN?
SURE.
AND EDDIE?
YEAH?
LET'S NOT GET TO THE STAGE WHERE WE CAN'T LOOK EACH OTHER IN THE EYE.
SURE.
OKAY...YOU WANT TO TAKE A GOOD BIG SHOT OF THAT SHIT, BITE ON A BULLET OR SOMETHING, AND HOLD ON TIGHT WHILE I TRY A LITTLE AMATEUR BRAIN SURGERY?
YEAH, YEAH, YEAH.
JESUS, LADY, LEAVE SOME FOR ME--!
"IT WOULDN'T BE ME THAT TOOK US DOWN. OR EDDIE OR DUKE OR GEORGE EITHER."
"WHEN THE HAPPY DAY CAME, IT'D BE SOMETHING ELSE ALTOGETHER."

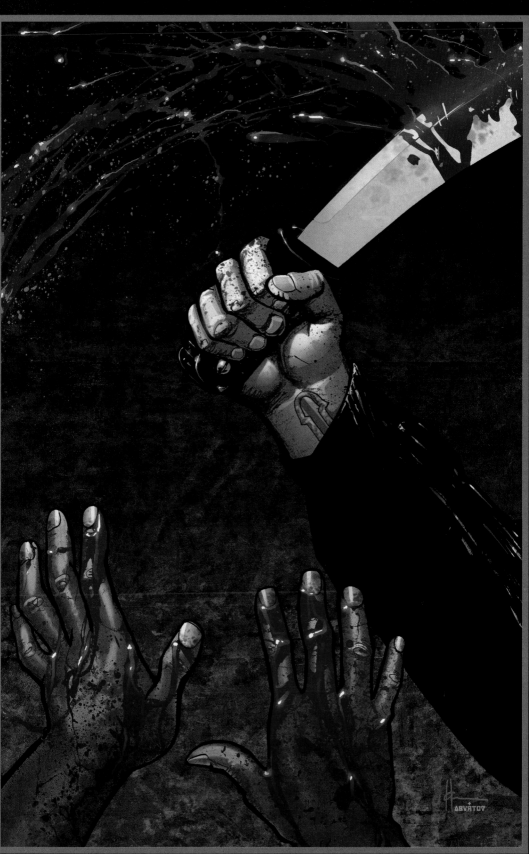

Issue #5 cover art by **HOWARD CHAYKIN** colors by **JESUS ABURTO**

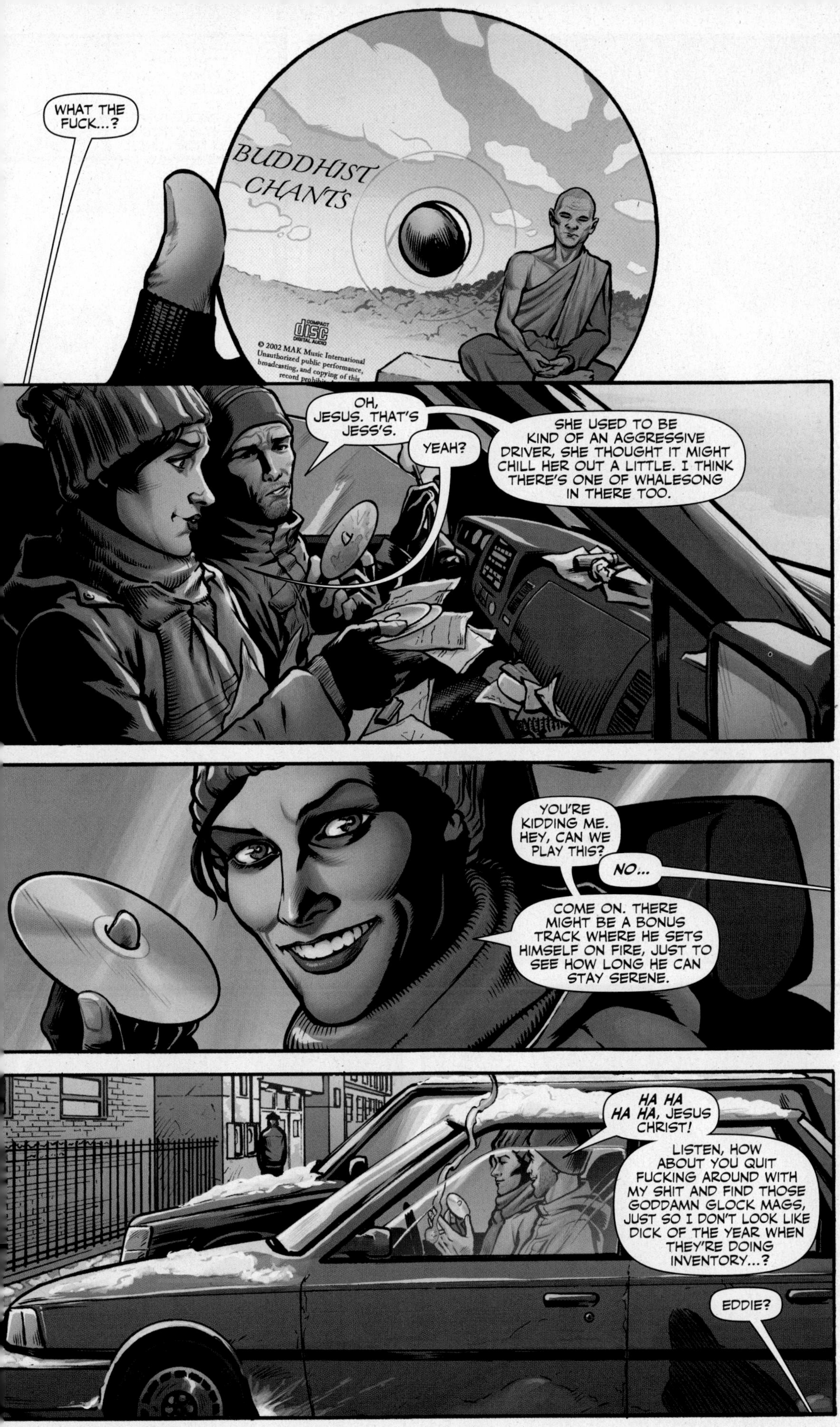
WHAT THE FUCK...?
BUDDHIST CHANTS
© 2002 MAK Music International Unauthorized public performance, broadcasting, and copying of this record prohibi
OH, JESUS. THAT'S JESS'S.
YEAH?
SHE USED TO BE KIND OF AN AGGRESSIVE DRIVER, SHE THOUGHT IT MIGHT CHILL HER OUT A LITTLE. I THINK THERE'S ONE OF WHALESONG IN THERE TOO.
YOU'RE KIDDING ME. HEY, CAN WE PLAY THIS?
NO...
COME ON. THERE MIGHT BE A BONUS TRACK WHERE HE SETS HIMSELF ON FIRE, JUST TO SEE HOW LONG HE CAN STAY SERENE.
HA HA HA HA, JESUS CHRIST!
LISTEN, HOW ABOUT YOU QUIT FUCKING AROUND WITH MY SHIT AND FIND THOSE GODDAMN GLOCK MAGS, JUST SO I DON'T LOOK LIKE DICK OF THE YEAR WHEN THEY'RE DOING INVENTORY...?
EDDIE?

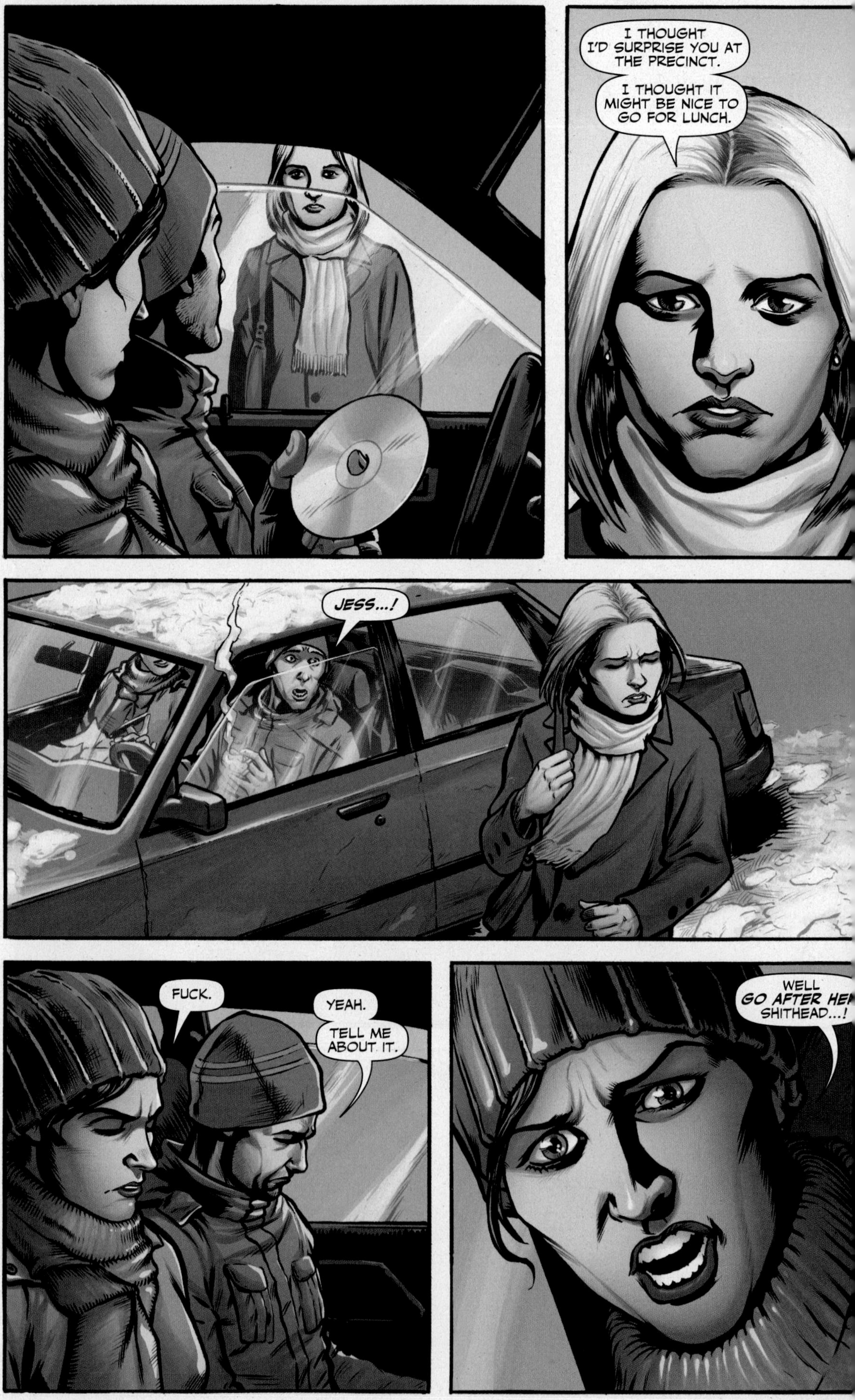
I THOUGHT I'D SURPRISE YOU AT THE PRECINCT.
I THOUGHT IT MIGHT BE NICE TO GO FOR LUNCH.
JESS...!
FUCK.
YEAH.
TELL ME ABOUT IT.
WELL GO AFTER HE SHITHEAD...!

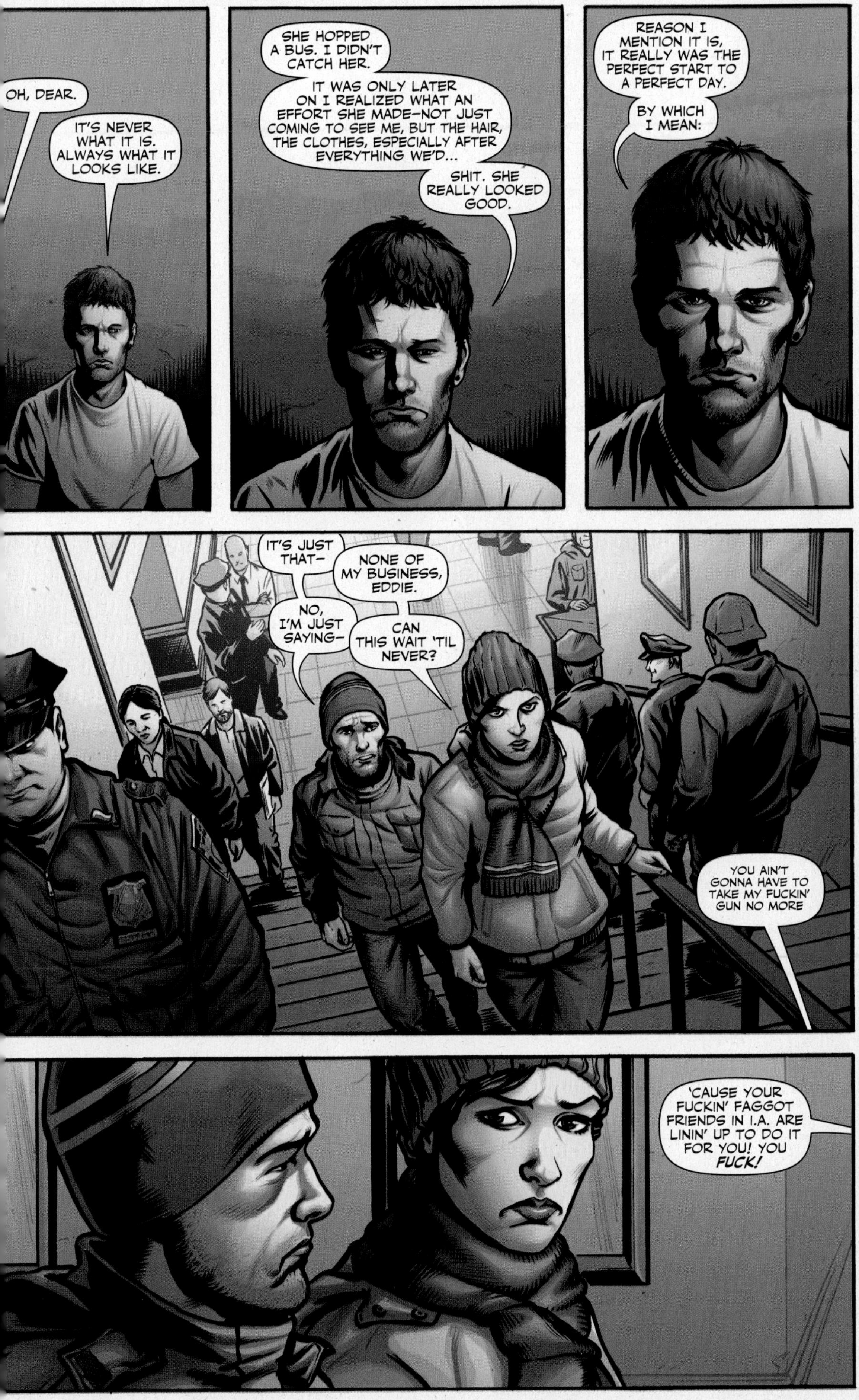
OH, DEAR.
IT'S NEVER WHAT IT IS. ALWAYS WHAT IT LOOKS LIKE.
SHE HOPPED A BUS. I DIDN'T CATCH HER.
IT WAS ONLY LATER ON I REALIZED WHAT AN EFFORT SHE MADE—NOT JUST COMING TO SEE ME, BUT THE HAIR, THE CLOTHES, ESPECIALLY AFTER EVERYTHING WE'D...
SHIT. SHE REALLY LOOKED GOOD.
REASON I MENTION IT IS, IT REALLY WAS THE PERFECT START TO A PERFECT DAY.
BY WHICH I MEAN:
IT'S JUST THAT—
NONE OF MY BUSINESS, EDDIE.
NO, I'M JUST SAYING—
CAN THIS WAIT 'TIL NEVER?
YOU AIN'T GONNA HAVE TO TAKE MY FUCKIN' GUN NO MORE
'CAUSE YOUR FUCKIN' FAGGOT FRIENDS IN I.A. ARE LININ' UP TO DO IT FOR YOU! YOU *FUCK!*

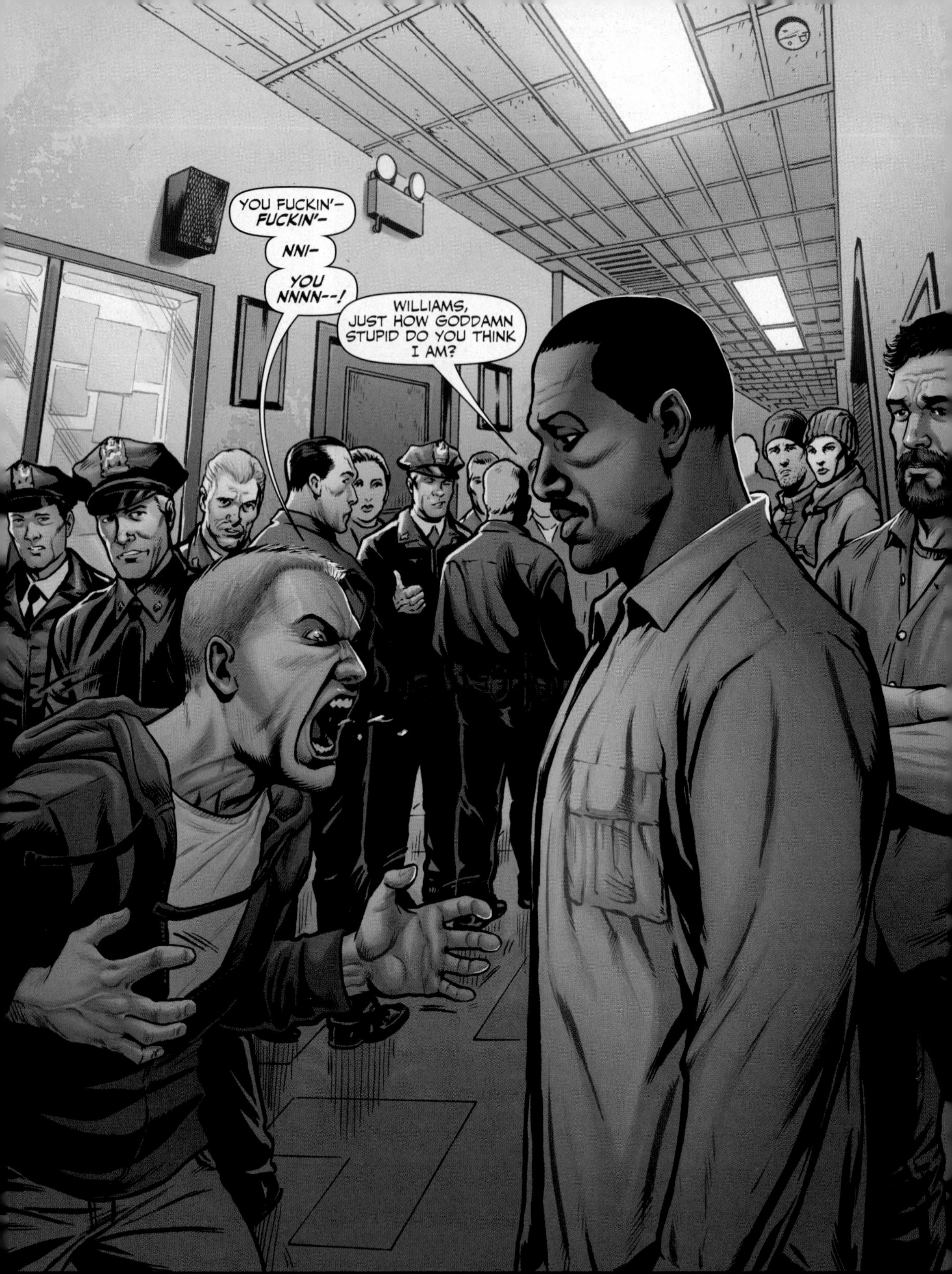
YOU FUCKIN'- FUCKIN'-
NNI-
YOU NNNN--!
WILLIAMS, JUST HOW GODDAMN STUPID DO YOU THINK I AM?

5: THE NIGHT OF NIGHTS

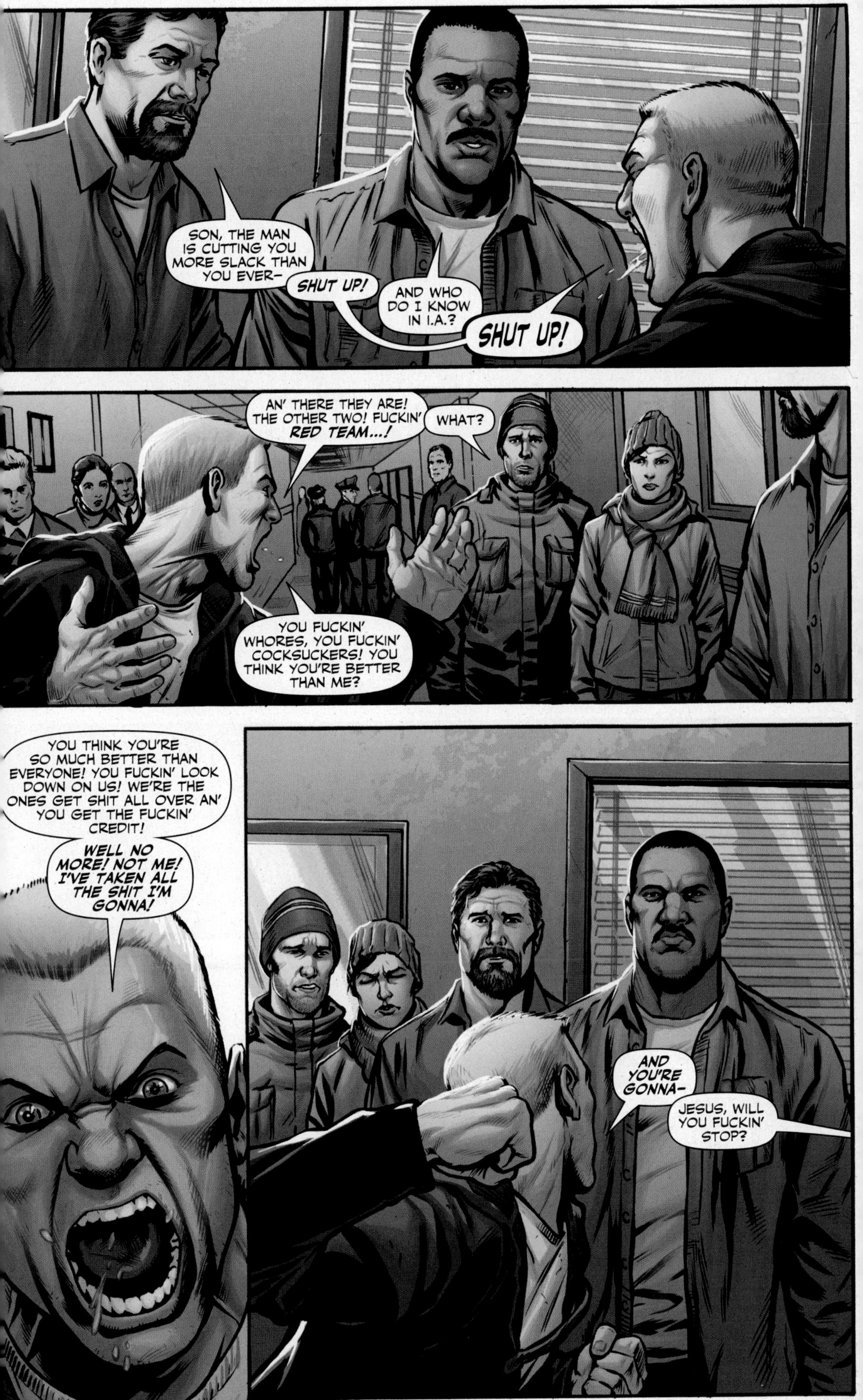
SON, THE MAN IS CUTTING YOU MORE SLACK THAN YOU EVER–
SHUT UP!
AND WHO DO I KNOW IN I.A.?
SHUT UP!
AN' THERE THEY ARE! THE OTHER TWO! FUCKIN' RED TEAM...!
WHAT?
YOU FUCKIN' WHORES, YOU FUCKIN' COCKSUCKERS! YOU THINK YOU'RE BETTER THAN ME?
YOU THINK YOU'RE SO MUCH BETTER THAN EVERYONE! YOU FUCKIN' LOOK DOWN ON US! WE'RE THE ONES GET SHIT ALL OVER AN' YOU GET THE FUCKIN' CREDIT!
WELL NO MORE! NOT ME! I'VE TAKEN ALL THE SHIT I'M GONNA!
AND YOU'RE GONNA–
JESUS, WILL YOU FUCKIN' STOP?

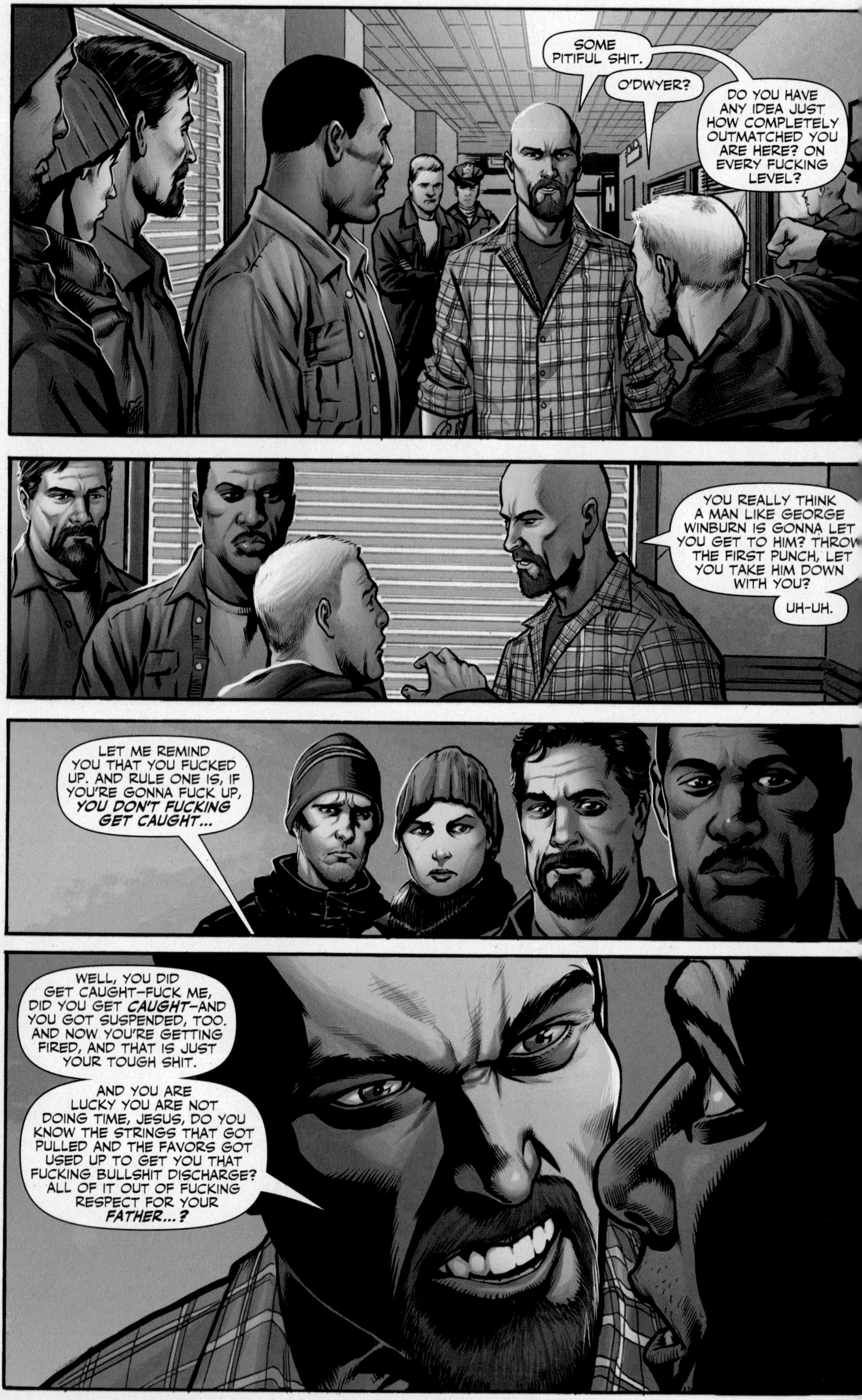

SOME PITIFUL SHIT.
O'DWYER?
DO YOU HAVE ANY IDEA JUST HOW COMPLETELY OUTMATCHED YOU ARE HERE? ON EVERY FUCKING LEVEL?
YOU REALLY THINK A MAN LIKE GEORGE WINBURN IS GONNA LET YOU GET TO HIM? THROW THE FIRST PUNCH, LET YOU TAKE HIM DOWN WITH YOU?
UH-UH.
LET ME REMIND YOU THAT YOU FUCKED UP. AND RULE ONE IS, IF YOU'RE GONNA FUCK UP, *YOU DON'T FUCKING GET CAUGHT...*
WELL, YOU DID GET CAUGHT—FUCK ME, DID YOU GET *CAUGHT*—AND YOU GOT SUSPENDED, TOO. AND NOW YOU'RE GETTING FIRED, AND THAT IS JUST YOUR TOUGH SHIT.
AND YOU ARE LUCKY YOU ARE NOT DOING TIME, JESUS, DO YOU KNOW THE STRINGS THAT GOT PULLED AND THE FAVORS GOT USED UP TO GET YOU THAT FUCKING BULLSHIT DISCHARGE? ALL OF IT OUT OF FUCKING RESPECT FOR YOUR *FATHER...?*

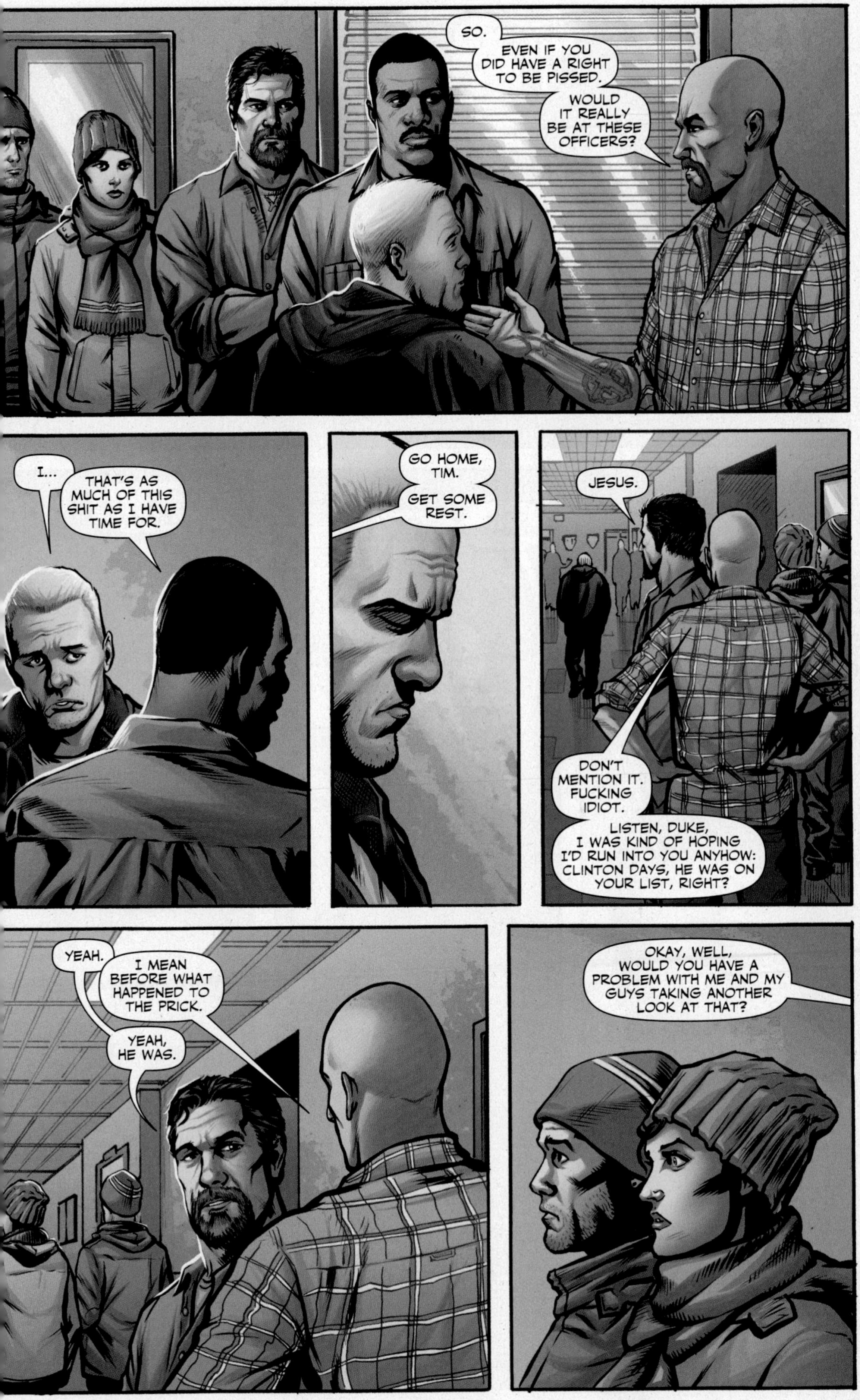
SO.
EVEN IF YOU DID HAVE A RIGHT TO BE PISSED.
WOULD IT REALLY BE AT THESE OFFICERS?
I...
THAT'S AS MUCH OF THIS SHIT AS I HAVE TIME FOR.
GO HOME, TIM.
GET SOME REST.
JESUS.
DON'T MENTION IT. FUCKING IDIOT.
LISTEN, DUKE, I WAS KIND OF HOPING I'D RUN INTO YOU ANYHOW: CLINTON DAYS, HE WAS ON YOUR LIST, RIGHT?
YEAH.
I MEAN BEFORE WHAT HAPPENED TO THE PRICK.
YEAH, HE WAS.
OKAY, WELL, WOULD YOU HAVE A PROBLEM WITH ME AND MY GUYS TAKING ANOTHER LOOK AT THAT?

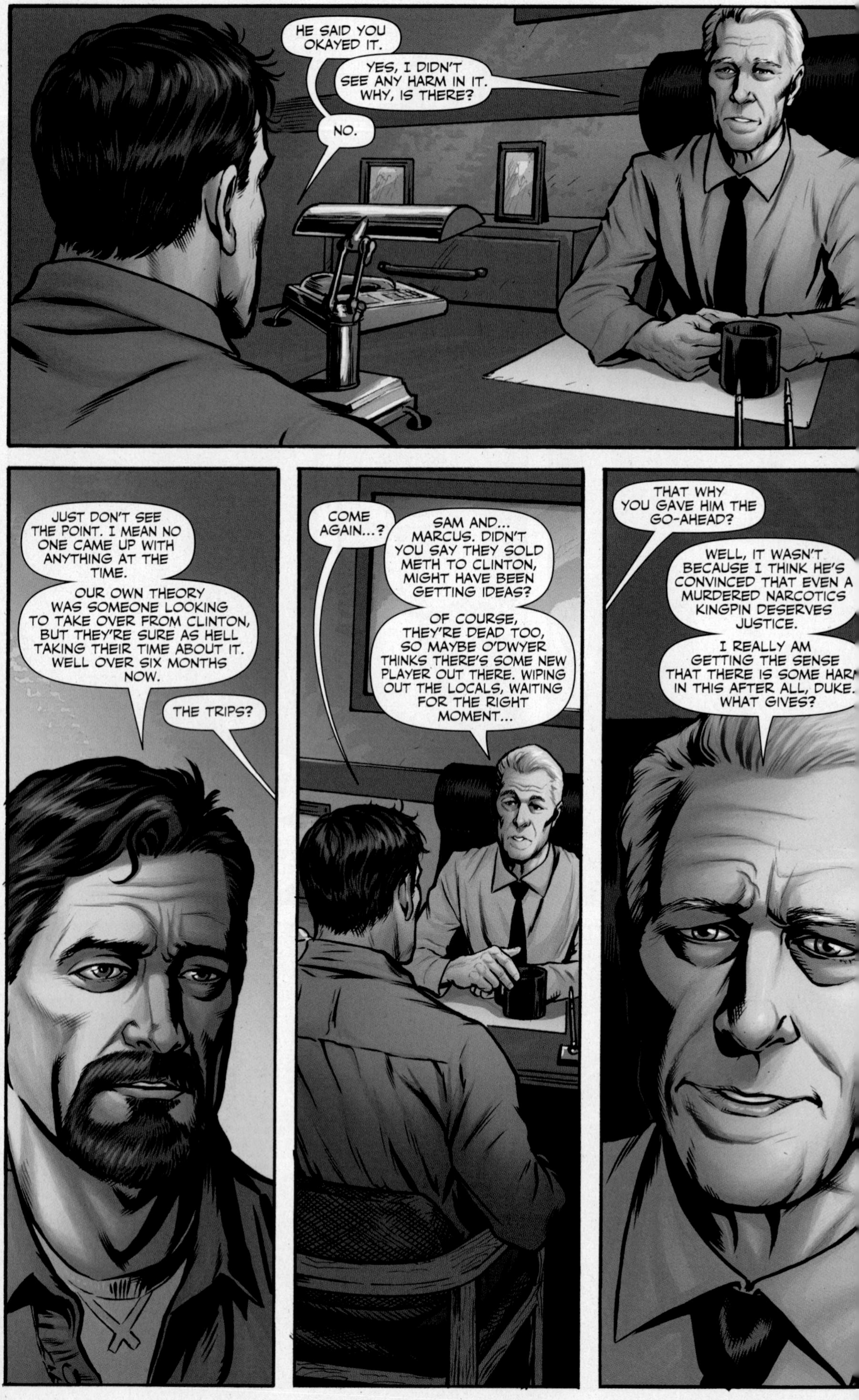
HE SAID YOU OKAYED IT.
YES, I DIDN'T SEE ANY HARM IN IT. WHY, IS THERE?
NO.
JUST DON'T SEE THE POINT. I MEAN NO ONE CAME UP WITH ANYTHING AT THE TIME.
OUR OWN THEORY WAS SOMEONE LOOKING TO TAKE OVER FROM CLINTON, BUT THEY'RE SURE AS HELL TAKING THEIR TIME ABOUT IT. WELL OVER SIX MONTHS NOW.
THE TRIPS?
COME AGAIN...?
SAM AND... MARCUS. DIDN'T YOU SAY THEY SOLD METH TO CLINTON, MIGHT HAVE BEEN GETTING IDEAS?
OF COURSE, THEY'RE DEAD TOO, SO MAYBE O'DWYER THINKS THERE'S SOME NEW PLAYER OUT THERE. WIPING OUT THE LOCALS, WAITING FOR THE RIGHT MOMENT...
THAT WHY YOU GAVE HIM THE GO-AHEAD?
WELL, IT WASN'T BECAUSE I THINK HE'S CONVINCED THAT EVEN A MURDERED NARCOTICS KINGPIN DESERVES JUSTICE.
I REALLY AM GETTING THE SENSE THAT THERE IS SOME HARM IN THIS AFTER ALL, DUKE. WHAT GIVES?

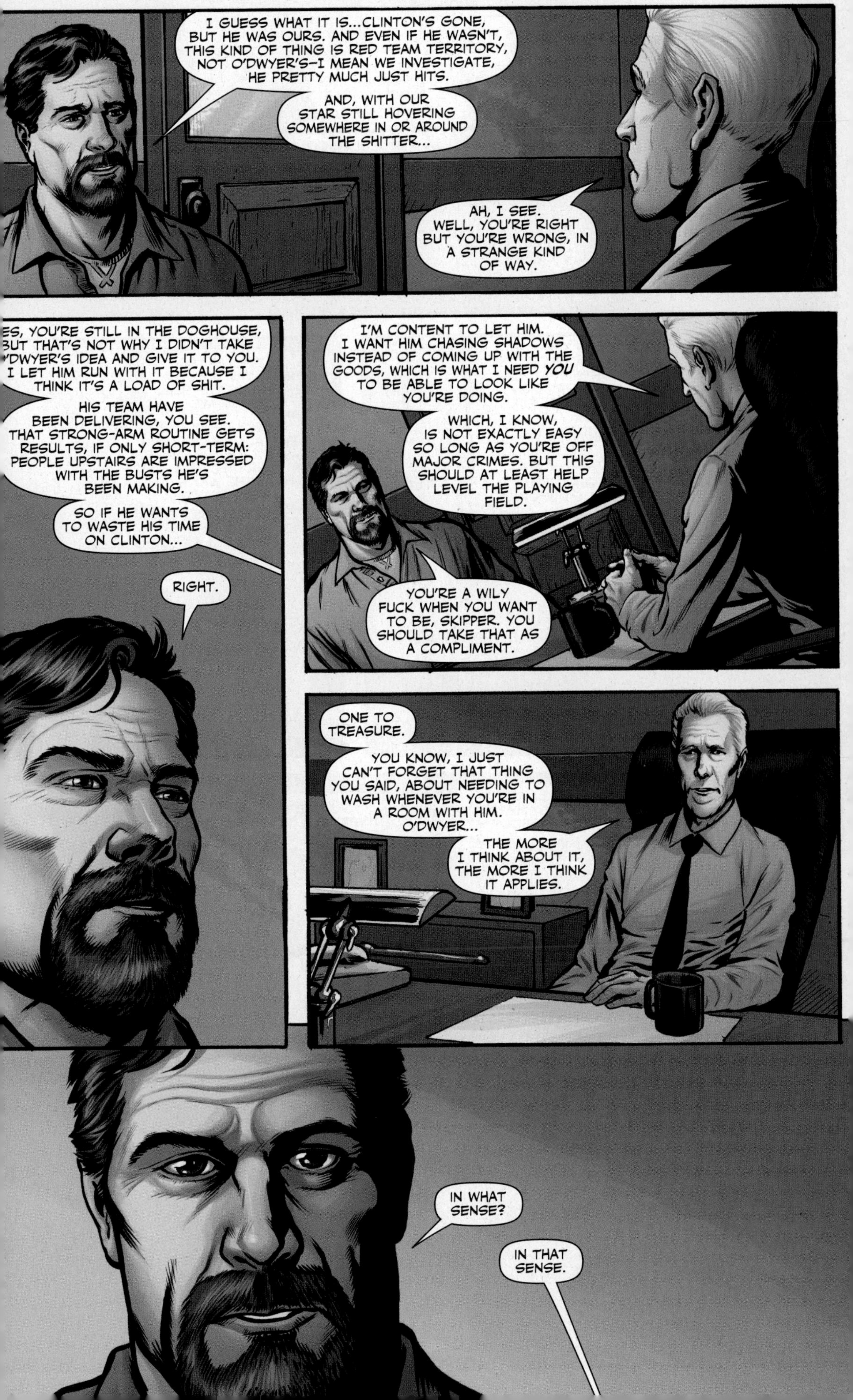
I GUESS WHAT IT IS...CLINTON'S GONE, BUT HE WAS OURS. AND EVEN IF HE WASN'T, THIS KIND OF THING IS RED TEAM TERRITORY, NOT O'DWYER'S–I MEAN WE INVESTIGATE, HE PRETTY MUCH JUST HITS.
AND, WITH OUR STAR STILL HOVERING SOMEWHERE IN OR AROUND THE SHITTER...
AH, I SEE. WELL, YOU'RE RIGHT BUT YOU'RE WRONG, IN A STRANGE KIND OF WAY.
ES, YOU'RE STILL IN THE DOGHOUSE, BUT THAT'S NOT WHY I DIDN'T TAKE 'DWYER'S IDEA AND GIVE IT TO YOU. I LET HIM RUN WITH IT BECAUSE I THINK IT'S A LOAD OF SHIT.
HIS TEAM HAVE BEEN DELIVERING, YOU SEE. THAT STRONG-ARM ROUTINE GETS RESULTS, IF ONLY SHORT-TERM: PEOPLE UPSTAIRS ARE IMPRESSED WITH THE BUSTS HE'S BEEN MAKING.
SO IF HE WANTS TO WASTE HIS TIME ON CLINTON...
I'M CONTENT TO LET HIM. I WANT HIM CHASING SHADOWS INSTEAD OF COMING UP WITH THE GOODS, WHICH IS WHAT I NEED YOU TO BE ABLE TO LOOK LIKE YOU'RE DOING.
WHICH, I KNOW, IS NOT EXACTLY EASY SO LONG AS YOU'RE OFF MAJOR CRIMES. BUT THIS SHOULD AT LEAST HELP LEVEL THE PLAYING FIELD.
YOU'RE A WILY FUCK WHEN YOU WANT TO BE, SKIPPER. YOU SHOULD TAKE THAT AS A COMPLIMENT.
RIGHT.
ONE TO TREASURE.
YOU KNOW, I JUST CAN'T FORGET THAT THING YOU SAID, ABOUT NEEDING TO WASH WHENEVER YOU'RE IN A ROOM WITH HIM. O'DWYER...
THE MORE I THINK ABOUT IT, THE MORE I THINK IT APPLIES.
IN WHAT SENSE?
IN THAT SENSE.

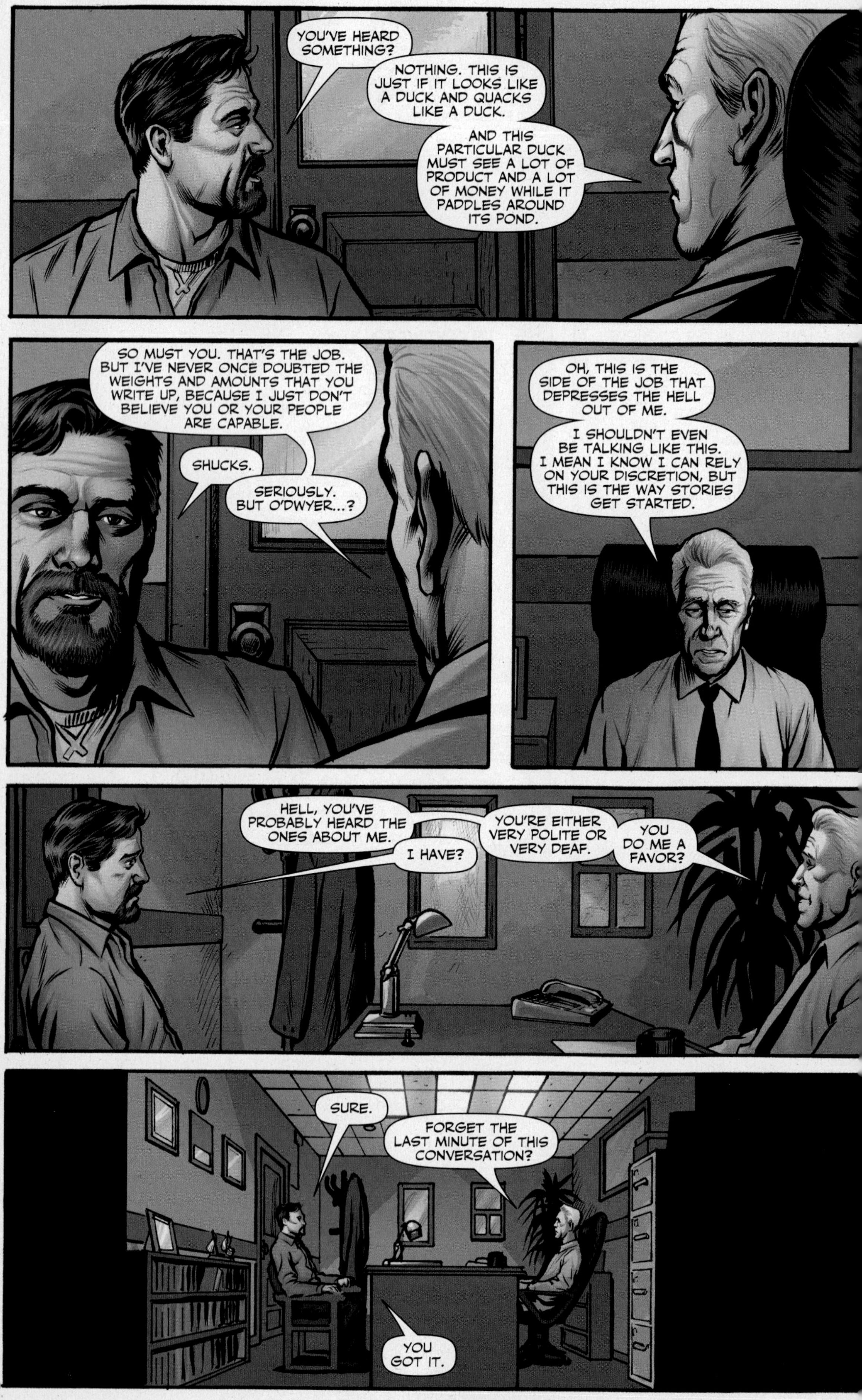
YOU'VE HEARD SOMETHING?
NOTHING. THIS IS JUST IF IT LOOKS LIKE A DUCK AND QUACKS LIKE A DUCK.
AND THIS PARTICULAR DUCK MUST SEE A LOT OF PRODUCT AND A LOT OF MONEY WHILE IT PADDLES AROUND ITS POND.
SO MUST YOU. THAT'S THE JOB. BUT I'VE NEVER ONCE DOUBTED THE WEIGHTS AND AMOUNTS THAT YOU WRITE UP, BECAUSE I JUST DON'T BELIEVE YOU OR YOUR PEOPLE ARE CAPABLE.
SHUCKS.
SERIOUSLY. BUT O'DWYER...?
OH, THIS IS THE SIDE OF THE JOB THAT DEPRESSES THE HELL OUT OF ME.
I SHOULDN'T EVEN BE TALKING LIKE THIS. I MEAN I KNOW I CAN RELY ON YOUR DISCRETION, BUT THIS IS THE WAY STORIES GET STARTED.
HELL, YOU'VE PROBABLY HEARD THE ONES ABOUT ME.
I HAVE?
YOU'RE EITHER VERY POLITE OR VERY DEAF.
YOU DO ME A FAVOR?
SURE.
FORGET THE LAST MINUTE OF THIS CONVERSATION?
YOU GOT IT.

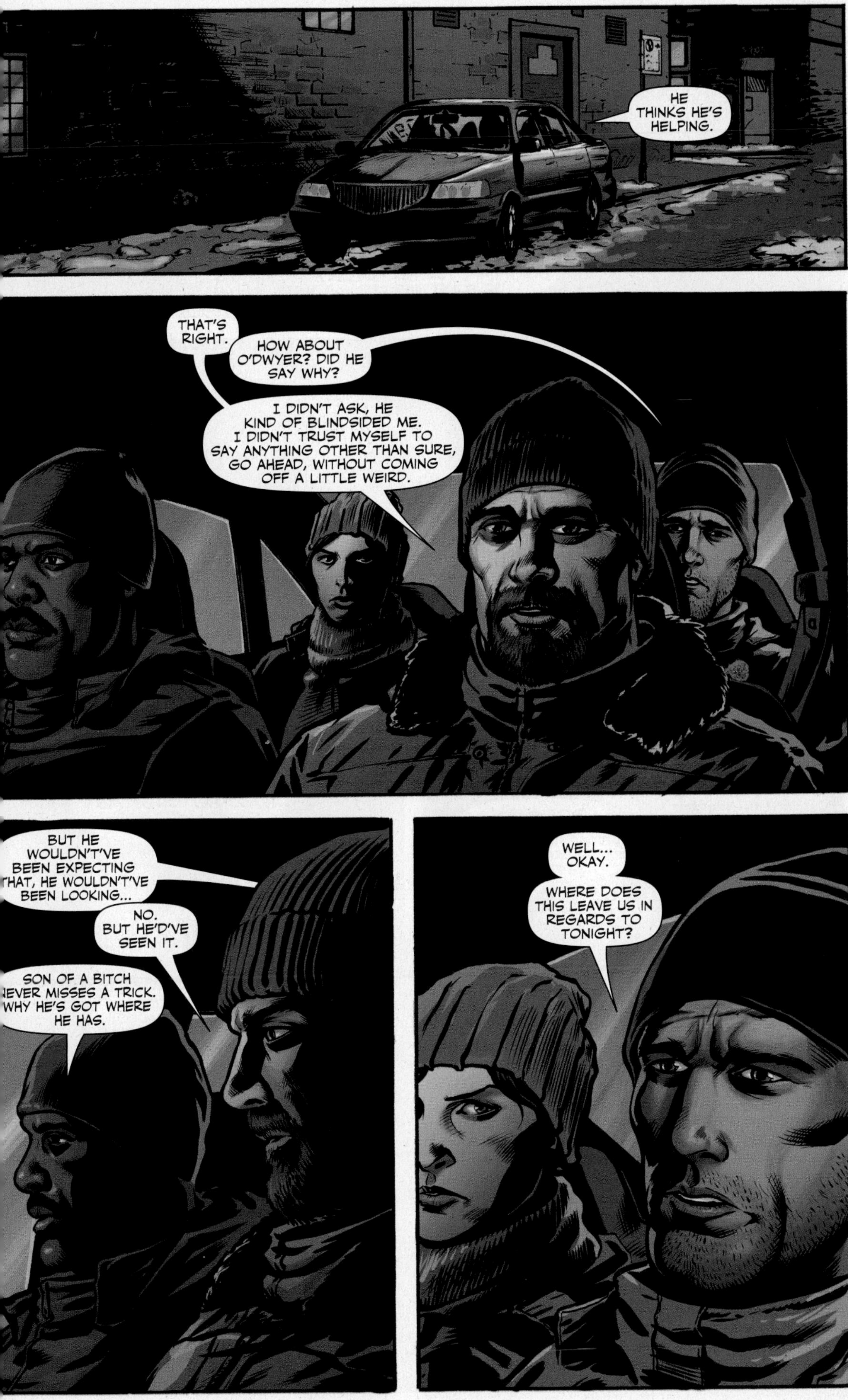
HE THINKS HE'S HELPING.
THAT'S RIGHT.
HOW ABOUT O'DWYER? DID HE SAY WHY?
I DIDN'T ASK, HE KIND OF BLINDSIDED ME. I DIDN'T TRUST MYSELF TO SAY ANYTHING OTHER THAN SURE, GO AHEAD, WITHOUT COMING OFF A LITTLE WEIRD.
BUT HE WOULDN'T'VE BEEN EXPECTING THAT, HE WOULDN'T'VE BEEN LOOKING...
NO. BUT HE'D'VE SEEN IT.
SON OF A BITCH NEVER MISSES A TRICK. WHY HE'S GOT WHERE HE HAS.
WELL... OKAY.
WHERE DOES THIS LEAVE US IN REGARDS TO TONIGHT?

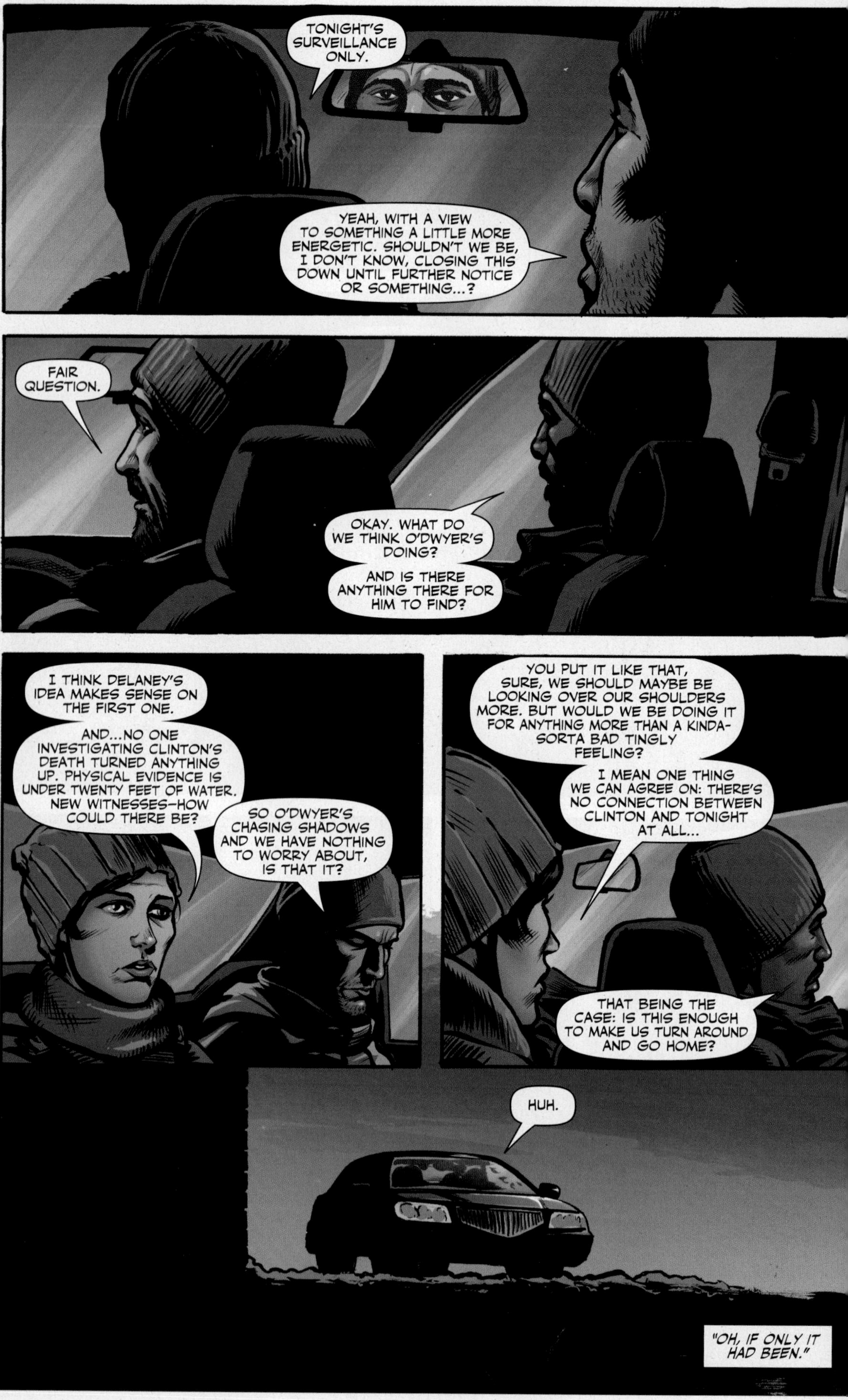
TONIGHT'S SURVEILLANCE ONLY.
YEAH, WITH A VIEW TO SOMETHING A LITTLE MORE ENERGETIC. SHOULDN'T WE BE, I DON'T KNOW, CLOSING THIS DOWN UNTIL FURTHER NOTICE OR SOMETHING...?
FAIR QUESTION.
OKAY. WHAT DO WE THINK O'DWYER'S DOING?
AND IS THERE ANYTHING THERE FOR HIM TO FIND?
I THINK DELANEY'S IDEA MAKES SENSE ON THE FIRST ONE.
AND...NO ONE INVESTIGATING CLINTON'S DEATH TURNED ANYTHING UP. PHYSICAL EVIDENCE IS UNDER TWENTY FEET OF WATER. NEW WITNESSES–HOW COULD THERE BE?
SO O'DWYER'S CHASING SHADOWS AND WE HAVE NOTHING TO WORRY ABOUT, IS THAT IT?
YOU PUT IT LIKE THAT, SURE, WE SHOULD MAYBE BE LOOKING OVER OUR SHOULDERS MORE. BUT WOULD WE BE DOING IT FOR ANYTHING MORE THAN A KINDA-SORTA BAD TINGLY FEELING?
I MEAN ONE THING WE CAN AGREE ON: THERE'S NO CONNECTION BETWEEN CLINTON AND TONIGHT AT ALL...
THAT BEING THE CASE: IS THIS ENOUGH TO MAKE US TURN AROUND AND GO HOME?
HUH.
"OH, IF ONLY IT HAD BEEN."

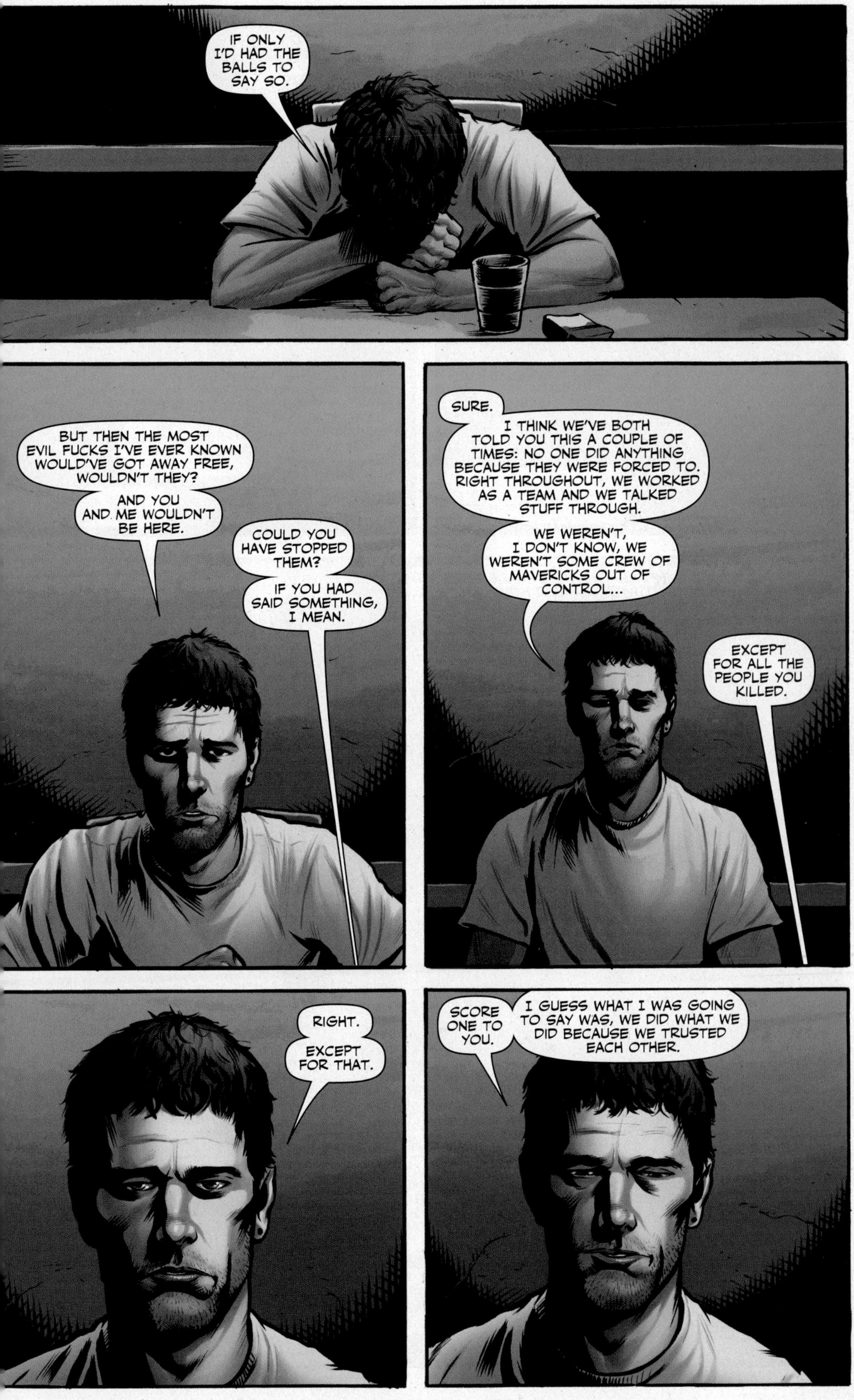
IF ONLY I'D HAD THE BALLS TO SAY SO.
BUT THEN THE MOST EVIL FUCKS I'VE EVER KNOWN WOULD'VE GOT AWAY FREE, WOULDN'T THEY?
AND YOU AND ME WOULDN'T BE HERE.
COULD YOU HAVE STOPPED THEM?
IF YOU HAD SAID SOMETHING, I MEAN.
SURE.
I THINK WE'VE BOTH TOLD YOU THIS A COUPLE OF TIMES: NO ONE DID ANYTHING BECAUSE THEY WERE FORCED TO. RIGHT THROUGHOUT, WE WORKED AS A TEAM AND WE TALKED STUFF THROUGH.
WE WEREN'T, I DON'T KNOW, WE WEREN'T SOME CREW OF MAVERICKS OUT OF CONTROL...
EXCEPT FOR ALL THE PEOPLE YOU KILLED.
RIGHT.
EXCEPT FOR THAT.
SCORE ONE TO YOU.
I GUESS WHAT I WAS GOING TO SAY WAS, WE DID WHAT WE DID BECAUSE WE TRUSTED EACH OTHER.

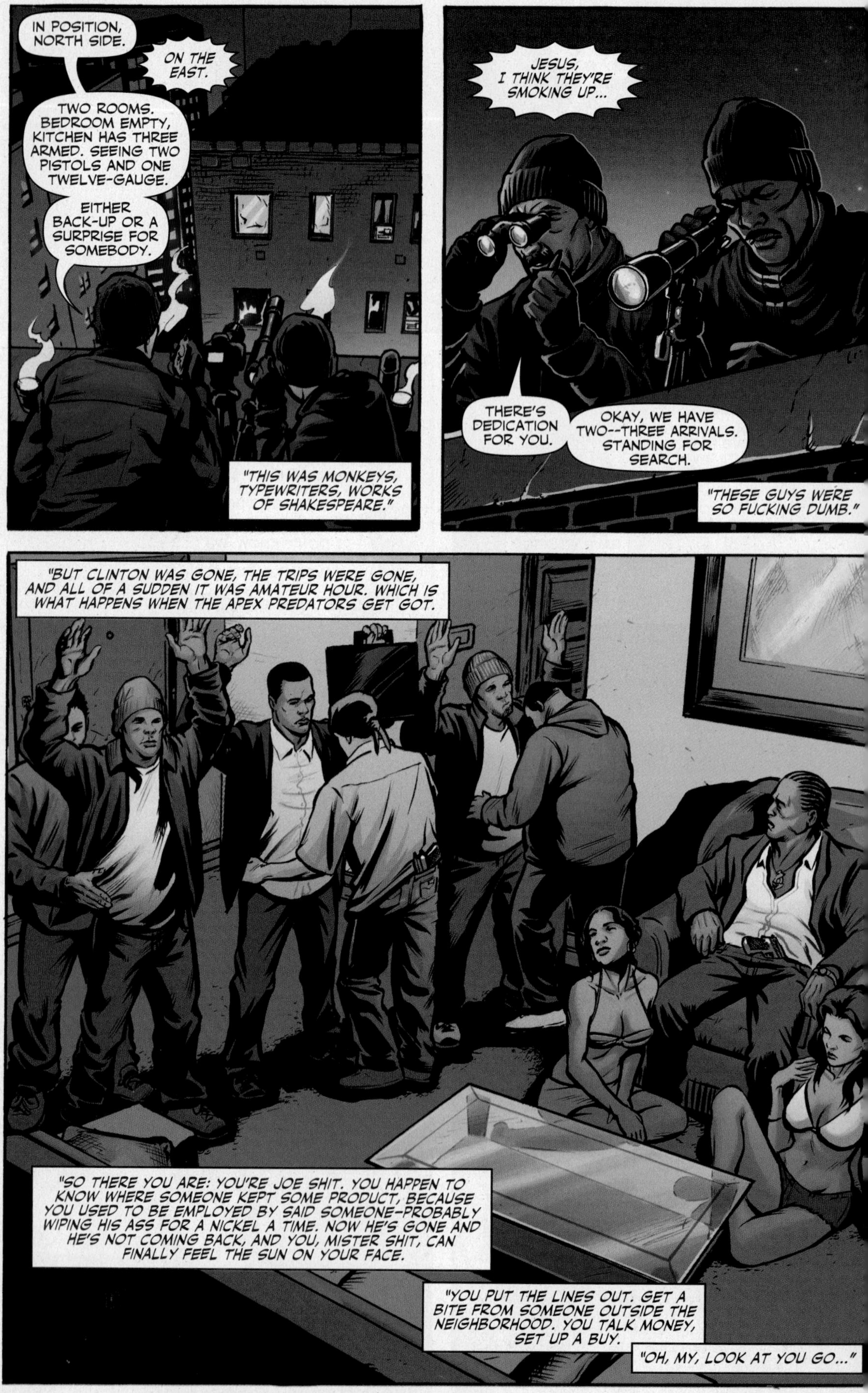
IN POSITION, NORTH SIDE.
ON THE EAST.
TWO ROOMS. BEDROOM EMPTY, KITCHEN HAS THREE ARMED. SEEING TWO PISTOLS AND ONE TWELVE-GAUGE.
EITHER BACK-UP OR A SURPRISE FOR SOMEBODY.
"THIS WAS MONKEYS, TYPEWRITERS, WORKS OF SHAKESPEARE."
JESUS, I THINK THEY'RE SMOKING UP...
THERE'S DEDICATION FOR YOU.
OKAY, WE HAVE TWO--THREE ARRIVALS. STANDING FOR SEARCH.
"THESE GUYS WERE SO FUCKING DUMB."
"BUT CLINTON WAS GONE, THE TRIPS WERE GONE, AND ALL OF A SUDDEN IT WAS AMATEUR HOUR. WHICH IS WHAT HAPPENS WHEN THE APEX PREDATORS GET GOT.
"SO THERE YOU ARE: YOU'RE JOE SHIT. YOU HAPPEN TO KNOW WHERE SOMEONE KEPT SOME PRODUCT, BECAUSE YOU USED TO BE EMPLOYED BY SAID SOMEONE--PROBABLY WIPING HIS ASS FOR A NICKEL A TIME. NOW HE'S GONE AND HE'S NOT COMING BACK, AND YOU, MISTER SHIT, CAN FINALLY FEEL THE SUN ON YOUR FACE.
"YOU PUT THE LINES OUT. GET A BITE FROM SOMEONE OUTSIDE THE NEIGHBORHOOD. YOU TALK MONEY, SET UP A BUY.
"OH, MY, LOOK AT YOU GO..."

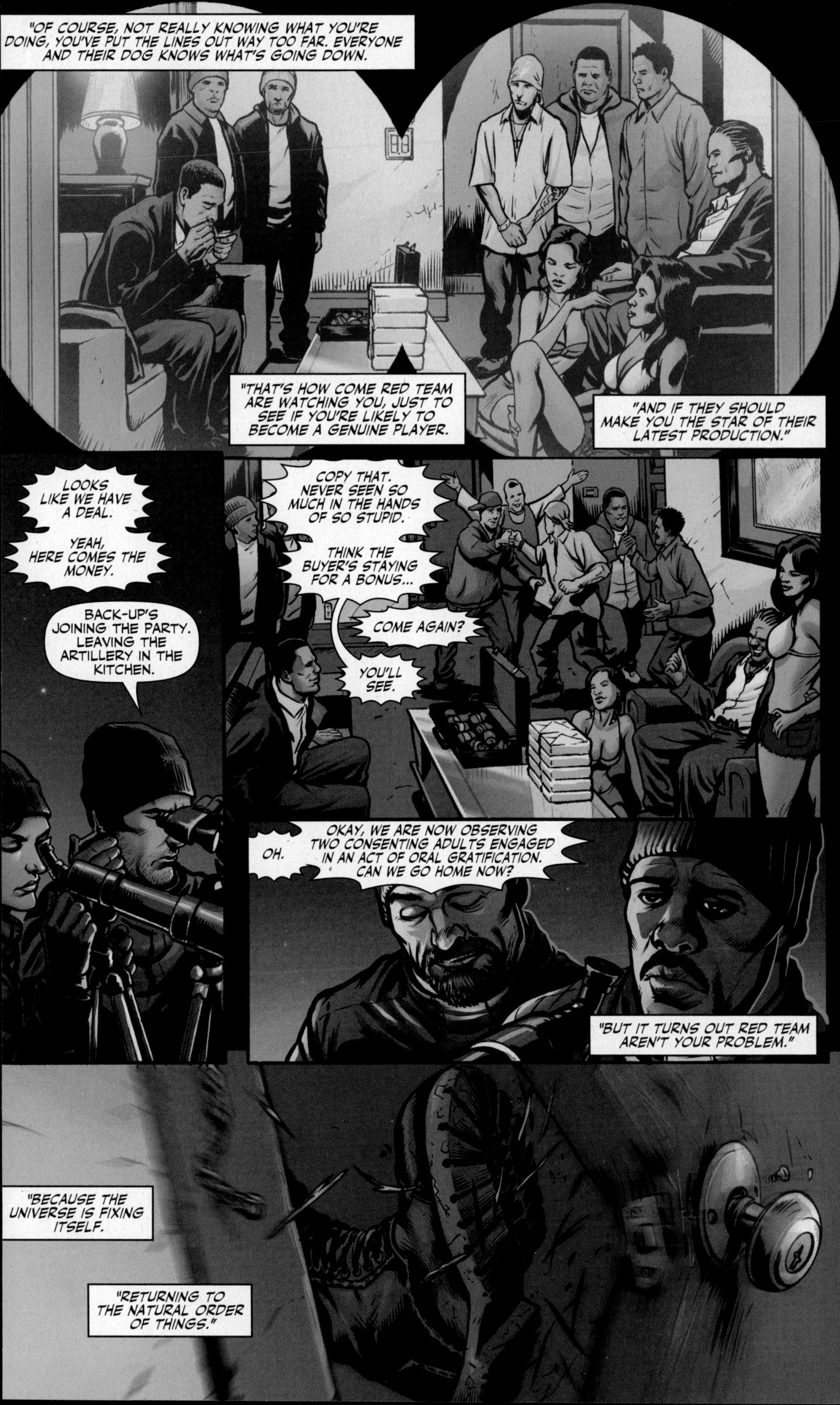
"OF COURSE, NOT REALLY KNOWING WHAT YOU'RE DOING, YOU'VE PUT THE LINES OUT WAY TOO FAR. EVERYONE AND THEIR DOG KNOWS WHAT'S GOING DOWN.
"THAT'S HOW COME RED TEAM ARE WATCHING YOU, JUST TO SEE IF YOU'RE LIKELY TO BECOME A GENUINE PLAYER.
"AND IF THEY SHOULD MAKE YOU THE STAR OF THEIR LATEST PRODUCTION."
LOOKS LIKE WE HAVE A DEAL.
YEAH, HERE COMES THE MONEY.
BACK-UP'S JOINING THE PARTY. LEAVING THE ARTILLERY IN THE KITCHEN.
COPY THAT. NEVER SEEN SO MUCH IN THE HANDS OF SO STUPID.
THINK THE BUYER'S STAYING FOR A BONUS...
COME AGAIN?
YOU'LL SEE.
OH.
OKAY, WE ARE NOW OBSERVING TWO CONSENTING ADULTS ENGAGED IN AN ACT OF ORAL GRATIFICATION. CAN WE GO HOME NOW?
"BUT IT TURNS OUT RED TEAM AREN'T YOUR PROBLEM."
"BECAUSE THE UNIVERSE IS FIXING ITSELF.
"RETURNING TO THE NATURAL ORDER OF THINGS."

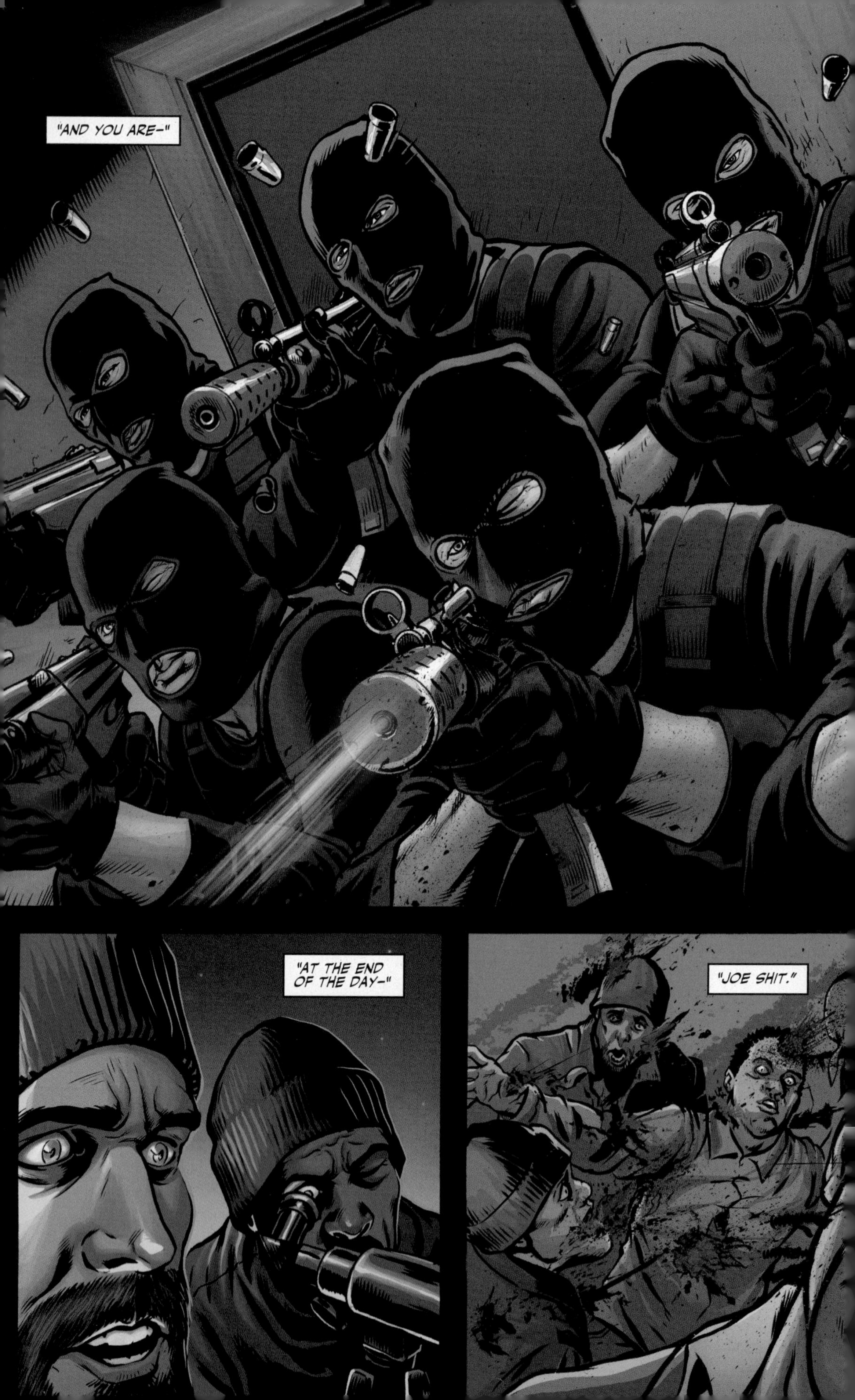
"AND YOU ARE-"
"AT THE END OF THE DAY-"
"JOE SHIT."

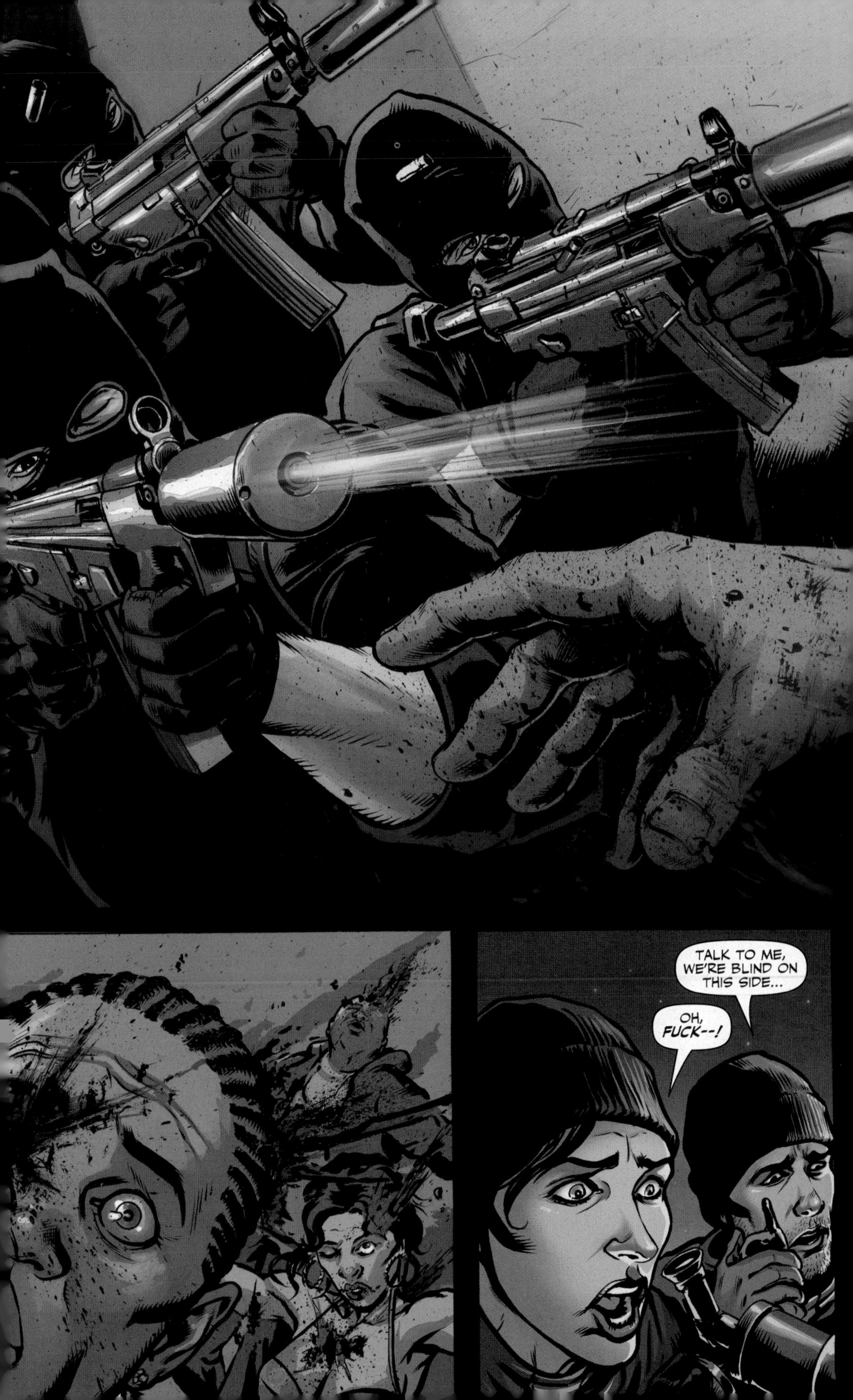
TALK TO ME, WE'RE BLIND ON THIS SIDE...
OH, *FUCK--!*

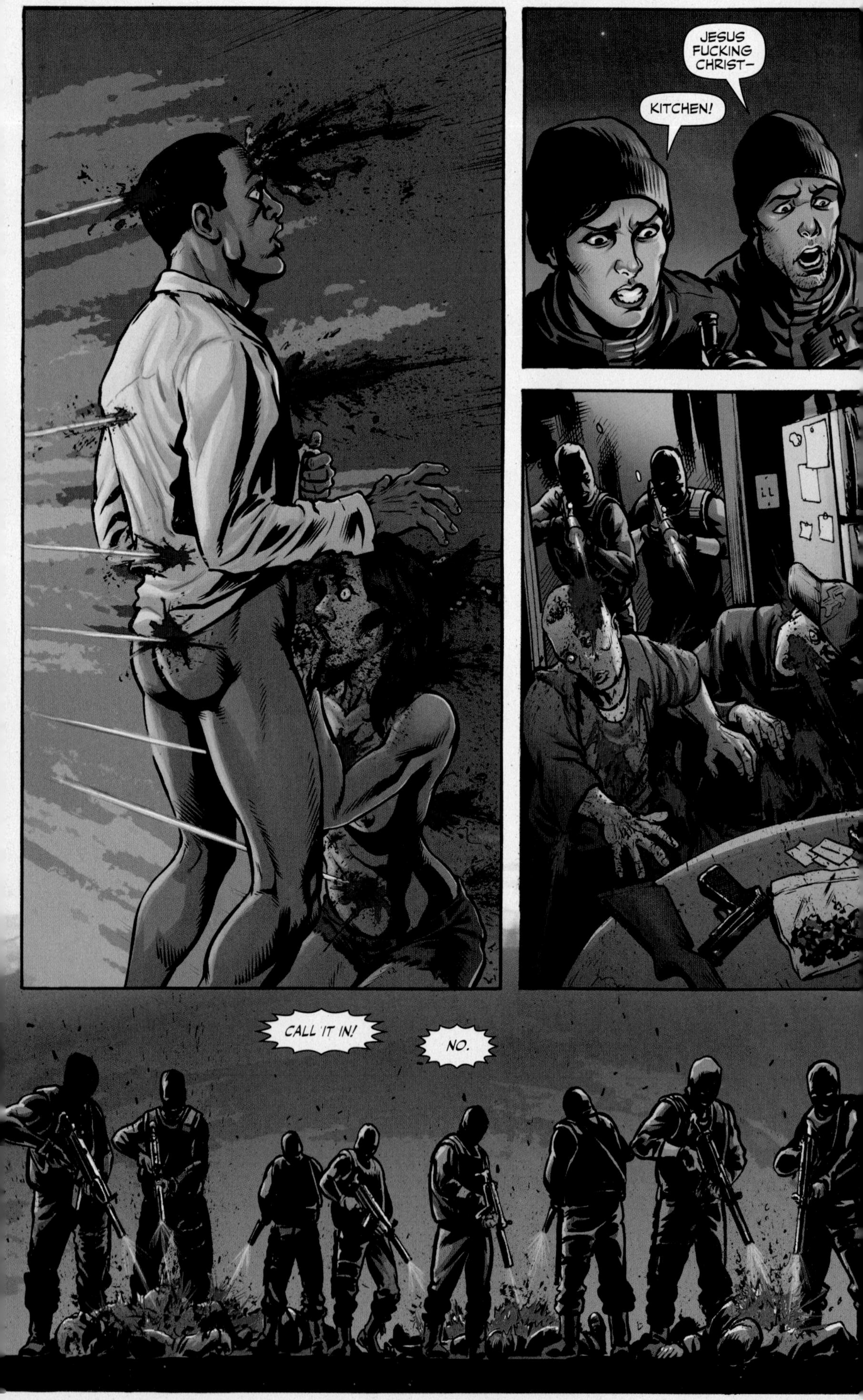
JESUS FUCKING CHRIST–
KITCHEN!
CALL IT IN!
NO.

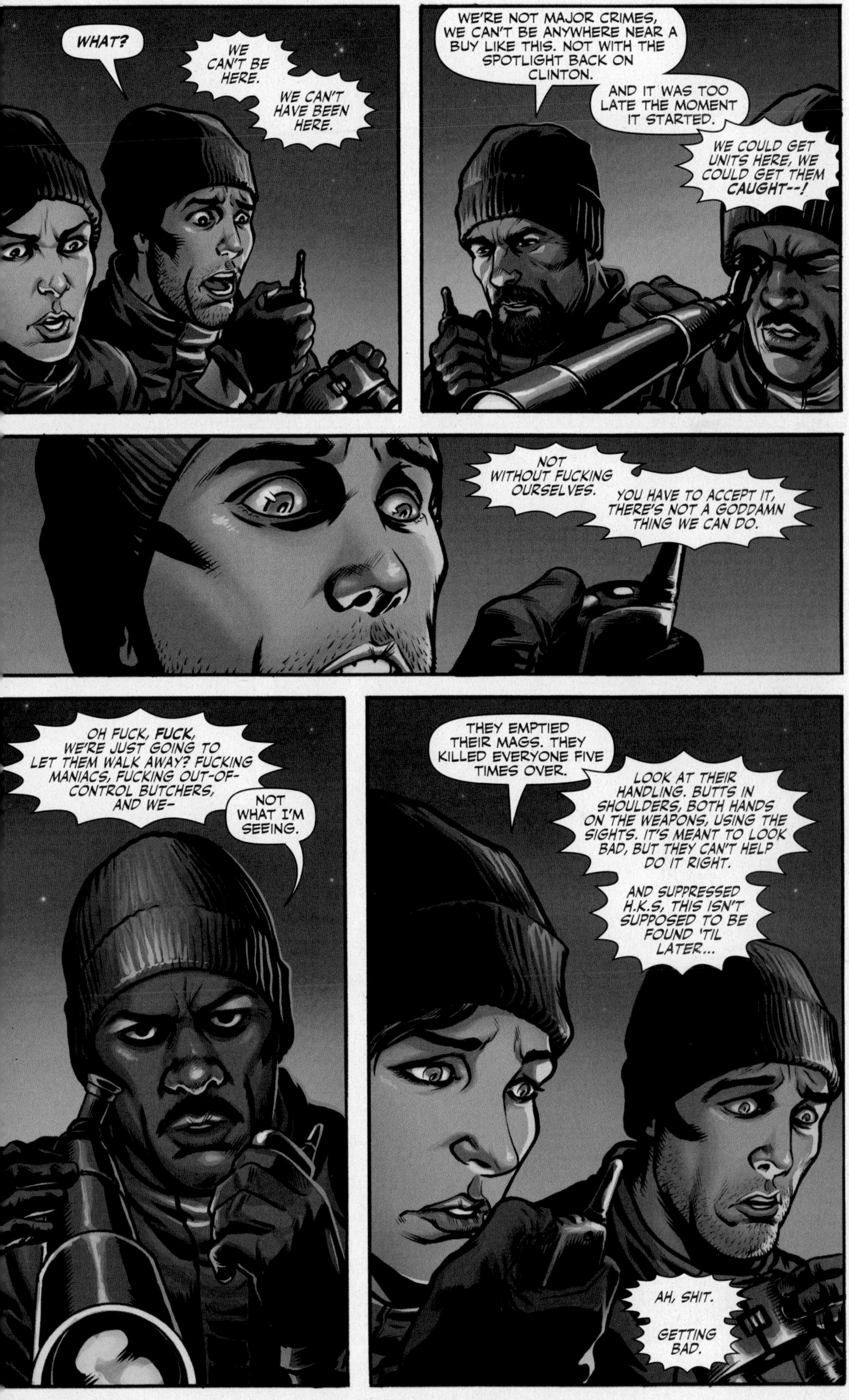

WHAT?
WE CAN'T BE HERE.
WE CAN'T HAVE BEEN HERE.
WE'RE NOT MAJOR CRIMES, WE CAN'T BE ANYWHERE NEAR A BUY LIKE THIS. NOT WITH THE SPOTLIGHT BACK ON CLINTON.
AND IT WAS TOO LATE THE MOMENT IT STARTED.
WE COULD GET UNITS HERE, WE COULD GET THEM CAUGHT--!
NOT WITHOUT FUCKING OURSELVES.
YOU HAVE TO ACCEPT IT, THERE'S NOT A GODDAMN THING WE CAN DO.
OH FUCK, FUCK, WE'RE JUST GOING TO LET THEM WALK AWAY? FUCKING MANIACS, FUCKING OUT-OF-CONTROL BUTCHERS, AND WE-
NOT WHAT I'M SEEING.
THEY EMPTIED THEIR MAGS. THEY KILLED EVERYONE FIVE TIMES OVER.
LOOK AT THEIR HANDLING. BUTTS IN SHOULDERS, BOTH HANDS ON THE WEAPONS, USING THE SIGHTS. IT'S MEANT TO LOOK BAD, BUT THEY CAN'T HELP DO IT RIGHT.
AND SUPPRESSED H.K.S, THIS ISN'T SUPPOSED TO BE FOUND 'TIL LATER...
AH, SHIT.
GETTING BAD.

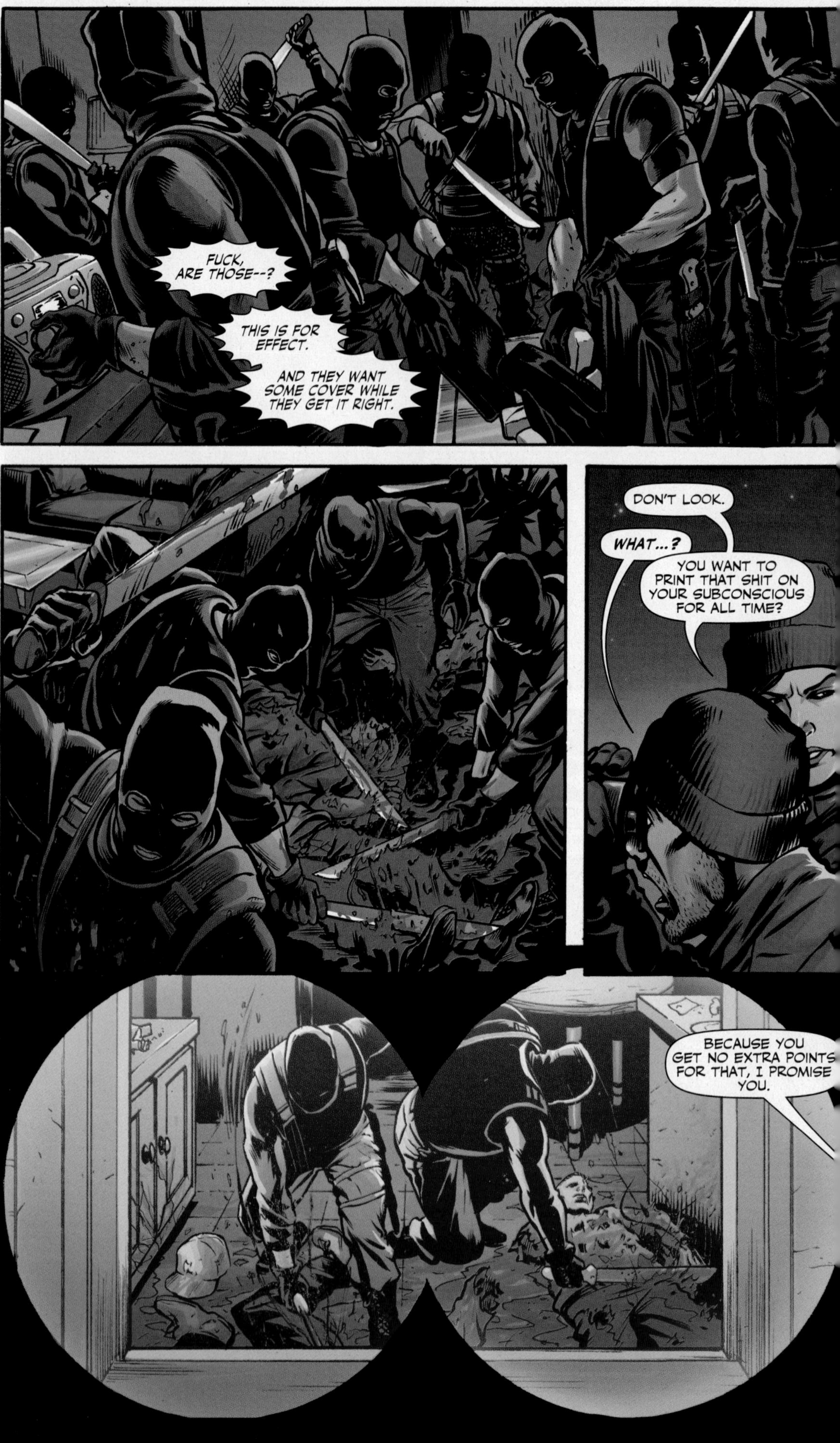
FUCK, ARE THOSE--?
THIS IS FOR EFFECT.
AND THEY WANT SOME COVER WHILE THEY GET IT RIGHT.
DON'T LOOK.
WHAT...?
YOU WANT TO PRINT THAT SHIT ON YOUR SUBCONSCIOUS FOR ALL TIME?
BECAUSE YOU GET NO EXTRA POINTS FOR THAT, I PROMISE YOU.

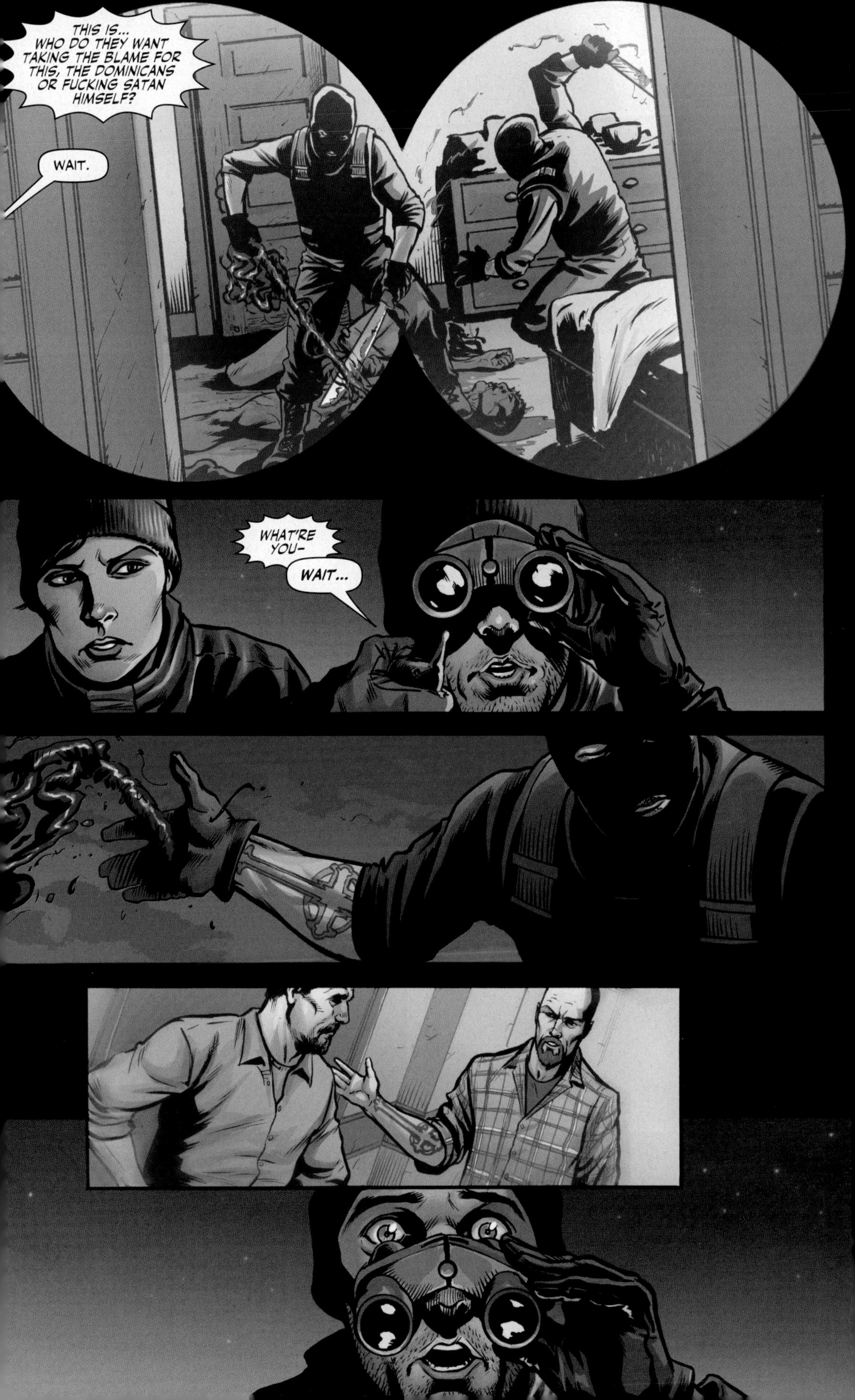
THIS IS... WHO DO THEY WANT TAKING THE BLAME FOR THIS, THE DOMINICANS OR FUCKING SATAN HIMSELF?
WAIT.
WHAT'RE YOU-
WAIT...

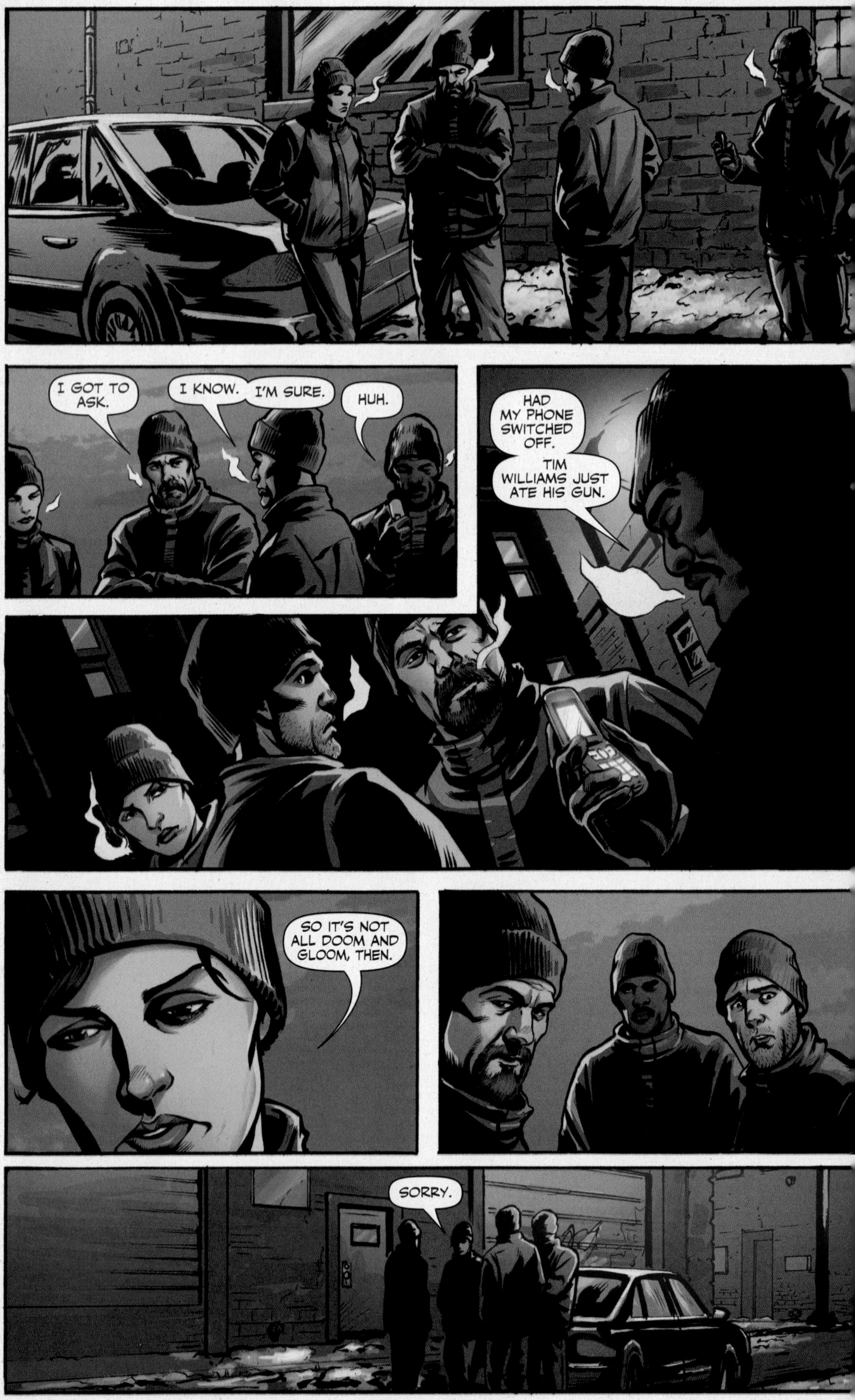
I GOT TO ASK.
I KNOW.
I'M SURE.
HUH.
HAD MY PHONE SWITCHED OFF.
TIM WILLIAMS JUST ATE HIS GUN.
SO IT'S NOT ALL DOOM AND GLOOM, THEN.
SORRY.

ISSUE SIX

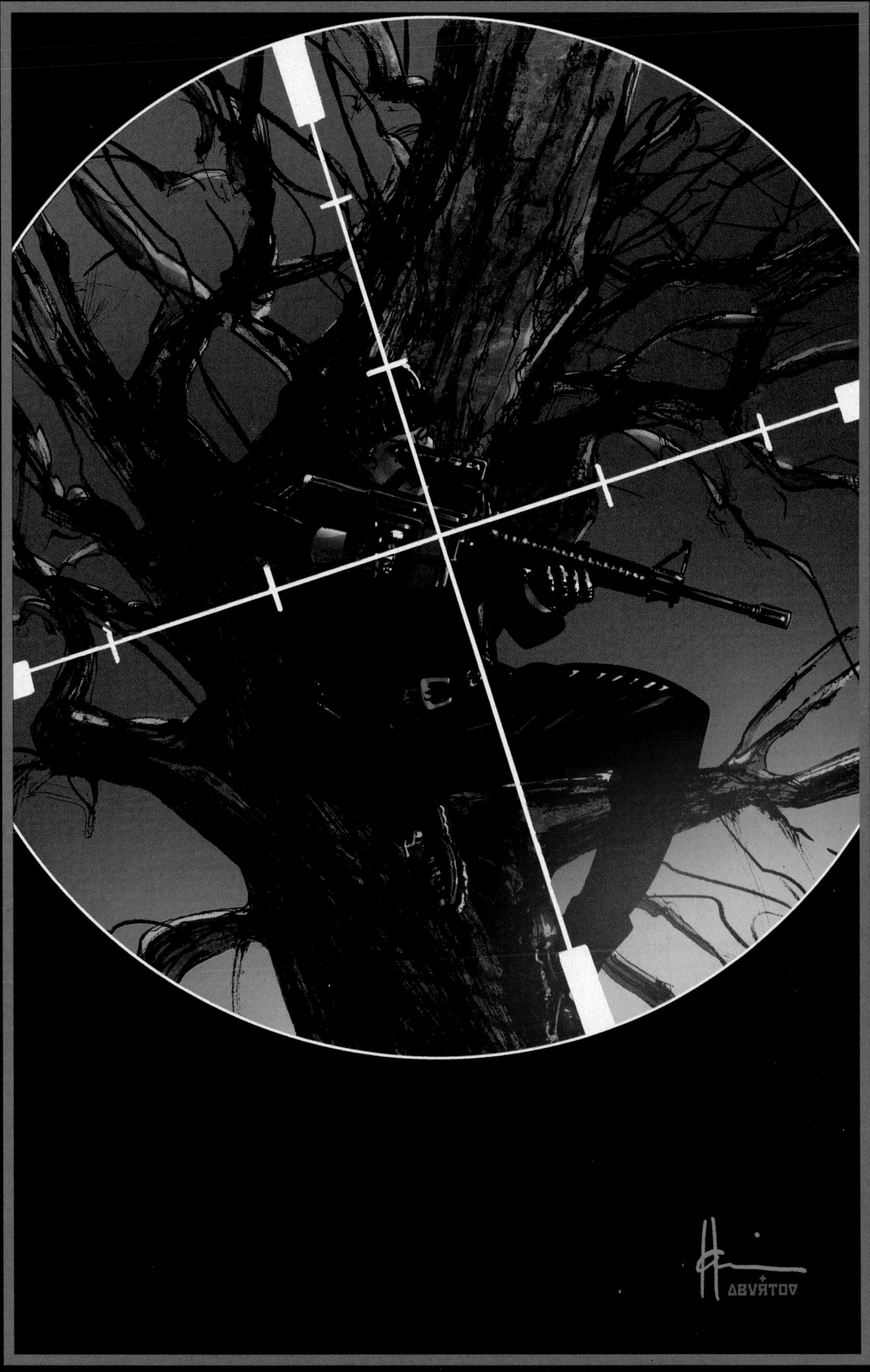

Issue #6 cover art by **HOWARD CHAYKIN** colors by **JESUS ABURTO**

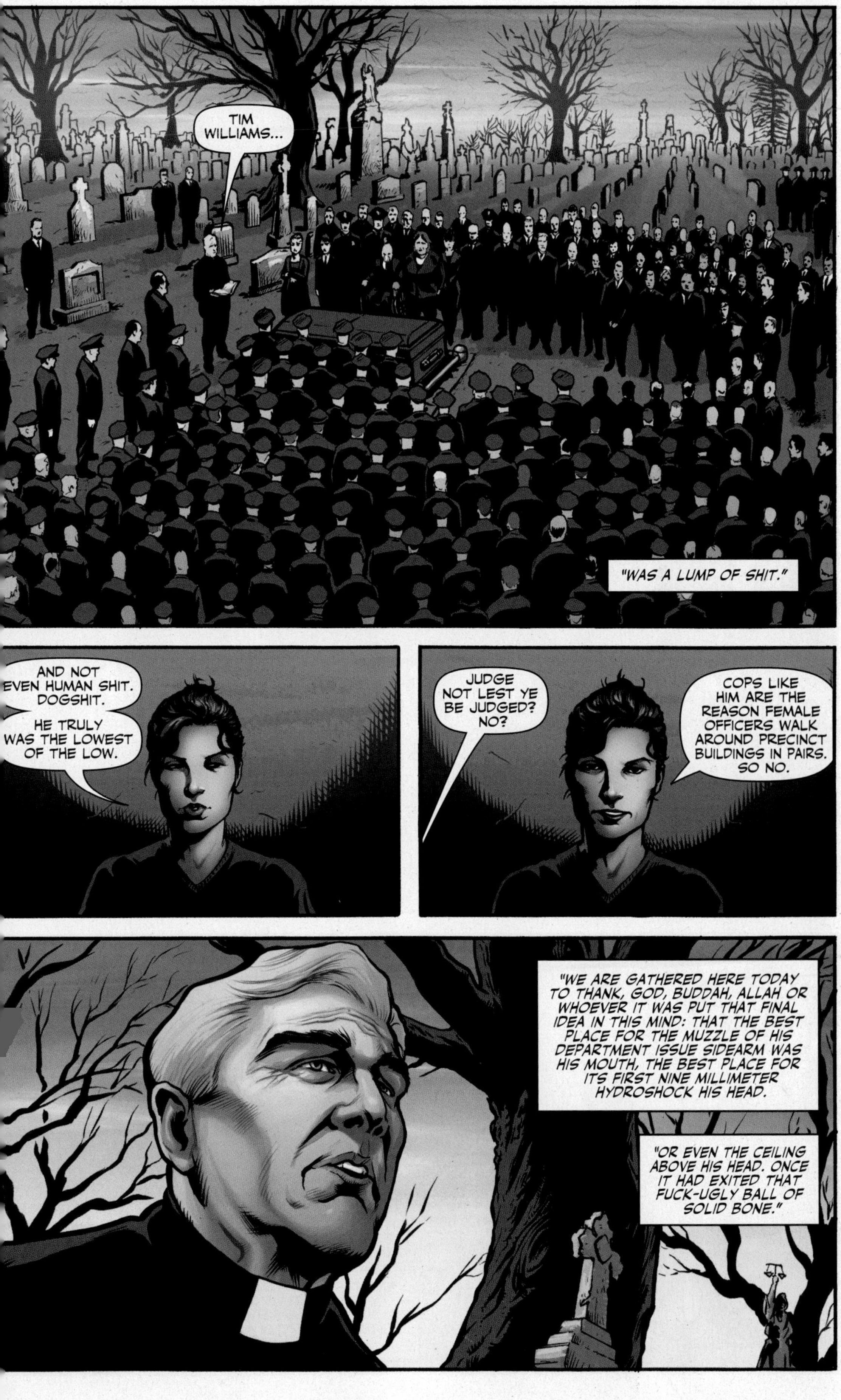
TIM WILLIAMS...
"WAS A LUMP OF SHIT."
AND NOT EVEN HUMAN SHIT. DOGSHIT.
HE TRULY WAS THE LOWEST OF THE LOW.
JUDGE NOT LEST YE BE JUDGED? NO?
COPS LIKE HIM ARE THE REASON FEMALE OFFICERS WALK AROUND PRECINCT BUILDINGS IN PAIRS. SO NO.
"WE ARE GATHERED HERE TODAY TO THANK, GOD, BUDDAH, ALLAH OR WHOEVER IT WAS PUT THAT FINAL IDEA IN THIS MIND: THAT THE BEST PLACE FOR THE MUZZLE OF HIS DEPARTMENT ISSUE SIDEARM WAS HIS MOUTH, THE BEST PLACE FOR ITS FIRST NINE MILLIMETER HYDROSHOCK HIS HEAD.
"OR EVEN THE CEILING ABOVE HIS HEAD. ONCE IT HAD EXITED THAT FUCK-UGLY BALL OF SOLID BONE."

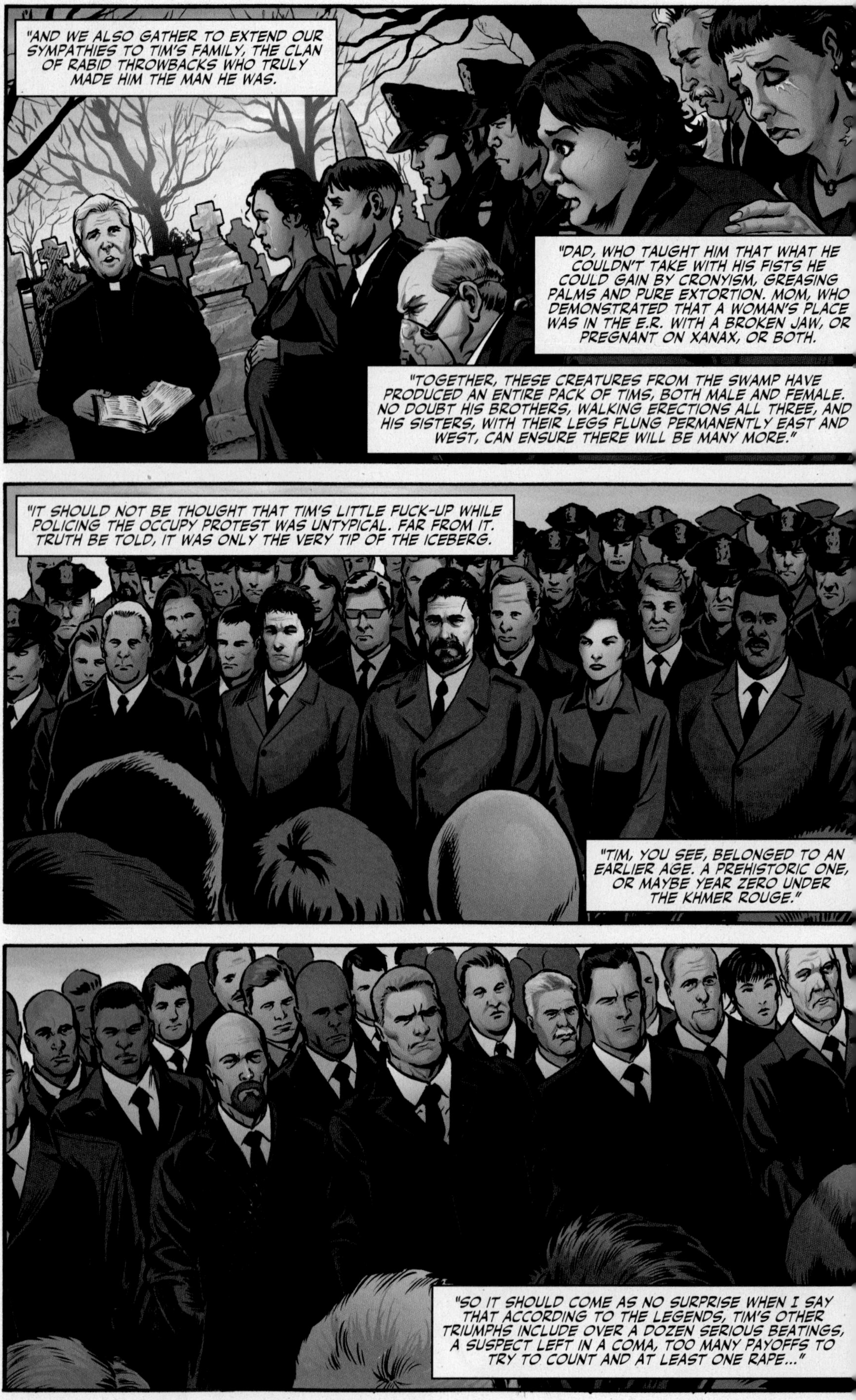
"AND WE ALSO GATHER TO EXTEND OUR SYMPATHIES TO TIM'S FAMILY, THE CLAN OF RABID THROWBACKS WHO TRULY MADE HIM THE MAN HE WAS.
"DAD, WHO TAUGHT HIM THAT WHAT HE COULDN'T TAKE WITH HIS FISTS HE COULD GAIN BY CRONYISM, GREASING PALMS AND PURE EXTORTION. MOM, WHO DEMONSTRATED THAT A WOMAN'S PLACE WAS IN THE E.R. WITH A BROKEN JAW, OR PREGNANT ON XANAX, OR BOTH.
"TOGETHER, THESE CREATURES FROM THE SWAMP HAVE PRODUCED AN ENTIRE PACK OF TIMS, BOTH MALE AND FEMALE. NO DOUBT HIS BROTHERS, WALKING ERECTIONS ALL THREE, AND HIS SISTERS, WITH THEIR LEGS FLUNG PERMANENTLY EAST AND WEST, CAN ENSURE THERE WILL BE MANY MORE."
"IT SHOULD NOT BE THOUGHT THAT TIM'S LITTLE FUCK-UP WHILE POLICING THE OCCUPY PROTEST WAS UNTYPICAL. FAR FROM IT. TRUTH BE TOLD, IT WAS ONLY THE VERY TIP OF THE ICEBERG.
"TIM, YOU SEE, BELONGED TO AN EARLIER AGE. A PREHISTORIC ONE, OR MAYBE YEAR ZERO UNDER THE KHMER ROUGE."
"SO IT SHOULD COME AS NO SURPRISE WHEN I SAY THAT ACCORDING TO THE LEGENDS, TIM'S OTHER TRIUMPHS INCLUDE OVER A DOZEN SERIOUS BEATINGS, A SUSPECT LEFT IN A COMA, TOO MANY PAYOFFS TO TRY TO COUNT AND AT LEAST ONE RAPE..."

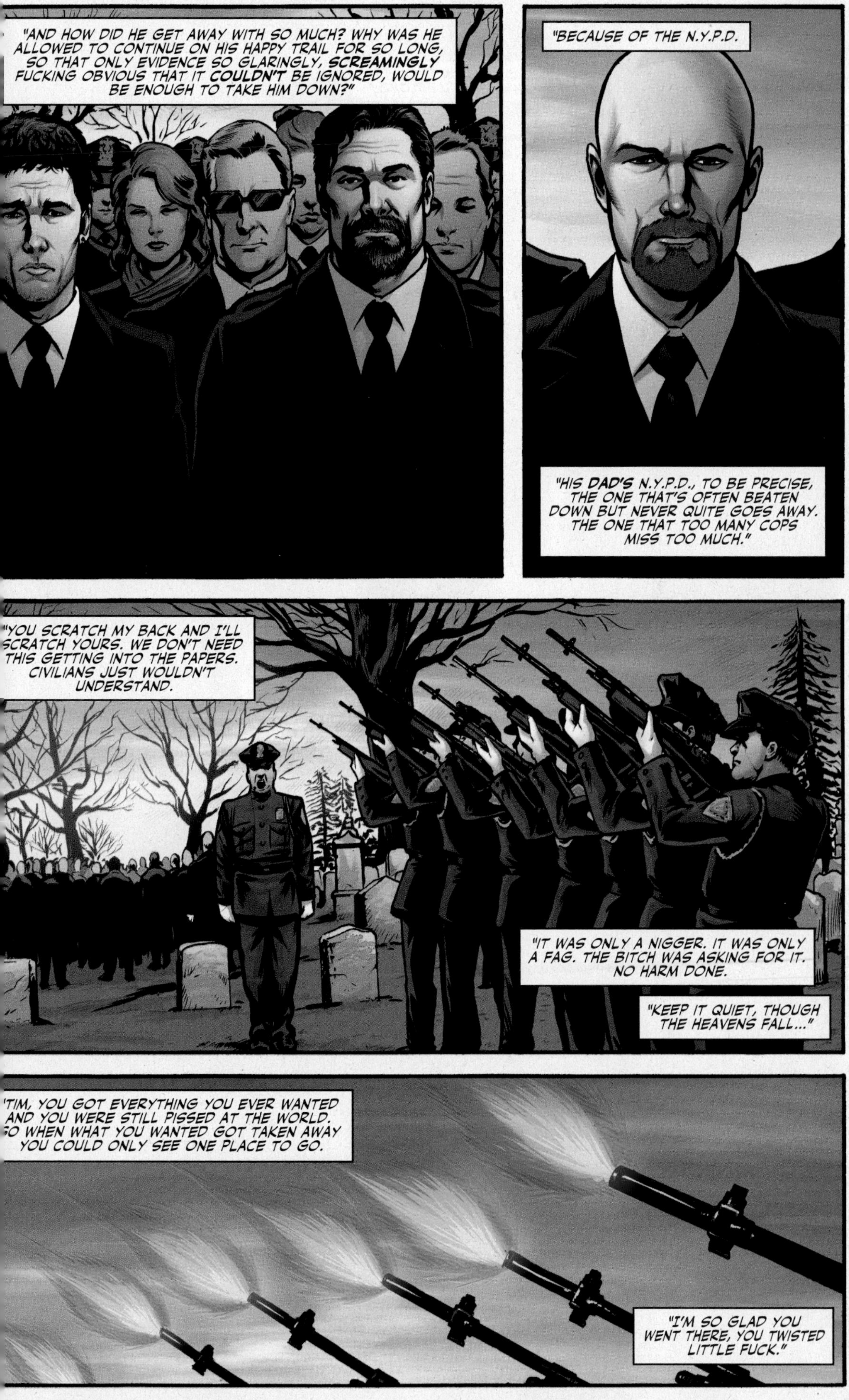
"AND HOW DID HE GET AWAY WITH SO MUCH? WHY WAS HE ALLOWED TO CONTINUE ON HIS HAPPY TRAIL FOR SO LONG, SO THAT ONLY EVIDENCE SO GLARINGLY, SCREAMINGLY FUCKING OBVIOUS THAT IT COULDN'T BE IGNORED, WOULD BE ENOUGH TO TAKE HIM DOWN?"
"BECAUSE OF THE N.Y.P.D.
"HIS DAD'S N.Y.P.D., TO BE PRECISE, THE ONE THAT'S OFTEN BEATEN DOWN BUT NEVER QUITE GOES AWAY. THE ONE THAT TOO MANY COPS MISS TOO MUCH."
"YOU SCRATCH MY BACK AND I'LL SCRATCH YOURS. WE DON'T NEED THIS GETTING INTO THE PAPERS. CIVILIANS JUST WOULDN'T UNDERSTAND.
"IT WAS ONLY A NIGGER. IT WAS ONLY A FAG. THE BITCH WAS ASKING FOR IT. NO HARM DONE.
"KEEP IT QUIET, THOUGH THE HEAVENS FALL..."
"TIM, YOU GOT EVERYTHING YOU EVER WANTED AND YOU WERE STILL PISSED AT THE WORLD. SO WHEN WHAT YOU WANTED GOT TAKEN AWAY YOU COULD ONLY SEE ONE PLACE TO GO.
"I'M SO GLAD YOU WENT THERE, YOU TWISTED LITTLE FUCK."

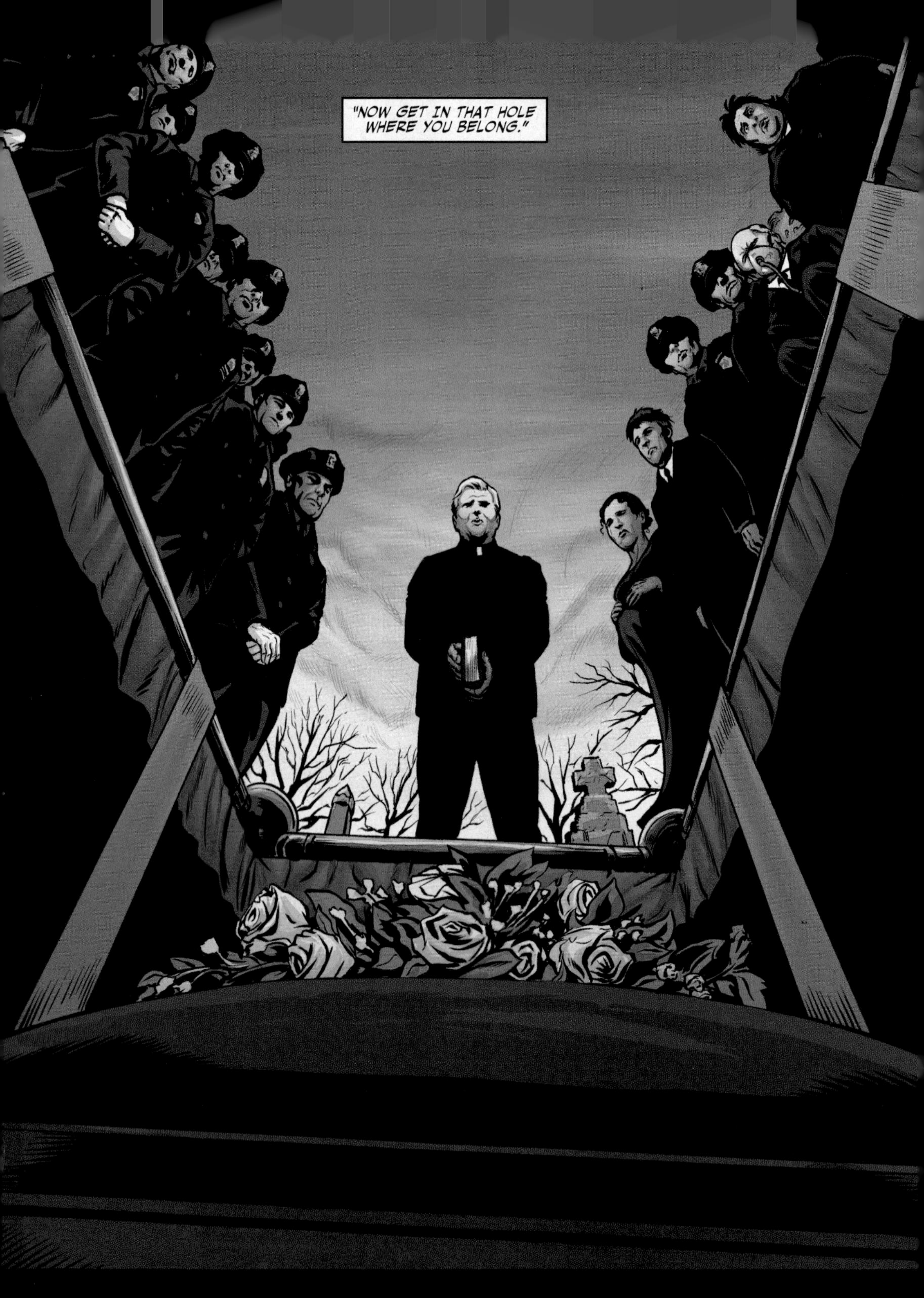
"NOW GET IN THAT HOLE WHERE YOU BELONG."

6: THE FALLEN

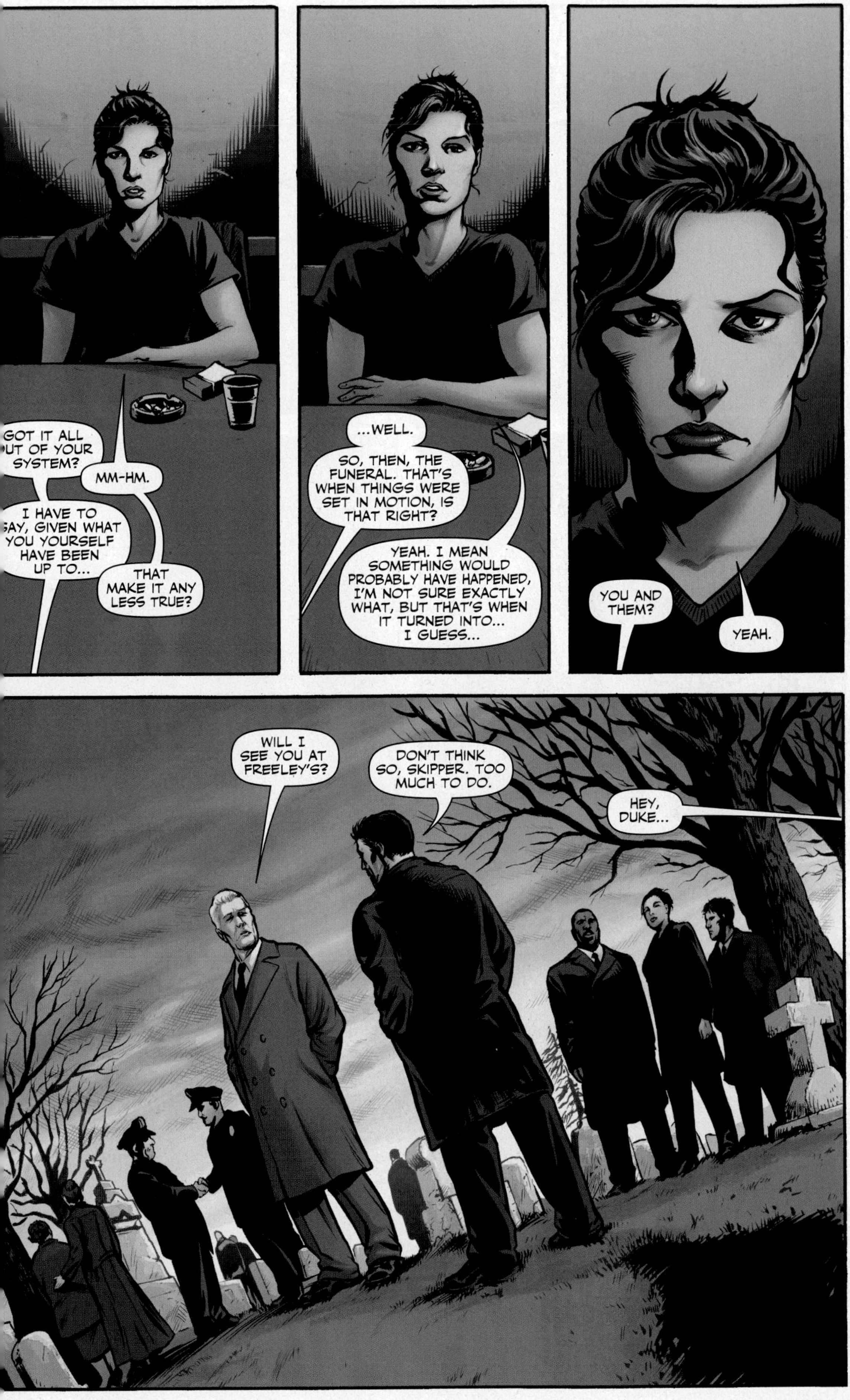
GOT IT ALL OUT OF YOUR SYSTEM?
MM-HM.
I HAVE TO SAY, GIVEN WHAT YOU YOURSELF HAVE BEEN UP TO...
THAT MAKE IT ANY LESS TRUE?
...WELL.
SO, THEN, THE FUNERAL. THAT'S WHEN THINGS WERE SET IN MOTION, IS THAT RIGHT?
YEAH. I MEAN SOMETHING WOULD PROBABLY HAVE HAPPENED, I'M NOT SURE EXACTLY WHAT, BUT THAT'S WHEN IT TURNED INTO... I GUESS...
YOU AND THEM?
YEAH.
WILL I SEE YOU AT FREELEY'S?
DON'T THINK SO, SKIPPER. TOO MUCH TO DO.
HEY, DUKE...

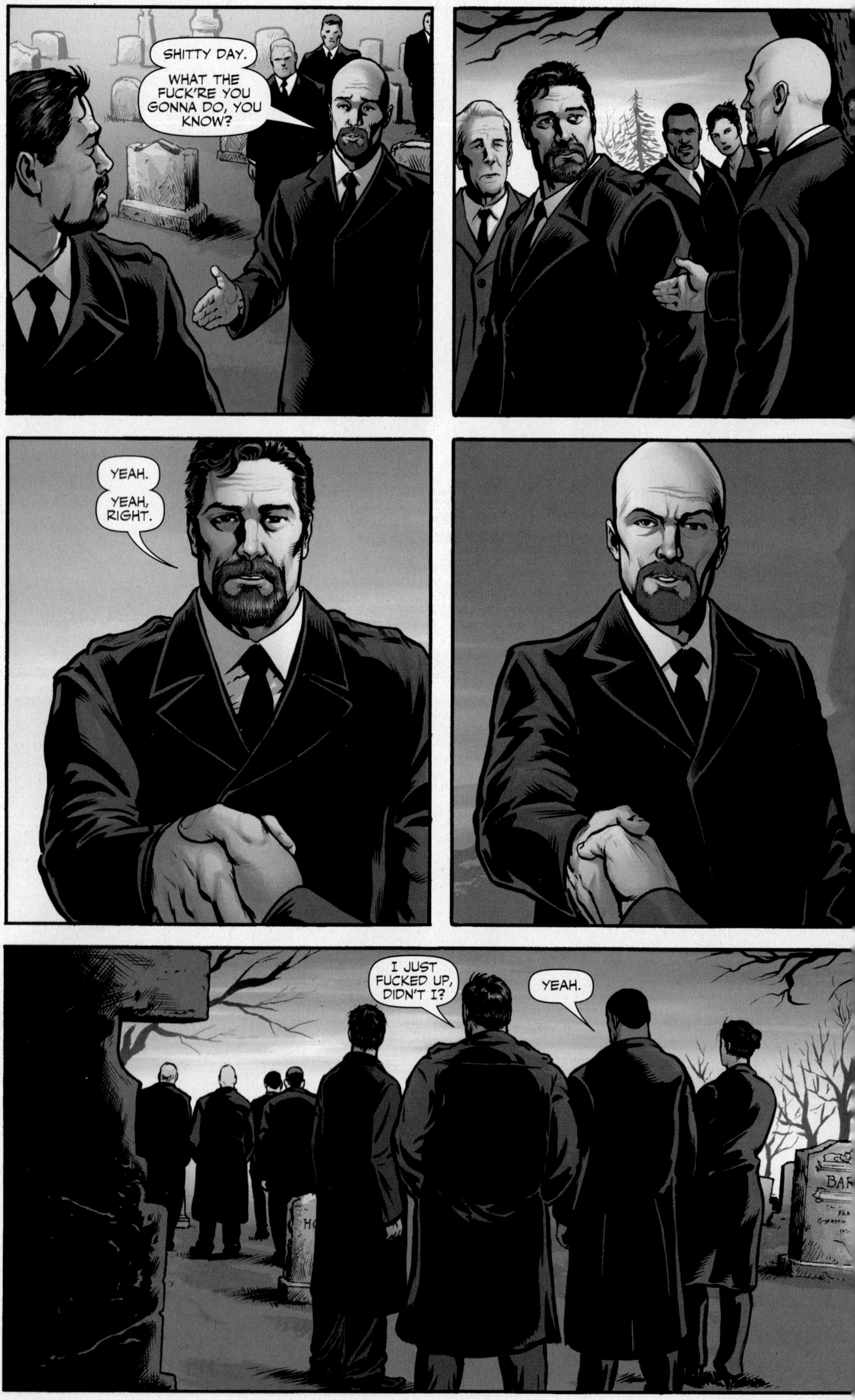
SHITTY DAY.
WHAT THE FUCK'RE YOU GONNA DO, YOU KNOW?
YEAH.
YEAH, RIGHT.
I JUST FUCKED UP, DIDN'T I?
YEAH.

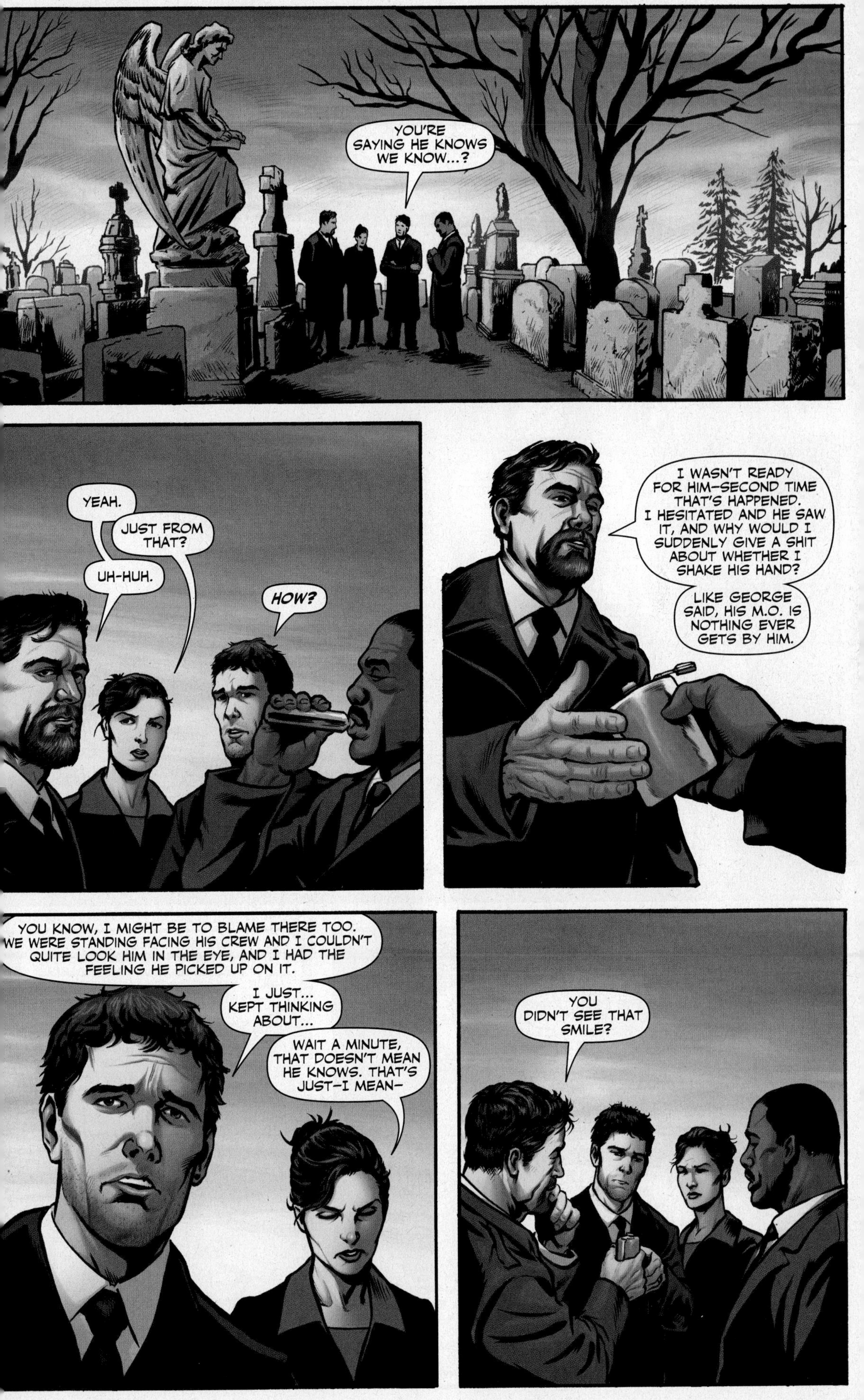
YOU'RE SAYING HE KNOWS WE KNOW...?
YEAH.
JUST FROM THAT?
UH-HUH.
HOW?
I WASN'T READY FOR HIM—SECOND TIME THAT'S HAPPENED. I HESITATED AND HE SAW IT, AND WHY WOULD I SUDDENLY GIVE A SHIT ABOUT WHETHER I SHAKE HIS HAND?
LIKE GEORGE SAID, HIS M.O. IS NOTHING EVER GETS BY HIM.
YOU KNOW, I MIGHT BE TO BLAME THERE TOO. WE WERE STANDING FACING HIS CREW AND I COULDN'T QUITE LOOK HIM IN THE EYE, AND I HAD THE FEELING HE PICKED UP ON IT.
I JUST... KEPT THINKING ABOUT...
WAIT A MINUTE, THAT DOESN'T MEAN HE KNOWS. THAT'S JUST—I MEAN—
YOU DIDN'T SEE THAT SMILE?

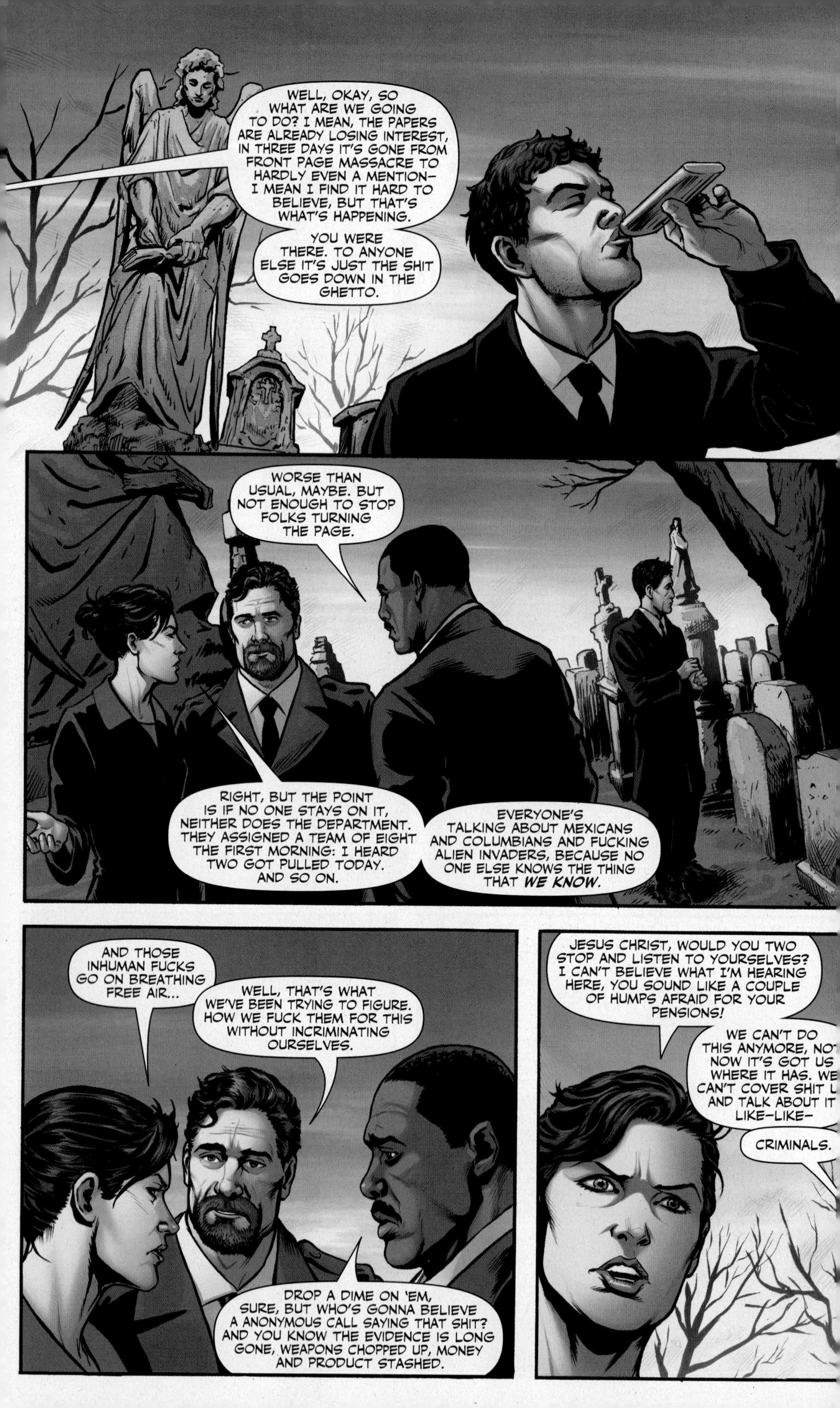
WELL, OKAY, SO WHAT ARE WE GOING TO DO? I MEAN, THE PAPERS ARE ALREADY LOSING INTEREST, IN THREE DAYS IT'S GONE FROM FRONT PAGE MASSACRE TO HARDLY EVEN A MENTION– I MEAN I FIND IT HARD TO BELIEVE, BUT THAT'S WHAT'S HAPPENING.
YOU WERE THERE. TO ANYONE ELSE IT'S JUST THE SHIT GOES DOWN IN THE GHETTO.
WORSE THAN USUAL, MAYBE. BUT NOT ENOUGH TO STOP FOLKS TURNING THE PAGE.
RIGHT, BUT THE POINT IS IF NO ONE STAYS ON IT, NEITHER DOES THE DEPARTMENT. THEY ASSIGNED A TEAM OF EIGHT THE FIRST MORNING: I HEARD TWO GOT PULLED TODAY. AND SO ON.
EVERYONE'S TALKING ABOUT MEXICANS AND COLUMBIANS AND FUCKING ALIEN INVADERS, BECAUSE NO ONE ELSE KNOWS THE THING THAT WE KNOW.
AND THOSE INHUMAN FUCKS GO ON BREATHING FREE AIR...
WELL, THAT'S WHAT WE'VE BEEN TRYING TO FIGURE. HOW WE FUCK THEM FOR THIS WITHOUT INCRIMINATING OURSELVES.
DROP A DIME ON 'EM, SURE, BUT WHO'S GONNA BELIEVE A ANONYMOUS CALL SAYING THAT SHIT? AND YOU KNOW THE EVIDENCE IS LONG GONE, WEAPONS CHOPPED UP, MONEY AND PRODUCT STASHED.
JESUS CHRIST, WOULD YOU TWO STOP AND LISTEN TO YOURSELVES? I CAN'T BELIEVE WHAT I'M HEARING HERE, YOU SOUND LIKE A COUPLE OF HUMPS AFRAID FOR YOUR PENSIONS!
WE CAN'T DO THIS ANYMORE, NOT NOW IT'S GOT US WHERE IT HAS. WE CAN'T COVER SHIT UP AND TALK ABOUT IT LIKE–LIKE–
CRIMINALS.

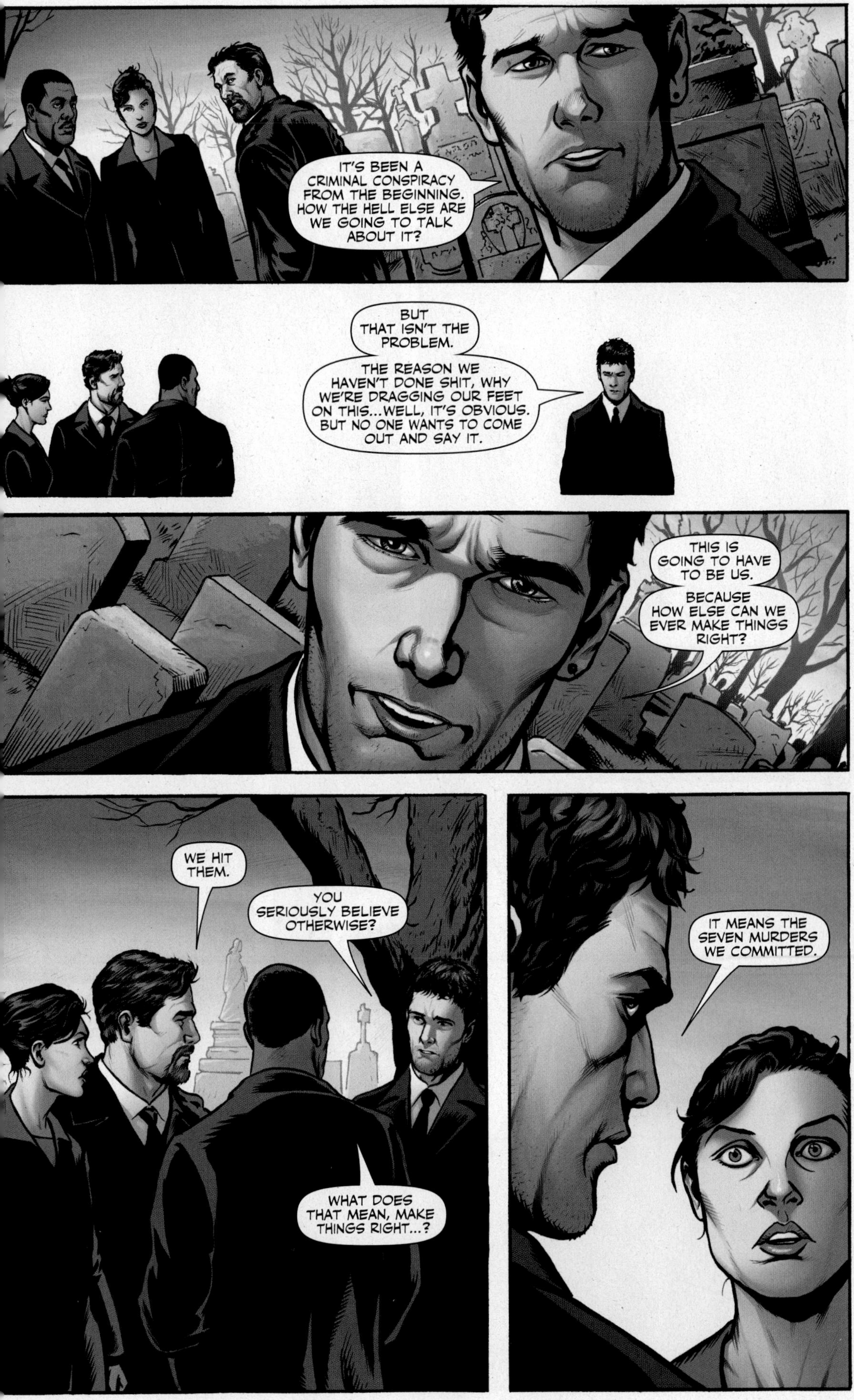
IT'S BEEN A CRIMINAL CONSPIRACY FROM THE BEGINNING. HOW THE HELL ELSE ARE WE GOING TO TALK ABOUT IT?
BUT THAT ISN'T THE PROBLEM.
THE REASON WE HAVEN'T DONE SHIT, WHY WE'RE DRAGGING OUR FEET ON THIS...WELL, IT'S OBVIOUS. BUT NO ONE WANTS TO COME OUT AND SAY IT.
THIS IS GOING TO HAVE TO BE US.
BECAUSE HOW ELSE CAN WE EVER MAKE THINGS RIGHT?
WHAT DOES THAT MEAN, MAKE THINGS RIGHT...?
WE HIT THEM.
YOU SERIOUSLY BELIEVE OTHERWISE?
IT MEANS THE SEVEN MURDERS WE COMMITTED.

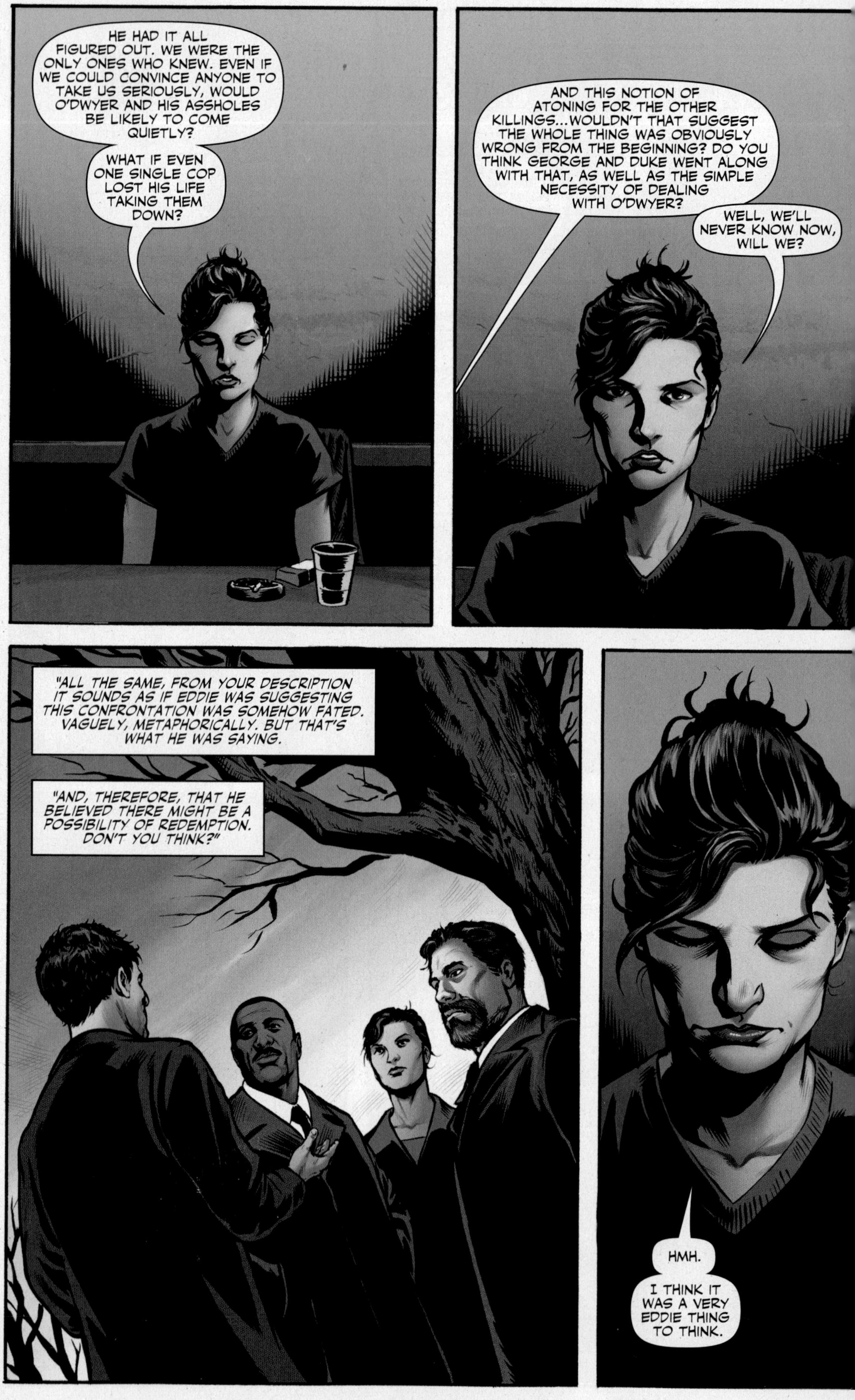
HE HAD IT ALL FIGURED OUT. WE WERE THE ONLY ONES WHO KNEW. EVEN IF WE COULD CONVINCE ANYONE TO TAKE US SERIOUSLY, WOULD O'DWYER AND HIS ASSHOLES BE LIKELY TO COME QUIETLY?
WHAT IF EVEN ONE SINGLE COP LOST HIS LIFE TAKING THEM DOWN?
AND THIS NOTION OF ATONING FOR THE OTHER KILLINGS...WOULDN'T THAT SUGGEST THE WHOLE THING WAS OBVIOUSLY WRONG FROM THE BEGINNING? DO YOU THINK GEORGE AND DUKE WENT ALONG WITH THAT, AS WELL AS THE SIMPLE NECESSITY OF DEALING WITH O'DWYER?
WELL, WE'LL NEVER KNOW NOW, WILL WE?
"ALL THE SAME, FROM YOUR DESCRIPTION IT SOUNDS AS IF EDDIE WAS SUGGESTING THIS CONFRONTATION WAS SOMEHOW FATED. VAGUELY, METAPHORICALLY. BUT THAT'S WHAT HE WAS SAYING.
"AND, THEREFORE, THAT HE BELIEVED THERE MIGHT BE A POSSIBILITY OF REDEMPTION. DON'T YOU THINK?"
HMH.
I THINK IT WAS A VERY EDDIE THING TO THINK.

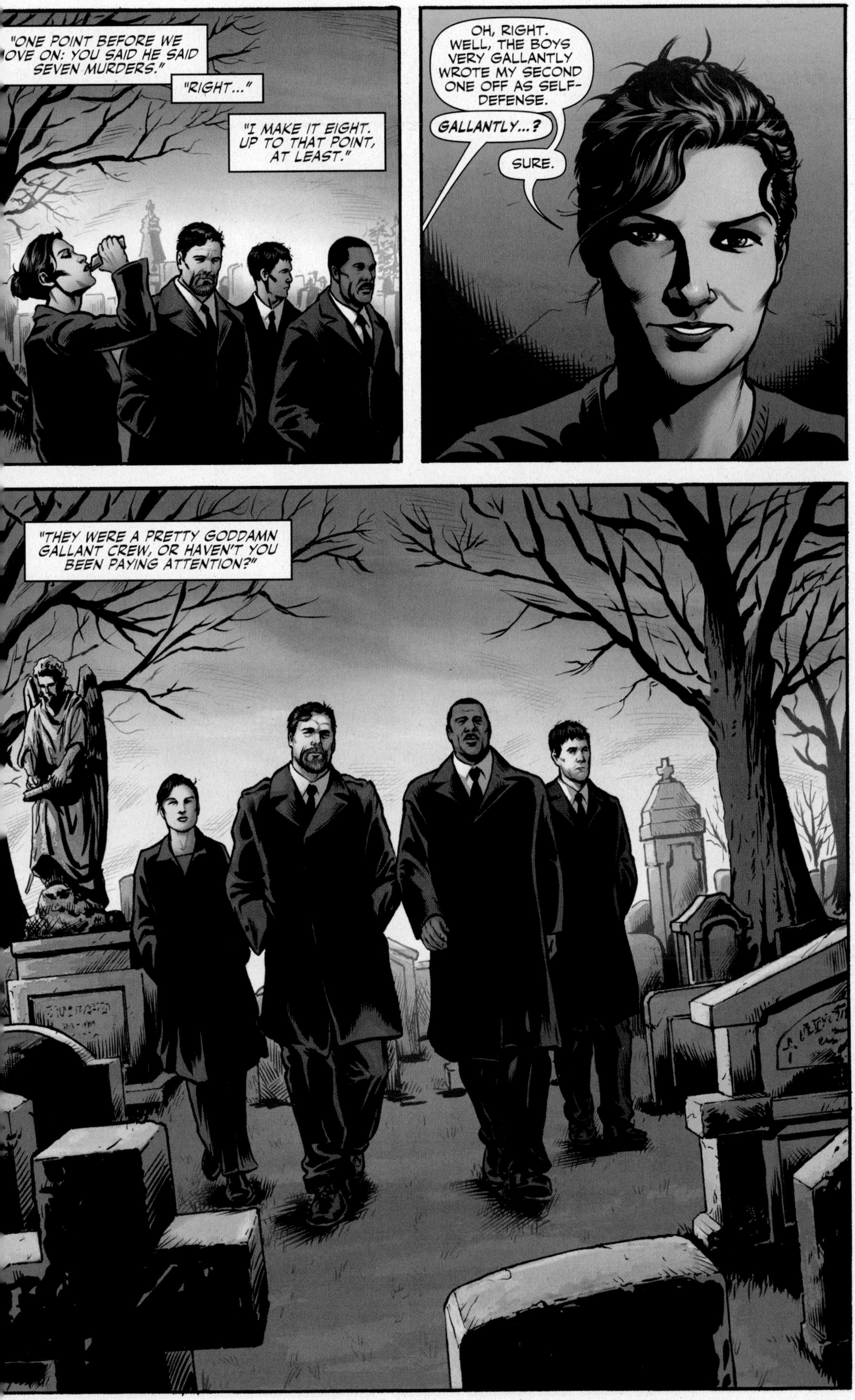
"ONE POINT BEFORE WE OVE ON: YOU SAID HE SAID SEVEN MURDERS."
"RIGHT..."
"I MAKE IT EIGHT. UP TO THAT POINT, AT LEAST."
OH, RIGHT. WELL, THE BOYS VERY GALLANTLY WROTE MY SECOND ONE OFF AS SELF-DEFENSE.
GALLANTLY...?
SURE.
"THEY WERE A PRETTY GODDAMN GALLANT CREW, OR HAVEN'T YOU BEEN PAYING ATTENTION?"

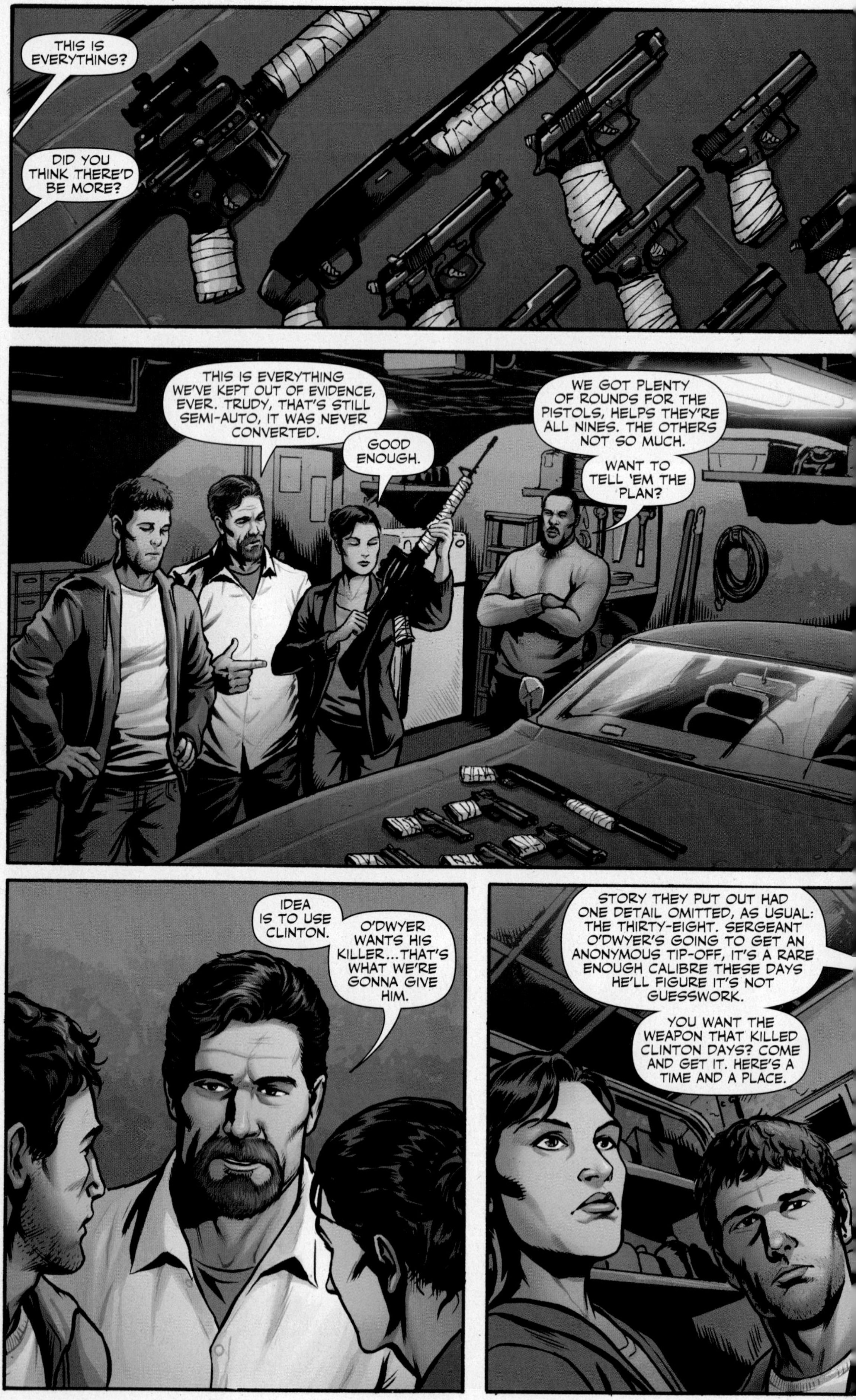
THIS IS EVERYTHING?
DID YOU THINK THERE'D BE MORE?
THIS IS EVERYTHING WE'VE KEPT OUT OF EVIDENCE, EVER. TRUDY, THAT'S STILL SEMI-AUTO, IT WAS NEVER CONVERTED.
GOOD ENOUGH.
WE GOT PLENTY OF ROUNDS FOR THE PISTOLS, HELPS THEY'RE ALL NINES. THE OTHERS NOT SO MUCH.
WANT TO TELL 'EM THE PLAN?
IDEA IS TO USE CLINTON.
O'DWYER WANTS HIS KILLER...THAT'S WHAT WE'RE GONNA GIVE HIM.
STORY THEY PUT OUT HAD ONE DETAIL OMITTED, AS USUAL: THE THIRTY-EIGHT. SERGEANT O'DWYER'S GOING TO GET AN ANONYMOUS TIP-OFF, IT'S A RARE ENOUGH CALIBRE THESE DAYS HE'LL FIGURE IT'S NOT GUESSWORK.
YOU WANT THE WEAPON THAT KILLED CLINTON DAYS? COME AND GET IT. HERE'S A TIME AND A PLACE.

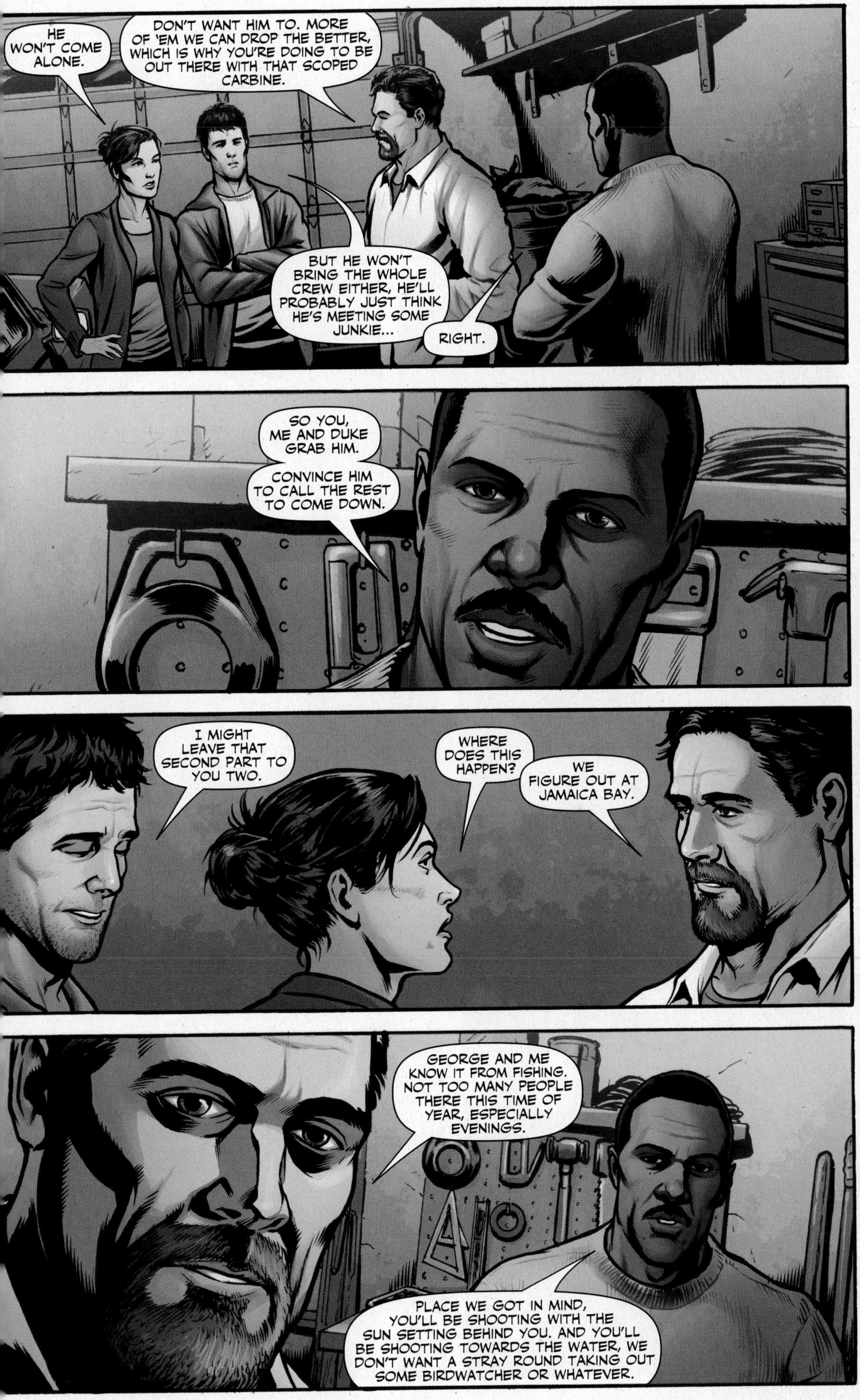
HE WON'T COME ALONE.
DON'T WANT HIM TO. MORE OF 'EM WE CAN DROP THE BETTER, WHICH IS WHY YOU'RE DOING TO BE OUT THERE WITH THAT SCOPED CARBINE.
BUT HE WON'T BRING THE WHOLE CREW EITHER, HE'LL PROBABLY JUST THINK HE'S MEETING SOME JUNKIE...
RIGHT.
SO YOU, ME AND DUKE GRAB HIM.
CONVINCE HIM TO CALL THE REST TO COME DOWN.
I MIGHT LEAVE THAT SECOND PART TO YOU TWO.
WHERE DOES THIS HAPPEN?
WE FIGURE OUT AT JAMAICA BAY.
GEORGE AND ME KNOW IT FROM FISHING. NOT TOO MANY PEOPLE THERE THIS TIME OF YEAR, ESPECIALLY EVENINGS.
PLACE WE GOT IN MIND, YOU'LL BE SHOOTING WITH THE SUN SETTING BEHIND YOU. AND YOU'LL BE SHOOTING TOWARDS THE WATER, WE DON'T WANT A STRAY ROUND TAKING OUT SOME BIRDWATCHER OR WHATEVER.

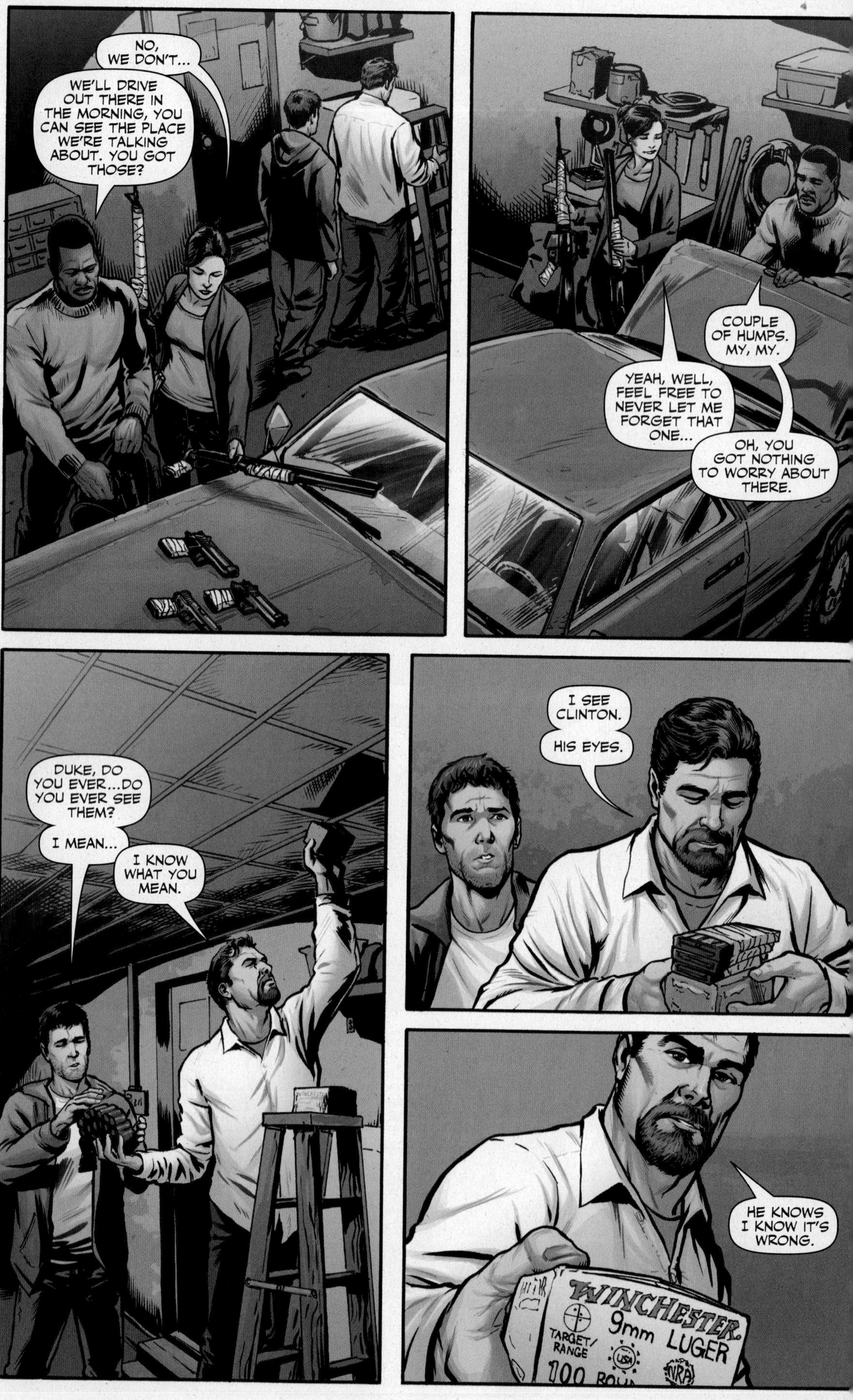
NO, WE DON'T...
WE'LL DRIVE OUT THERE IN THE MORNING, YOU CAN SEE THE PLACE WE'RE TALKING ABOUT. YOU GOT THOSE?
COUPLE OF HUMPS. MY, MY.
YEAH, WELL, FEEL FREE TO NEVER LET ME FORGET THAT ONE...
OH, YOU GOT NOTHING TO WORRY ABOUT THERE.
DUKE, DO YOU EVER...DO YOU EVER SEE THEM?
I MEAN...
I KNOW WHAT YOU MEAN.
I SEE CLINTON.
HIS EYES.
HE KNOWS I KNOW IT'S WRONG.
WINCHESTER
9mm LUGER
TARGET/ RANGE
USA
NRA

HOW WE DOING?
COPY.
COPY.
STILL FREEZING MY ASS OFF UP A FUCKING TREE.
GOT TO FIGURE THEY'LL SCOPE THE PLACE A WHILE BEFORE THEY SHOW. PROBABLY LOOKING AT US RIGHT NOW.
I CAN'T SEE YOU FROM HERE. THEY COME BY THE ROAD, THEY'LL HAVE NO ANGLE ON YOU.
THEY DON'T SHOW SOON, YOU WANT TO DO THIS IN THE DARK?
NOT CRAZY ABOUT IT. DEPENDS ON NUMBERS.
CAR.
JUST THE ONE. AT LEAST TWO OCCUPANTS.
CONFIRM?

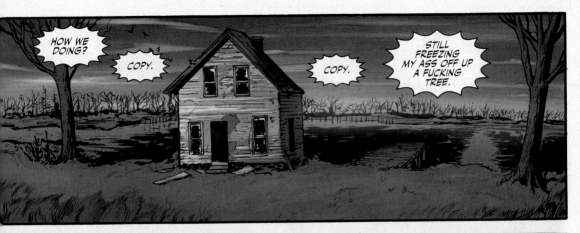

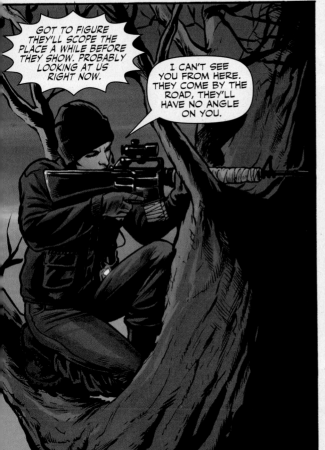

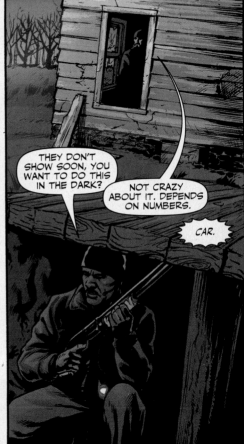

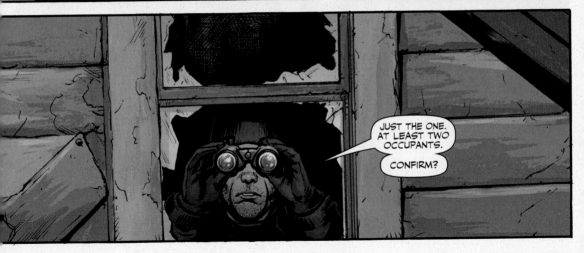

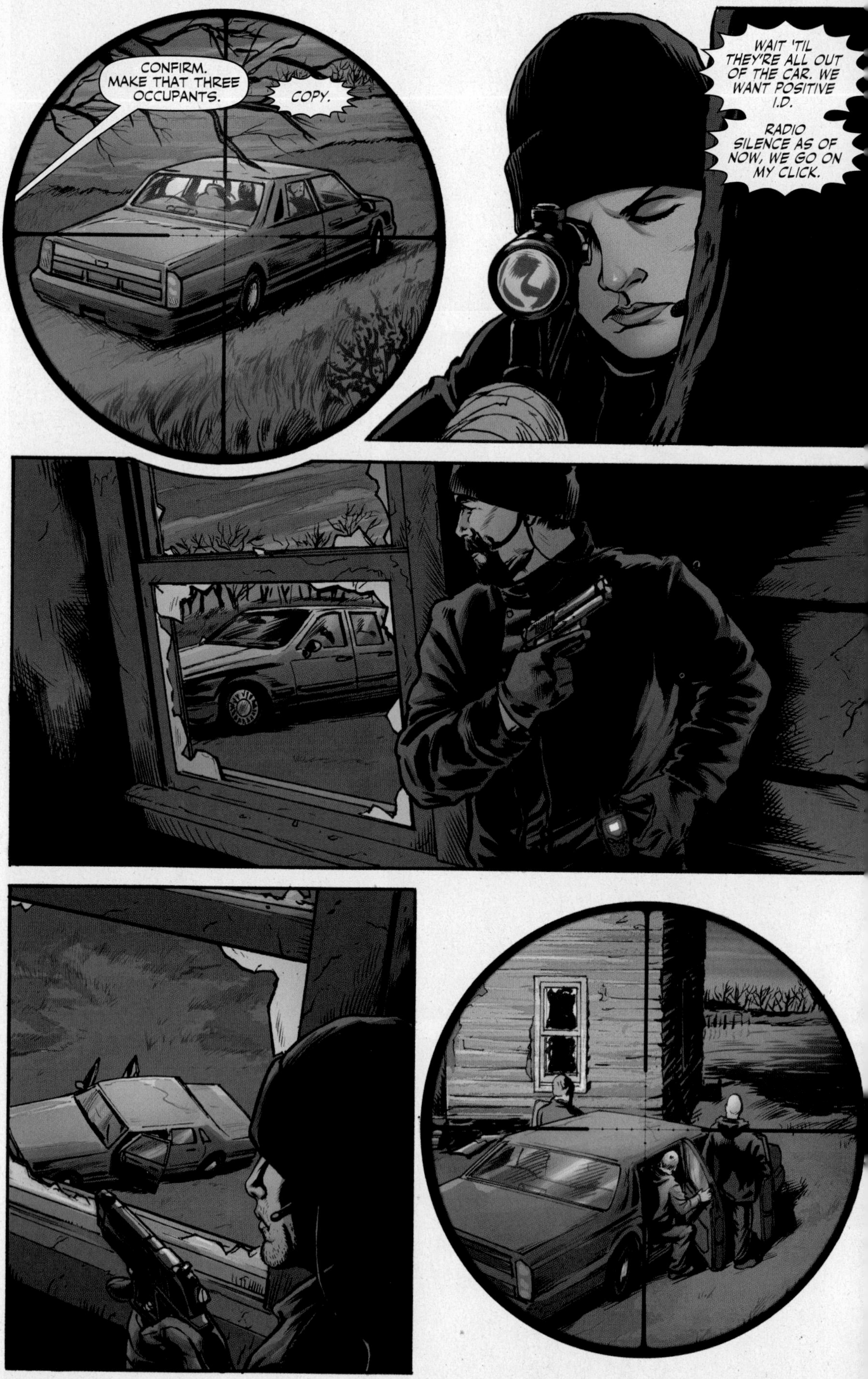
CONFIRM. MAKE THAT THREE OCCUPANTS.
COPY.
WAIT 'TIL THEY'RE ALL OUT OF THE CAR. WE WANT POSITIVE I.D.
RADIO SILENCE AS OF NOW, WE GO ON MY CLICK.

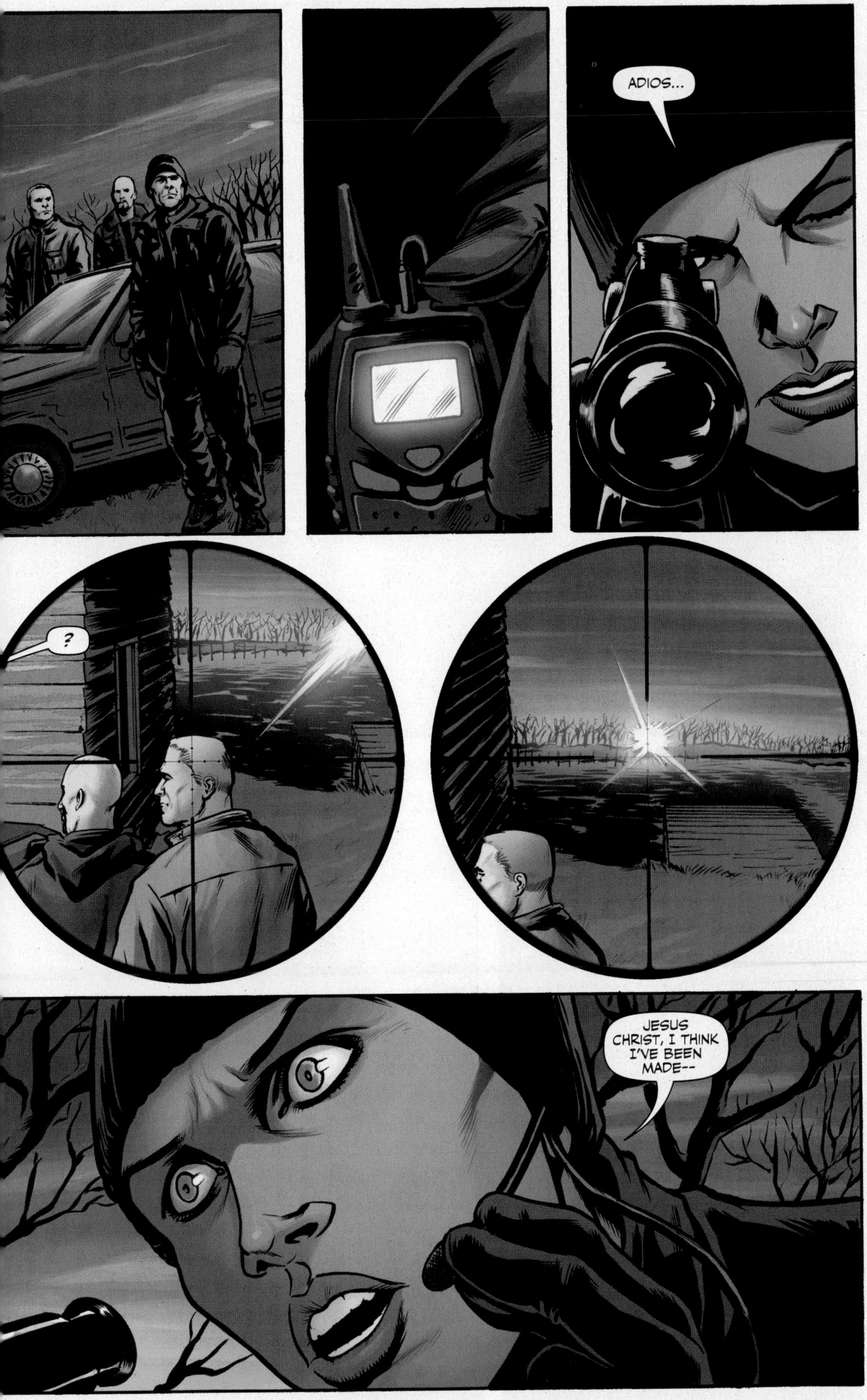
ADIOS...
?
JESUS CHRIST, I THINK I'VE BEEN MADE--

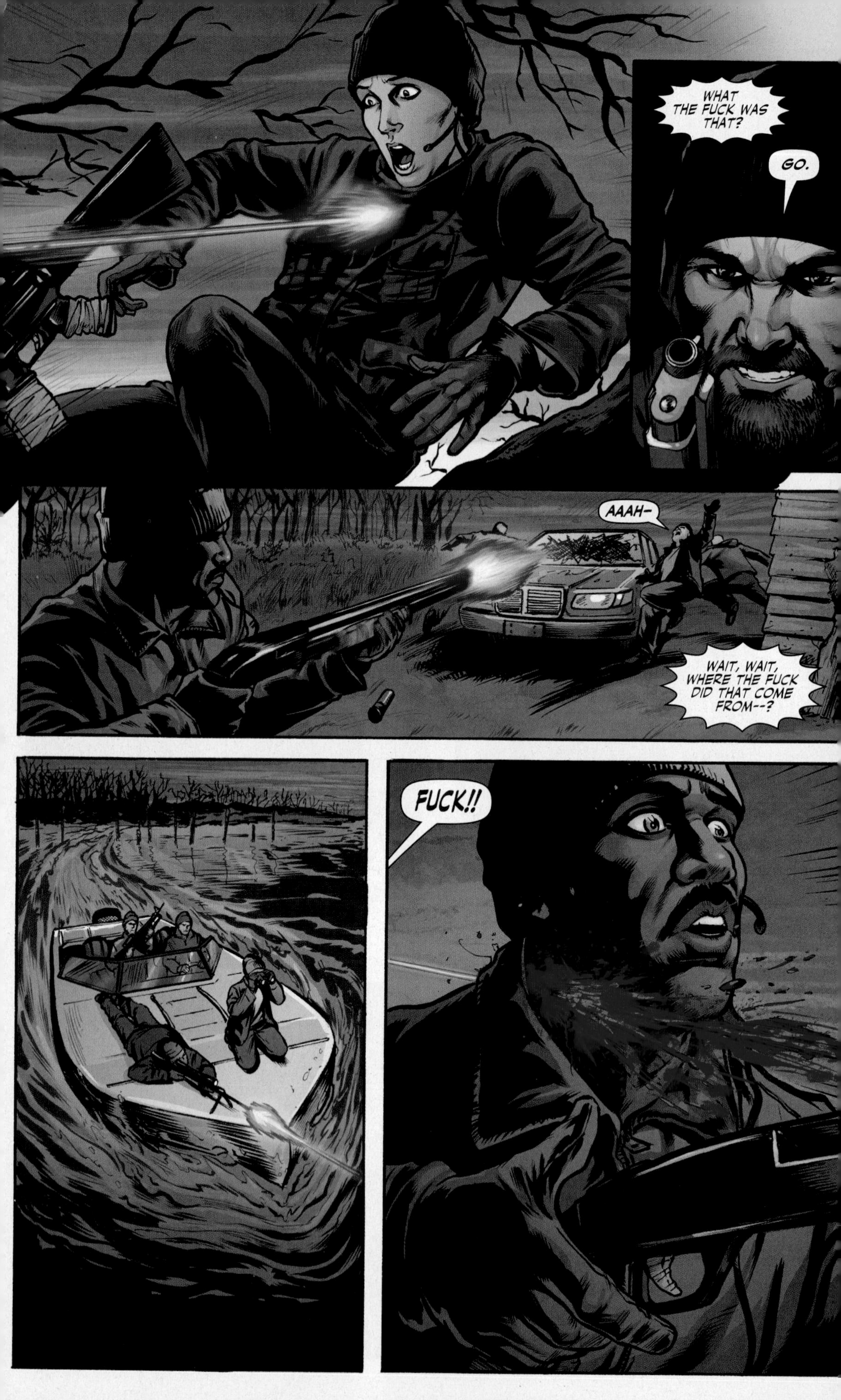
WHAT THE FUCK WAS THAT?
GO.
AAAH-
WAIT, WAIT, WHERE THE FUCK DID THAT COME FROM--?
FUCK!!

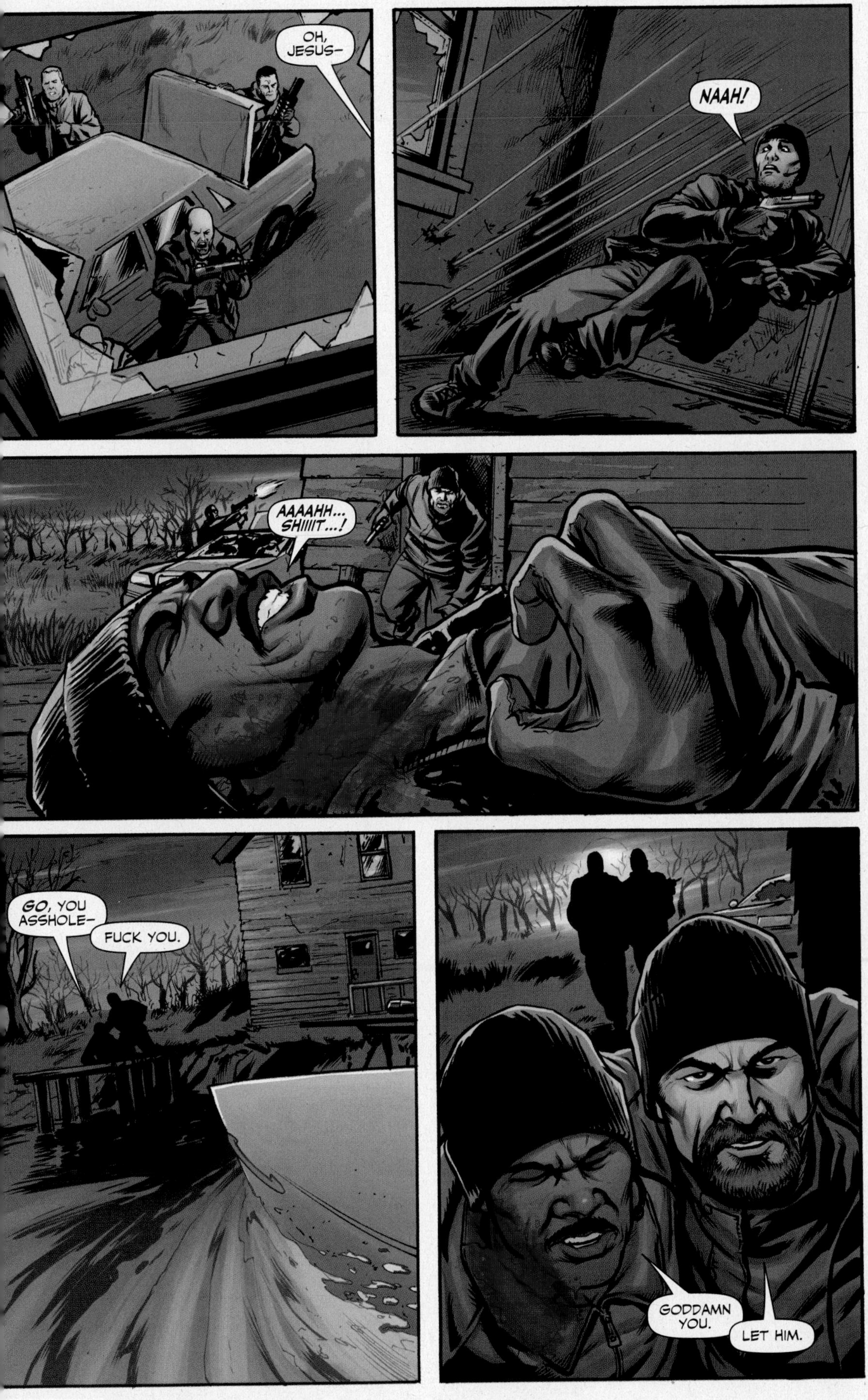
OH, JESUS-
NAAH!
AAAAHH... SHIIIIT...!
GO, YOU ASSHOLE-
FUCK YOU.
GODDAMN YOU.
LET HIM.

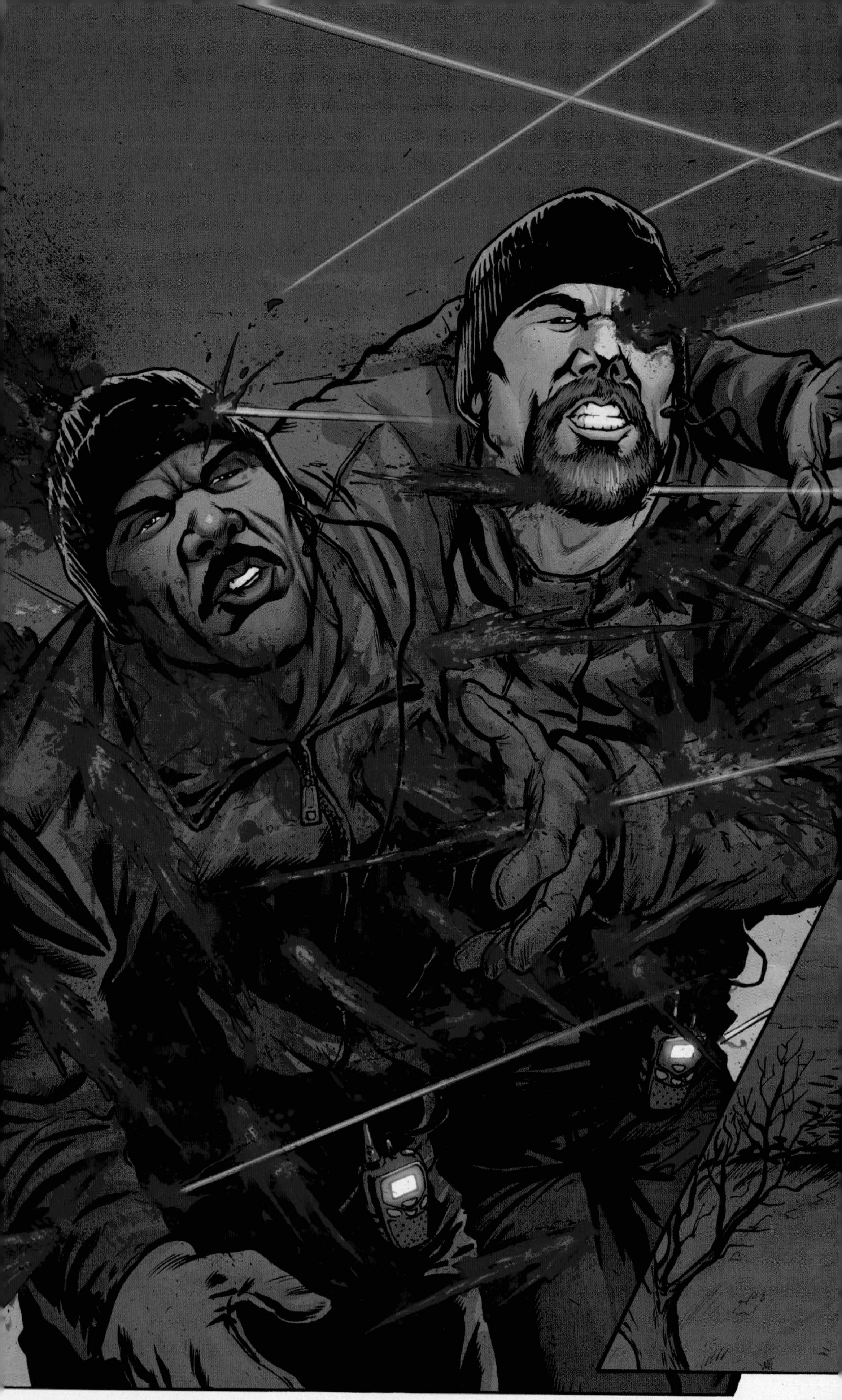

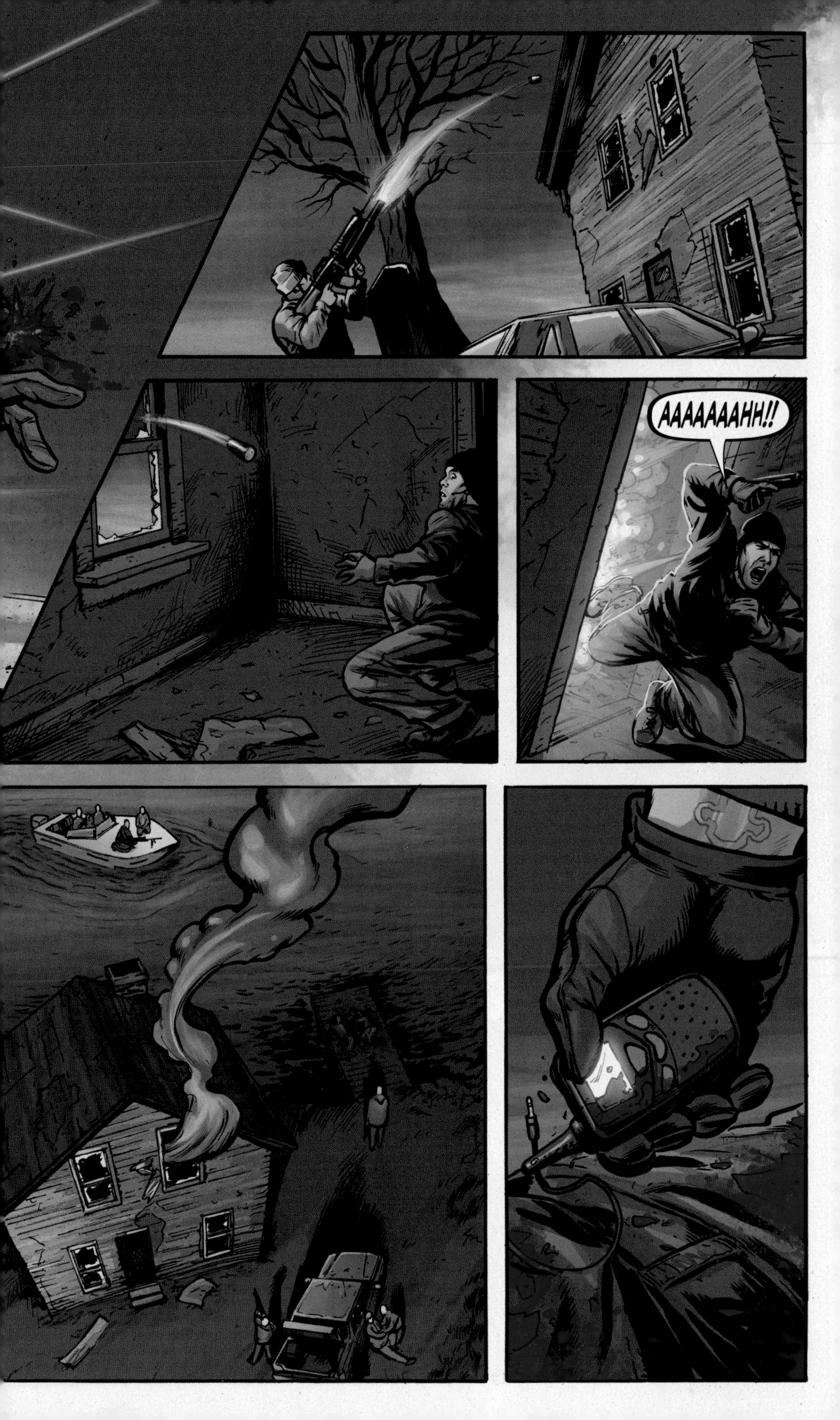
AAAAAAAHH!!

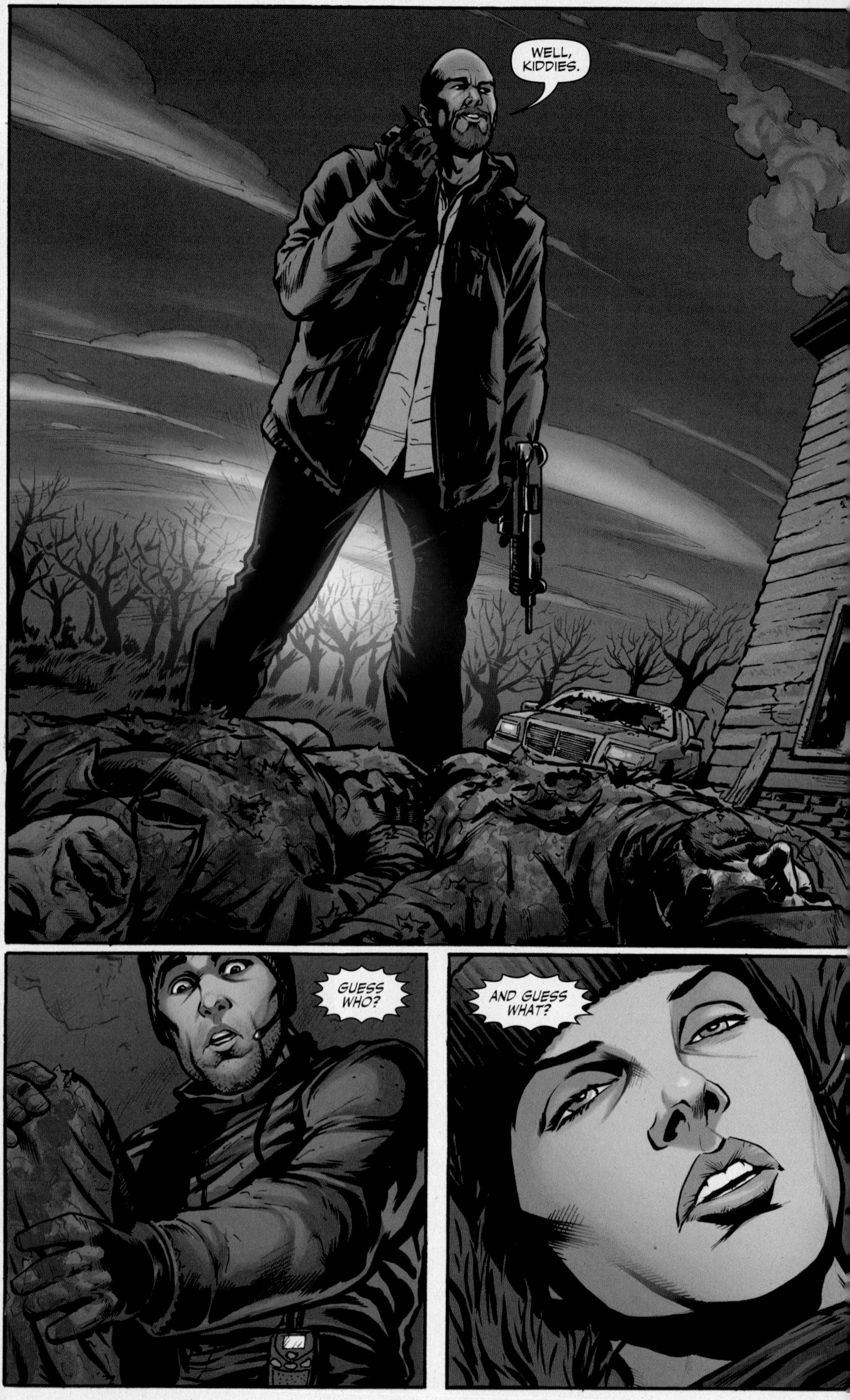
WELL, KIDDIES.
GUESS WHO?
AND GUESS WHAT?

ISSUE SEVEN

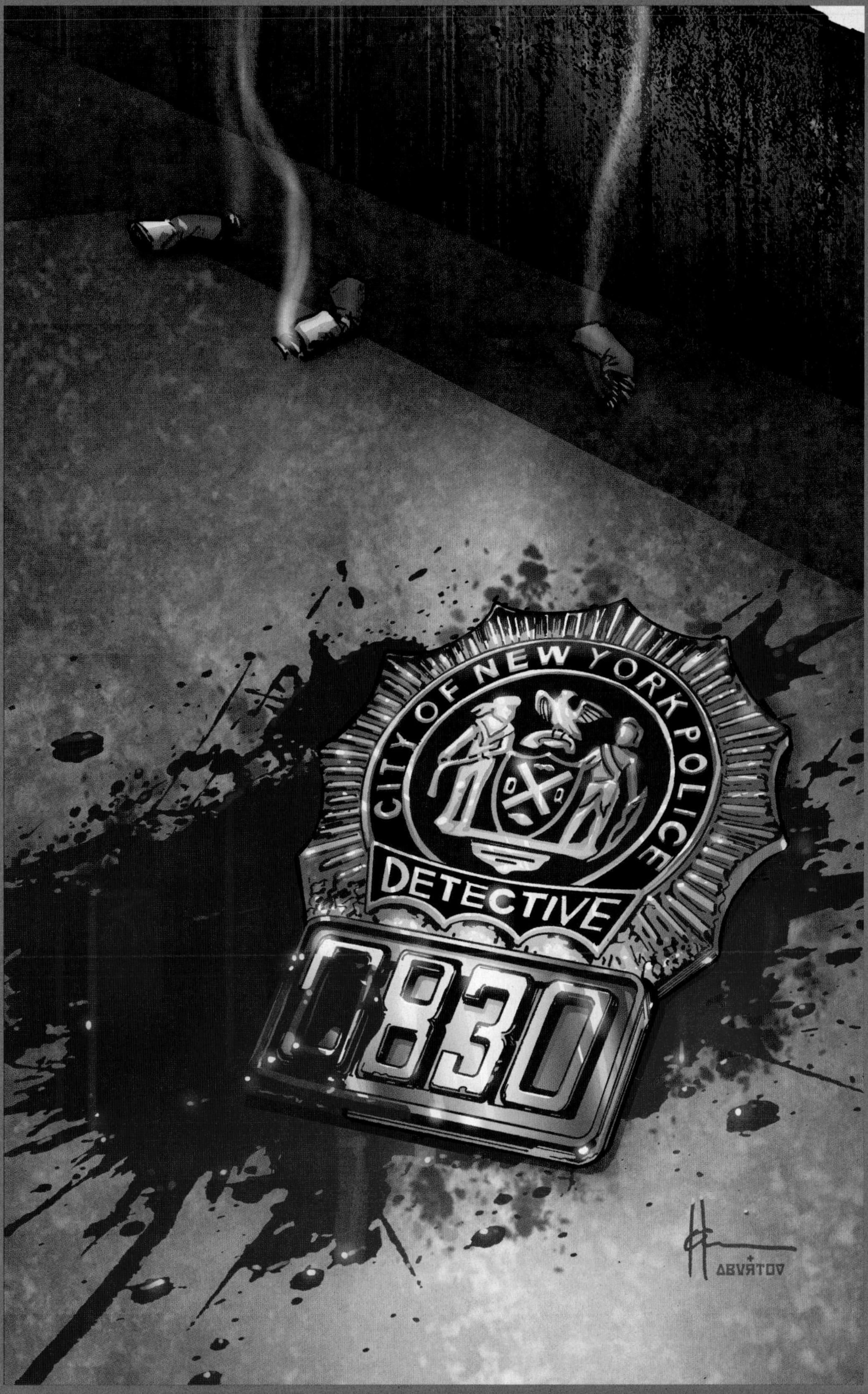

CITY OF NEW YORK POLICE
DETECTIVE
0830

Issue #7 cover art by **HOWARD CHAYKIN** colors by **JESUS ABURTO**

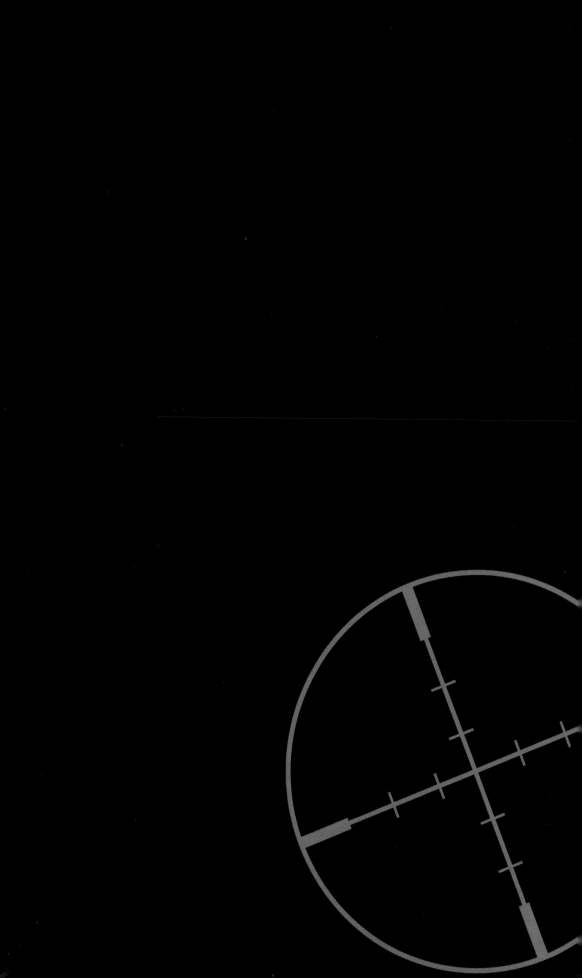

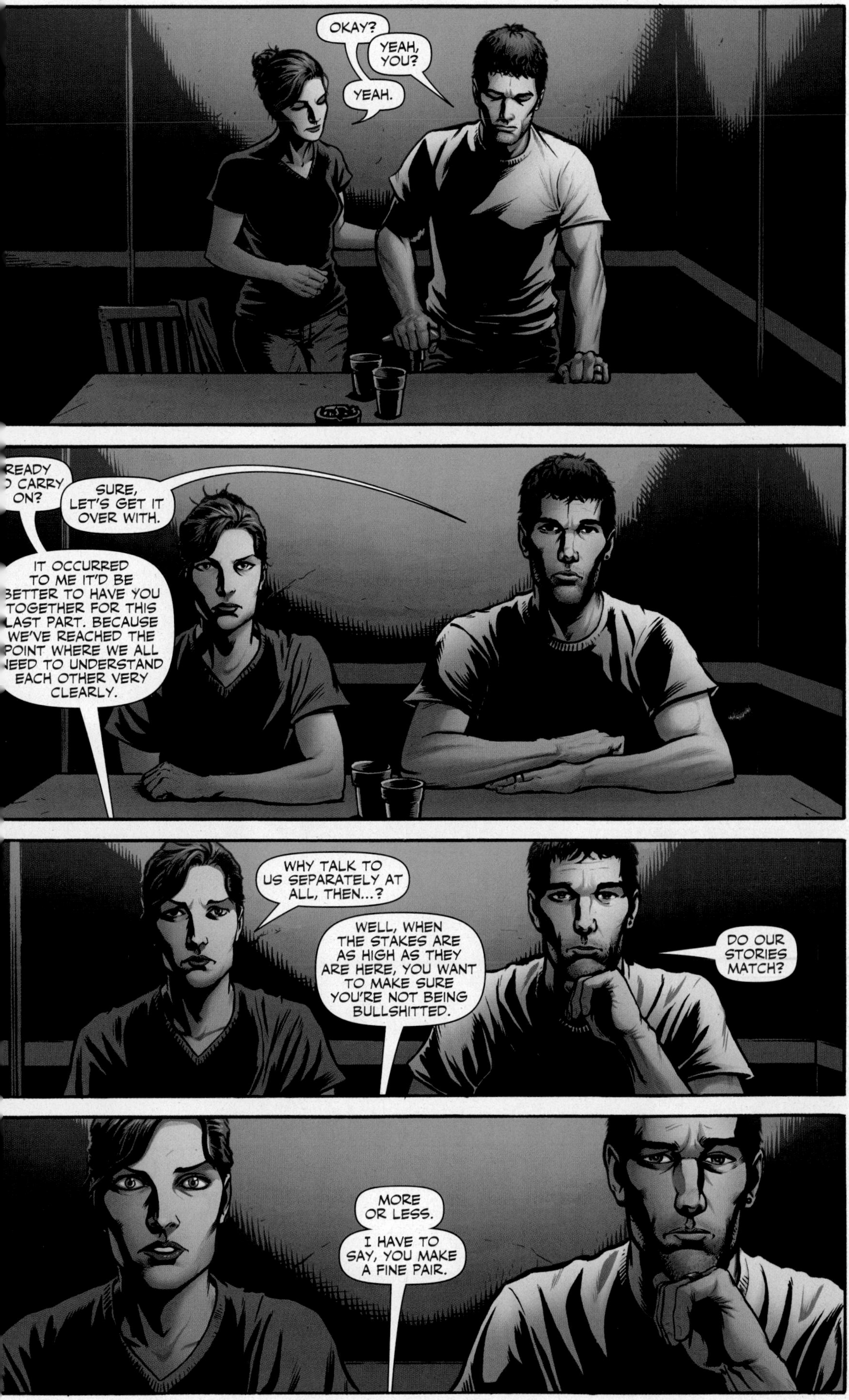

OKAY?
YEAH, YOU?
YEAH.
READY TO CARRY ON?
SURE, LET'S GET IT OVER WITH.
IT OCCURRED TO ME IT'D BE BETTER TO HAVE YOU TOGETHER FOR THIS LAST PART. BECAUSE WE'VE REACHED THE POINT WHERE WE ALL NEED TO UNDERSTAND EACH OTHER VERY CLEARLY.
WHY TALK TO US SEPARATELY AT ALL, THEN...?
WELL, WHEN THE STAKES ARE AS HIGH AS THEY ARE HERE, YOU WANT TO MAKE SURE YOU'RE NOT BEING BULLSHITTED.
DO OUR STORIES MATCH?
MORE OR LESS.
I HAVE TO SAY, YOU MAKE A FINE PAIR.

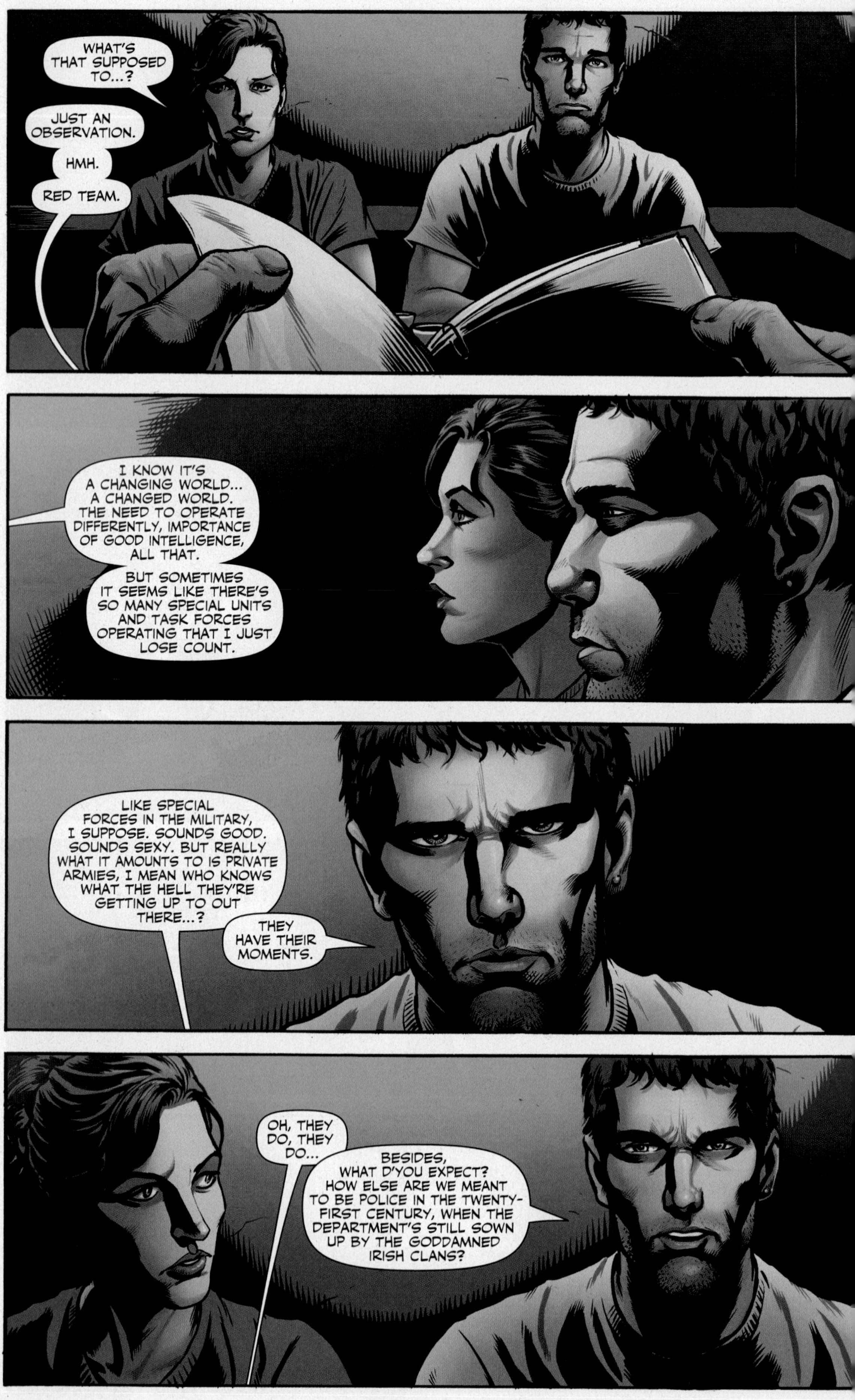
WHAT'S THAT SUPPOSED TO...?
JUST AN OBSERVATION.
HMH.
RED TEAM.
I KNOW IT'S A CHANGING WORLD... A CHANGED WORLD. THE NEED TO OPERATE DIFFERENTLY, IMPORTANCE OF GOOD INTELLIGENCE, ALL THAT.
BUT SOMETIMES IT SEEMS LIKE THERE'S SO MANY SPECIAL UNITS AND TASK FORCES OPERATING THAT I JUST LOSE COUNT.
LIKE SPECIAL FORCES IN THE MILITARY, I SUPPOSE. SOUNDS GOOD. SOUNDS SEXY. BUT REALLY WHAT IT AMOUNTS TO IS PRIVATE ARMIES, I MEAN WHO KNOWS WHAT THE HELL THEY'RE GETTING UP TO OUT THERE...?
THEY HAVE THEIR MOMENTS.
OH, THEY DO, THEY DO...
BESIDES, WHAT D'YOU EXPECT? HOW ELSE ARE WE MEANT TO BE POLICE IN THE TWENTY-FIRST CENTURY, WHEN THE DEPARTMENT'S STILL SOWN UP BY THE GODDAMNED IRISH CLANS?

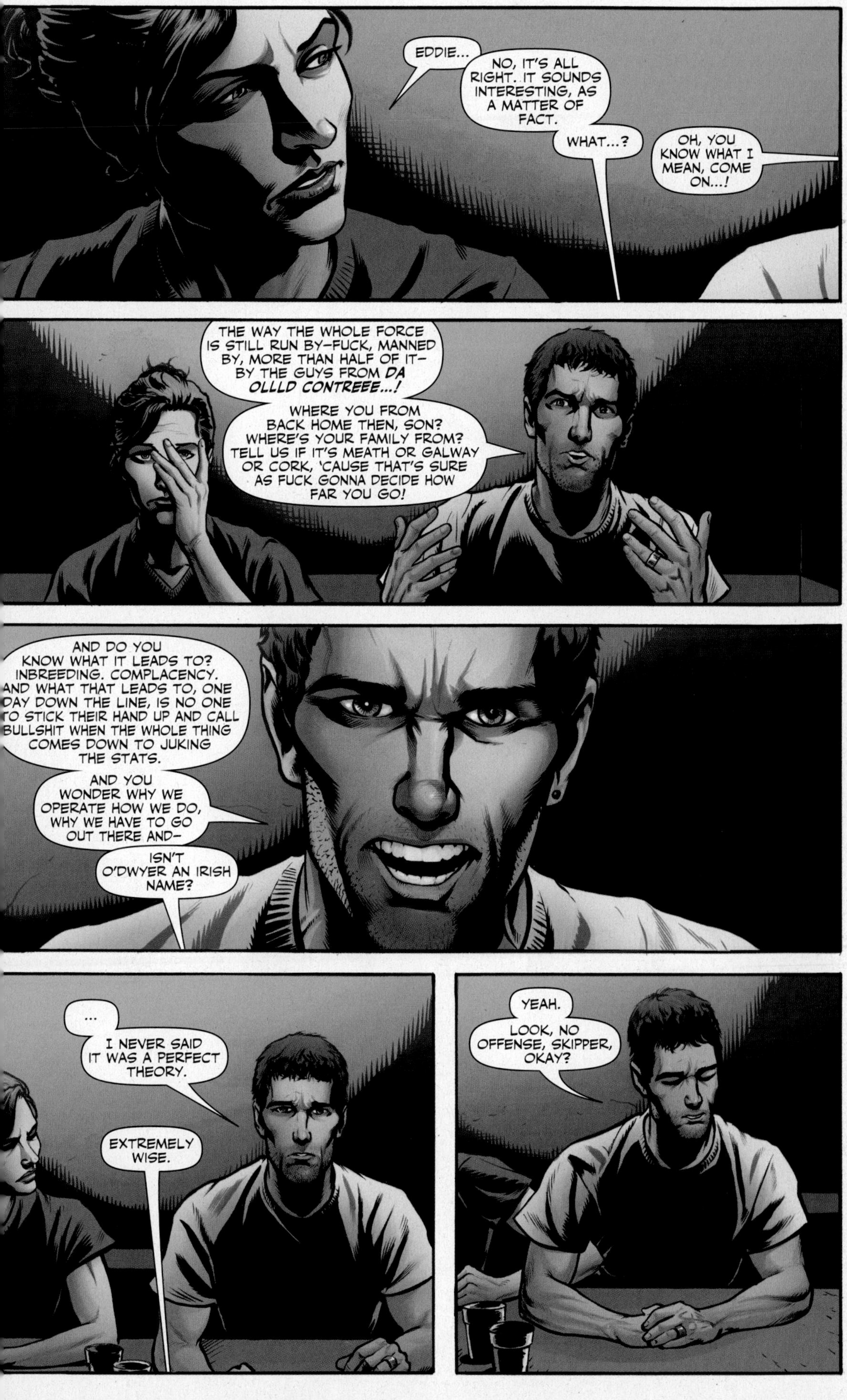
EDDIE...
NO, IT'S ALL RIGHT. IT SOUNDS INTERESTING, AS A MATTER OF FACT.
WHAT...?
OH, YOU KNOW WHAT I MEAN, COME ON...!
THE WAY THE WHOLE FORCE IS STILL RUN BY—FUCK, MANNED BY, MORE THAN HALF OF IT—BY THE GUYS FROM *DA OLLLD CONTREEE...!*
WHERE YOU FROM BACK HOME THEN, SON? WHERE'S YOUR FAMILY FROM? TELL US IF IT'S MEATH OR GALWAY OR CORK, 'CAUSE THAT'S SURE AS FUCK GONNA DECIDE HOW FAR YOU GO!
AND DO YOU KNOW WHAT IT LEADS TO? INBREEDING. COMPLACENCY. AND WHAT THAT LEADS TO, ONE DAY DOWN THE LINE, IS NO ONE TO STICK THEIR HAND UP AND CALL BULLSHIT WHEN THE WHOLE THING COMES DOWN TO JUKING THE STATS.
AND YOU WONDER WHY WE OPERATE HOW WE DO, WHY WE HAVE TO GO OUT THERE AND—
ISN'T O'DWYER AN IRISH NAME?
...
I NEVER SAID IT WAS A PERFECT THEORY.
EXTREMELY WISE.
YEAH.
LOOK, NO OFFENSE, SKIPPER, OKAY?

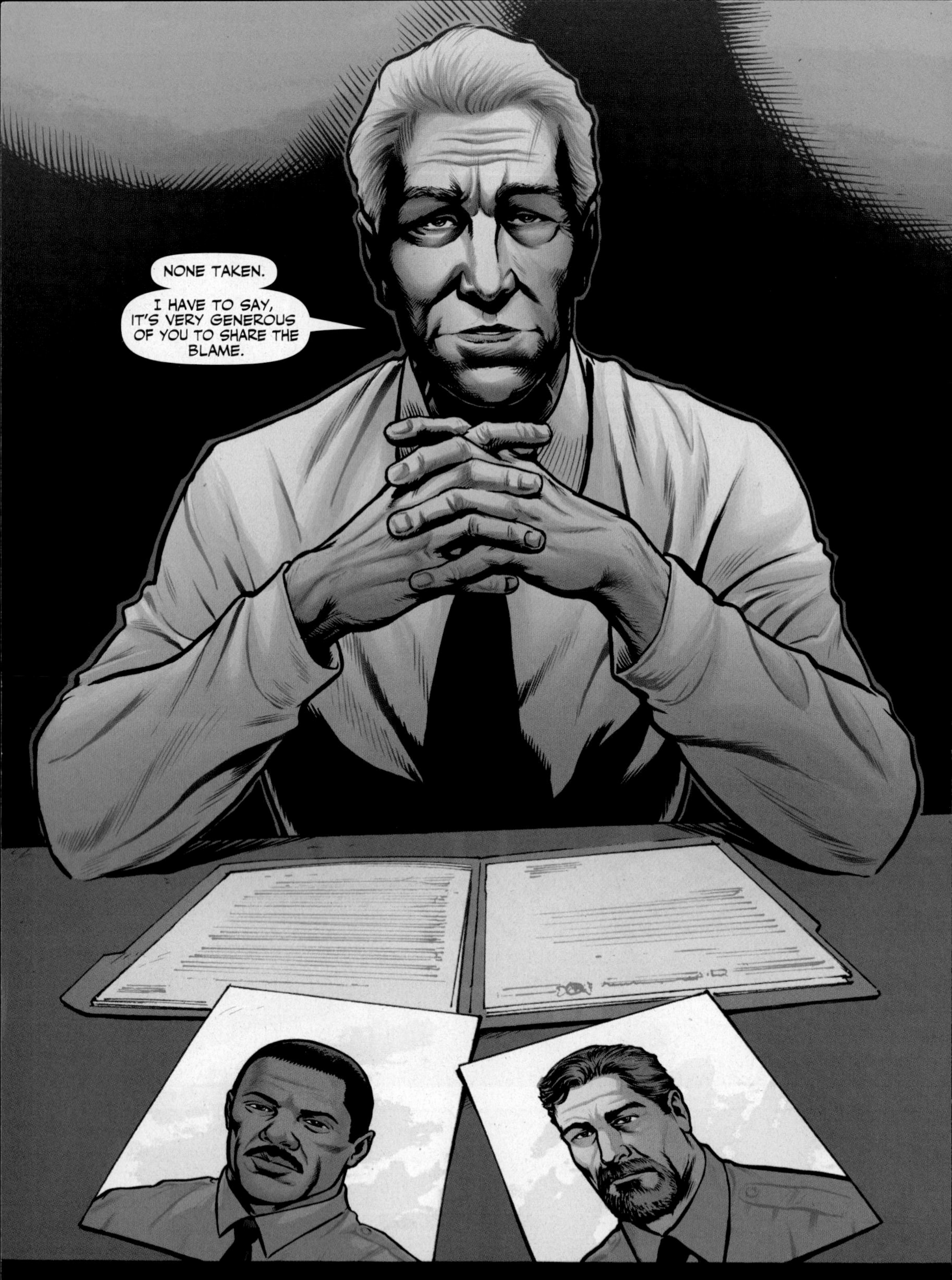
NONE TAKEN.
I HAVE TO SAY, IT'S VERY GENEROUS OF YOU TO SHARE THE BLAME.

7: THE RULES (REPRISE)

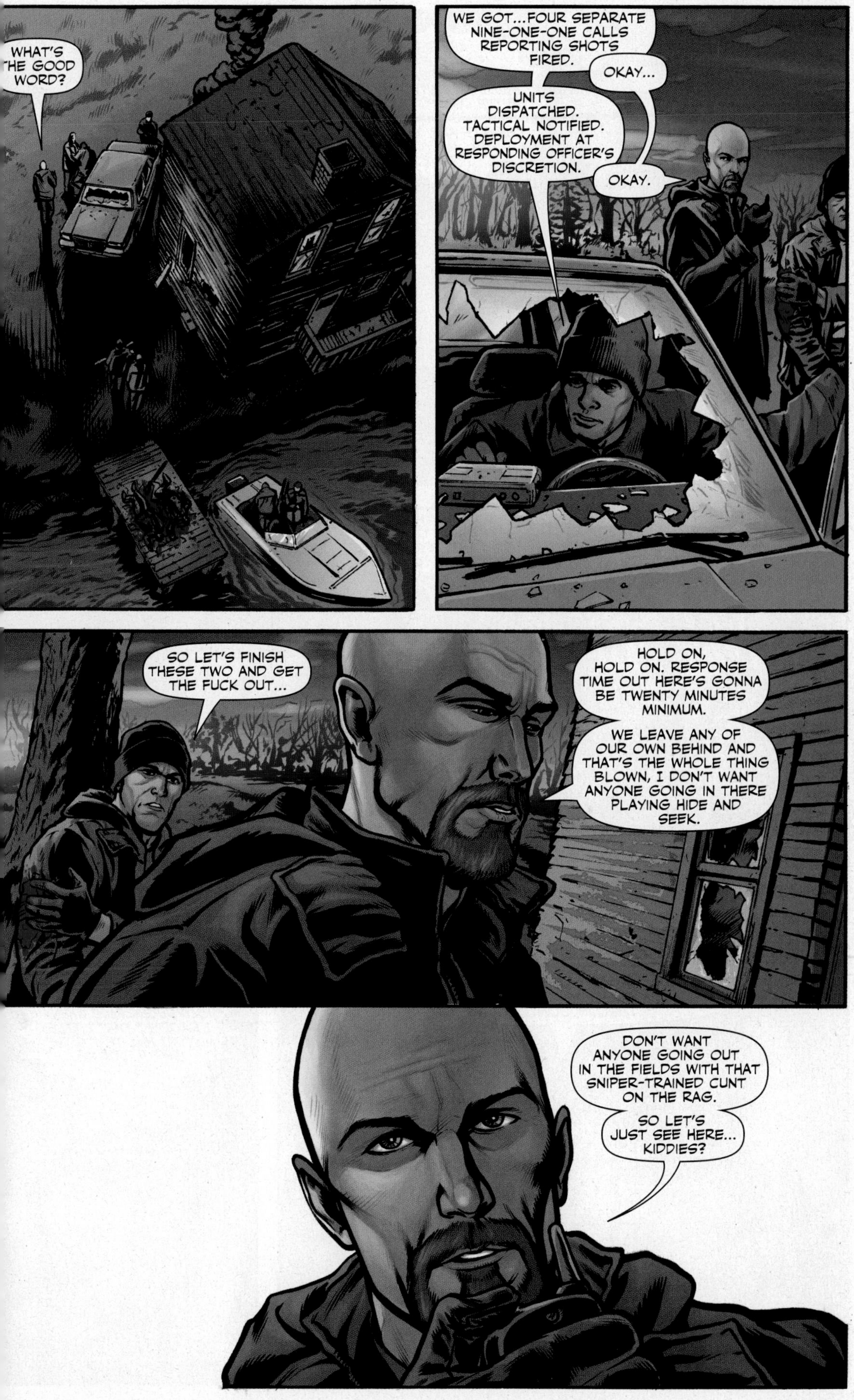
WHAT'S THE GOOD WORD?
WE GOT...FOUR SEPARATE NINE-ONE-ONE CALLS REPORTING SHOTS FIRED.
OKAY...
UNITS DISPATCHED. TACTICAL NOTIFIED. DEPLOYMENT AT RESPONDING OFFICER'S DISCRETION.
OKAY.
SO LET'S FINISH THESE TWO AND GET THE FUCK OUT...
HOLD ON, HOLD ON. RESPONSE TIME OUT HERE'S GONNA BE TWENTY MINUTES MINIMUM.
WE LEAVE ANY OF OUR OWN BEHIND AND THAT'S THE WHOLE THING BLOWN, I DON'T WANT ANYONE GOING IN THERE PLAYING HIDE AND SEEK.
DON'T WANT ANYONE GOING OUT IN THE FIELDS WITH THAT SNIPER-TRAINED CUNT ON THE RAG.
SO LET'S JUST SEE HERE... KIDDIES?

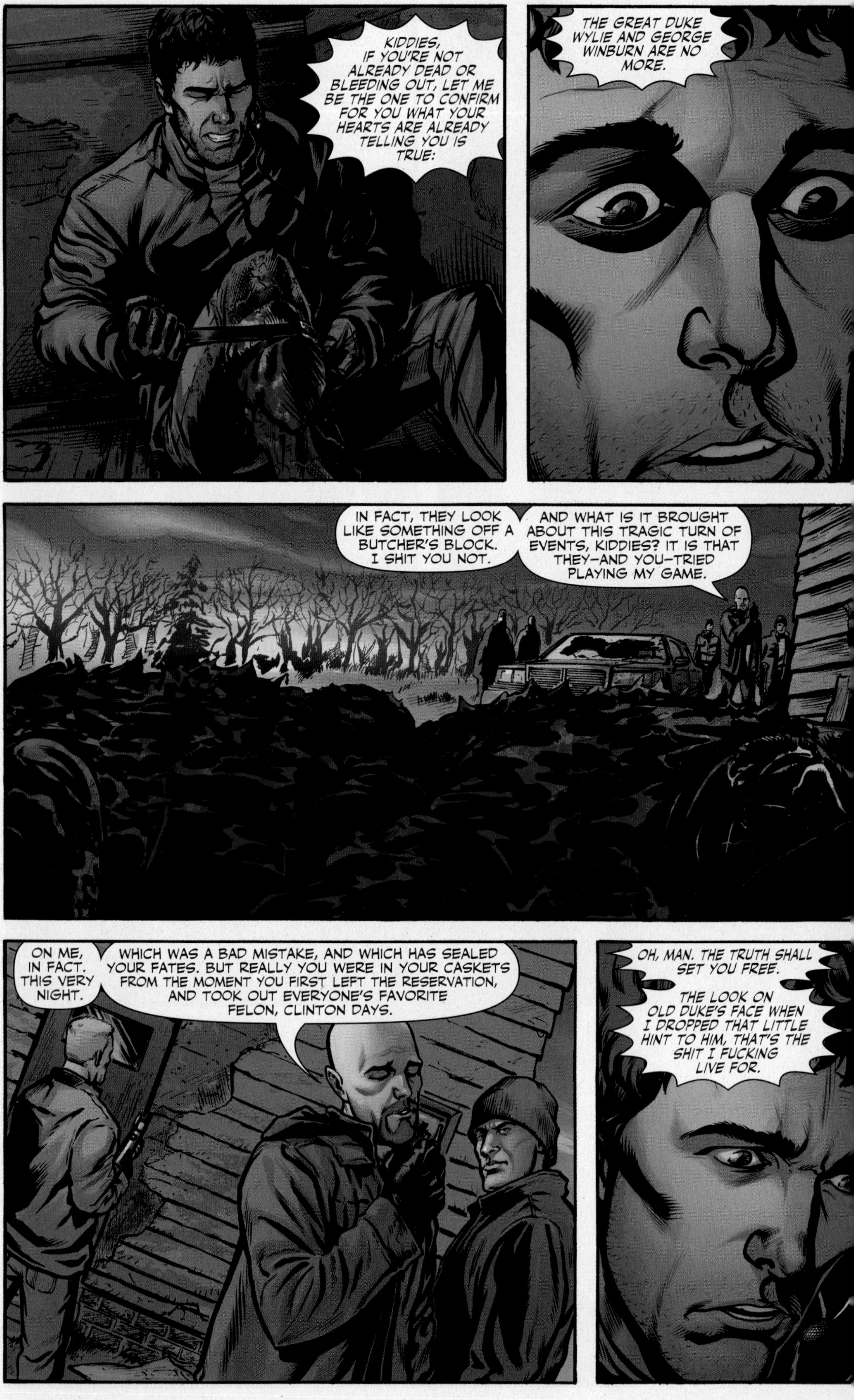
KIDDIES, IF YOU'RE NOT ALREADY DEAD OR BLEEDING OUT, LET ME BE THE ONE TO CONFIRM FOR YOU WHAT YOUR HEARTS ARE ALREADY TELLING YOU IS TRUE:
THE GREAT DUKE WYLIE AND GEORGE WINBURN ARE NO MORE.
IN FACT, THEY LOOK LIKE SOMETHING OFF A BUTCHER'S BLOCK. I SHIT YOU NOT.
AND WHAT IS IT BROUGHT ABOUT THIS TRAGIC TURN OF EVENTS, KIDDIES? IT IS THAT THEY—AND YOU—TRIED PLAYING MY GAME.
ON ME, IN FACT. THIS VERY NIGHT.
WHICH WAS A BAD MISTAKE, AND WHICH HAS SEALED YOUR FATES. BUT REALLY YOU WERE IN YOUR CASKETS FROM THE MOMENT YOU FIRST LEFT THE RESERVATION, AND TOOK OUT EVERYONE'S FAVORITE FELON, CLINTON DAYS.
OH, MAN. THE TRUTH SHALL SET YOU FREE.
THE LOOK ON OLD DUKE'S FACE WHEN I DROPPED THAT LITTLE HINT TO HIM, THAT'S THE SHIT I FUCKING LIVE FOR.

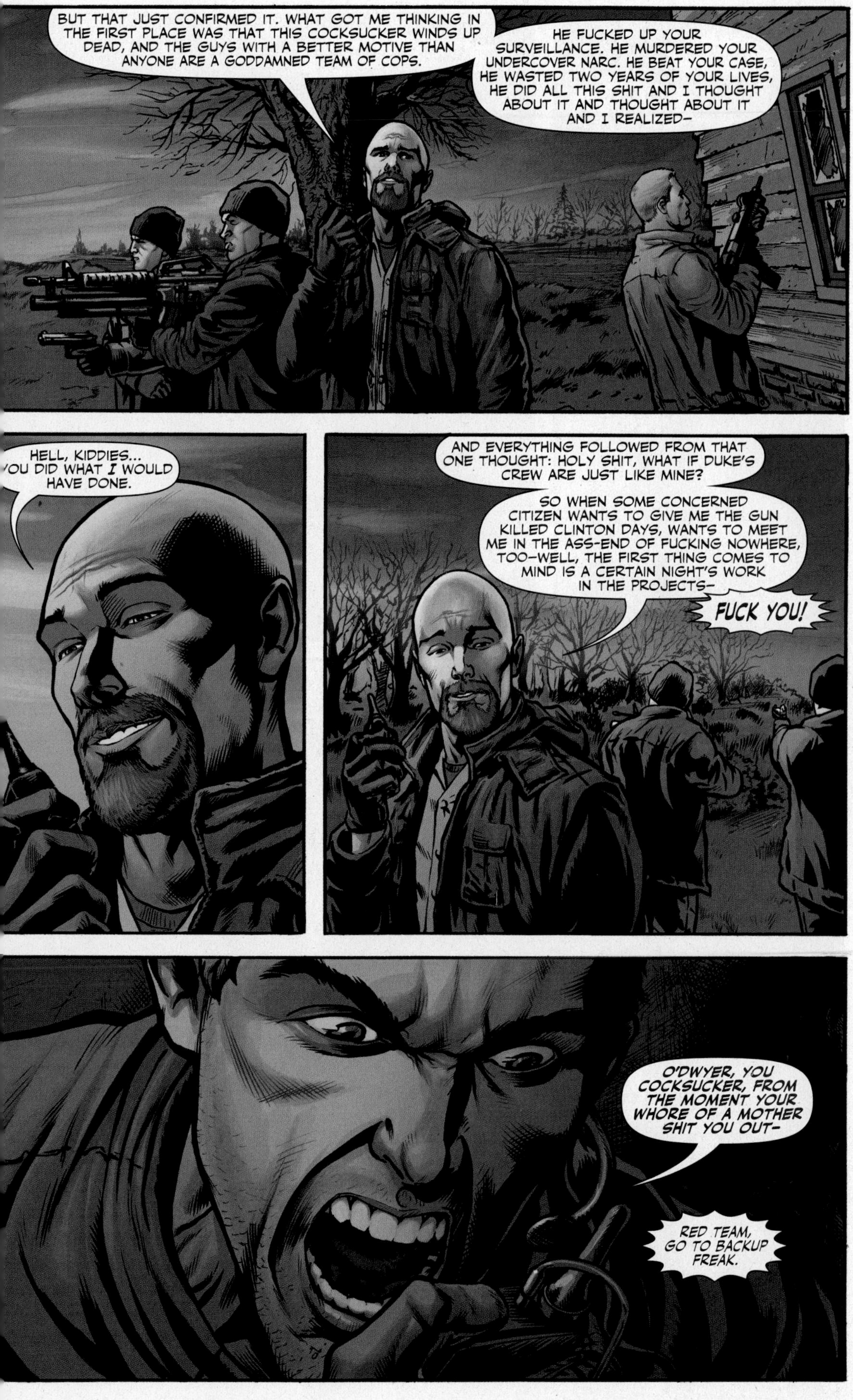

BUT THAT JUST CONFIRMED IT. WHAT GOT ME THINKING IN THE FIRST PLACE WAS THAT THIS COCKSUCKER WINDS UP DEAD, AND THE GUYS WITH A BETTER MOTIVE THAN ANYONE ARE A GODDAMNED TEAM OF COPS.
HE FUCKED UP YOUR SURVEILLANCE. HE MURDERED YOUR UNDERCOVER NARC. HE BEAT YOUR CASE, HE WASTED TWO YEARS OF YOUR LIVES, HE DID ALL THIS SHIT AND I THOUGHT ABOUT IT AND THOUGHT ABOUT IT AND I REALIZED–
HELL, KIDDIES... YOU DID WHAT *I* WOULD HAVE DONE.
AND EVERYTHING FOLLOWED FROM THAT ONE THOUGHT: HOLY SHIT, WHAT IF DUKE'S CREW ARE JUST LIKE MINE?
SO WHEN SOME CONCERNED CITIZEN WANTS TO GIVE ME THE GUN KILLED CLINTON DAYS, WANTS TO MEET ME IN THE ASS-END OF FUCKING NOWHERE, TOO–WELL, THE FIRST THING COMES TO MIND IS A CERTAIN NIGHT'S WORK IN THE PROJECTS–
FUCK YOU!
O'DWYER, YOU COCKSUCKER, FROM THE MOMENT YOUR WHORE OF A MOTHER SHIT YOU OUT–
RED TEAM, GO TO BACKUP FREAK.

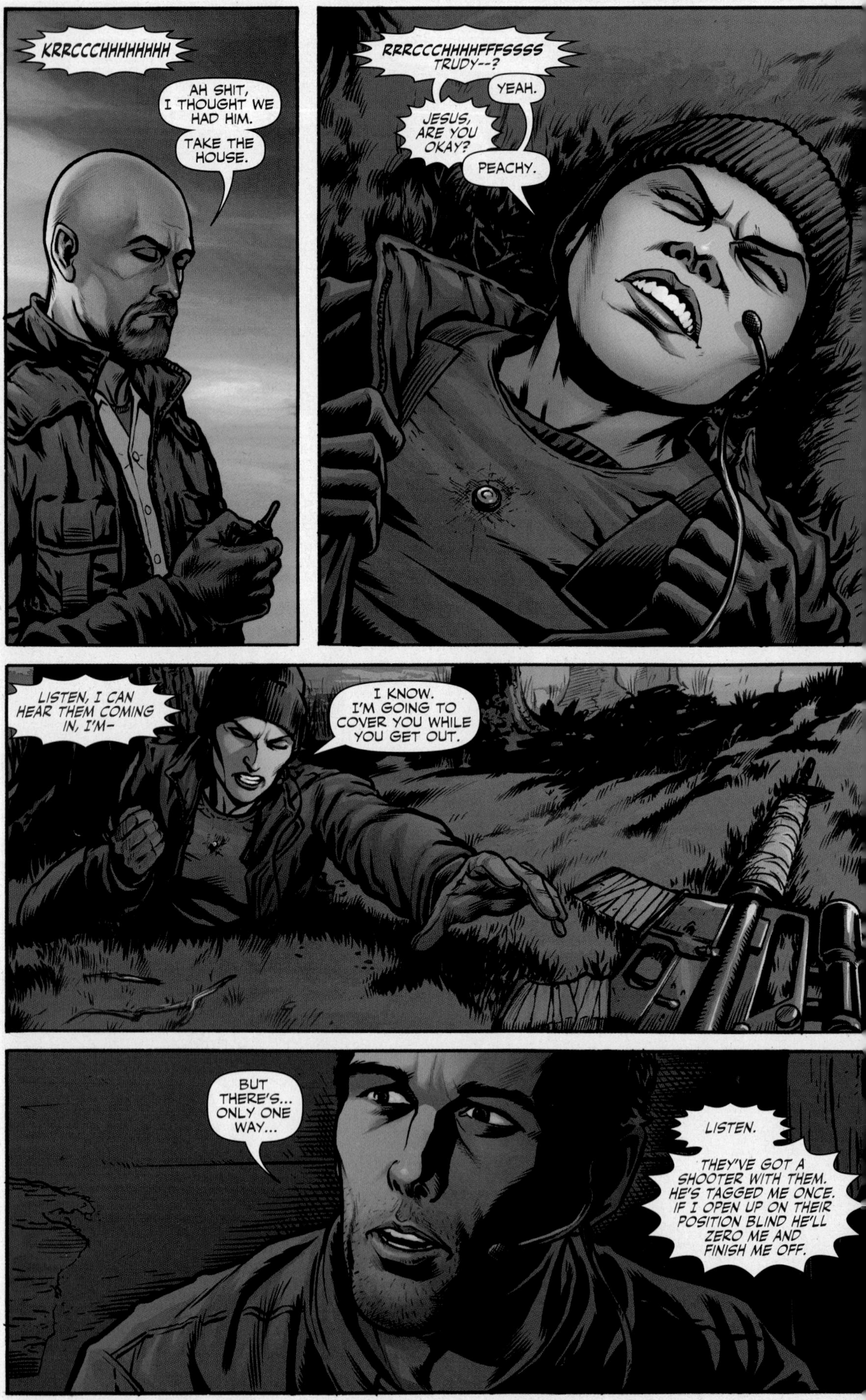
KRRCCCHHHHHHHH
AH SHIT, I THOUGHT WE HAD HIM.
TAKE THE HOUSE.
RRRCCCHHHHFFFSSSS TRUDY--?
YEAH.
JESUS, ARE YOU OKAY?
PEACHY.
LISTEN, I CAN HEAR THEM COMING IN, I'M-
I KNOW. I'M GOING TO COVER YOU WHILE YOU GET OUT.
BUT THERE'S... ONLY ONE WAY...
LISTEN.
THEY'VE GOT A SHOOTER WITH THEM. HE'S TAGGED ME ONCE. IF I OPEN UP ON THEIR POSITION BLIND HE'LL ZERO ME AND FINISH ME OFF.

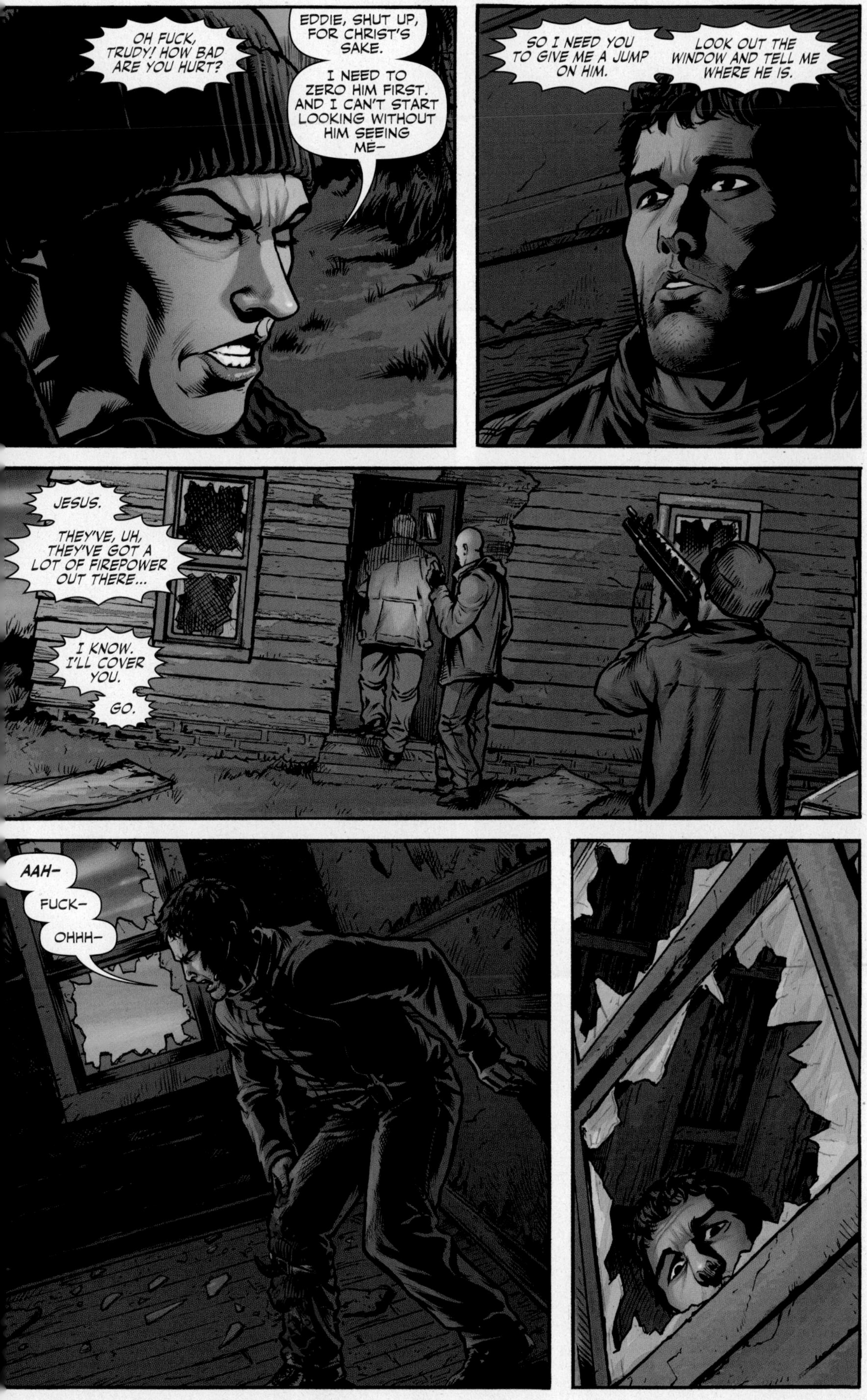
OH FUCK, TRUDY! HOW BAD ARE YOU HURT?
EDDIE, SHUT UP, FOR CHRIST'S SAKE.
I NEED TO ZERO HIM FIRST. AND I CAN'T START LOOKING WITHOUT HIM SEEING ME–
SO I NEED YOU TO GIVE ME A JUMP ON HIM.
LOOK OUT THE WINDOW AND TELL ME WHERE HE IS.
JESUS.
THEY'VE, UH, THEY'VE GOT A LOT OF FIREPOWER OUT THERE...
I KNOW. I'LL COVER YOU.
GO.
AAH–
FUCK–
OHHH–

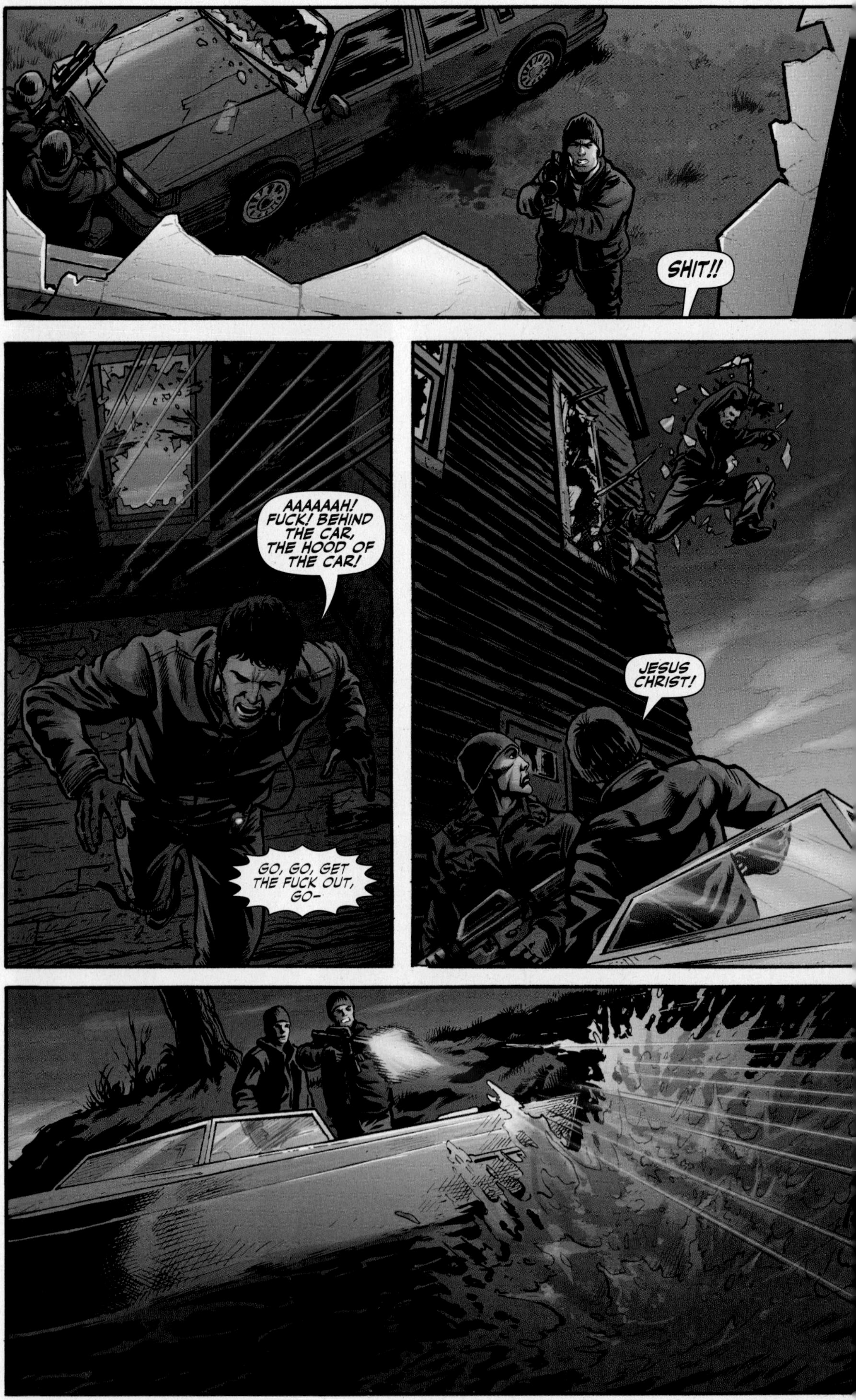
SHIT!!
AAAAAAH! FUCK! BEHIND THE CAR, THE HOOD OF THE CAR!
GO, GO, GET THE FUCK OUT, GO–
JESUS CHRIST!

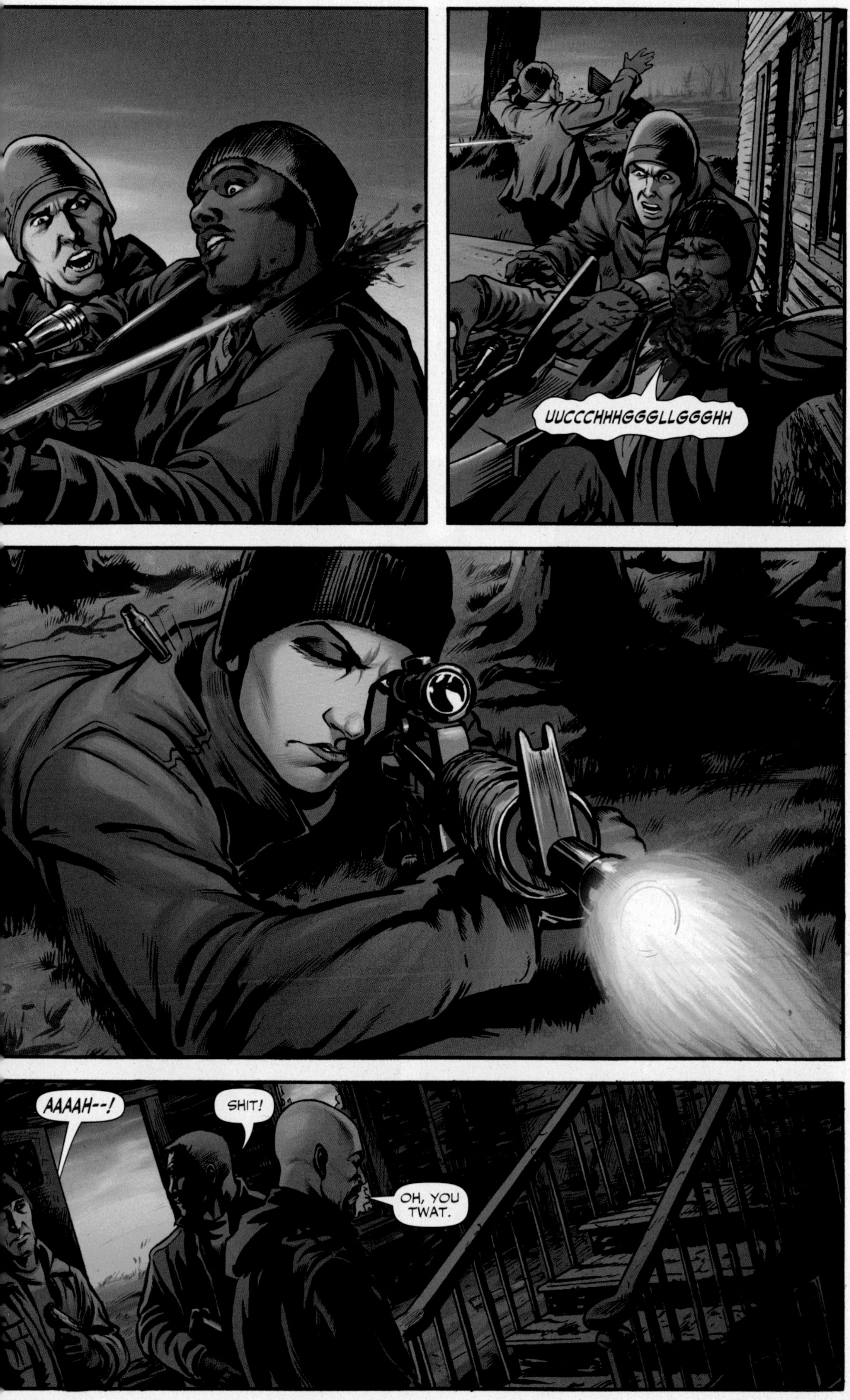
UUCCCHHHGGGLLGGGHH
AAAAH--!
SHIT!
OH, YOU TWAT.

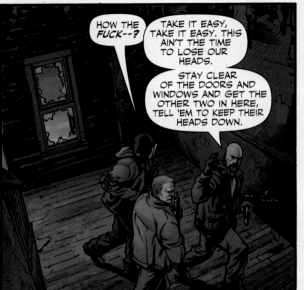

HOW THE **FUCK--?**

TAKE IT EASY, TAKE IT EASY. THIS AIN'T THE TIME TO LOSE OUR HEADS.

STAY CLEAR OF THE DOORS AND WINDOWS AND GET THE OTHER TWO IN HERE, TELL 'EM TO KEEP THEIR HEADS DOWN.

THIS CAN STILL COME OUT ALL RIGHT, SO LONG AS WE'RE THE ONLY ONES TALKING...

MOVE IT!

TOO FUCKING DARK, I CAN'T SEE BLOOD, I CAN'T SEE BUBBLES...

COME ON, HE WANTS US!

I WANT TO CONFIRM THIS PRICK...

MOTHERFUCKER--

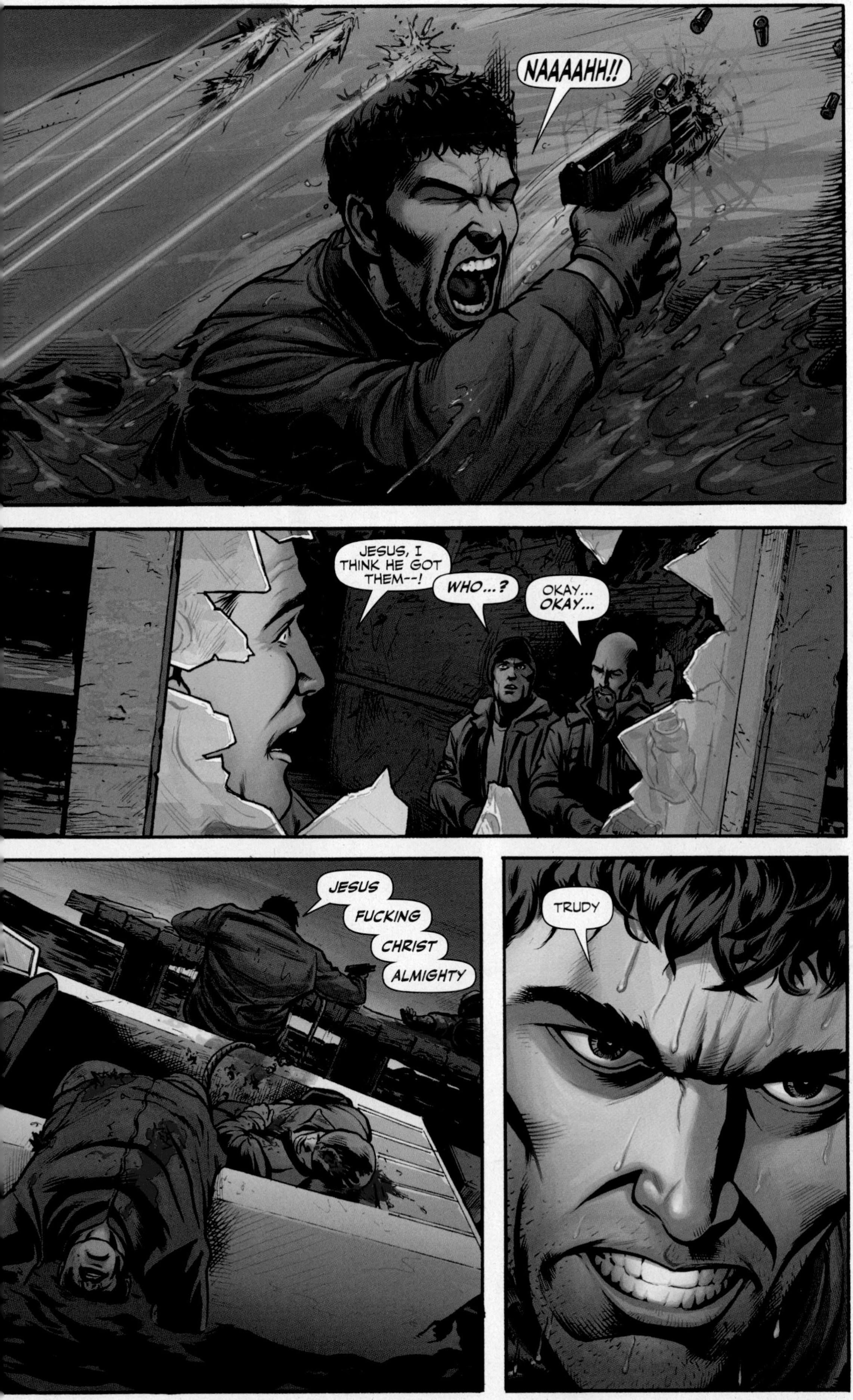
NAAAAHH!!
JESUS, I THINK HE GOT THEM--!
WHO...?
OKAY... OKAY...
JESUS
FUCKING
CHRIST
ALMIGHTY
TRUDY

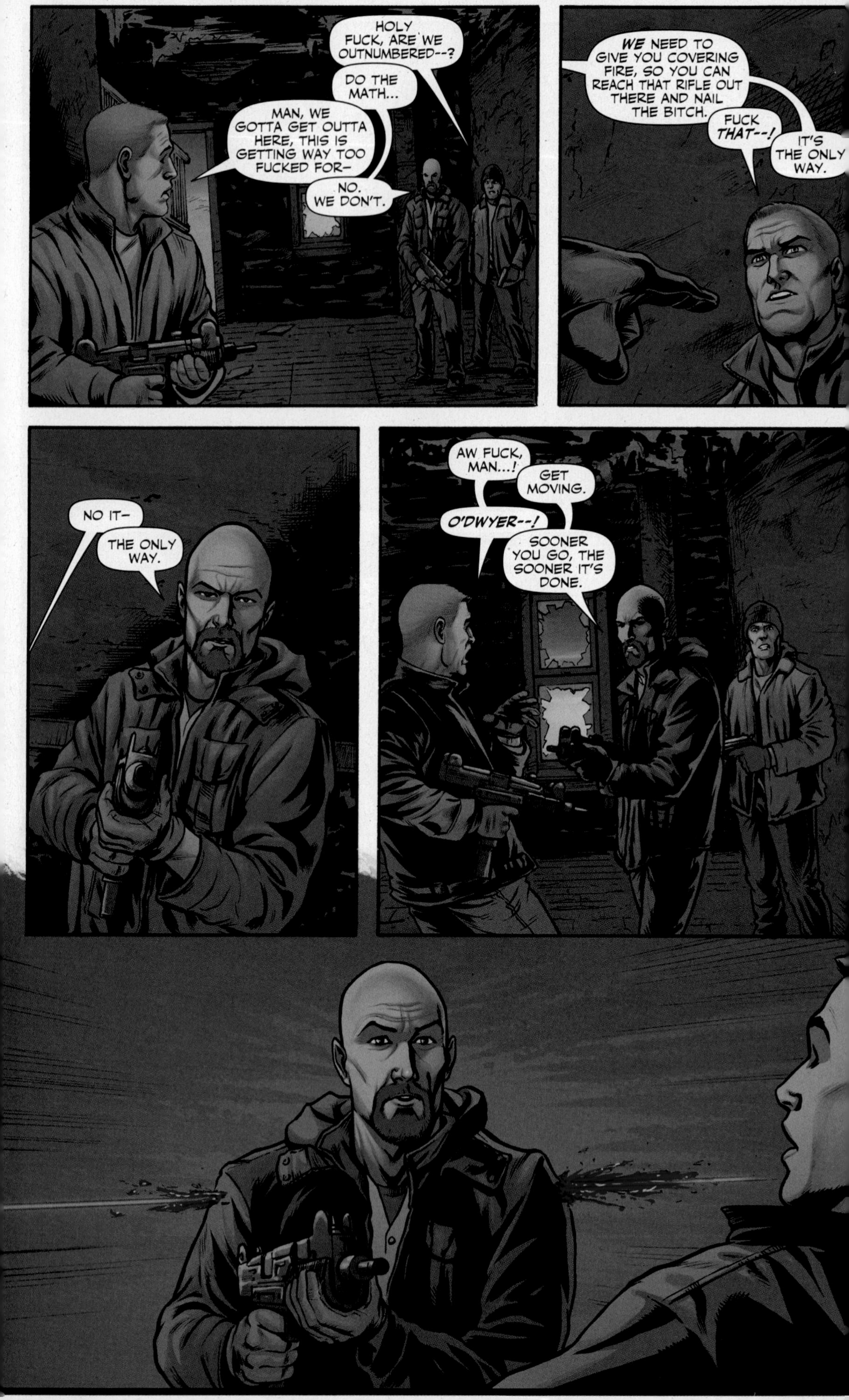

HOLY FUCK, ARE WE OUTNUMBERED--?
DO THE MATH...
MAN, WE GOTTA GET OUTTA HERE, THIS IS GETTING WAY TOO FUCKED FOR–
NO. WE DON'T.
WE NEED TO GIVE YOU COVERING FIRE, SO YOU CAN REACH THAT RIFLE OUT THERE AND NAIL THE BITCH.
FUCK *THAT*--!
IT'S THE ONLY WAY.
NO IT–
THE ONLY WAY.
AW FUCK, MAN...!
GET MOVING.
O'DWYER--!
SOONER YOU GO, THE SOONER IT'S DONE.

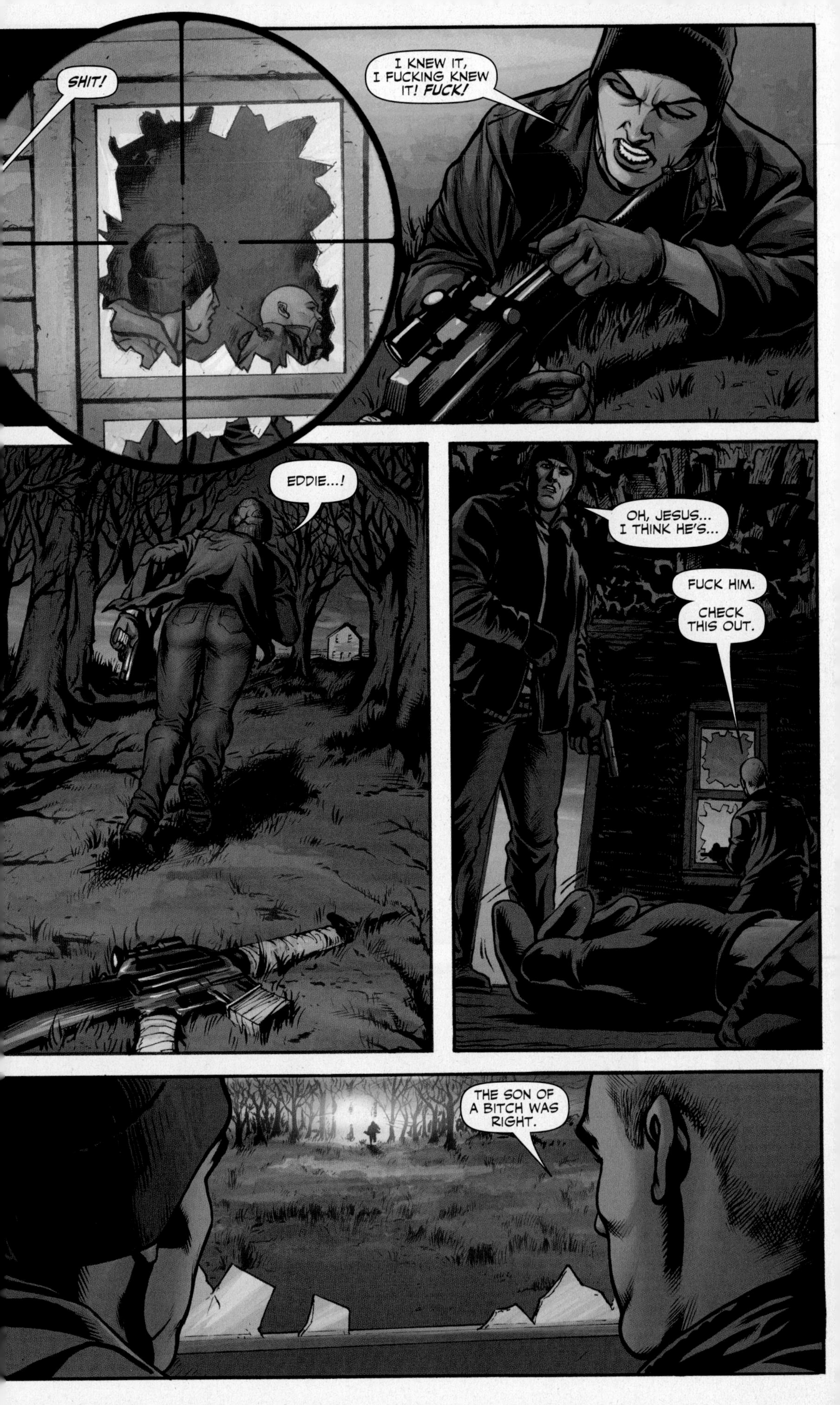
SHIT!
I KNEW IT, I FUCKING KNEW IT! FUCK!
EDDIE...!
OH, JESUS... I THINK HE'S...
FUCK HIM.
CHECK THIS OUT.
THE SON OF A BITCH WAS RIGHT.

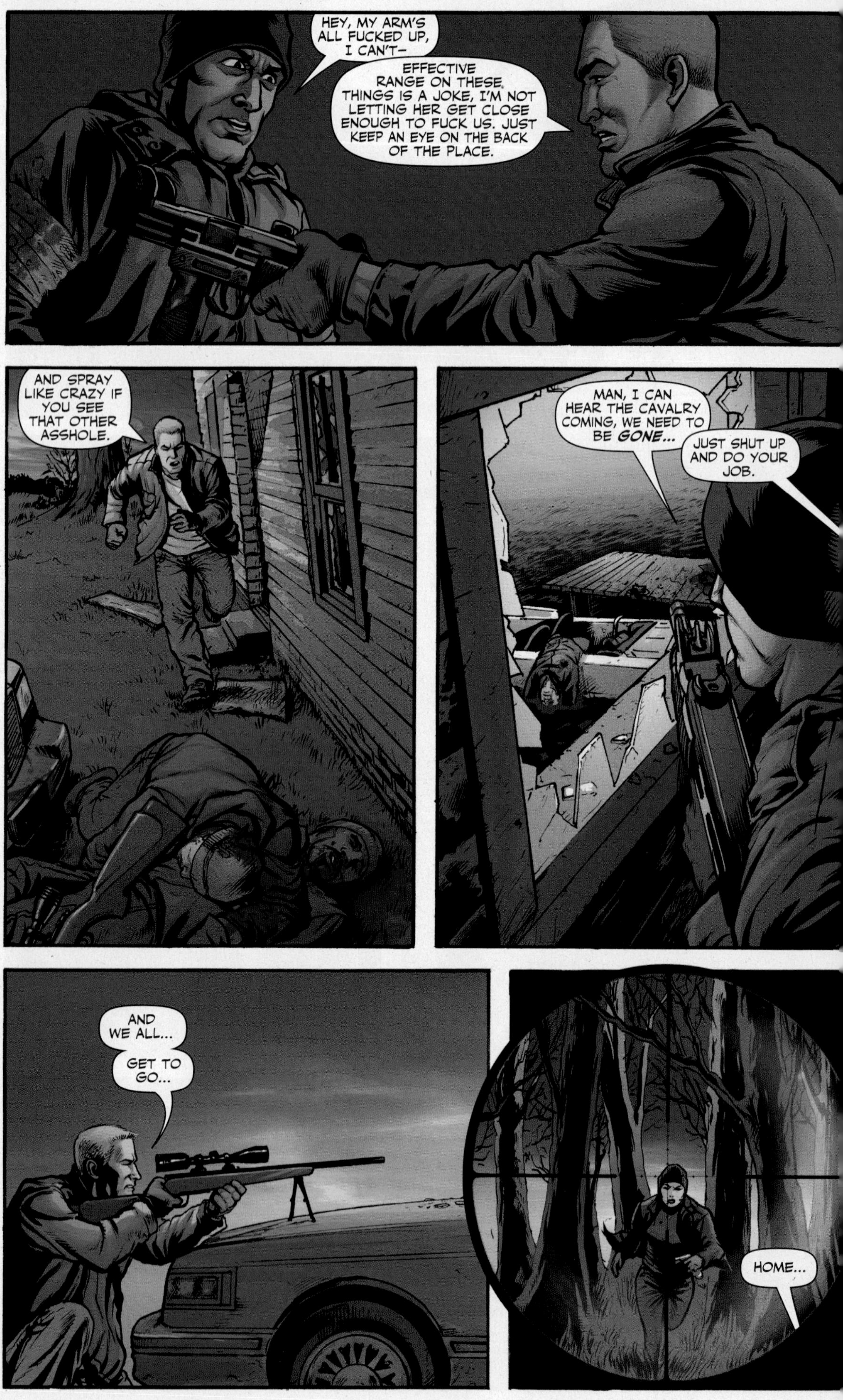
HEY, MY ARM'S ALL FUCKED UP, I CAN'T–
EFFECTIVE RANGE ON THESE THINGS IS A JOKE, I'M NOT LETTING HER GET CLOSE ENOUGH TO FUCK US. JUST KEEP AN EYE ON THE BACK OF THE PLACE.
AND SPRAY LIKE CRAZY IF YOU SEE THAT OTHER ASSHOLE.
MAN, I CAN HEAR THE CAVALRY COMING, WE NEED TO BE *GONE*...
JUST SHUT UP AND DO YOUR JOB.
AND WE ALL...
GET TO GO...
HOME...

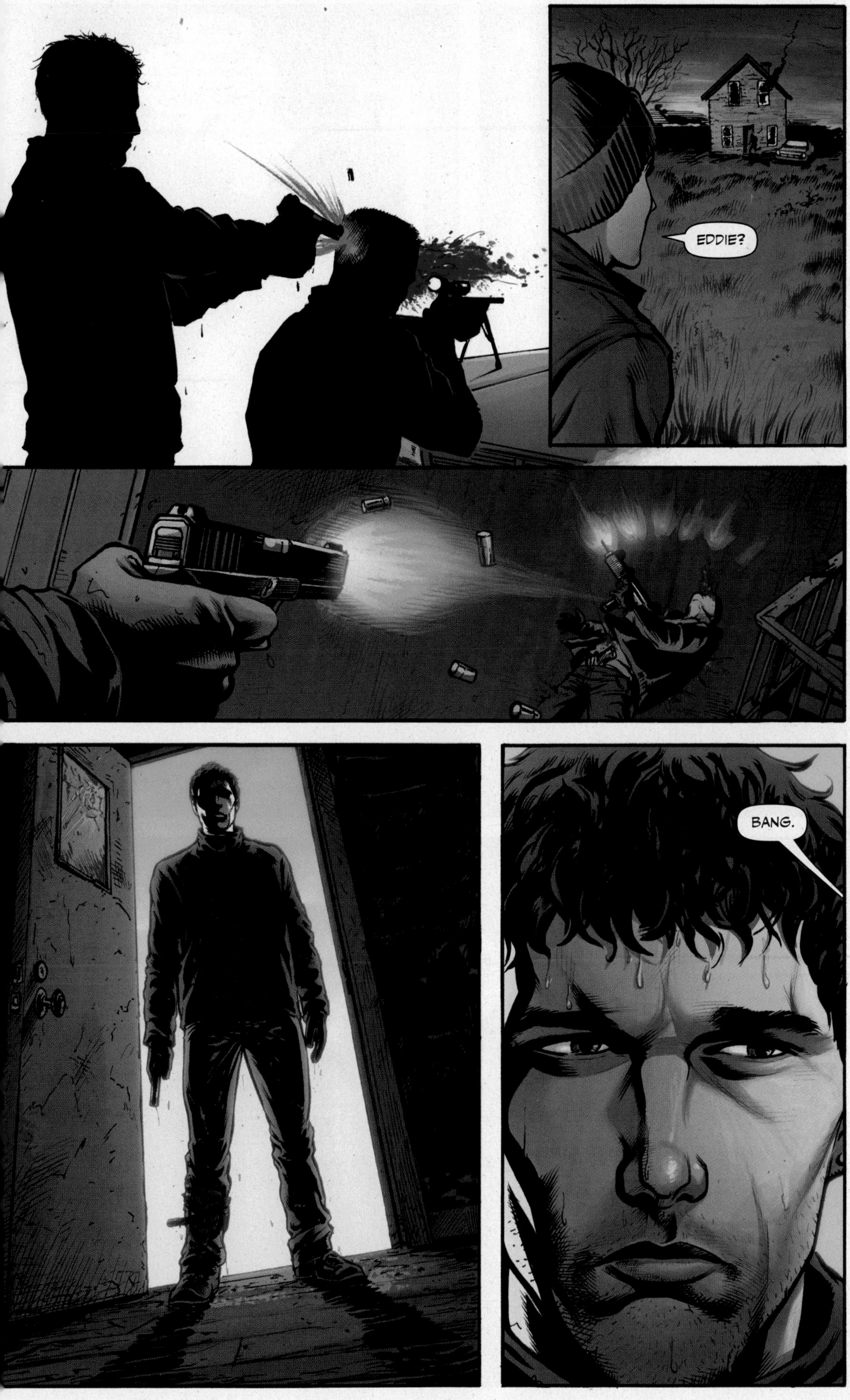
EDDIE?
BANG.

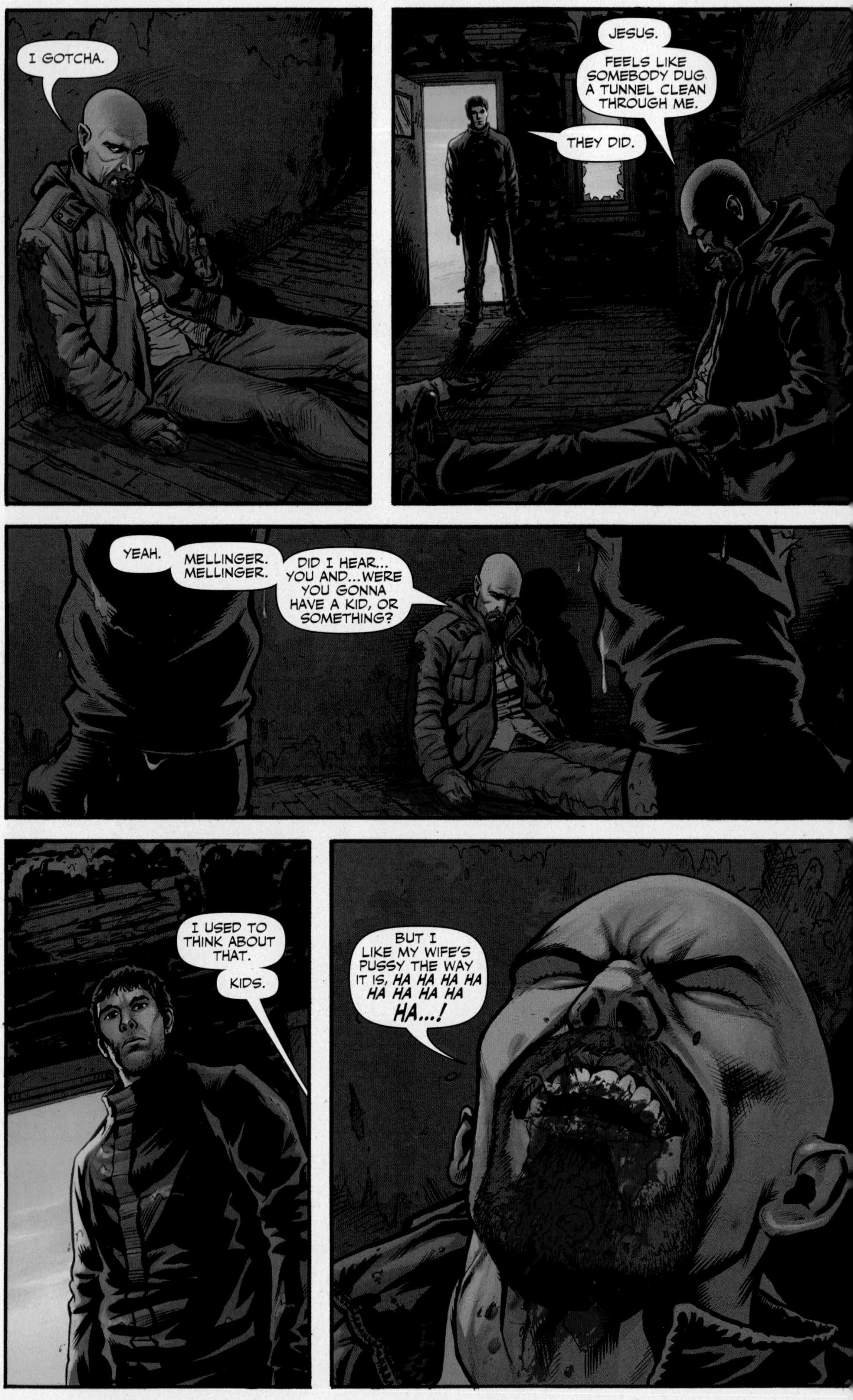
I GOTCHA.
JESUS.
FEELS LIKE SOMEBODY DUG A TUNNEL CLEAN THROUGH ME.
THEY DID.
YEAH.
MELLINGER. MELLINGER.
DID I HEAR... YOU AND...WERE YOU GONNA HAVE A KID, OR SOMETHING?
I USED TO THINK ABOUT THAT.
KIDS.
BUT I LIKE MY WIFE'S PUSSY THE WAY IT IS, HA HA HA HA HA HA HA HA HA...!

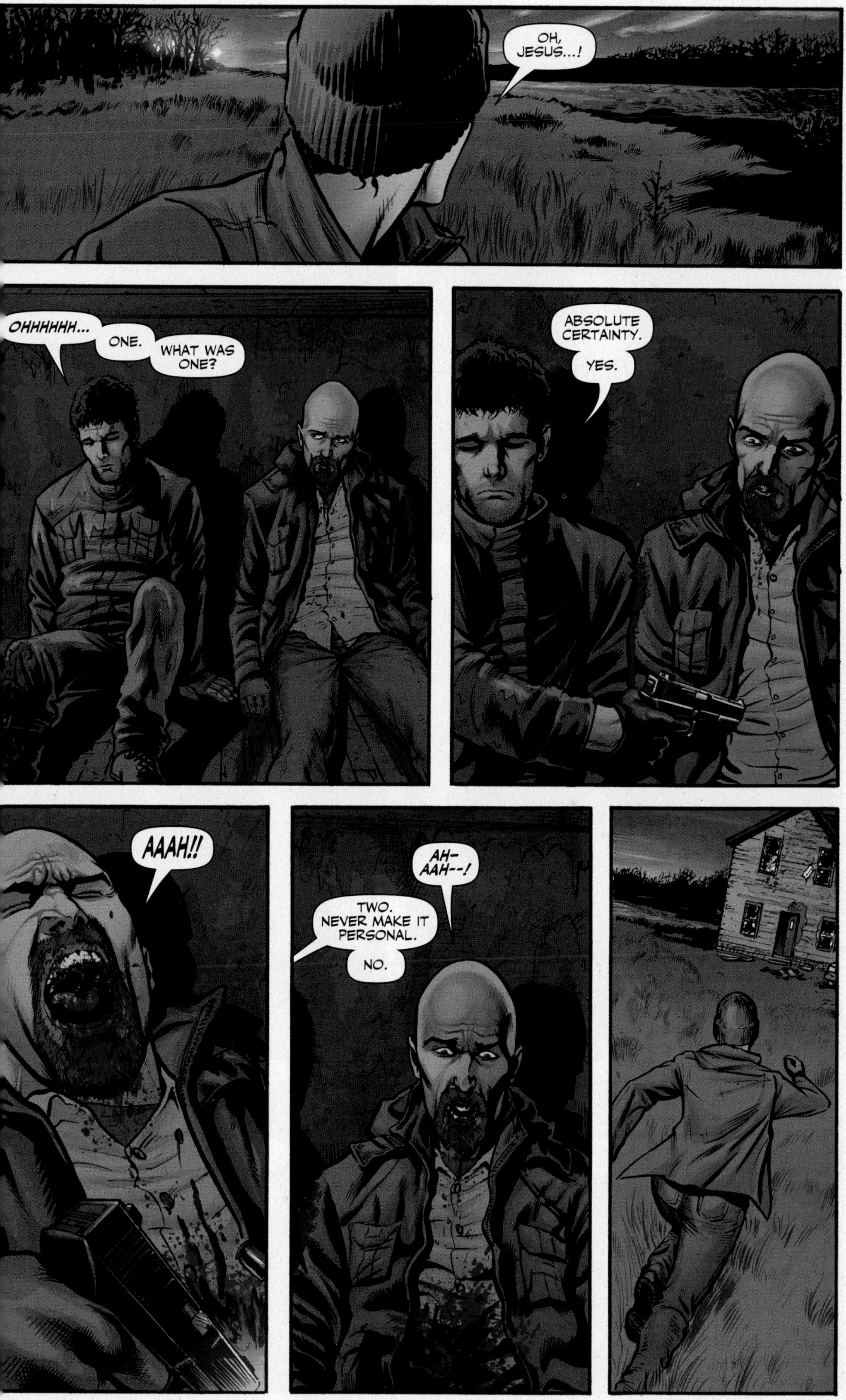
OH, JESUS...!
OHHHHHH...
ONE.
WHAT WAS ONE?
ABSOLUTE CERTAINTY.
YES.
AAAH!!
AH-AAH--!
TWO. NEVER MAKE IT PERSONAL.
NO.

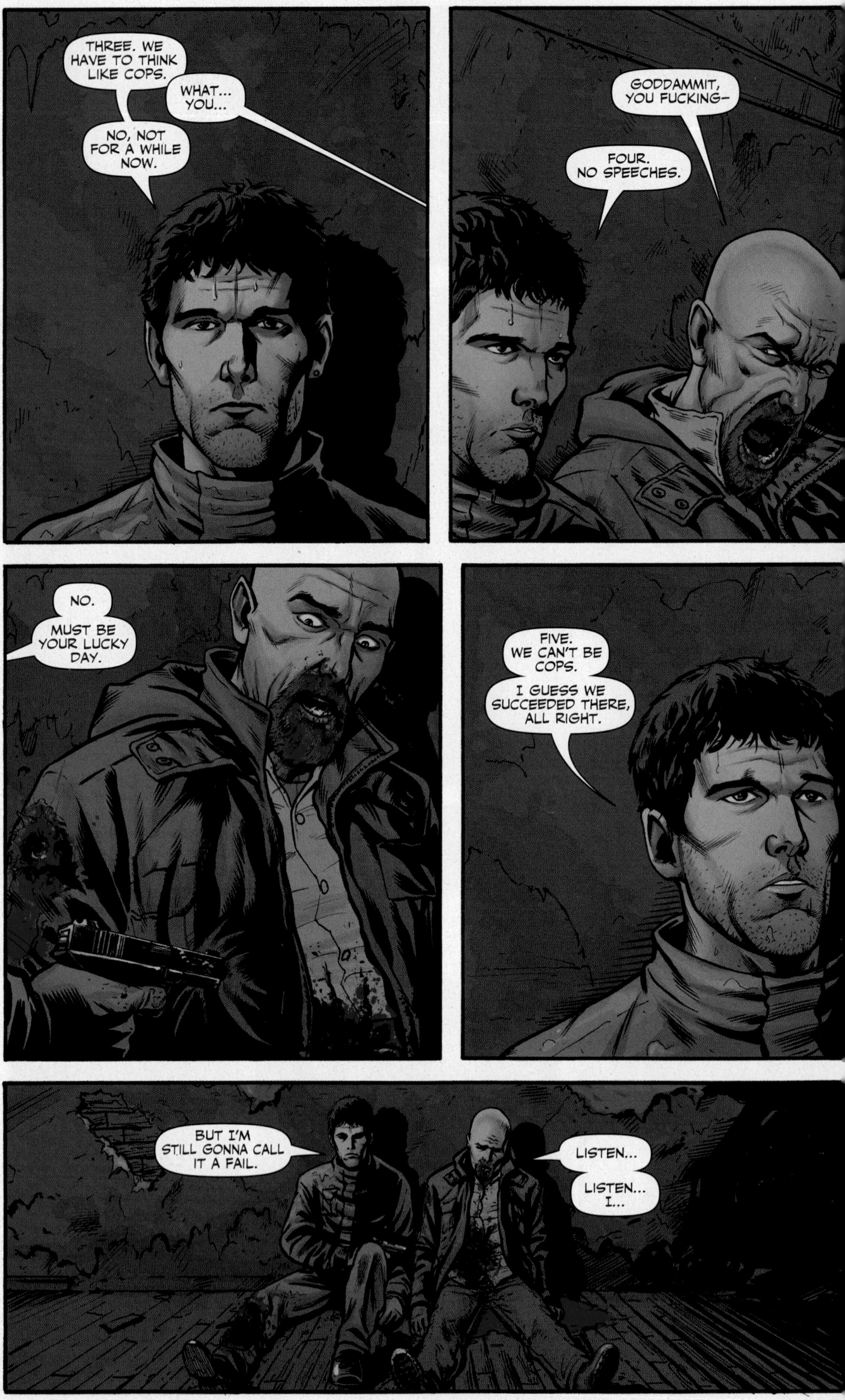
THREE. WE HAVE TO THINK LIKE COPS.
WHAT... YOU...
NO, NOT FOR A WHILE NOW.
GODDAMMIT, YOU FUCKING–
FOUR. NO SPEECHES.
NO.
MUST BE YOUR LUCKY DAY.
FIVE. WE CAN'T BE COPS.
I GUESS WE SUCCEEDED THERE, ALL RIGHT.
BUT I'M STILL GONNA CALL IT A FAIL.
LISTEN...
LISTEN... I...

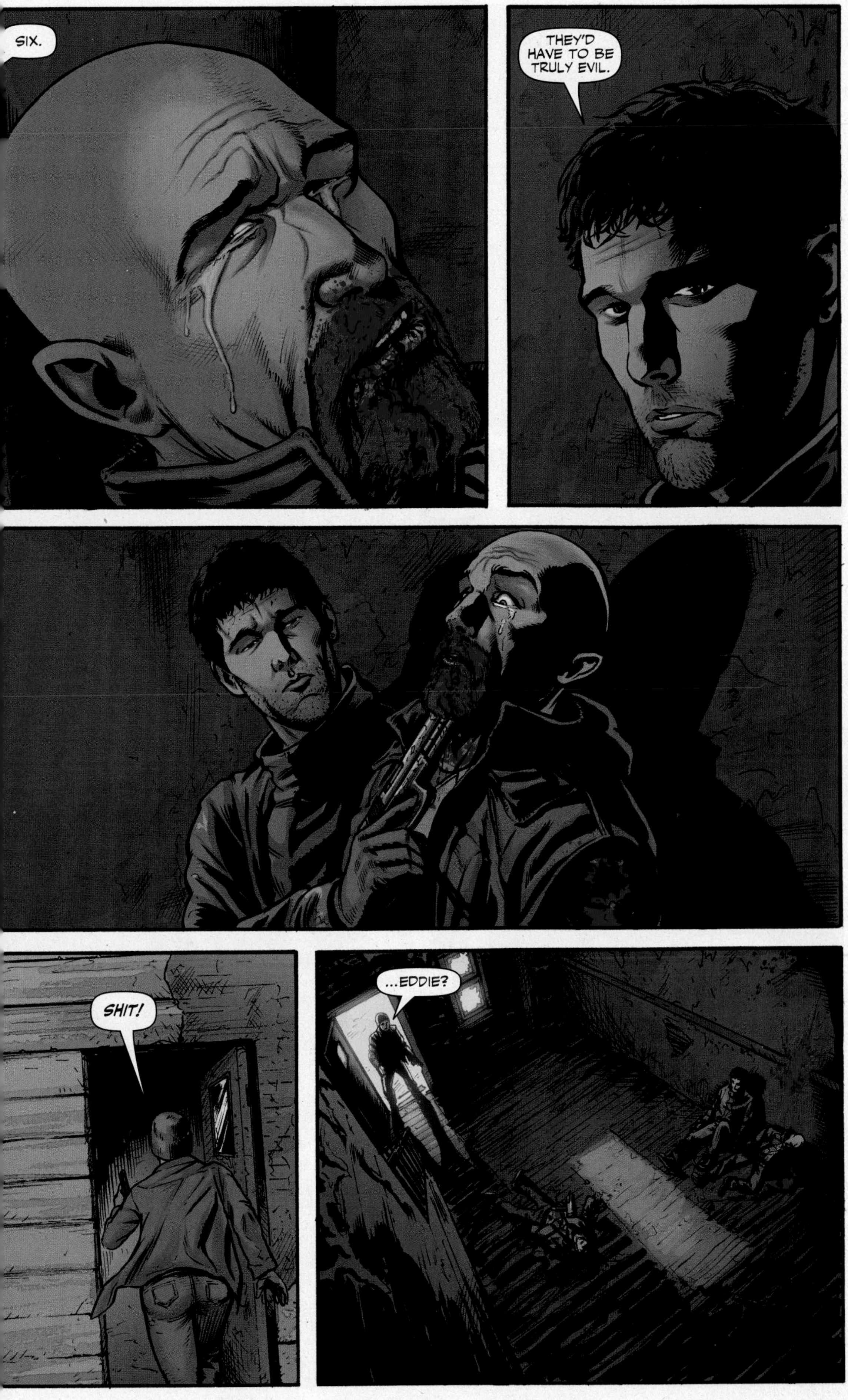
SIX.
THEY'D HAVE TO BE TRULY EVIL.
SHIT!
...EDDIE?

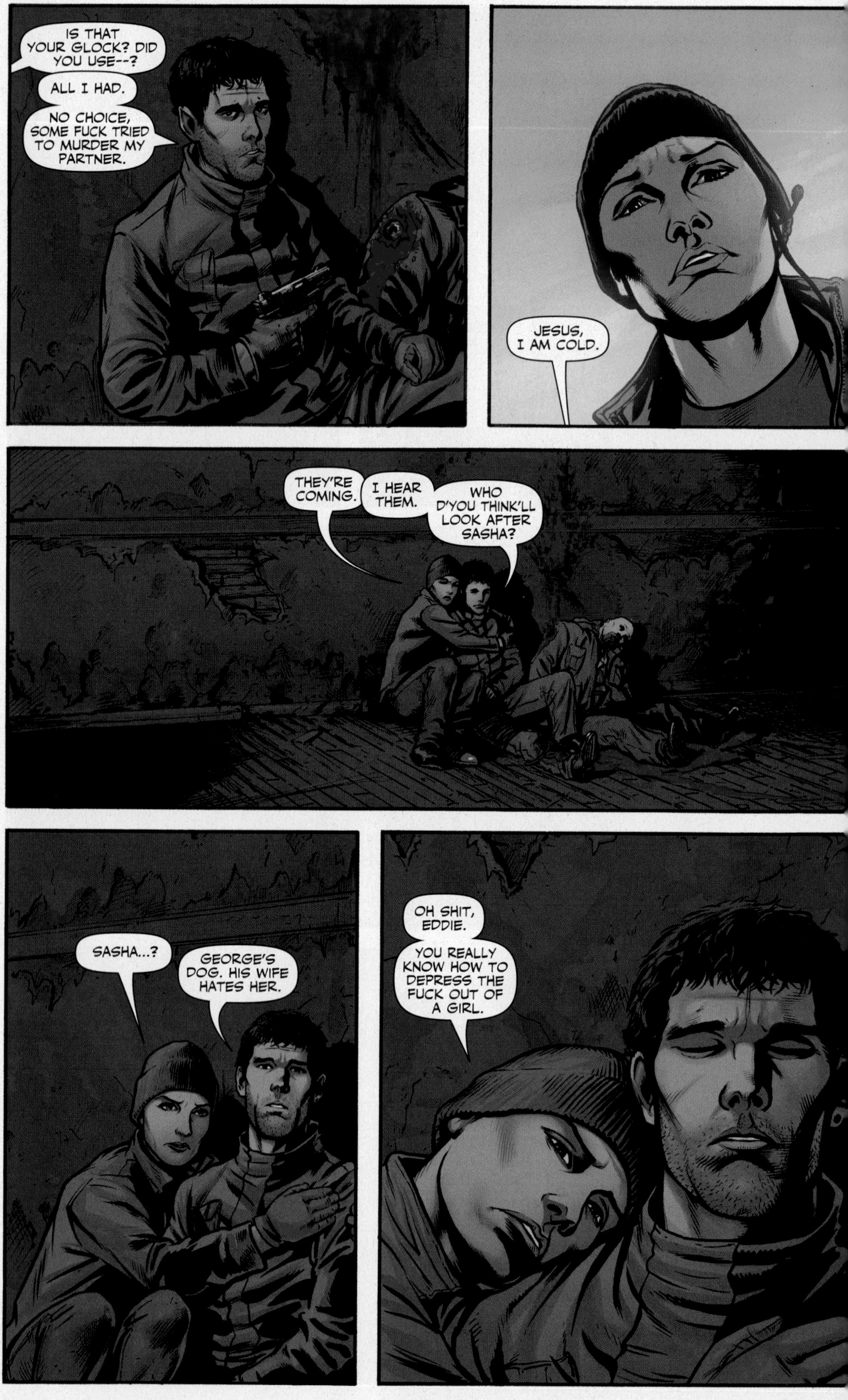
IS THAT YOUR GLOCK? DID YOU USE--?
ALL I HAD.
NO CHOICE, SOME FUCK TRIED TO MURDER MY PARTNER.
JESUS, I AM COLD.
THEY'RE COMING.
I HEAR THEM.
WHO D'YOU THINK'LL LOOK AFTER SASHA?
SASHA...?
GEORGE'S DOG. HIS WIFE HATES HER.
OH SHIT, EDDIE.
YOU REALLY KNOW HOW TO DEPRESS THE FUCK OUT OF A GIRL.

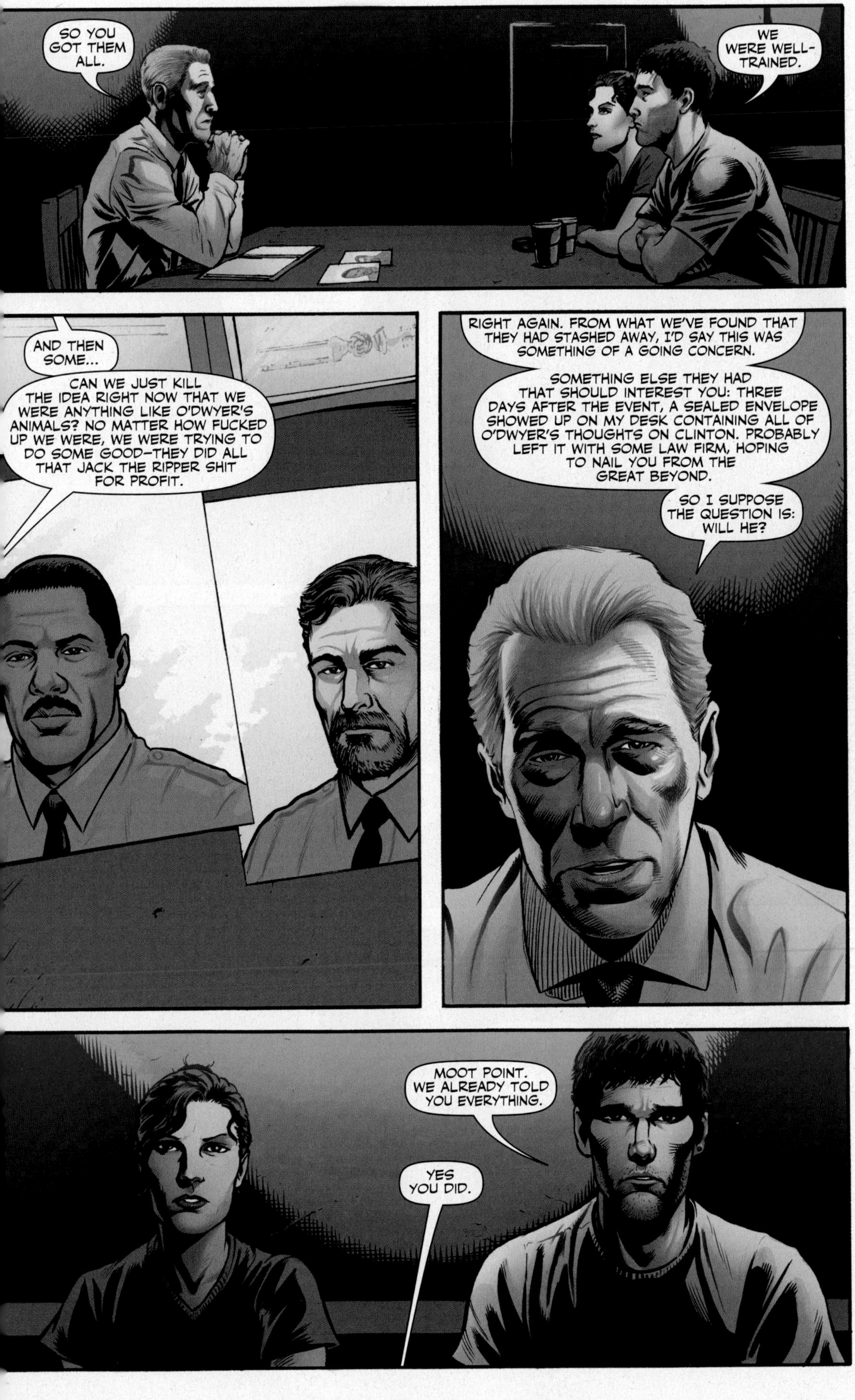
SO YOU GOT THEM ALL.
WE WERE WELL-TRAINED.
AND THEN SOME...
CAN WE JUST KILL THE IDEA RIGHT NOW THAT WE WERE ANYTHING LIKE O'DWYER'S ANIMALS? NO MATTER HOW FUCKED UP WE WERE, WE WERE TRYING TO DO SOME GOOD—THEY DID ALL THAT JACK THE RIPPER SHIT FOR PROFIT.
RIGHT AGAIN. FROM WHAT WE'VE FOUND THAT THEY HAD STASHED AWAY, I'D SAY THIS WAS SOMETHING OF A GOING CONCERN.
SOMETHING ELSE THEY HAD THAT SHOULD INTEREST YOU: THREE DAYS AFTER THE EVENT, A SEALED ENVELOPE SHOWED UP ON MY DESK CONTAINING ALL OF O'DWYER'S THOUGHTS ON CLINTON. PROBABLY LEFT IT WITH SOME LAW FIRM, HOPING TO NAIL YOU FROM THE GREAT BEYOND.
SO I SUPPOSE THE QUESTION IS: WILL HE?
MOOT POINT. WE ALREADY TOLD YOU EVERYTHING.
YES YOU DID.

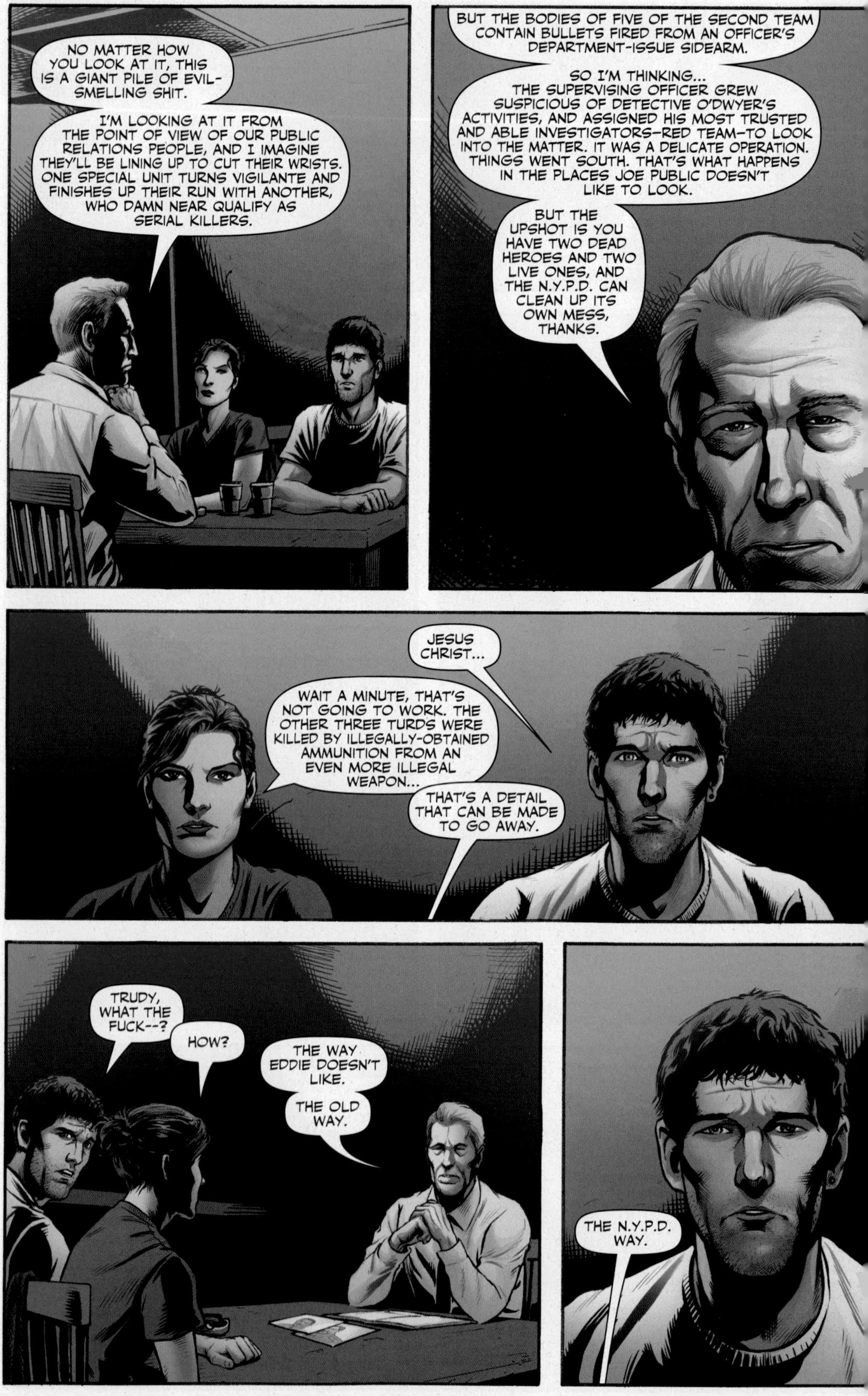
NO MATTER HOW YOU LOOK AT IT, THIS IS A GIANT PILE OF EVIL-SMELLING SHIT.
I'M LOOKING AT IT FROM THE POINT OF VIEW OF OUR PUBLIC RELATIONS PEOPLE, AND I IMAGINE THEY'LL BE LINING UP TO CUT THEIR WRISTS. ONE SPECIAL UNIT TURNS VIGILANTE AND FINISHES UP THEIR RUN WITH ANOTHER, WHO DAMN NEAR QUALIFY AS SERIAL KILLERS.
BUT THE BODIES OF FIVE OF THE SECOND TEAM CONTAIN BULLETS FIRED FROM AN OFFICER'S DEPARTMENT-ISSUE SIDEARM.
SO I'M THINKING... THE SUPERVISING OFFICER GREW SUSPICIOUS OF DETECTIVE O'DWYER'S ACTIVITIES, AND ASSIGNED HIS MOST TRUSTED AND ABLE INVESTIGATORS–RED TEAM–TO LOOK INTO THE MATTER. IT WAS A DELICATE OPERATION. THINGS WENT SOUTH. THAT'S WHAT HAPPENS IN THE PLACES JOE PUBLIC DOESN'T LIKE TO LOOK.
BUT THE UPSHOT IS YOU HAVE TWO DEAD HEROES AND TWO LIVE ONES, AND THE N.Y.P.D. CAN CLEAN UP ITS OWN MESS, THANKS.
JESUS CHRIST...
WAIT A MINUTE, THAT'S NOT GOING TO WORK. THE OTHER THREE TURDS WERE KILLED BY ILLEGALLY-OBTAINED AMMUNITION FROM AN EVEN MORE ILLEGAL WEAPON...
THAT'S A DETAIL THAT CAN BE MADE TO GO AWAY.
TRUDY, WHAT THE FUCK--?
HOW?
THE WAY EDDIE DOESN'T LIKE.
THE OLD WAY.
THE N.Y.P.D. WAY.

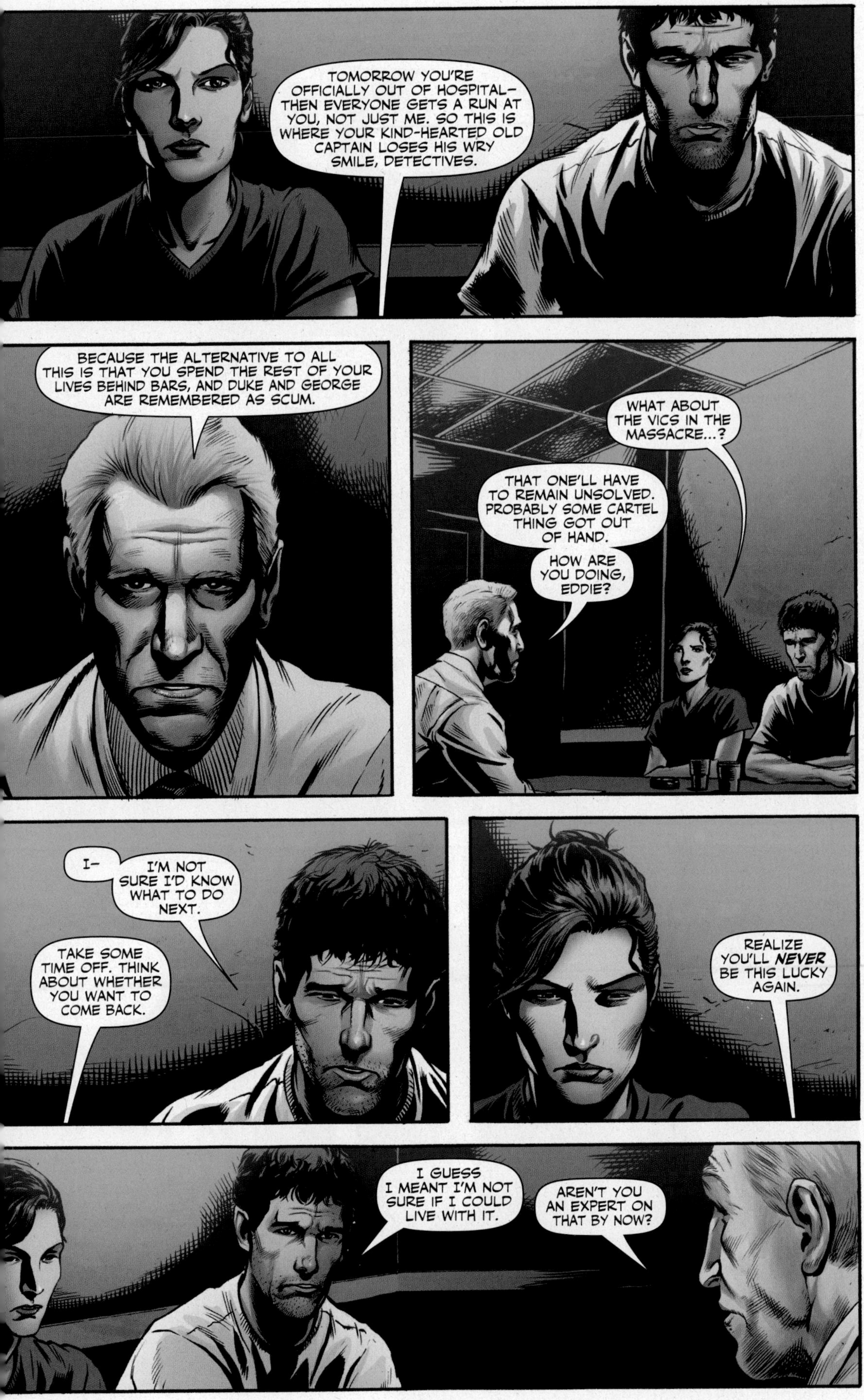
TOMORROW YOU'RE OFFICIALLY OUT OF HOSPITAL– THEN EVERYONE GETS A RUN AT YOU, NOT JUST ME. SO THIS IS WHERE YOUR KIND-HEARTED OLD CAPTAIN LOSES HIS WRY SMILE, DETECTIVES.
BECAUSE THE ALTERNATIVE TO ALL THIS IS THAT YOU SPEND THE REST OF YOUR LIVES BEHIND BARS, AND DUKE AND GEORGE ARE REMEMBERED AS SCUM.
WHAT ABOUT THE VICS IN THE MASSACRE...?
THAT ONE'LL HAVE TO REMAIN UNSOLVED. PROBABLY SOME CARTEL THING GOT OUT OF HAND.
HOW ARE YOU DOING, EDDIE?
I–
I'M NOT SURE I'D KNOW WHAT TO DO NEXT.
TAKE SOME TIME OFF. THINK ABOUT WHETHER YOU WANT TO COME BACK.
REALIZE YOU'LL *NEVER* BE THIS LUCKY AGAIN.
I GUESS I MEANT I'M NOT SURE IF I COULD LIVE WITH IT.
AREN'T YOU AN EXPERT ON THAT BY NOW?

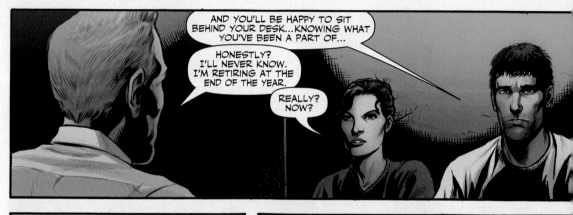

AND YOU'LL BE HAPPY TO SIT BEHIND YOUR DESK...KNOWING WHAT YOU'VE BEEN A PART OF...

HONESTLY? I'LL NEVER KNOW. I'M RETIRING AT THE END OF THE YEAR.

REALLY? NOW?

WHY NOT NOW?

IT'S JUST KIND OF SUDDEN. OR MAYBE NOT, WITH O'DWYER OUT OF THE PICTURE.

SKIPPER, DID HE HAVE SOMETHING ON YOU?

WHAT IS IT MAKES YOU SAY THAT, EXACTLY?

DUKE MENTIONED THERE'D ALWAYS BEEN TALK.

YES, ABOUT PAYOFFS. THERE ALWAYS HAS.

THE FUNNY THING IS THAT NONE OF IT'S TRUE.

UP TO YOU IF YOU BELIEVE ME OR NOT. BUT I RECOMMEND YOU DEVOTE YOUR ENERGIES TO CONSIDERING YOUR OWN SITUATION.

I'LL BE BACK IN HALF AN HOUR.

WASN'T O'DWYER'S DAD A COP?

YES...

DID YOU EVER HEAR AN OLD STORY... FROM BACK AROUND THE EARLY EIGHTIES...

SOMETHING ABOUT A BUNCH OF COPS WHO WIPED OUT SOME MOB CREW OR OTHER?

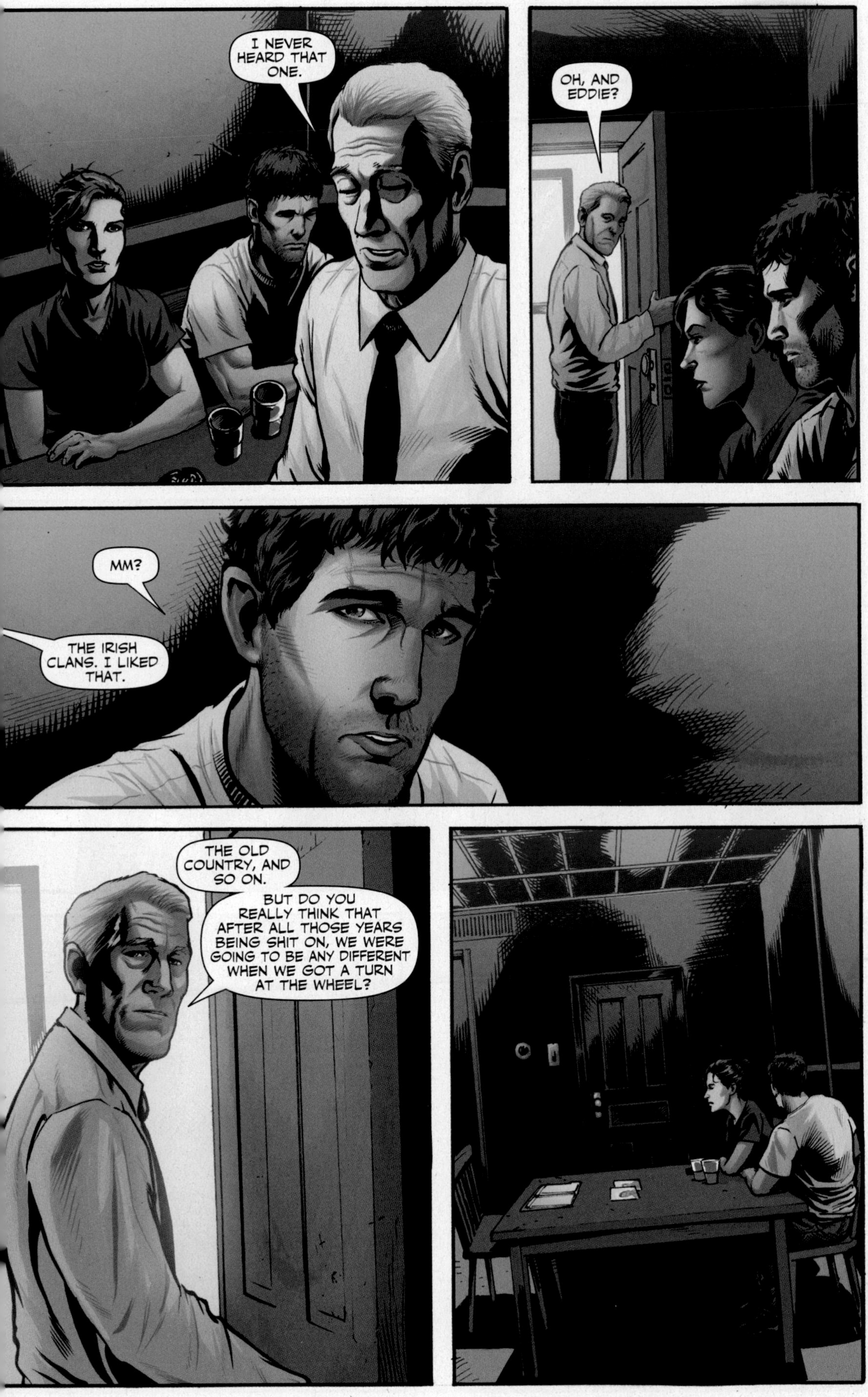
I NEVER HEARD THAT ONE.
OH, AND EDDIE?
MM?
THE IRISH CLANS. I LIKED THAT.
THE OLD COUNTRY, AND SO ON.
BUT DO YOU REALLY THINK THAT AFTER ALL THOSE YEARS BEING SHIT ON, WE WERE GOING TO BE ANY DIFFERENT WHEN WE GOT A TURN AT THE WHEEL?

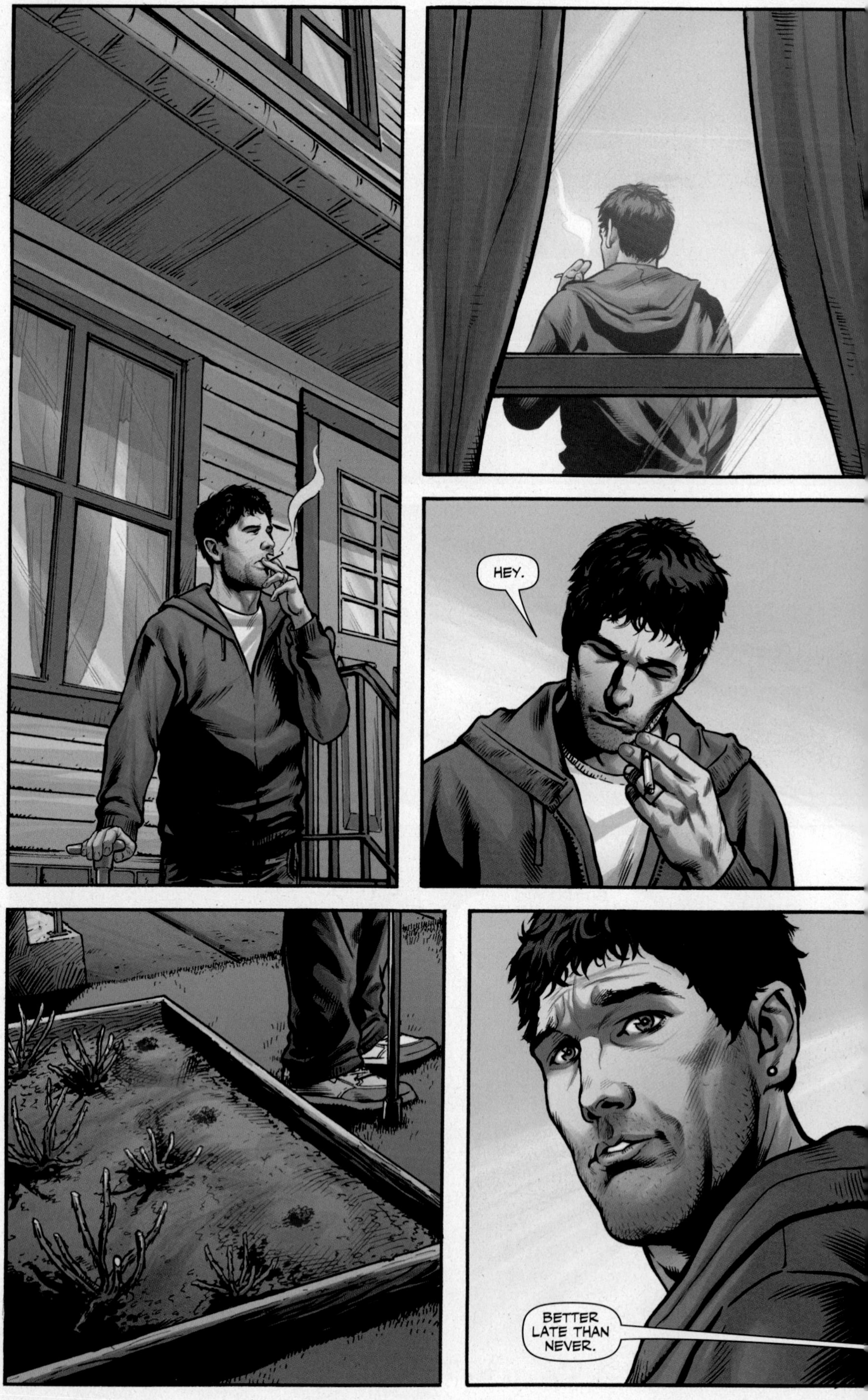
HEY.
BETTER LATE THAN NEVER.

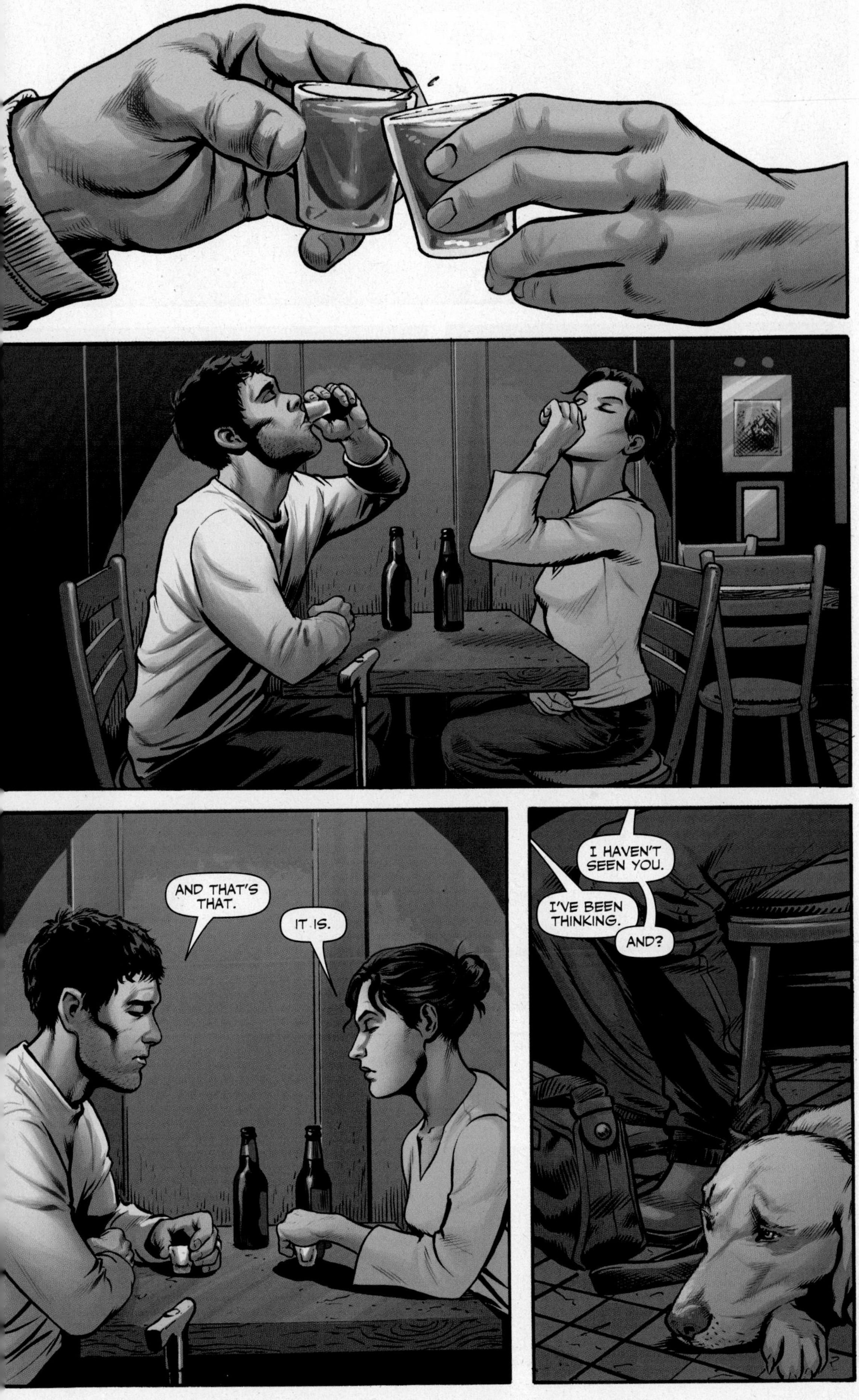
AND THAT'S THAT.
IT IS.
I HAVEN'T SEEN YOU.
I'VE BEEN THINKING.
AND?

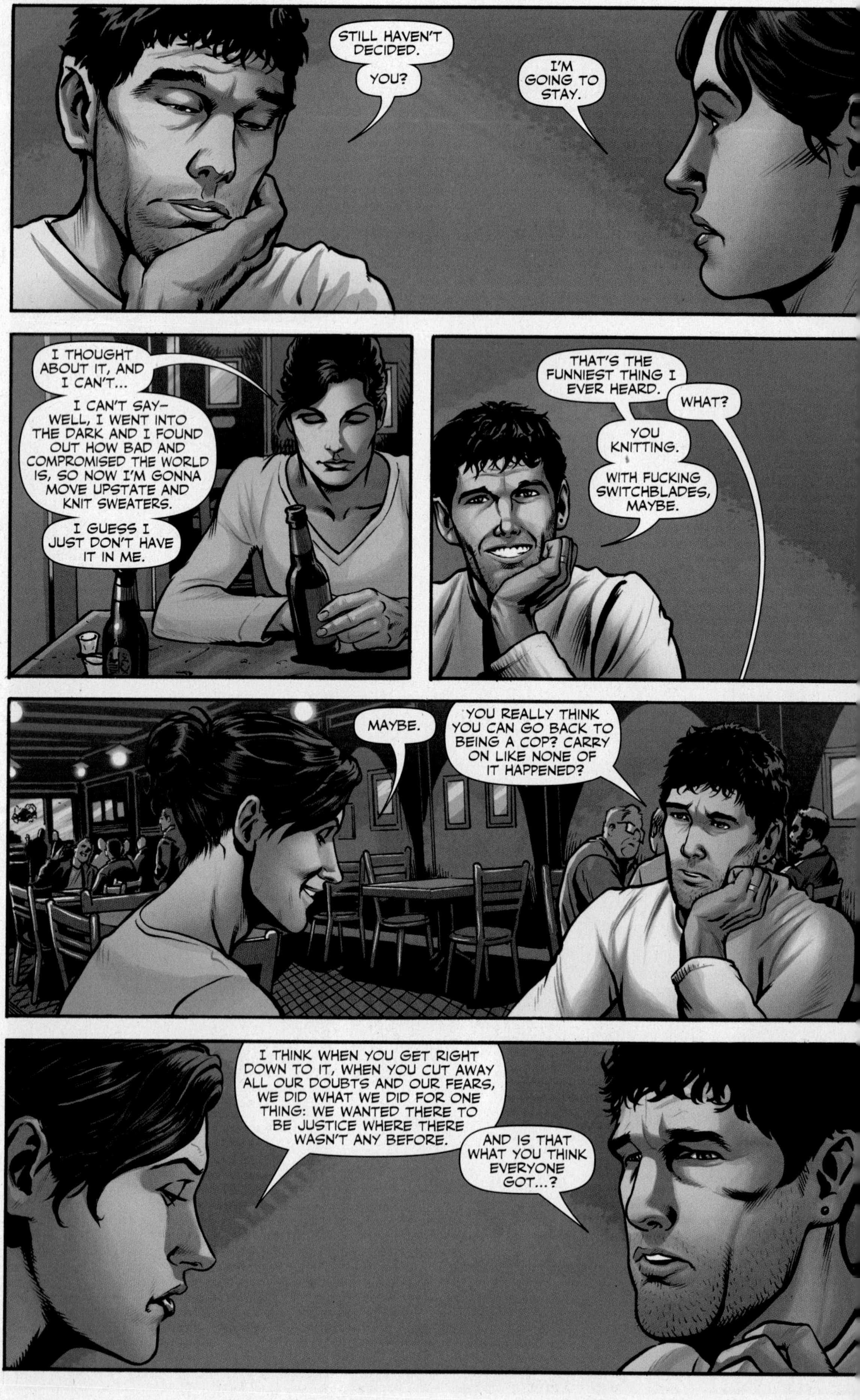

STILL HAVEN'T DECIDED.
YOU?
I'M GOING TO STAY.
I THOUGHT ABOUT IT, AND I CAN'T...
I CAN'T SAY— WELL, I WENT INTO THE DARK AND I FOUND OUT HOW BAD AND COMPROMISED THE WORLD IS, SO NOW I'M GONNA MOVE UPSTATE AND KNIT SWEATERS.
I GUESS I JUST DON'T HAVE IT IN ME.
THAT'S THE FUNNIEST THING I EVER HEARD.
WHAT?
YOU KNITTING.
WITH FUCKING SWITCHBLADES, MAYBE.
MAYBE.
YOU REALLY THINK YOU CAN GO BACK TO BEING A COP? CARRY ON LIKE NONE OF IT HAPPENED?
I THINK WHEN YOU GET RIGHT DOWN TO IT, WHEN YOU CUT AWAY ALL OUR DOUBTS AND OUR FEARS, WE DID WHAT WE DID FOR ONE THING: WE WANTED THERE TO BE JUSTICE WHERE THERE WASN'T ANY BEFORE.
AND IS THAT WHAT YOU THINK EVERYONE GOT...?

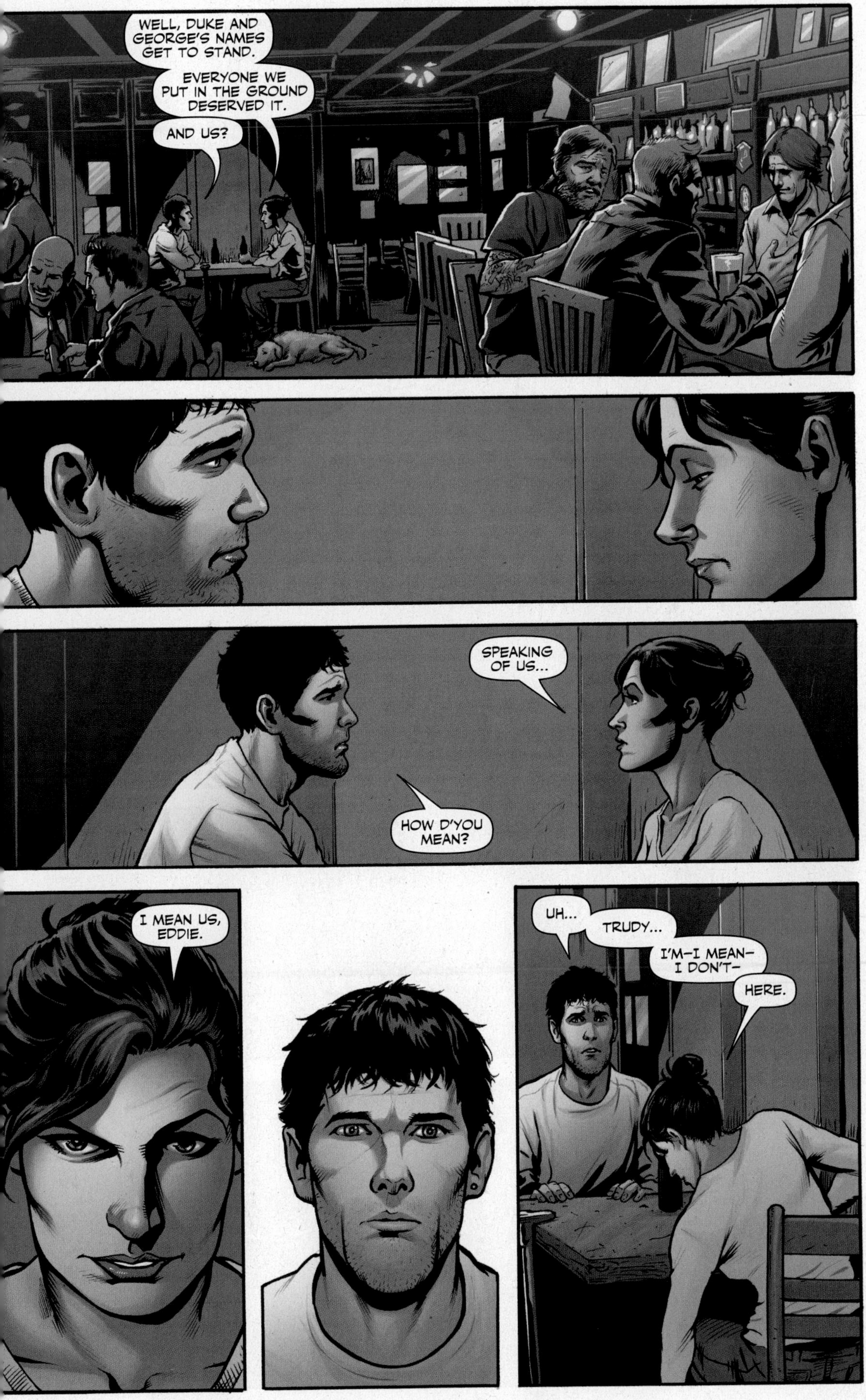
WELL, DUKE AND GEORGE'S NAMES GET TO STAND.
EVERYONE WE PUT IN THE GROUND DESERVED IT.
AND US?
SPEAKING OF US...
HOW D'YOU MEAN?
I MEAN US, EDDIE.
UH...
TRUDY...
I'M—I MEAN— I DON'T—
HERE.

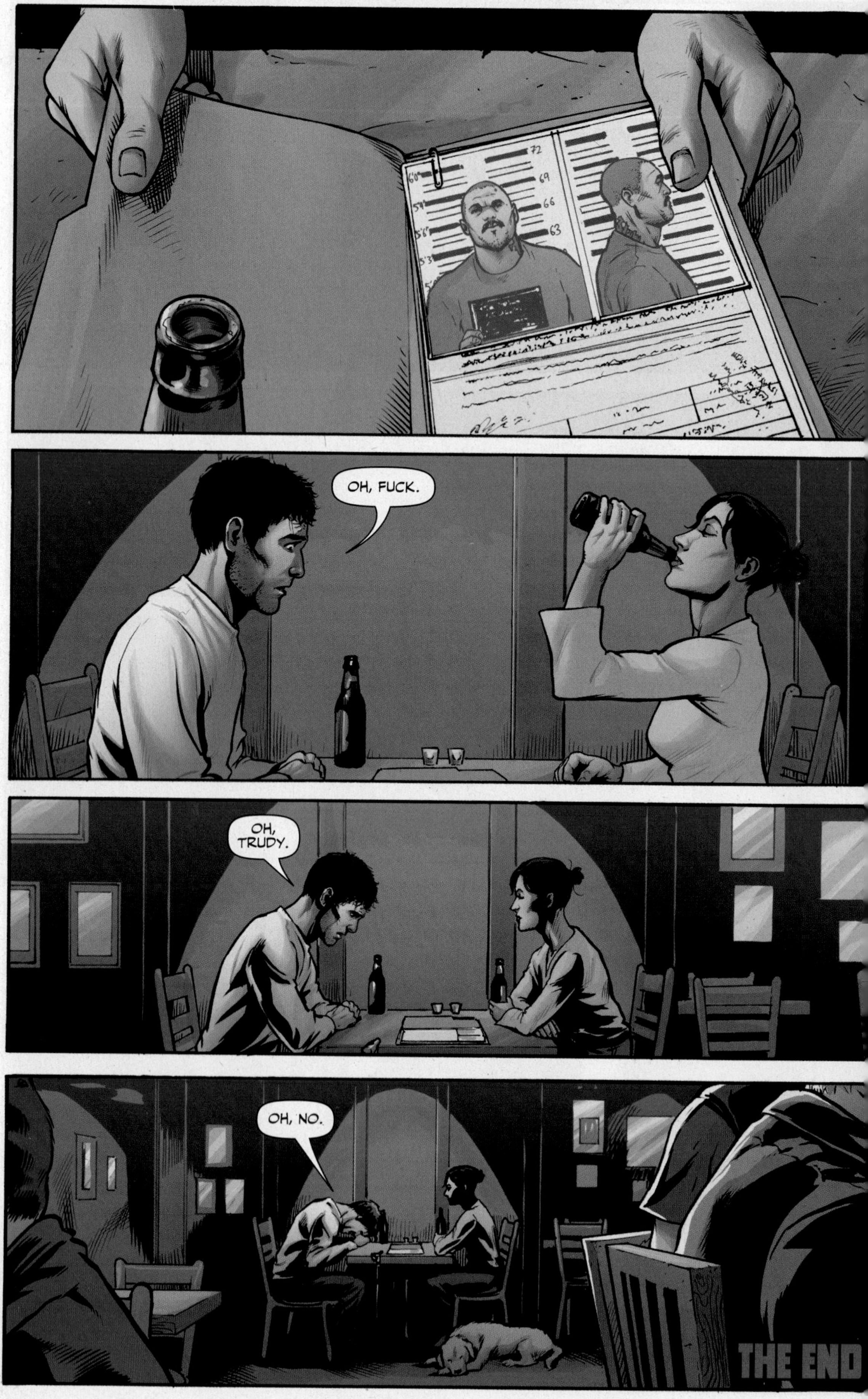
OH, FUCK.
OH, TRUDY.
OH, NO.
THE END

BONUS MATERIAL

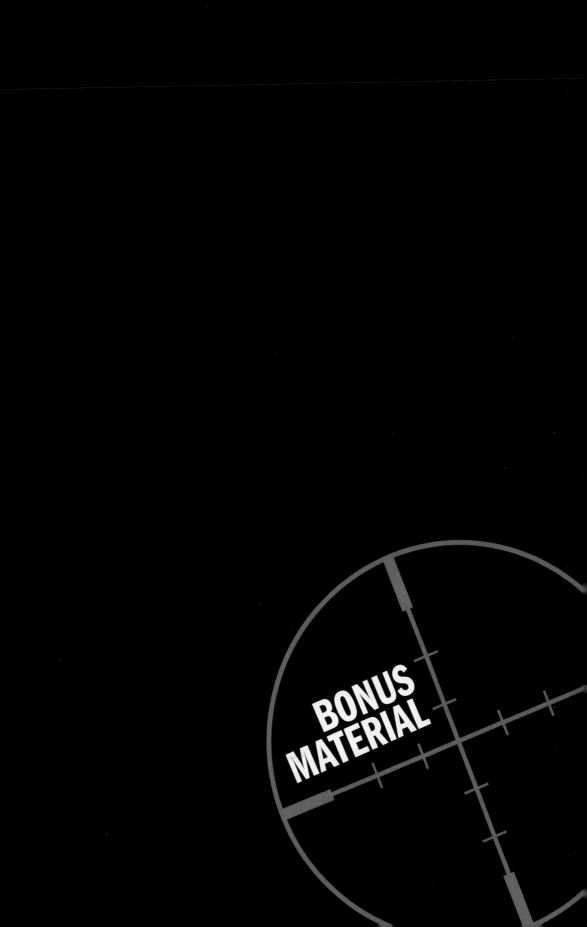

original character designs by CRAIG CERMAK

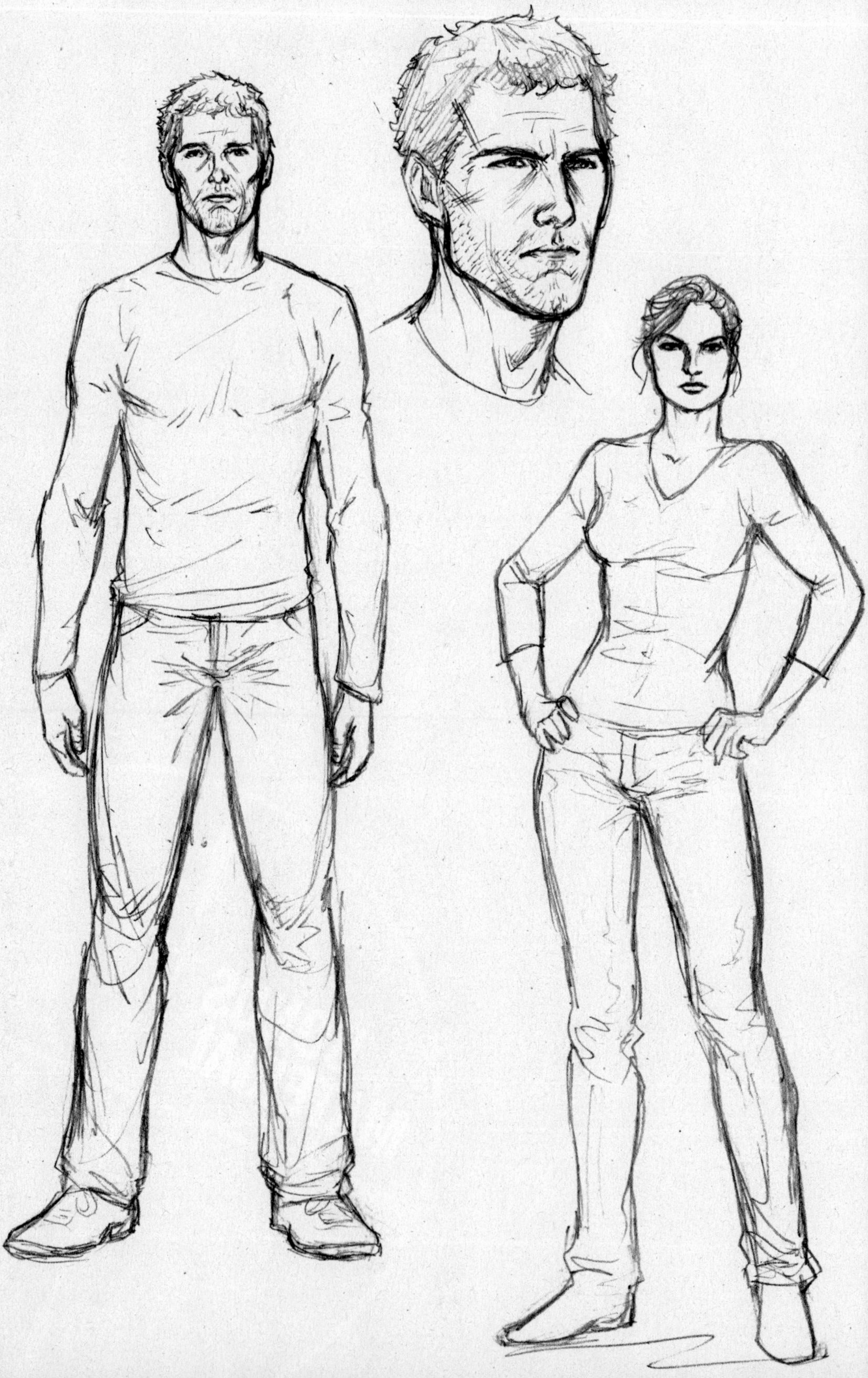

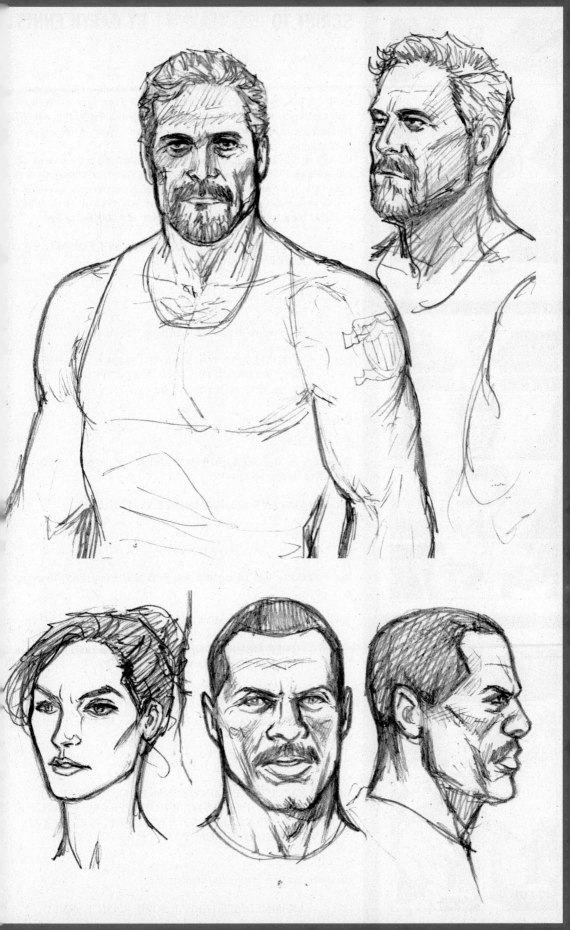

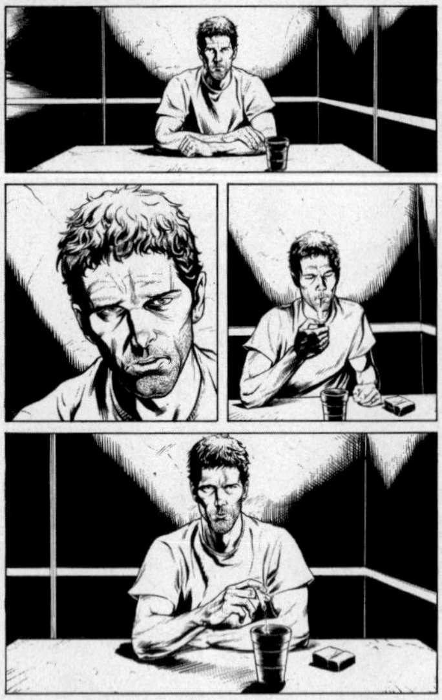

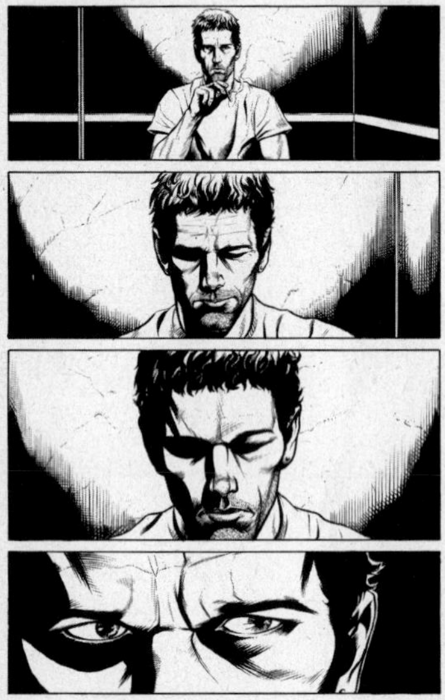

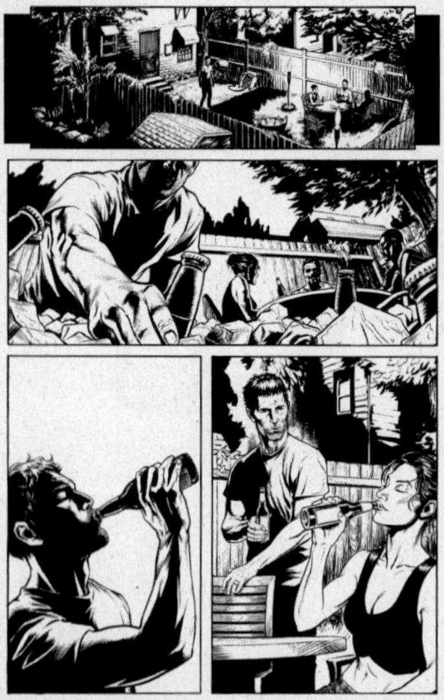

SCRIPT TO RED TEAM #1 BY GARTH ENNIS

PAGE ONE

1.

Eddie Mellinger sits across a table from us in a gloomy interrogation room. No windows, door presumably offshot. Facing us with a slightly resigned expression, more weary than anything else. He's calm, relaxed, but there's a sense he wants this over with. Just a paper coffee cup in front of him.

Eddie's an NYPD detective aged about 30, something in the manner of Ethan Hawke. Wiry, but not ripped. Cyclones t-shirt, no tattoos, short curly dark hair. Single earring, wedding ring. Unshaven but not slobby. Tricky though this is, we don't want to show too much of the room he's in during these sequences- certainly no sense of who's facing him.

Off: DETECTIVE MELLINGER, WHY DON'T YOU MAKE A START?

Eddie: SURE.

2.

Close in. Eddie seems to think of something, frowns at us.

Eddie: ACTUALLY, DO YOU MIND IF I SMOKE? I MEAN I KNOW I CAN'T, IN A NEW YORK CITY MUNICIPAL BUILDING... BUT AT THIS POINT...

Off: GO AHEAD.

3.

Eddie lights a Marlboro Light with a zippo, leaves the pack on the table. Not looking up.

Eddie: MAY AS WELL GET ME RELAXED, HUH?

" MM—

4.

Big. He exhales, taps his cigarette ash in the coffee cup. Faces us evenly.

Eddie: ABOUT EIGHT MONTHS AGO, AROUND THE END OF JUNE TWO THOUSAND TWELVE, MYSELF AND THE OTHER MEMBERS OF MAJOR CRIMES UNIT **RED TEAM** DECIDED TO MURDER A SUSPECT.

PAGE TWO

1.

Eddie faces us evenly, cigarette in hand. Not backing down, but staying cool.

Off: MURDER?

Eddie: EXECUTE, TERMINATE, WASTE, BLOW AWAY. THE POINT IS THAT AS POLICE OFFICERS WE BROKE THE LAW: WE KILLED A MAN WHO DIDN'T PRESENT AN IMMEDIATE THREAT TO US OR ANYONE ELSE.

2.

He lowers his gaze, smiles, no humour in it.

Off: AN IMMEDIATE THREAT. SO HE WASN'T ARMED.

Eddie: AT THE TIME? PROBABLY. WE NEVER STOPPED TO FIND OUT.

"   BUT HE DID PRESENT A THREAT TO KEEPING YOUR LUNCH DOWN, IF YOU THOUGHT ABOUT SOMEONE LIKE HIM BEING ALIVE AND FREE TO GO ABOUT HIS BUSINESS. HE WAS… A PIECE OF WORK…

3.
Same angle as he stops smiling, bleak now.

Eddie: AND THAT WAS WHAT THE TEAM WAS SET UP TO DEAL WITH: THE WORST OF THE WORST. WE JUST DECIDED TO TAKE IT A STAGE FURTHER.

"   LIKE I SAID, WE DECIDED TO MURDER A SUSPECT.

4.
Close up. His eyes narrow, a certain weary bitterness flickers across his face. Not looking at us, reflective.

Eddie: AND THE WORST POSSIBLE THING—I MEAN THE **WORST** POSSIBLE THING—

"   THAT'S WHAT HAPPENED.

PAGE THREE
1.
Summer night somewhere in the suburban wilds of Brooklyn- way, way out, Sheepshead bay or similar. Three people sit at a table at the end of a long, thin back yard, fenced off from a row of similar. A fourth person walks towards them from the house.

Fourth: I DON'T THINK I WOKE ANYBODY…

Table: GOOD MAN.

"   GRAB A BEER.

2.
The newcomer turns out to be Eddie, who stops to extract a Bud from a cooler full of ice and bottles, opener on top. Dressed similarly to previous. The other three are further back- we can make out two large men and a rather more slightly built woman. All three drink Buds and smoke.

Eddie: ANYONE ELSE?

Man: UH-UH.

Man 2: YOU KNOW, I'M JUST THINKING: YOU ABSOLUTELY HAVE TO DRESS LIKE THAT?

Woman: LIKE WHAT?

Man 2: YOU DON'T THINK MY WIFE HATES YOU ENOUGH?

3.
Eddie takes a long pull on the beer. Hot night.

Off: ALL YOUR WIVES HATE ME. YOU SHOULD TELL THEM I'M LIKE A SURROGATE DAUGHTER, I LOOK UP TO YOU AS FATHER FIGURES.

Off 2: I'LL TRY THAT WITH GINA. IF MY HEAD'S STILL ON MY SHOULDERS I'LL LET YOU KNOW HOW IT WENT.

4.
Eddie approaches the table. Nearest us Trudy Giroux sips her beer- about Eddie's age, quite a looker, shock of black hair and black vest top. Tall and lanky, but not the bulimic model look. Obviously works out but, like Eddie, hasn't overdone it. He glances at her, raises an eye.

Eddie: I MISS ANYTHING?

Trudy: MM-MM.

Off: WE WAITED FOR YOU.

PAGE FOUR
1.
Eddie pulls back a chair next to Trudy, and we see all four of the team together. The two nearest are Duke Wylie and George Winburn- for placing, Duke was talking to Trudy about her attire. Nice and dark here, not much light. Atmosphere is cool, not quite grim, everyone waiting to get down to what they know will be dark business. None of them is the type to pose or glare dramatically, they're all pretty low-key.

Duke is about 6'2" and built like a brick wall, about 45, black hair going grey. Moustache and goatee, also graying. Couple of small tattoos, long-faded. Swarthy look about him. Old scar running along his jawline. Hair kept short.

George could be Duke's twin, except that he's black and lacks the tats and scar, and has a moustache rather than the goatee. Apart from that they're the same breed of old-school, hard-as-nails tough guy, with the same keen intelligence obvious in their eyes.

(NB- all title pages should have a thick black bar at the bottom for the title, which always reads last)

Duke: HAVE A SEAT AND LET'S GET STARTED THINKING THE UNTHINKABLE.

Title: **1: THE FIRST-TIMERS**

PAGE FIVE
1.
Pull back, wide view of the four of them sitting there talking. Again, no sense of drama or conspiratorial huddling. All that counts that they're alone and obviously have a clear view around them, there's no way anyone could sneak up or listen from cover.

Caption: "IT WAS THE NIGHT AFTER JUG TOPPINS WAS DECLARED D.O.A. AT SAINT VINCENT'S. JUG WASN'T ONE OF US, DON'T FORGET, HE WAS ON LOAN FROM NARCOTICS — BUT IT WAS OUR OPERATION, SO TECHNICALLY HE DIED ON OUR WATCH.

"   "AND, AT THE END OF THE DAY — CANCELLING AND OVERRIDING EVERYTHING — HE WAS A COP."

2.
Close in. Eddie listens intently as Duke speaks calmly and seriously- not very expressive, just gesturing with one finger on the hand he holds his bottle in.

Caption: "JUG HAD SET HIMSELF UP AS A BUYER AND WAS LINING THINGS UP NICELY WITH CLINTON DAYS: THE LUMP OF SHIT WHO WAS THE OBJCT OF THE EXERCIZE. THIS WASN'T DEEP COVER, NOT SOME LONG TERM THING, BUT JUG WAS AN EXPERIENCED MAN AND HE LIKED HOW THE DEAL WAS COMING TOGETHER. SO DID WE.

"   "HE PROBABLY JUST MADE… ONE LITTLE MISTAKE."

3.
Duke only, cool.

Duke: COULD BE WE'LL NEVER KNOW.

"   HOW CLINTON DID IT WAS, HE GAVE THE JOB TO BOOGIE BENSON. YOU CAN GUESS WHAT BOOGIE SAID.

4.
Eddie looks bleak. Trudy frowns slightly.

Eddie: JUMPED AT IT.

Trudy: I ONCE TALKED TO BOOGIE'S HIGH SCHOOL PRINCIPAL. HIS I.Q. IS SEVENTY-NINE.

PAGE SIX

1.
Trudy stops short at this next bit, frowning.

Duke: WAS.

Trudy: WHAT?

Duke: NOT HARD TO SEE HOW IT WENT DOWN. CREW'S RESIDENT PISSBOY GETS A CHANCE TO IMPRESS THE BIG KIDS.

" JUG HAD A GLOCK NINETEEN EMPTIED AT HIM POINT BLANK. TWO HITS.

2.
Duke only, quietly meaningful look.

Duke: ANONYMOUS CALL CAME IN THIS AFTERNOON, ARMED BLACK MALE SEEN ENTERING A ROW HOUSE ON SUTTER. TACTICAL RESPONDED. THEY FOUND BOOGIE WITH A BIG BAG OF ROCK, A KID'S COLORING BOOK, AND A GLOCK NINETEEN—WHICH HE ATTEMPTED TO USE.

" AFTERWARDS, COUPLE OF RESIDENTS SAID THEY DIDN'T KNOW ABOUT **ARMED**—BUT THREE MEN HAD GONE IN AND TWO CAME OUT NOT LONG AFTERWARDS.

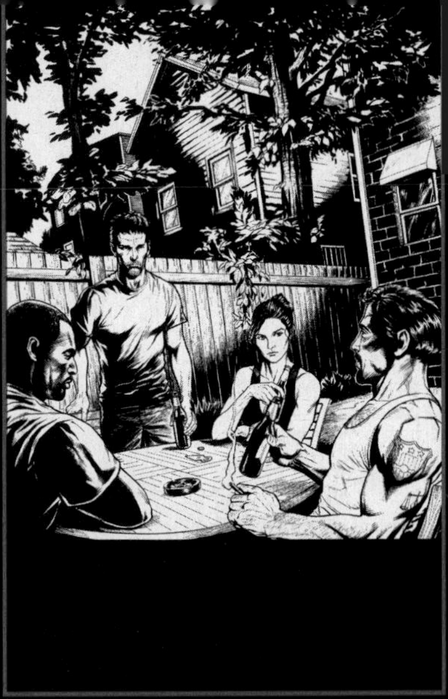

3.
Eddie smiles sadly. Trudy looks bleak, no surprises for her in this. Tough cookie, but not cold or inhuman.

Eddie: I BET THEY DIDN'T EVEN GIVE THE POOR PRICK ANY CRAYONS.

Trudy: NICE AND NEAT AND SELF-CONTAINED. WHOLE THING STARTS AND ENDS INSIDE TWENTY-FOUR HOURS.

" WE'RE LEFT WITH NOWHERE TO GO. IT'S... CLASSIC CLINTON.

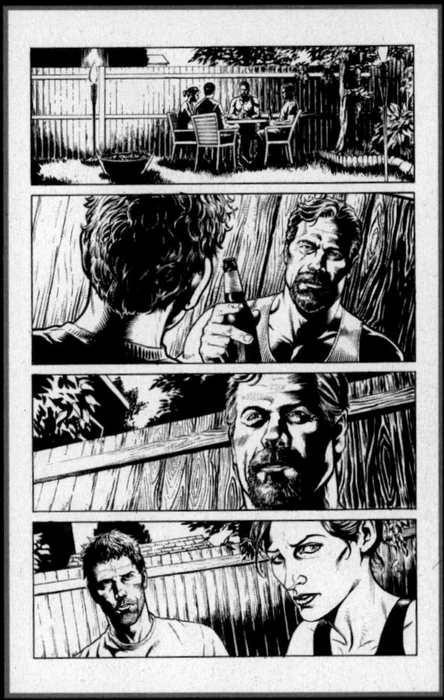

4.
George speaks for the first time, cool, at ease. Waiting calmly to see how people react.

George: IT IS.

" WE GOING TO TALK ABOUT KILLING HIM NOW?

PAGE SEVEN

1.
View past George as he lights a cigarette. Duke is calm. Eddie has gone still- not frozen in any dramatic way, just silent. Trudy is more at ease but isn't looking at anyone else.

Caption: "THERE IT WAS, RIGHT ON THE TABLE IN FRONT OF US. NOT THAT ANYONE WASN'T EXPECTING IT, OR ELSE WHY WOULD WE COME TO DUKE'S IN THE FIRST PLACE?

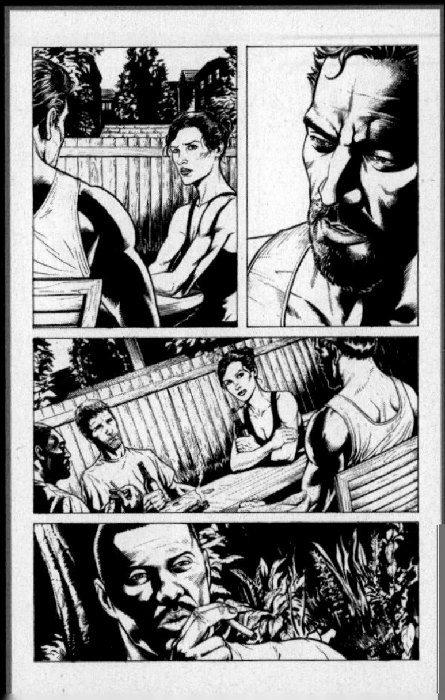

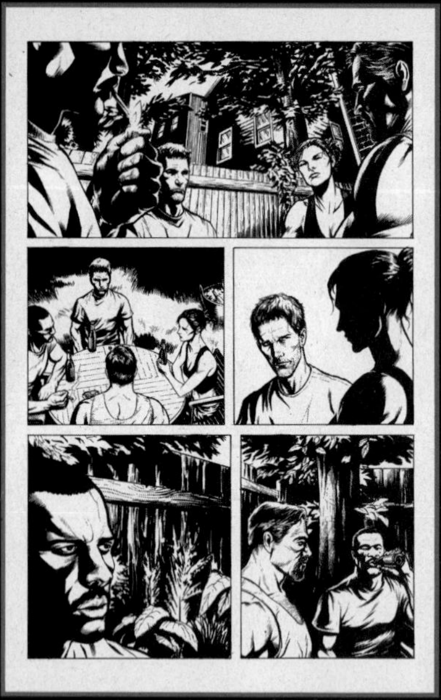

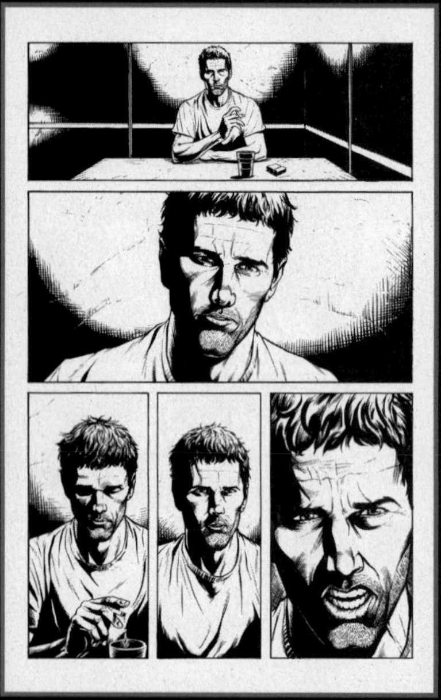

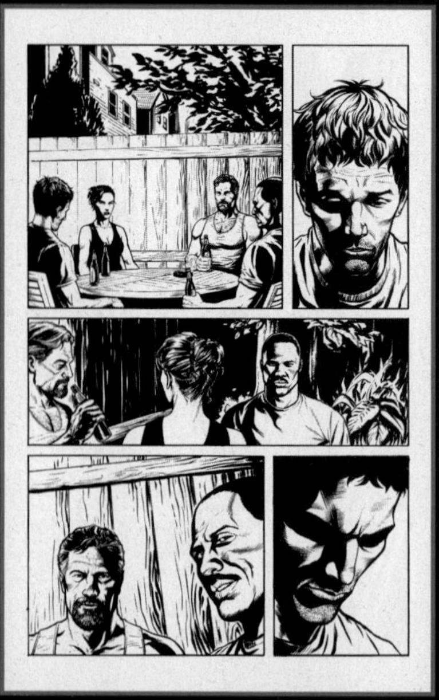

“ “BUT THIS MADE IT REAL. THIS TOOK THE ANGER OVER WHAT HAPPENED TO JUG AND COOLED IT WAY, WAY DOWN, FROM **WE HAVE GOT TO DO SOMETHING** TO— YEAH? WHAT?”

2.
Eddie raises an eye, watching the others carefully. Duke is calm, matter of fact. Trudy stubs out her cigarette.

Eddie: IS THIS WHERE WE GO ROUND IN A CIRCLE AND SAY IN OR OUT?

Duke: IN.

Trudy: ME TOO.

3.
Eddie stares at Trudy, smiling but with no humour in it. She doesn’t look at him.

Eddie: THAT WAS QUICK…

Off: EDDIE.

4.
George faces us nearest, cool, matter of fact.

George: THIS IS STILL US, UNDERSTAND? SAME TEAM. NO ONE’S BACKING ANYONE INTO A CORNER.

“ WE BEEN ON CLINTON TWO HARD, SHITTY YEARS, AND ALL WE GOT TO SHOW FOR IT IS MORE SHIT. THERE’S THE NARCOTICS, THE GIRLS HE TRAF FICKED, THE CHILD PORN, AND ON TOP OF THAT THERE’S THE BODIES HE DROPS WHEN HE DOES BUSINESS. LATEST OF WHICH IS JUG TOPPINS.

“ **DETECTIVE** TOPPINS. I’M IN.

5.
View past Duke at George, who swigs his beer while Duke takes up the cause. Same cool, reasoned approach.

Duke: WE TRIED EVERYTHING, AND EITHER CLINTON OR HIS SCUMBAG LAWYER BEAT US. KEEP ON HIM NOW AND THAT SON OF A BITCH’LL MAKE HARASSMENT STICK, AND THEN…

“ I TELL YOU STRAIGHT OUT, I HATE THE FACT THAT HE’S ALIVE. ANYBODY FEEL OTHERWISE?

Caption: “DUKE AND GEORGE CAME UP TOGETHER…”

PAGE EIGHT

1.
Eddie in the interview room again, cool.

Eddie: THEY WERE THE BEST I EVER KNEW. THEY’D TAKEN FIRE AND TAKEN LIVES; IF THEY SAID THE ONLY WAY LEFT WAS TO KILL CLINTON DAYS, THEN IT WASN’T A DECISION THEY CAME TO LIGHTLY.

“ THEY WERE WHY I SAID WHAT I SAID. WHICH IS

NOT TO BLAME THEM, BY THE WAY.

Off: WHAT ABOUT DETECTIVE GIROUX?

2.
Eddie looks a little bleak, even awkward. Not keen on going here.

Eddie: TRUDY WAS… SHE'D GONE FROM BEAT COP TO PLAIN CLOTHES TO MAJOR CRIMES TO
           ELITE UNIT, AND SHE'D DONE IT COMPLETELY ON MERIT. BUT BEING A FEMALE IN THAT
           SITUATION, I THINK SHE WAS A LITTLE INSECURE ABOUT IT.

"   SHE WAS ALWAYS THINKING, HOW DO PEOPLE **REALLY** THINK I GOT HERE/ SHE KNEW
           THE TRUTH, BUT SHE STILL WORKED HARDER THAN ANYBODY ELSE. STILL TOOK THE
           HARDEST POSSIBLE CHOICE EVERY TIME, MAYBE WITHOUT THINKING IT THROUGH AS
           MUCH AS SHE MIGHT HAVE.

"   AS IN THIS INSTANCE.

3.
He looks down, taps ash in the coffee cup.

Off: INTERESTING VIEWPOINT.

Eddie: JUST MY OPINION.

4.
He looks up at us again, calm. Not iron-cast certain, like the others when they decided. But not afraid, either.

Off: SO WHAT DID YOU SAY, WHEN YOU SAID WHAT YOU SAID?

Eddie: YES.

"   EVENTUALLY.

5.
He stares at us, frowns in disbelief, caught off guard for a second. A flicker of genuine anger crosses his face.

Off: WHY EVENTUALLY?

Eddie: BECAUSE IT WAS FUCKING **WRONG…!**

PAGE NINE
1.
Eddie sits nearest us at the table, head down, thinking it through. George and Duke wait patiently, calmly. Trudy
watches Eddie, but he hasn't noticed.

Caption: "DON'T THINK THAT JUST BECAUSE WE SAT TALKING OVER BEERS, RATIONAL AND
           REASONABLE, NOT ONE VOICE RAISED, THAT WE DIDN'T KNOW EXACTLY WHERE WE
           WERE GOING WITH THIS. WE WEREN'T A BUNCH OF BURNOUTS GETTING LAZY, OR SOME
           MEATHEAD LOSING IT WITH A GUY IN A HOLDING CELL: WE'D BEEN ASSIGNED BECAUSE
           WE THOUGHT SHIT THROUGH.

"   "THE SAME UNSPOKEN RULE THAT GAVE JUG HIS SPECIAL STATUS APPLIED TO US, TOO.
           COPS INVESTIGATE, THEY AMASS EVIDENCE, THEY ARREST SUSPECTS, AND **THAT'S
           SUPPOSED TO BE IT**—AND HERE WE WERE CROSSING OVER TO FUCKING CLINTON'S
           SIDE…'

2.
Eddie only, musing thoughtfully, not quite looking up.

Caption: "BUT IT HAD BEEN TWO YEARS.

"   "AND HE KNEW WE WERE HURTING.

"   "AND IT WAS TOO MUCH TO BEAR.

"   "AND... WELL, DON'T WORRY, I TALKED MYSELF INTO IT."

Eddie: I GUESS IT WOULDN'T EXACTLY BE THE FIRST TIME, WOULD IT?

3.
Duke shrugs, looks thoughtfully into his beer. Trudy is interested. George glances at her.

Duke: NO IT WOULD NOT.

Trudy: MM?

George: THING IN THE EIGHTIES.

4.
George explains. Nearest us Duke looks calmly past us.

George: SOME UNIFORMS TEAMED UP TO TAKE OUT A IRISH MOB CREW. SO THE STORY GOES.

"   THERE'S MORE, YOU WANT TO GO BACK FAR ENOUGH.

Duke: ALWAYS SOMETHING, RIGHT?

5.
Eddie smiles slightly, not looking at us. Quietly giving in.

Eddie: HMH.

"   RIGHT.

PAGE TEN
1.
Shitty day. A Precinct building in the rundown district of East New York, Brooklyn.

From in: UNOFFICIALLY, I KNOW THERE'S NOT A GOD DAMN THING YOU COULD HAVE DONE
          BETTER. ANY MISTAKES WERE NOT YOURS.

2.
Captain Delaney sits behind his desk, wearily facing Duke. Late fifties, a smart and decent man reaching retirement, jacket off but tie tight and sleeves rolled down- he'll only relax so far even here. Full head of white hair, clean shaven, a slightly younger Max Von Sydow with oddly sad eyes. His office is fairly neat and tidy. Mug of coffee each.

Delaney: OFFICIALLY... THERE'S ABOUT A HUNDRED POUNDS OF SHIT ABOUT TO LAND IN YOUR
         FILE. AN OFFICER DIED, IS HOW THEY'RE GOING TO SEE IT.

Duke: UNDERSTOOD, SKIPPER.

Delaney: IF IT WAS UP TO ME...

Duke: UNDERSTOOD.

3.
Wide. The two men are pretty relaxed with each other, even now. Duke looks meaningfully at Delaney, who clearly understands.

Duke: CAN WE MAKE SURE IT IS MY FILE? NOT THE OTHER THREE?

Delaney: 'COURSE. HOW THEY DOING?

Duke: LIKE YOU'D THINK.

Delaney: HOW ABOUT MELLINGER'S WIFE, IS THAT GOING ANY BETTER…?

4.
Delaney smiles with slight regret.

Off: HE HASN'T SAID. I'M GUESSING NO BETTER AND NO WORSE.

" I'LL TELL HIM YOU WERE ASKING, HE'LL APPRECIATE IT.

Delaney: SHE'S A SWEET KID.

" I HATE TO DO THE BUSINESS AS USUAL THING…

PAGE ELEVEN
1.
Duke, reflective, not quite looking at us.

Duke: SURE.

" CLINTON WE'LL HAVE TO BACK OFF OF FOR THE TIME BEING. IF NOTHING ELSE IT FREES US UP TO TAKE ANOTHER RUN AT JIMMY JAY AND HIS BROTHERS.

" WE'LL START WITH THE PLACE ON ATLANTIC, WAIT FOR THE RIGHT EVIDENCE TO SHOW… BUT…

2.
Delaney smiles, sympathetic. Duke sets down his mug, bit bleak.

Delaney: I'VE NO DOUBT IT WILL.

" LIKE USING A SLEDGEHAMMER ON A PEANUT, I KNOW. I'M SORRY, DUKE.

Duke: THAT'S NOT EVEN IT. I MEAN YOU'VE GOT US, YOU USE US.

3.
Duke only, weary, meaningful look to him.

Duke: FACT IS, BEFORE WE STARTED TO RAMP THINGS UP ON CLINTON A YEAR AND A HALF AGO, WE'D PRETTY MUCH TAKEN CARE OF EVERYONE ELSE. IDEA WAS TO GET RID OF THE SMALL FRY SO AS TO ISOLATE HIM, THEN MAKE OUR MOVE.

" WHAT IT BOILS DOWN TO NOW IS WE PRETTY MUCH JUST CLEARED AWAY HIS COMPETITION, WHICH JIMMY JAY IS THE LAST OF. AND THAT AIN'T SAYING TOO MUCH.

4.
Delaney slumps a bit, gloomy. Duke raises an eye.

Delaney: MM.

" THE MORE YOU THINK ABOUT THIS, THE WORSE IT GETS…

Duke: WE DID A LOT OF GOOD, THESE LAST SIX YEARS. EVEN IF WE ONLY STOPPED THE PLACE FROM GETTING WORSE.

5.
Delaney only, bleak smile.

Delaney: THE SHIT A MAN HAS TO SWALLOW, DOING THIS JOB.

" YOU GETTING ANYWHERE NEAR YOUR LIMIT?

PAGE TWELVE
1.
Wide view of the office, Duke smiling thinly, Delaney serious.

Duke: UH-UH.

Delaney: GLAD TO HEAR IT.

" BECAUSE THIS WILL PASS, I PROMISE YOU. I NEED YOU, AND I NEED YOUR TEAM.

Off: SKIPPER!

2.
View past Delaney as Paul O'Dwyer strolls in, leaves the door open behind him- CAPT. F.D. DELANEY printed thereon. Duke looks away but otherwise doesn't react.

O'Dwyer's as tall as Duke but wiry rather than heavy. Head shaved, sharply shaven goatee, huge Celtic cross tattooed along the length of one forearm- as well as numerous other tattoos. Works out, ripped- a man of many angles and few curves. About 40. Sleeves rolled up on check shirt over t-shirt, jeans, Glock in a shoulder holster. Squinty, nasty piece of work despite his blithe manner. He dumps a couple of files on the desk.

Delaney: PAUL. KAREN AWAY FROM HER DESK OUT THERE?

O'Dwyer: HEY, DUKE…

Duke: HEY.

O'Dwyer: THE THING IN CYPRESS HILLS, THE LAST MONTH'S WORTH OF BUY-BUSTS, THE REDBALL YOU GAVE TO US WITH THE DEAD FAG. SHOULDA STUCK TO COCK, NOT ROCK. ALL DONE.

3.
O'Dwyer only, smiling wearily at us. Give us a good look at him here.

Off: THANK YOU VERY MUCH. I WAS GOING TO TALK TO YOU ANYWAY…

O'Dwyer: ABOUT WILLIAMS? WILD FUCKING GUESS.

" DON'T WORRY ABOUT IT, THE LAST THING I WANT IS A GUY AS DUMB AS THAT ON MY TEAM. I MEAN IF I'D KNOWN WOULDN'T'VE EVEN FILED THE APPLICATION.

" CONSIDER IT WITHDRAWN, UNLESS YOU WANT TO

KEEP IT TO WIPE YOUR ASS WITH…?

4.
Duke only, watching calmly.

Off: I'LL FOREGO THAT PLEASURE. OH, AND YOU SHOULD KNOW THAT DUKE'S UNIT ARE
         GOING TO BE LOOKING AT JIMMY JAY PRETTY SOON.

Off 2:   THAT'S COOL, WE'LL KEEP OUR DISTANCE. DUKE'S GUYS AND MY GUYS, WE'RE GOOD AT
         NOT STEPPING ON EACH OTHERS' TOES, RIGHT?

"   SEE YOU.

PAGE THIRTEEN
1.
Wide view again. The door is closed, O'Dwyer's gone. The two men face each other across the room. Duke coolly
raises an eye, Delaney smiles wryly.

Delaney: HMH.

2.
Delaney smiles at us, amused.

Delaney; YOU THINK THERE'S A MAN IN THE DEPARTMENT **DOESN'T KNOW** WHAT A WASTE OF
         SPACE TIM WILLIAMS IS? IS, ALWAYS WAS, ALWAYS WILL BE?

"   APART FROM ANYTHING ELSE… HOW MANY TIMES HAS HE HE BEEN BROUGHT UP FOR
         LETTING HIS SIDEARM OFF INTO THE CEILING IN FREELEY'S…?

3.
Duke shrugs, bleak.

Duke: LAST TIME GEORGE HAD TO TAKE IT OFF HIM, HE WAS POINTING IT AT THE DARTS TEAM
         FROM THE SEVEN-THREE. EVEN HIS OLD MAN'S BUDDIES WOULDN'T'VE GOT HIM OUT
         OF THAT ONE.

Off: HE TOOK IT OFF HIM…

Duke: THE WAY YOU'D EXPECT GEORGE TO TAKE IT OFF HIM. NO LOVE LOST THERE.

4.
Delaney smiles at Duke, curious. Duke looks away, shrugs.

Delaney: NOT MUCH WITH YOU AND OUR FRIEND, EITHER.

Duke: OH, I DON'T KNOW, SKIPPER.

5.
Duke frowns, trying to pin down a thought.

Duke: IT'S NOT LIKE HE **ACTS** LIKE AN ASSHOLE. HE COULD, HE COULD'VE GIVEN ME SHIT
         ABOUT CLINTON OR CROWED ABOUT HIS GUYS' RECORD RECENTLY, BUT HE DIDN'T.
         HE'S RIGHT, WE DON'T STEP ON EACH OTHERS' TOES.

"   BUT EVERY TIME I'M IN A ROOM WITH HIM?

6.
He gazes out the window, bleak, slightly preoccupied. Delaney studies him, interested.

Duke: I END UP FEELING LIKE I NEED TO WASH.

PAGE FOURTEEN

1.
Close up on four pistols set on a metal surface: two Glocks, a Beretta 92 and an old-fashioned snubnose .38 revolver. All have handgrips, triggers and hammers covered with white tape.

Off: WE'LL USE THE THIRTY-RIGHT TO DO IT, KEEP THE CASINGS FROM GETTING AWAY FROM US. THE REST ARE LAST RESORT ONLY.

" WE DON'T USE OUR OWN WEAPONS OR OUR OWN WHEELS, WE DON'T EVEN WEAR OUR OWN CLOTHES. WHAT WE DO WEAR WE BURN.

" I MEAN IT, TRUDY, NOT EVEN A KNUCKLEDUSTER. CLEAR?

2.
The four are gathered around an unmarked car next to the subway tracks, where the only way they could really be observed is from a passing train. Shitty day, but warm enough for t-shirts or shirtsleeves (Trudy tones it down a little when she's on duty). George eyes Trudy, who looks a little surprised. Duke watches Eddie look at the guns.

Trudy: SURE.

George: CLEAR?

Trudy: YES...!

Eddie: THESE'RE FROM...?

3.
Close in. Eddie smiles, no humour in it. Duke raises an eye.

Eddie: OH YEAH. FOR WHEN THE RIGHT EVIDENCE NEEDS TO SHOW UP.

Duke: PROBLEM?

Eddie: NOT REALLY.

4.
Eddie only, slightly pained.

Eddie: ONLY... YOU THINK MAYBE WHEN THEY PUT THE SMARTEST COPS THEY COULD FIND ON A TEAM DOES THE STUFF WE DO, THE WHOLE POJNT WAS WE'D KNOW **NEVER** TO GO DOWN THIS ROAD...?

5.
Duke only, calm.

Duke: I THINK WE LEFT WHAT THEY INTENDED BEHIND A LONG TIME BACK.

PAGE FIFTEEN

1.
Eddie in the interrogation room again, thoughtful.

Eddie: WE'D PUT TOGETHER A LOT OF INTEL ON CLINTON WHEN WE WERE BUILDING THE CASE. AS COPS, THERE WASN'T A WHOLE LOT WE COULD DO WITH IT NOW.

" BUT AS... WELL...

Off: PRIVATE CITIZENS?

2.
Big. A terrified young black woman lies on the bed in the bedroom of a suburban house, wrists secured behind her, ankles tied, eyes and ears covered, mouth gagged, all of it done with heavy tape. She wears a pink silk nightie, obviously been expecting different company. George stands at the bedroom door- closed- with one of the Glocks, wearing black or dark blue from head to foot, including gloves and ski-mask. Drapes pulled. Framed photo on bed-

side table nearest, same woman in a nice dress next to a tall black man in army dress uniform, both smiling.

Caption: "YEAH, HA HA. ONE OF THE THINGS WE FOUND UP WAS HE'D BEEN CHECKING UP ON HIS BROTHER'S WIFE, WHILE STAFF SERGEANT DAYS WAS OTHER WISE OCCUPIED IN KANDAHAR. HE WAS VERY, VERY THOROUGH.

" "USING IT WAS ON OUR **MAYBE IF WE HAVE TO** LIST, JUST BECAUSE WE DIDN'T WANT TO MESS UP A SERVING AMERICAN SOLDIER **AND** THE DECENT ONE OF THE DAYS BROTHERS. NOW, ALL OF A SUDDEN, IT WAS OUR WAY IN.

" "CLINTON WAS BEING SO CAREFUL BIG BRO NEVER FOUND OUT, HE TENDED TO VISIT THE LADY EITHER ALONE OR WITH JUST ONE GUY WATCHING HIS BACK. ONLY HIS MOST TRUSTED ASSHOLES WERE PRIVY TO THIS SHIT.

" "AND—OF COURSE—HE DIDN'T KNOW WE KNEW ABOUT IT."

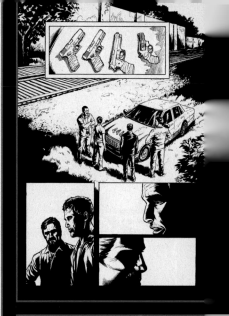

3.
Close up on George, cool and grim. The ski-mask hides his features but we can see skin at eyes and mouth.

Caption: "GEORGE HANDLED THE WOMAN SOLO. ONE FLASH OF WHITE SKIN AND SHE'D HAVE A HELL OF A STORY TO TELL."

4.
Duke and Eddie wait in the hallway in similar attire. Duke has the 38, Eddie the other Glock.

Eddie: WHAT'D YOU SAY TO DELANEY?

Duke: MM?

Eddie: YOU KNOW.

PAGE SIXTEEN
1.
Duke deadpans this. Eddie glances offshot.

Duke: I DID MY BEST DIRTY HARRY. I SAID—WELL, I JUST HOPE NOTHING… **HAPPENS**… TO CLINTON.

" YOU THINK HE'LL MAYBE GET SUSPICIOUS?

Eddie: OKAY, I WAS ONLY—

" ENGINE.

2.
Outside, in a quiet Brooklyn street- somewhere a little nicer than the precinct's neighbourhood- we see a tall black man in a tracksuit exit a black range-rover outside the house. Nearest us is a battered, nondescript Toyota (this is not the car they laid the guns out on), maybe 100 yards back on the other side of the street. Night, no one around.

Caption: "WE WERE ON RADIO SILENCE. ANYONE SCANNING

PICKING UP A WOMAN'S VOICE—ANY VOICE—
MIGHT JUST PUT IT TOGETHER AFTER THE NEWS
BROKE.

"   "ONE CLICK FOR CLINTON, ONE EXTRA FOR EACH
MAN WITH HIM IN THE CAR. HOLD DOWN THE
SWITCH AND THEY WERE COMING IN TOO, AND
THAT MEANT ABOART AND OUT THE BACK."

3.
Trudy at the wheel of the Toyota, ski-mask rolled up on her head like a
wool cap. She lowers her binoculars, coolly depresses the send switch
on her walkie-talkie nearest- a wire links the walkie to her earpiece.

Caption: "CLICK."

4.
Headshot on Clinton as he enters- and freezes partway through the door.
A gloved hand puts a taped-up Glock to his head. He isn't scared, just
goes completely still. Clinton's medium height, muscular build, braided
dreads. About 30. Not too much gold, just an earring and simple neck
chain. As intelligent as he is tough.

Clinton: JOANNE—

PAGE SEVENTEEN
1.
Clinton calmly puts his hands up as Eddie pushes him forward into the
hall with the Glock at the back of his head, pushes the door shut behind
him with his free hand. Duke steps forward nearest. Our heroes move
quickly but without drama or urgent expressions, being careful to get it
right.

Clinton: OKAY.

"   OKAY.

"   Y'ALL GOT MY ATTENTION.

2.
Big, close. Eddie's hand clamps over Clinton's mouth and pushes his
head back against the wall. Duke's hand puts the 38 to his chest- direct-
ly over his heart- and fires. Clinton's
eyes bulge in total amazement.

3.
Close up on Clinton, headshot, shaking and juddering under multiple
impacts. His eyes betray shock and real terror now, he knows exactly
what's happening to him. Eddie's hand remains clamped over his
mouth.

Caption: "DUKE PUT ALL FIVE STRAIGHT INTO HIS HEART."

PAGE EIGHTEEN
1.
Eddie opens the door again, peeks out. Duke steps over the awkwardly
sprawled body of Clinton. George exits the bedroom nearest.

Eddie: SHE'S HERE.

2.
View past Trudy at the wheel of the Toyota, ski-mask on, stopped paral-
lel to the house. The three men run towards her, leaving the front door

closed behind them. She doesn't look at them, stays calm.

3.
Rear view past the Range Rover as the Toyota speeds off up the street- not too fast, but not hanging about either.

4.
Trudy and Duke face front, both cool. Behind them George shows no reaction, but Eddie's eyes narrow as he watches her. Ski-masks still on.

Trudy: WE GOOD?

Duke: MM.

5.
Long shot, high view on the Toyota as it proceeds along a main street like Atlantic, bit more traffic here despite the hour. Lights of Manhattan just visible off in the distance.

Caption: "IT WAS ALL IN HIS EYES.

"   "FROM EASY GRACE AT WHAT HE THOUGHT WOULD BE NEGOTIATION, TO SHOCK AS THINGS MOVED FAR TOO FAST, TO UNDERSTANDING, DISBELIVING, **KNOWING**: THIS WAS IT.

"   "AND ON DOWN INTO THE DARK."

PAGE NINETEEN
1.
Big. Eddie in the back seat of the Toyota, grim, face still, but eyes staring- obviously having real trouble. Next to him George isn't at all. Ski-masks up off their faces now.

Caption: "IN MY HEAD I CYCLED THROUGH THE PICTURES, MEMORIES, NAMES, EVENTS, EVERY LOUSY THING HE'D EVER DONE. JUST TO WIPE AWAY THOSE GODDAMNED EYES OF HIS.

"   "TOO MANY O.D.S. TOO MANY MURDERS. THE KIDS DESTROYED IN THE MOVIES HE FINANCED. THE PRODUCT CUT WITH POISON, SOLD ON A RIVAL'S PATCH TO DRAW NEW CUSTOMERS TO HIS.

"   "THE HOOKER WHOSE BODY CAME APART IN MY HANDS, AFTER ONE OF CLINTON'S CHRISTMAS PARTIES.

"   "JUG TOPPINS.

"   "POOR RETARDED BOOGIE BENSON."

2.
Eddie now, in the interrogation room, facing us thoughtfully.

Eddie: I DON'T KNOW IF YOU REMEMBER THIS... THERE WAS A NIGERIAN WOMAN ABOUT TWO YEARS BACK, PART OF A SHIPMENT CLINTON BROUGHT IN THROUGH BAYONNE. SHE GOT PICKED UP AT THE LINDEN HOUSES, SAID SHE'D TALK. AND SHE KNEW **LOTS**.

"   THING WAS, SHE WASN'T TOO DISCREET ABOUT WHO SHE TALKED TO IN THE TANK. CLINTON HEARD. INK WAS STILL DRYING ON THE SAFE CUSTODY ORDER WHEN SOME ONE STUCK HER WITH A HYPO FULL OF MERCURY.

3.
He smiles bleakly, sadly.

Eddie: I SAW HER BEFORE THEY ZIPPED THE BAG UP, AND... TURNED OUT THE LOOK IN HER EYES CANCELLED HIS.

"   CONGRATULATIONS, SWEETHEART. YOU MADE IT ALL THE WAY TO THE U.S. JUST TO MAKE A COP FEEL BETTER ABOUT HIS FIRST KILL.

4.
The Toyota sinks in a canal nearest, almost under, our four heroes walking away across a patch of wasteground further back. Still night, no one else around. Nearest buildings are half a mile away.

Caption: "MANY THANKS, WHOEVER YOU WERE."

PAGE TWENTY
1.
Eddie in the interrogation room, raising an eye. Pull back a bit.

Off: THERE'S SOMETHING I'M CONFUSED ABOUT.

Eddie: YEAH?

2.
Closer on him, realizing, understanding.

Off: YOU SAID... LET'S SEE, YOU SAID YOU DECIDED TO MURDER A SUSPECT...

Eddie: RIGHT.

Off: AND THEN YOU SAID—"THE WORST POSSIBLE THING HAPPENED."

Eddie: RIGHT...

3.
He faces us, bleak but open and honest, hiding nothing.

Off: SO...?

Eddie: THE WORST POSSIBLE THING WAS THAT IT WENT LIKE CLOCKWORK.

4.
Close up on Duke's hands holding open a plastic shopping bag, 38 and Glock within, Eddie's hand dropping in the other Glock, Trudy's hand waiting with the Beretta.

Caption: "NOTHING WENT WRONG. NOTHING.

"   "WE FOUND OUT FOR SURE OVER THE NEXT COUPLE DAYS, BUT REALLY WE KNEW THERE AND THEN."

5.
Eddie watches the others carefully as Duke ties off the bag. They're all at ease, haven't seen how he's watching them. Ski masks off. George and Trudy pull their gloves off.

Caption: "THE BROTHER'S WIFE DIDN'T SEE OR HEAR SHIT. CLINTON DIDN'T GRAB THE PIECE.

"   "HE DIDN'T HAVE BACK-UP ARRIVING LATER. NO ONE WASTED TIME TELLING HIM HE HAD IT COMING. THE GUN DIDN'T JAM. THE CAR DIDN'T STALL. THERE WASN'T EVEN ANYONE ON THE STREET.

"   "IT WENT JUST LIKE WE PLANNED IT BECAUSE THAT'S HOW FUCKING GOOD WE WERE: BECAUSE WE WERE RED TEAM."

PAGE TWENTY-ONE
1.
Eddie now, grimacing as he looks down at the table, slowly tapping it with a fingertip.

Eddie: WE DIDN'T EVEN HAVE A CLOSE SHAVE, SOMETHING WHERE WE COULD SAY—JESUS, THAT WOULD'VE SCREWED US FOR SURE. WE'LL NEVER BE THAT LUCKY TWICE.

Off: AH.

2.

Long shot as the four walk off across the wasteground.

Caption: "YEAH. **AH**.

"   "I COULD FEEL IT COMING. CLINTON WAS GONE,
        BUT THIS WAS SOMETHING WE WERE HEADED
        TOWARDS, NOT AWAY FROM."

3.

Eddie then, head lowered, eyes closed as he walks. There's a slightly
sick look about him, like he's steeling himself to face something he
really doesn't want to.

Caption: "WE MURDERED A SUSPECT AND THE WORST
          POSSIBLE THING HAPPENED: IT WENT LIKE GOD
          DAMNED CLOCKWORK."

PAGE TWENTY-TWO

1.

Trudy, George and Duke walk towards us, calm and collected, the bag
of guns hanging from Duke's hand. They're not cold and heartless here,
no ruthless stormtrooper stuff- just relaxed and at ease with no reason to
be agitated. Behind them Eddie follows, raising his head to look at them
with a look of deep foreboding. Still night, nice dark shot.

Caption: "AND I JUST KNEW WE WERE GOING TO DO IT
          AGAIN."

TO BE CONTINUED